The Uses of Haiti

Paul Farmer

Common Courage Press   Monroe, Maine 04951

Copyright © Paul Farmer 2006
First published in 1994, updated 2005
All Rights Reserved
Cover design by Matt Wuerker with Erica Bjerning
Cover photo by Maggie Steber
Map by Katy Farmer
Book design by Mary Trew
Updated index by Alice Yang

Library of Congress Cataloging-in-Publication Data
is available from the publisher on request.

ISBN 1-56751-344-1 paper
ISBN 1-56751-345-x hardcover

ISBN 13 9781567513448 paper
ISBN 13 978567513455 hardcover

Common Courage Press
P.O. Box 702
Monroe ME 04951
207-525-0900
Fax: 207-525-3068

See www.commoncouragepress.com for more
information on the book and electronic editions.
Printed in Canada

Third Edition

Third Printing

For Tom and Jim, whom I pulled

into this maelstrom.

For Loune, whom I found already there.

For Frico and Mamito, who went down with me.

Everyone in Haiti was always criticizing the American government, and I'd say 'You're not there, so how do you know they really wish us harm?' They'd say, 'but look what they did to us in 1915, and I'd respond, 'But that was a long time ago; things have changed.' And yet I've come to see that there hasn't really been any change. My experience on Guantánamo allowed me to discover that it was true — these things are their doing. I have no idea what we are to them — their bêtes noires, *or perhaps devils. We're not human to them, but I don't know what we are. It's as if they see us as a part of the world born to serve as American lackeys. And that's just what's come to pass. They use us as they see fit.*

— Yolande Jean, detained on Guantánamo

Acknowledgments

On the night of December 5, 1992, Jean-Sony Philogène and six other young men were arrested by a group of heavily armed men in civilian clothing. They were taken to Titanyen, a small village to the north of Port-au-Prince, and led to a common grave, a preferred dumping ground for the death squads. There the men were shot with automatic weapons and left for dead. But Philogène, 20 years old, was not mortally wounded; he had been shot in the legs. After his assailants left the area, the young man knotted his shirt sleeves around his most heavily bleeding wounds and dragged himself to a nearby road. Some hours later, he was picked up by a truck driver, who took him to St-François de Sales Hospital in Port-au-Prince. For unknown reasons, Philogène was not admitted, but a physician admitted him to the Hôpital du Canapé-Vert, a private facility not far from the center of the city.

The next morning, Jean-Sony Philogène was taken to the hospital's operating room. Philogène, it was decided, was a fortunate man: his thighs had been pierced by five bullets, one of which remained lodged in his left leg, but no major artery had been severed. The remaining bullet was extracted uneventfully, and Philogène was sent to a room, where his grandmother anxiously awaited him (Philogène's mother was living out of the country).

At three o'clock that afternoon, a group of uniformed soldiers came to the hospital asking for Philogène. The nurse at the front desk informed them that no such patient was registered in her ledger, and the soldiers left. At approximately 10 p.m. that evening, a group of five men — this time in civilian garb — entered the hospital. Two of them went directly to Room 3, where they found Jean-Sony Philogène and his grandmother. The young man was executed with two nine-millimeter bullets, fired at point-blank range.

According to the nurses on duty, the police were summoned immediately, but did not arrive until fully 30 minutes later.

It was not my intention to write a book, however modest, about the current "political situation" in Haiti and how it came to be. Thoroughly engaged in other work regarding tuberculosis and AIDS, and, most of all, busy working with a group committed to improving the health of a score of villages in rural Haiti, I was an unlikely candidate for the task of chronicling and analyzing the events and processes described here. Such a project was far from my mind when it was suggested to me by Noam Chomsky and by Greg Bates of Common Courage Press.

But deaths such as Jean-Sony Philogène's have become commonplace in Haiti. One does not have to be a physician to be incensed by crimes committed, with utter impunity, against the sick and the poor. *The Uses of Haiti* was written under the influence of this indignation, and it suffers, no doubt, from the shortcomings of any work of passion.

But surely indignation should not be absent from a consideration of such events. Writing of English historian E.P. Thompson's *The Poverty of Theory*, one reviewer observed that in it, "the tygers of wrath fraternise with the horses of instruction." It is just this sort of mixture that someone who has worked among the Haitian poor — the poor who will never read this book — might strive to concoct. It is the mixture of one who is grateful for victories, but more accustomed to defeats.

This essay was not written for a scholarly press, as I then would have felt compelled to abandon not the arguments, which are easily buttressed, but the passion. In times of strife, when hospitals become charnel houses, the university has seemed bucolic; tygers are rare in the groves of academe. At the same time, I have no delusions about writing for a large readership. *The Uses of Haiti* is a critique of U.S. foreign policy towards the poor not only of Haiti, but of all of Latin America. Such critiques, especially when they underline the complicity of the mainstream media, have not, as a rule, had broad appeal.

Although not written primarily for an academic audience, some of my arguments have been tried out in scholarly forums. The chapter on Guantánamo took shape after I presented a similar account during a conference on "AIDS and Its Unforeseen Consequences," organized by the American Historical Association, to which I am grateful. The material was further developed for the faculty seminar of the Department of Anthropology of Harvard University, and I thank Stanley Tambiah for the invitation. Discussion of the roots of human rights abuses in Haiti continued at the invitation of Jonathan Mann and the François-Xavier Bagnoud Center for Health and Human Rights of the Harvard School of Public Health.

I've also accumulated debts to individuals. It's no exaggeration to say that this particular book would not have been written without the encouragement and assistance of Bill Rodriguez, who both suggested its format and edited the uneven prose. Thank you, Bill, and sorry.

Other key readers were Haun Saussy (as usual), Noam Chomsky, and Kristin Nelson; Kristin, in addition, provided great moral support. Parts of the text or oral expositions of its arguments were commented upon by Didi Bertrand, Allan Brandt, John Donnelly, Kris Heggenhougen, Oaksook Kim, and Amy Wilentz. Ophelia Dahl supported this endeavor in many ways, as did Jennifer Farmer, Roger Grande, Kate Elliott, and John Hines. Virginia Farmer found documents that only a librarian-mother would have uncovered. As a long-time admirer of Maggie Steber's photographs, I will thank her for the use of one of them by despairing of ever being able, with mere words, to capture what she does on film. Greg Bates of Common Courage Press used his fax machine and enthusiasm to keep this fast-paced project on schedule.

Haitian friends have commented on parts of this text, but all, with the exception of Yolande Jean, have asked to remain anonymous. One valiant nurse will recognize, I hope, the influence of her own example.

Of course, Tom White, Jim Kim, and Loune Viaud were a part of this effort, as they are of any project in which I am involved. They have some idea, I expect, of how grateful I am to them. In case of doubt, they should refer to this book's frontispiece.

As ever, I am thankful to be a part of the Department of Social Medicine at the Harvard Medical School, of the Brigham and Women's Hospital, and of Partners In Health.

It is perfunctory, in acknowledgments like these, to claim sole responsibility for a work. *The Uses of Haiti* was written in anxious haste, and no one (with the exception of Bill) bears much responsibility for its final form. Certainly, no one with whom I am associated should be held accountable for the ideas or analyses expressed here.

Let me close the preliminaries and open this book with a quotation from E.P. Thompson: "Isolated within intellectual enclaves, the drama of 'theoretical practice' may become a *substitute* for more difficult practical engagements," he wrote in 1978. Thompson concludes his withering attack on the French philosopher Louis Althusser and other scholar-demagogues by accusing them of taking young men and women of good will on a ride: "The terminus of that ride is outside the city of human endeavor and outside the domain of knowledge. So we can expect them to be absent from both."

It is every scholar's wish to remain within both the city of human endeavor and the domain of knowledge. It is every physician's hope to avoid feeling as if he were merely plugging holes in a straining dike. Author's royalties, in the event there are any, will go to the Institute for Health and Social Justice.

Port-au-Prince
January 15, 1994

Contents

Foreword

Jonathan Kozol

Powerful books that bravely challenge citadels of cultural deception are not welcomed by the orchestrating forces they condemn. *The Uses of Haiti* is a classic instance of this kind of brave iconoclastic work; and it is no surprise that it has been consigned by those who shape American opinion to the critical oblivion that is reserved for books that threaten the accepted lies by which we live.

Paul Farmer has given us a devastating document that strips away the pretense of benevolence from U.S. policy on Haiti and reveals the limitless brutality with which the richest nation in the Western Hemisphere has fostered misery and death within the poorest. In an utterly compelling analytic narrative that reaches back across 200 years of history, Dr. Farmer demonstrates the ruthlessness with which the U.S. government has preyed upon the people of the world's first black republic and then courageously unveils our government's collusion with the agents of state terror in the recent era of the two Duvalier dictatorships and in the reign of military terror that ensued after the younger of the two Duvaliers had been overthrown.

Writing from his vantage point as founder and director of a hospital in one of Haiti's poorest rural sectors, Dr. Farmer draws upon the words of his own patients and his own eye-witness observations to portray the consequences of our nation's policies and sets the stage for the contemporary stranglehold in which the U.S. government is crushing Haiti's people in an effort to destabilize a popularly elected president who, unique in Haiti's modern history, is not a servile viceroy of U.S. interest and does not routinely genuflect before American demands.

Jean-Bertrand Aristide, a former priest who worked for years with children in the slums of Port-au-Prince, spoke softly to me earlier this year within his office in the presidential palace. Scarcely eight weeks prior to our conversation, more than 30 men, several believed to have been former military officers, had stormed the palace on a Sunday night on which the president, fortuitously, was not in the building. American heavy-weaponry, apparently abandoned by them in their flight, was on display before the sandbagged palace on the day I talked with Aristide, who made only passing reference to the multiple attempts that have been made upon his life but offered a meticulous and detailed briefing on the educational and economic needs of Haiti's people and the critical health status of its children.

An American-imposed embargo on $500 million in external aid, most of which had been intended for humanitarian relief, has paralyzed the president's ability to reconstruct the physical and social infrastructure of the nation and has gravely undermined attempts to raise the nation's literacy levels, to deliver basic public services such as clean water, and develop comprehensive health-care networks that can lower the alarming levels of mortality in children. The embargo is defended by the U.S. State Department as a means of punishing the Aristide administration for refusal to accept our economic dictates and our morally unjustifiable insistence that the president "negotiate" collaboration on an equal basis with a tiny unelected opposition hand-selected by the U.S. government and funded, in large part, by U.S. interests.

No such strong-arm tactics were employed by the United States during the 30 years of the corrupt Duvalier dictatorships in which vast sums of U.S. aid were funneled without question or conditions to a murderous regime that was considered a strategic asset by the U.S. State Department. Only now, when an elected president with massive popular support among the poorest of the poor speaks truth to power in the small but well-connected upper-class kleptocracy of Haiti, does the U.S. government resort to economic blackmail and political manipulation to destabilize a democratic process it pretends to honor.

I met some of the youngest victims of these policies within the medieval-looking pediatric wards of Haiti's University State Hospital in Port-au-Prince. Children afflicted with the reddish hair and puffy limbs that indicate the most extreme degrees of malnutrition, many afflicted too with polio, tuberculosis, HIV infection, typhoid fever, and malaria, others with heart failure, brain tumors, diabetes, and leukemia, were lying patiently, but listlessly, on beds that looked to be the rusted relics of pre-modern medicine.

Adjustable beds or bedside monitors to check a child's vital signs were luxuries beyond the nation's budget possibilities, the chief of surgery informed me. Mothers of children had to go out on their own into the streets to purchase medical essentials such as penicillin, intravenous tubes and needles, sometimes even sterile gauze and sutures. Blood transfusions were impossible unless a patient had the money to buy blood outside the hospital. No intensive-care facilities existed. Pediatric neurosurgery was unavailable to children with brain tumors and to those whose foreheads were grotesquely swollen by hydrocephalus. Even brain shunts to relieve the pressure on the children's skulls were unavailable unless a parent had the funds to buy one on the private market for $400. In the neonatal ward there were no respirators.

When I later asked a U.S. diplomat in Port-au-Prince why the United States, with all its wealth and power, could not bring itself to set aside its fierce political hostility to Aristide in order to release even some portion of the funds that would relieve not only these but many other needless miseries of Haiti's people, the answer I was given was as cold as polished steel: The United States would not support the public services administered by governmental agencies in Haiti until Haiti's government accepted ultimatums set in Washington, no matter how these ultimatums were perceived, by those who had elected Aristide, to compromise their sovereignty. The lives of millions of poor children, I was made to understand, had been assigned no place in these political determinations.

Paul Farmer, who is both a world-renowned clinician and an utterly respectful and engaged participant within the lives of those he serves in Haiti, offers us the undiluted and uncensored story of the underpinnings and the consequences of these policies. The eloquence and earned authority with which he writes have, not surprisingly, created major problems for opinion makers in the U.S. government and for their allies in the mainstream U.S. media. Hence, perhaps, the fear voiced by Noam Chomsky in the introduction to this volume, which he wrote in 1994, that Dr. Farmer's work was "fated for oblivion."

We may justly celebrate the fact that this has proven not to be the case. Even after being out of print for several years, Dr. Farmer's work retains so strong a following that it continues to be widely read and now will be available again in this updated and expanded version to a new and, I expect, much larger readership. For this, not only ardent and progressive intellectuals invested in the policy debates but ordinary citizens whose lives are rooted in the simplest and most transparent principles of justice, mercy, and fair play ought to be grateful.

In the final words of this intensely moving book, the author recommends the virtues of "old-fashioned penitence" to U.S. citizens who contemplate the tragic misdirection of our nation's policies and actions as they bear upon the Haitian people. Penitence is surely not too much to ask of us. Shame and indignation, certainly, would be in order too—and with them, a revitalized determination to deny to any agency of U.S. government the power or the right to compromise our nation's honor and betray its ethical foundations with impunity.

—Jonathan Kozol,
Byfield, Massachusetts, August 2002

Introduction

Noam Chomsky

This is a book that I fear is fated for oblivion. The reason is that it tells the truth about uncomfortable matters—uncomfortable, that is, for the structures of power and the doctrinal framework that protects them from critical scrutiny. It tells the truth about what has been happening in Haiti, and the U.S. role in its bitter fate.

The reigning intellectual and moral culture portrays the world in a far different light. Adopting its perspective, why should we even care about Haiti? After all, we are the richest and most powerful country in the world, while Haiti is at the opposite extreme of human existence: miserable, horrifying, black, ugly. We may pity Haitians and other backward peoples who have, unaccountably, failed to achieve our nobility and wealth, and we may even try to lend them a helping hand, out of humanitarian impulse. But responsibility stops there.

Our power and fortune are a tribute to our virtue, and we are, perhaps more than ever, the beacon of freedom, democracy, markets, and all wonderful things. So one learns daily from every respectable source. "America's victory in the cold war was a victory for a set of political and economic principles: democracy and the free market," *The New York Times* instructs us with pride, and we grandly lead "the wave of the future—a future for which America is both the gatekeeper and the model." A century ago things might have been a bit different, but today "American motives are largely humanitarian;" the present danger is that we might err in an excess of benevolence, carrying out yet another humanitarian intervention even though no clear self-interest can be demonstrated, failing to understand that "there are limits to what outsiders can do," even marvels of good will like us, and that "the armies we dispatch to foreign soil for humanitarian reasons" may not be able "to save people from others or from themselves."[1]

Since these are Plain Truths, no evidence or analysis is necessary, and the pronouncements, which abound, are typically devoid of anything of the sort. That is fair enough, given that the truths are self-evident. Serious thinkers even inform us that the perfection of our leaders and institutions is a *necessary* truth. In a prestigious journal, the Eaton Professor of the Science of Government at Harvard explains that the United States must maintain its "international primacy" for the benefit of the world; the reason is that its "national identity is defined by a set of universal political and economic values," namely "liberty, democracy, equality, private property, and markets" (Samuel Huntington). Since this is a matter of *definition*, so the Science of Government teaches, it would be an error of logic to bring up the factual record, as if one were to conduct experiments to determine whether even numbers are in fact divisible by two.[2]

Admittedly there are flaws and errors in the record, but these have no bearing on what lies before us. That conclusion is firmly established by a device that is invoked with impressive regularity: the doctrine of "change of course." In the past, it is true, we may have strayed from the path of righteousness—for understandable reasons—but now we have "changed course" so the past is irrelevant. We are returning to our fundamental nature and "national identity." The doctrine plays a critical role in current debate over "humanitarian intervention," which remains unsullied by any inquiry into the actual record of intervention to the present day, by the United States or any other state, or the ways intellectuals have recast history to efface the most sordid crimes. Nor do respectable people deign to ask why institutions that have not changed should be expected to function differently in the future. Review of the historical record is nothing more than "sound-bites and invectives about Washington's historically evil foreign policy," Brown

University professor Thomas Weiss writes with derision, hence "easy to ignore."[3]

The Cold War provides the favored current formula, as Paul Farmer observes. Any lapse in recent years can be attributed to the cosmic struggle with the Russians. Thus if experimental subjects for radiation studies were chosen from a school for the mentally retarded rather than an elite prep school, that was unfortunate, but understandable in the atmosphere of the Cold War, so it is alleged—about as plausibly as in most other cases. And we have now "changed course," so that history may rest in peace.

Reality is a bit different, wherever we look. In the case of Haiti, the European conquerers half a millenium ago regarded the island of Hispanolia (today's Haiti and Dominican Republic) as a virtual paradise: opulent, peaceful, densely populated, rich in resources, much like today's Bangladesh, the first part of India conquered by the British and now, along with Haiti, the very symbol of hopelessness and despair. The observation generalizes in interesting ways, another of those politically incorrect lessons, better suppressed. The centuries since have seen terror, oppression, and looting that devastated the victims and vastly enriched the conquerors, who were finally expelled while keeping their grip in other ways. We inherit from them not only the fruits of their crimes but also the moral cowardice that is the standard accompaniment of conquest, including the wondrous capacity for self-adulation whatever horrors the victors have left in their wake and an intellectual armory to ensure that nothing is learned from what they have done.

The experience of Haiti shows just how significant a factor the Cold War has been. As Farmer records, U.S. relations with Haiti are not a thing of yesterday. Two centuries ago the American Republic, which had just gained its own independence, joined European powers in aiding France's violent repression of Haiti's slave rebellion. When the rebellion nevertheless succeeded, the U.S.

exceeded all others in the harshness of its reaction, refusing to recognize Haiti until 1862, in the context of the American Civil War. At that moment, Haiti's strategic location was important for Lincoln's armies and the Black country gained a new attractiveness as a place to dump freed slaves so that the American Republic could be free of "blot or mixture" in Thomas Jefferson's picturesque phrase, the Red Indians eliminated or removed and the Blacks expelled to the Caribbean or Africa; Liberia was recognized in the same year, in part for the same reasons. Haiti then became a plaything for international power politics. Numerous U.S. interventions culminated in Woodrow Wilson's invasion of Haiti and the Dominican Republic, where his warriors—as viciously racist as the Administration in Washington—murdered and destroyed, reinstituted virtual slavery, dismantled the constitutional system because the backward Haitians were unwilling to turn their country into a U.S. plantation, and established the National Guards that ran the countries by violence and terror after the Marines finally left.

Wilson's thuggery has entered history in two different ways: here and there. Here the events illustrate U.S. "humanitarian intervention," and its difficulties (for us). "Haiti's tragic history should be a cautionary tale for those now eagerly pursuing Operation Restore Hope in Somalia," Robert Kaplan warned, recalling the difficulties we face as we seek "to heal the body politic of a land that lacks the basis of a modern political culture." Elaine Sciolino recalls that the Marines "kept order, collected taxes, arbitrated disputes, distributed food and medicine, and even censored criticism in the press and tried political offenders in military courts," the worst sin of the occupation. Mark Danner writes that "six decades have passed since the Marines departed Haiti, leaving behind a few well-paved roads, a handful of new agricultural and vocational schools, and an American-trained 'non-political army'," nothing more. For USAID official Lawrence Harrison, who thinks that Haiti's problem is that it needs a new culture and more kind tutelage of the kind he provided as director of the USAID mission in 1977–79, the occupation merits only the words: "And some of the Marines abused their power." Harvard historian David Landes recounts that the occupation "provided the stability needed to make the political system work and to facilitate trade with the outside." Another noted scholar, Professor Hewson Ryan of the Fletcher School of Law and Diplomacy at Tufts University, is effusive in his praise for what the U.S. accomplished in "two centuries of well-intentioned involvement," beginning with U.S. support for France's merciless terror. "Few nations have been the object over such a sustained period of so much well-intentioned guidance and support," he writes—so that Haiti's current state is something of a mystery. Ryan is particularly impressed with Wilson's kind insistence on eliminating such "unprogressive" features of the constitutional system as the provisions against takeover of lands by foreigners, referring to his forceful dissolution of the National Assembly because it refused to ratify the U.S.-designed constitution. Further odes are recorded below.[4]

Haitians have somewhat different memories of American solicitude. Grassroots organizations, priests in hiding, and others suffering bitterly from the violence of the security forces expressed marked opposition to the plan to dispatch 500 United Nations (U.N.) police to the terrorized country in 1993, seeing them as a cover for a U.S. intervention that evokes bitter memories of the 19-year Marine occupation—a strange view held only by "radical leftists," according to U.S. doctrine. Under the heading "unhealed sores," Haitian anthropologist Michel-Rolph Trouillot points out that "Most observers agree that the achievements of the occupation were minor; they disagree only as to the amount of damage it inflicted," including the acceleration of Haiti's economic, military, and political centralization, its economic dependence and sharp class divisions, the vicious exploitation of the peasantry, the internal conflicts much intensified by the extreme racism of the occupying forces, and perhaps worst of all, the establishment of "an army to fight the people." If ever noted, such reactions may be attributed to the backwardness and ignorance of Haitians, or the fact that "even a benevolent occupation creates resistance... among the beneficiaries."[5]

The occupation left Haiti a U.S. dependency, hence a fine example of what we can accomplish when we have a free hand, standing alongside the Philippines, Brazil, and much of the rest of the Central America-Caribbean region. Just think how much we could learn about ourselves by looking at the results, an unpopular exercise, for some reason.

In the case of Haiti, Washington reacted with ambivalence to the brutal dictatorship of "Papa Doc" Duvalier. He was a bit too independent for U.S. tastes, though John F. Kennedy did promise to provide aid for the François Duvalier International Airport in exchange for the Haitian vote to expel Cuba from the Organization of American States (OAS). Kennedy also provided the bloodthirsty killer with military assistance as part of the general program of extending U.S. control over the security forces in Latin America, a long-standing project carried a long step forward by the Kennedy intellectuals, who recognized that "in the Latin American cultural environment" the military must be prepared "to remove government leaders from office whenever, in the judgment of the military, the conduct of those leaders is injurious to the welfare of the nation." So Robert McNamara pointed out to McGeorge Bundy shortly after the Brazilian generals had performed the mission for which the groundwork had been carefully laid by the Kennedy Administration, instituting a neo-Nazi regime that was highly praised by Washington and the business community. Thanks to the entrenchment of U.S. control, McNamara continued, the military throughout the continent approach their task of defending sovereignty and democracy with a proper "understanding of, and orientation toward, U.S. objectives." Many people south of the border can testify to the perspicuity of these words.[6]

When "Baby Doc" Jean-Claude Duvalier took over in 1971, relations rapidly improved, and Haiti joined Brazil as a "darling" of the American business community. USAID undertook to turn Haiti into the "Taiwan of the Caribbean," forecasting "a historic change toward deeper market interdependence with the United States." U.S. taxpayers funded major efforts to establish assembly plants for U.S. manufacturers, who were able to benefit from such advantages as enormous unemployment (thanks in part to USAID policies emphasizing agroexport), no unions, ample terror, workers at wages of 14 cents an hour (mainly women, as elsewhere considered more docile), and the other usual amenities.

Having acquired a proper "understanding of, and orientation toward, U.S. objectives," the military performed the mission required in "the Haitian cultural environment." It was "standard operating procedure for employers to call in armed forces, either uniformed troops or groups of thugs, to frighten workers who have begun an organizing effort" or to terrorize workers who sought to bargain or go on strike, union activists informed U.S. labor rights investigators. A U.S. Embassy official explained the conventional pattern: "You have to understand, the army here is like the police at home," he said. "It's not that big a deal. It's not like calling out the National Guard" when factories are invaded by what union activists describe as squads of "Uzi-bearing, combat-booted soldiers from the notorious Dessalines barracks or Leopard commando units, who have been implicated in the shootings of hundreds of Haitians in recent years." No big deal.

The consequences were profits for U.S. manufacturers and the Haitian superrich, and a decline of 56% in Haitian wages through the 1980s—in short, an "economic miracle" of the usual sort. Haiti remained Haiti, not Taiwan.[7]

Washington's much-admired "yearning for democracy" was also well illustrated in those years. In June 1985, the Haitian legislature unanimously adopted a law requiring that every political party recognize President-for-Life Duvalier as the supreme arbiter of the nation, outlawing the Christian Democrats, and granting the government the right to suspend the rights of any party without reasons. The law was ratified by a majority of 99.98%. Deeply impressed by this "encouraging step forward," the Reagan Administration certified to Congress that "democratic development" was progressing so that military and economic aid could continue to flow—mainly into the pockets of Baby Doc and his entourage. It also informed Congress that the human rights situation was improving, an automatic concomitant of a decision to provide military aid. The House Foreign Affairs Committee, controlled by Democrats, had given its approval in advance, calling on the Administration "to maintain friendly relations with Duvalier's non-Communist government."

To justify their view of the vote as an "encouraging step forward" in "democratic development," the Reaganites could have recalled the vote held under Woodrow Wilson's rule after he had disbanded the Haitian parliament in punishment for its refusal to turn the country over to American corporations under the terms of the U.S.-designed Constitution. Wilson's Marines organized a plebiscite in which the Constitution was ratified by a 99.9% vote, with 5% of the population participating, using "rather high handed methods to get the Constitution adopted by the people of Haiti," the State Department conceded a decade later. Baby Doc, in contrast, allowed a much broader franchise, though it is true that he demanded a slightly higher degree of acquiescence than Wilsonian idealists. A case can be made, then, that the lessons in democracy that Washington had been laboring to impart were finally sinking in.

Unfortunately, matters did not proceed as planned.

As the *Wall Street Journal* explained, "huge demonstrations" convinced the White House "that the regime was unraveling" and "U.S. analysts learned that Haiti's ruling inner circle had lost faith in" Baby Doc. "As a result, U.S. officials, including Secretary of State George Shultz, began openly calling for a 'democratic process' in Haiti." So that no one could mistake the reasons for its sudden embrace of democracy, Washington followed the very same scenario in the Philippines at the same time, turning against its long-time favorite Ferdinand Marcos and calling for a "democratic process" when the army and elite made it clear that it was determined to rid the country of the bloodthirsty and rapacious gangster for whom Reagan and Bush had expressed their admiration, even "love," not long before. The doctrine of "change of course" ensures that absolutely nothing is learned from any of this.[8]

Washington proceeded to support the post-Duvalier Conseil National de Gouvernement (CNG), providing $2.8 million in military aid in its first year, while the CNG, "generously helped by the U.S. taxpayer's money, had openly gunned down more civilians than Jean-Claude Duvalier's government had done in fifteen years," Trouillot comments. Despite repeated coups and massacres, things remained pretty much on course, while Reagan's Ambassador explained to U.S. human rights investigators that "I don't see any evidence of a policy against human rights"; there may be violence, it is true, but it is just "part of the culture." Whose, one might ask.

A serious problem did arise in December 1990, however. Washington made the mistake of allowing a free election, expecting an easy victory for its candidate, Marc Bazin, a former World Bank official. Shocking outside observers, Father Jean-Bertrand Aristide was elected with two-thirds of the vote (Bazin was second with 14%), swept into office by a remarkable collection of grassroots organizations, Lavalas ("flood"), which had escaped the notice of the rich folk. Aristide held office from February to September, when his government was overthrown by a military coup, plunging the country into even deeper barbarism than before.

There are two versions of what happened since Aristide was elected, though they converge on certain facts. Both versions agree that the rampant state terror of earlier years radically declined while "the flow of boat people all but dried up,"[9] and that both the terror and the refugee flow surged anew with the September 1991 coup. These are "economic refugees," hence not entitled to political asylum, according to official doctrine. Beyond that, the versions differ.

The approved version is offered by *New York Times* Haiti correspondent Howard French. He reports that Aristide governed "with the aid of fear," leaning "heavily on Lavalas, an unstructured movement of affluent idealists and long-exiled leftists" whose model was China's Cultural Revolution. Aristide's power hunger led to "troubles with civil society." Furthermore, "Haitian political leaders and diplomats say, the growing climate of vigilantism as well as increasingly strident statements by Father Aristide blaming the wealthier classes for the poverty of the masses encouraged" the coup. "Although he retains much of the popular support that enabled him to win 67% of the popular vote in the country's December 1990 elections, Father Aristide was overthrown in part because of concerns among politically active people over his commitment to the Constitution, and growing fears of political and class-based violence, which many believe the President endorsed."[10]

The assumptions are worth contemplating: two-thirds of the population and their organizations are outside of "civil society"; the politically active people involved in the popular organizations and in local and national politics are not among the "politically active people"; it is scandalous to tell the truth about the responsibility of the kleptocracy for the poverty of the masses; "fears of political and class-based violence" are limited to the months when such violence sharply declined. We detect, perhaps, a few more lessons from which respectable society must be defended.

A different version is put forward by various extremists who see Lavalas as a "remarkably advanced" array of popular organizations that gave the large majority of the population a "considerable voice in local affairs" and even in national politics (Americas Watch), and who were impressed by Aristide's policies as he "acted quickly to restore order to the government's finances" after taking power when "the economy was in an unprecedented state of disintegration" (Inter-American Development Bank, IDB). The World Bank was also in the extremist camp. International lending agencies offered aid, endorsing Aristide's investment program and noting his reduction of foreign debt; the increase of foreign exchange reserves from near zero to $12 million, increased government revenues thanks to Aristide's anti-corruption campaign and tax collection measures that infringed on the traditional rights of the kleptocracy; the streamlining of the bloated government bureaucracy; his determined efforts to end contraband trade, including narcotrafficking, and to improve the customs system; measures that sharply reduced inflation; and the establishment of a responsible fiscal system. These actions were "welcomed by the international financial community," the IDB noted, leading to "a substantial increase in assistance."[11]

The same deviant version was provided by the Council on Hemispheric Affairs in Washington. "Under Aristide," it reported, "for the first time in the republic's tortured history, Haiti seemed to be on the verge of tearing free from the fabric of despotism and tyranny which had smothered all previous attempts at democratic expression and self-determination." His victory "represented more than a decade of civic engagement and education on his part," spearheaded by local activists of the Church, small grassroots-based communities, and other popular organizations that formed the basis of the Lavalas movement that swept him into power, "a textbook example of participatory, 'bottom-up' and democratic political development." His government sought "the empowerment of the poor," a "populist model" committed to "social and economic justice, popular political participation and openness in all governmental affairs." Aristide's balancing of the budget and "trimming of a bloated bureaucracy" led to a "stunning success" that also made White House planners "extremely uncomfortable": he secured over half a billion dollars in aid from the international lending community, indicating "that Haiti was slipping out of Washington's financial orbit" and "demonstrating a degree of sovereignty in its political affairs."[12]

Sober commentators, however, generally endorse *The New York Times* version. Arguing "the case for pragmatism," the editor of *Foreign Affairs*, William Hyland, observed that "In Haiti it has not been so easy to differentiate among the democrats and the dictators"— between Aristide, on the one hand, and the Duvaliers and their contemporary clones, on the other. Pragmatism thus requires that we seek some middle way between the various extremists.

Also writing in *Foreign Affairs*, the Dean of the Paul Nitze School of Advanced International Studies at Johns Hopkins, Paul Wolfowitz, agrees with French and Hyland. President Clinton, he argues, took Bush's "dubious commitment to President Aristide and deepened it," a mistake all along given Aristide's limited credentials as a "democrat." These credentials are "meager," Lawrence Harrison explains, and his "human rights record" was "far from exemplary." It might be wise, Harrison suggests, to undertake a "new start on building democratic institutions, with at least symbolic participation by Aristide," but surely nothing more.[13]

The actual facts are presented in the chapters that follow, and I need not review them here. It might, however, be useful to comment on the standards of those who find Aristide lacking. Wolfowitz was Defense

Undersecretary during the Reagan-Bush years, hence a direct participant in the terror and atrocities they conducted, organized, and supported in Central America. As Assistant Secretary of State for East Asian Affairs in mid-1985, he lauded the dictator Marcos for his "revitalization of political institutions" and the "broad press freedom" under his benign rule; shortly before, 14 journalists had been murdered by his security forces. As noted, a few months later, the Reagan Administration changed its tune when the army and elite turned against their beloved friend.

As for Harrison, it may suffice to have a look at the achievements in the region of the Administration he served, notably those of the current U.S. special envoy to Haiti, Lawrence Pezzullo, appointed Ambassador to Nicaragua while Harrison was presiding over the USAID projects that were to turn Haiti into Taiwan. As Pezzullo took charge in Nicaragua, it was becoming difficult to sustain the vicious Somoza dictatorship. Pezzullo's task was to ensure that nothing changed even if our favored friend had to be sacrificed like Marcos, Baby Doc, and others who had outlived their usefulness. At the time, Somoza's National Guard was busy slaughtering tens of thousands of civilians. Pezzullo recommended that the bloodbath continue: "I believe it ill-advised," he cabled Washington, "to go to Somoza and ask for a bombing halt." He advised further that "with careful orchestration we have a better than even chance of preserving enough of the [National Guard] to maintain order and hold the FSLN in check after Somoza resigns," even though this plan would "smack somewhat of Somocismo sin Somoza." A few weeks later he informed the Carter State Department that the "survivability" of the Guard was doubtful unless Somoza left, as he did, fleeing to Miami with what remained of the national treasury. Pezzullo and his associates then established the Guard at the border, with consequences that we need not review here.

If any of this offends Harrison's delicate sensibilities,

we have yet to learn about it, though he is not without compassion for Haitians, as they suffer under the ill-advised embargo with its "appalling" costs, leading to deaths that are "surely much higher than the number of victims of military and police violence," not to speak of the "cost in terms of Haitians self-respect and self-reliance" of U.S. humanitarian efforts "to cushion the impact" of the embargo.[14]

As for Pezzullo, he explained in December 1993 that Washington was seeking a "centrist" solution to the problem of leadership in Haiti, a solution that amounts to "a soft coup," the Council on Hemispheric Affairs observes, which would put Aristide and his supporters to the side while placing effective power in the hands of elements of the military and the business classes that had lost the election by a huge margin. "Pezzullo has implemented the Administration's two-track policy of trying to placate the Congressional Black Caucus and the other critics who have made Aristide's cause their own, while under-cutting the Haitian president at every opportunity." To insure that "the populist Aristide" is kept "on a short tether," Pezzullo "insists that Aristide must enter into a power-sharing relationship with the military and his political enemies by broadening his cabinet, which already is far more pluralistic than the one which serves Mr. Clinton." The Haitian military, meanwhile, are treating Pezzullo "with the contempt that, perhaps, he deserves."[15]

In reality, the differences between the two versions of what happened during the brief moment of democracy and an end to terror are much less than they appear. The description by Americas Watch of a "remarkably advanced" array of popular organizations that brought the large majority of the population into the political arena is precisely what frightened Washington and the mainstream generally (French, Harrison, etc.). That is not their concept of "democracy," "civil society," or proper "political leaders." The preferred picture is sketched by

Reagan insider Thomas Carothers, a State Department official who took part in the "democracy enhancement" projects for Latin America and the Caribbean and has written informatively (if ruefully) on the consequences of these programs, which he is sure were "sincere," despite what he sees as their failure. Carothers notes a correlation between U.S. influence and the rise of democracy in the hemisphere: where U.S. influence was least, in the southern cone, steps towards democracy took place, opposed by the Reagan Administration, which later hastened to take credit for them. Where U.S. influence was greatest, the effects were worst. Washington adopted "prodemocracy policies as a means of relieving pressure for more radical change," he writes, "but inevitably sought only limited, top-down forms of democratic change that did not risk upsetting the traditional structures of power with which the United States has long been allied." Its "impulse is to promote democratic change, but the underlying objective is to maintain the basic order of what, historically at least, are quite undemocratic societies." The U.S. keeps to "very limited, controlled forms of democratic change" because of its "deep fear...of populist-based change in Latin America—with all its implications for upsetting established economic and political orders and heading off in a leftist direction."[16]

"In other words," Carothers concludes, "the United States works with the existing power structures and tries to teach or persuade them to be democratic rather than working from the bottom up to spread the ideas and principles of a democratic society among the citizenries." Of course, persuading these power structures "to be democratic" makes about as much sense as persuading the persuaders "to be democratic." The thought could only horrify them. In the elite political culture, "democracy" is determined by outcome, not process. And the outcome must be "top-down" rule, with some degree of public endorsement to ensure stability if that can be obtained, but nothing that would "risk upsetting the traditional structures of power." These should be truisms, taught in elementary school.

The "existing power structures" are "civil society," the "moderates," the proper "political leaders." Popular organizations that threaten to offer the overwhelming majority a voice in managing their own affairs are a threat to democracy. Their spokespersons have only "meager" democratic credentials and can be allowed only "symbolic participation" in the true "democratic institutions" that we will construct.

These simple truths are the key to understanding of policy quite generally. They suffice to explain just what has happened in Haiti. Trouillot concludes his study by observing that "In Haiti, the peasantry is the nation." But for policymakers, the peasantry are only instruments for maximizing corporate profits, otherwise worthless objects. They may produce food for export and enrich local affiliates of U.S. agribusiness, or flock to the city to provide supercheap labor for assembly plants. They have no further function. It is, then, entirely natural that USAID, while providing $100 million in assistance to the private sector, should never have provided a penny to the leading popular peasant organization, the Peasant Movement of Papaye (MPP); and that a former USAID director should see no special problem when MPP members are massacred by the military forces and should dismiss with contempt its call for the imposition of a real, not symbolic, embargo to reinstitute the popularly elected President who was committed to "bottom-up" rather than "top-down" democracy. Again, no big deal.

Similarly, it is hardly surprising that USAID should have denounced the labor reforms Aristide sought to institute and opposed his efforts to raise the minimum wage to a princely 37 cents an hour. Nor should we find it odd that USAID invested massively in the low wage assembly sector while wages sharply declined and working conditions fell to abysmal levels, but terminated all efforts to promote investment as the democratically elected government took office. Rather, USAID reacted to this catastrophe by dedicating itself still more firmly to providing the Haitian business community with what it called "technical assistance in labor relations, development of a business oriented public relations campaign, and intensified efforts to attract U.S. products assembly operations to Haiti." Given the unfortunate democratic deviation, USAID's task, in its own words, was to "work to develop sustainable dialogue between the government and the business community"; comparable efforts for workers and peasants during the days when Haiti was run by U.S.-backed killers and torturers are, to date, unknown.[17]

Similarly, there is no reason to be surprised that U.S. elites suddenly began to show such sensitive concern for human rights and democracy just as human rights violations precipitously decline and democracy (though not in the preferred "top-down" sense) begins to flower. Amy Wilentz, who has done some of the best reporting from Haiti, observes that during Aristide's brief term, Washington suddenly became concerned with "human rights and the rule of law in Haiti." "During the four regimes that preceded Aristide," she writes, "international human-rights advocates and democratic observers had begged the State Department to consider helping the democratic opposition in Haiti. But no steps were taken by the United States to strengthen anything but the executive and the military until Aristide won the presidency. Then, all of a sudden, the United States began to think about how it could help those Haitians eager to limit the powers of the executive or to replace the government constitutionally." The State Department "Democracy Enhancement" project was "specifically designed to fund those sectors of the Haitian political spectrum where opposition to the Aristide government could be encouraged."[18]

All as would be expected by anyone with eyes open.

Wilentz reports further that immediately after the September 30 coup, the State Department apparently "circulated a thick notebook filled with alleged human rights violations" under Aristide—"something it had not done under the previous rulers, Duvalierists and military men," who were deemed proper recipients for aid, including military aid, "based on unsubstantiated human-rights improvements." Linda Diebel adds details. A "thick, bound dossier" on Aristide's alleged crimes was presented by the coup leader, General Cédras, to OAS negotiators. On October 3, U.S. Ambassador Alvin Adams summoned reporters from *The New York Times*, *Washington Post*, and other major U.S. journals to private meetings where he briefed them on these alleged crimes, reportedly presenting them with the "dossier"— which, we may learn some day, was compiled by U.S. intelligence and offered to its favorite generals. The Ambassador and his helpers began leaking the tales that have since been used to demonstrate Aristide's "meager" democratic credentials and his psychological defects and instability; to borrow the terms of *New York Times* headlines right after the coup, his "Autocratic Ways" that "ended Haiti's Embrace of Democracy," that is, "Haiti's Democracy, Such as it Was." Much of the "evidence" that has become part of the now-familiar litany, Diebel reports, was provided by a Canadian, Lynn Garrison, who "masterminded the smear campaign" while staying in close contact with U.S. Embassy "military attaché" Pat Collins.[19]

After the coup, the OAS instituted an embargo, which the Bush Administration reluctantly joined, while making clear to its allies and clients that it was not to be taken seriously. The official reasons were explained a year later by Howard French: "Washington's deep-seated ambivalence about a leftward-tilting nationalist whose style diplomats say has sometimes been disquietingly erratic" precludes any meaningful support for sanctions against the military rulers. "Despite much blood on the army's hands, United States diplomats consider it a vital counterweight to Father Aristide, whose class-struggle rhetoric...threatened or antagonized traditional power centers at home and abroad." Aristide's "call for punishment of the military leadership" that had slaughtered and tortured thousands of people "reinforced a view of him as an inflexible and vindictive crusader," and heightened Washington's "antipathy" towards the "clumsy" and "erratic" extremist who has aroused great "anger" in Washington because of "his tendency toward ingratitude."[20]

The "vital counterweight" is therefore to hold total power while the "leftward tilting nationalist" remains in exile, awaiting the "eventual return" that Bill Clinton promised on the eve of his inauguration. Meanwhile, the "traditional power centers" in Haiti and the U.S. will carry on with class struggle as usual, employing such terror as may be needed in order for plunder to proceed unhampered. And as the London *Financial Times* added at the same time, Washington was proving oddly ineffective in detecting the "lucrative use of the country in the transhipment of narcotics" by which "the military is funding its oil and other necessary imports," financing the necessary terror and rapacity—though U.S. forces seem able to find every fishing boat carrying miserable refugees. Nor had Washington figured out a way to freeze the assets of "civil society" or to hinder their shopping trips to Miami and New York, or to induce its Dominican clients to monitor the border to impede the flow of goods that takes care of the wants of "civil society" while the embargo remains "at best, sieve-like."[21]

Little has changed since, and these late-1992 observations understate the facts. Thus Washington continues to provide Haitian military leaders with intelligence on narcotics trafficking—which they will naturally use to expedite their activities and tighten their grip on power. It's not easy to intercept narcotraffickers here, the press explains, because "Haiti has no radar," and evidently the

U.S. Navy and Air Force, hard hit by military cutbacks, cannot figure out a way to remedy this deficiency. The military and police command are U.S.-trained, and doubtless retain their contacts with U.S. military and intelligence. According to Church sources, officers of the Haitian military were seen at the U.S. Army base in Fort Benning, Georgia, home of the notorious School of the Americas, as recently as October 1993.[22]

On February 4, 1992, the Bush Administration lifted the embargo for assembly plants, "under heavy pressure from American businesses with interests in Haiti," the *Washington Post* reported. The editors judged the decision wise: the embargo was a "fundamental political miscalculation" that "has caused great suffering, but not among the gunmen. Since it hasn't served its purpose, it is good that it is being relaxed"—not tightened so as to serve its professed purpose, as those who endure the "great suffering" were pleading. A few months later, it was noted in the small print that Washington "is apparently continuing to relax controls on goods going to Port-au-Prince from the United States," allowing export of seeds, fertilizers and pesticides. For January-October 1992, U.S. trade with Haiti came to $265 million, according to the Department of Commerce, apparently unreported here in the mainstream.[23]

The New York Times also gave a positive cast to the undermining of the embargo, reported under the headline "U.S. Plans to Sharpen Focus of Its Sanctions Against Haiti." "The Bush Administration said today that it would modify its embargo against Haiti's military Government to punish anti-democratic forces and ease the plight of workers who lost jobs because of the ban on trade," Barbara Crossette reported. The State Department was "fine tuning" its economic sanctions, the "latest move" in Administration efforts to find "more effective ways to hasten the collapse of what the Administration calls an illegal Government in Haiti."[24] We are to understand that the "fine tuning" is designed to punish the "illegal Government" that applauds it and to benefit the workers who strenuously oppose it (not to speak of U.S. investors, unmentioned). Orwell would have been impressed, once again.

During the presidential campaign, Clinton bitterly assailed George Bush's cruel Haitian policies, particularly his harsh treatment of refugees. Clinton moved quickly to change these policies as he took office, harshening them still further by extending the (flatly illegal) blockade on Haiti to prevent refugees from escaping the mounting terror—all for humanitarian reasons; the goal was to save lives. Those who fled remained "economic refugees." Clinton's increased brutality proved to be a grand success. Refugee flow, which had reached over 30,000 in 1992, sharply declined under Clinton's ministrations, to about the level of 1989, before the decline under Aristide.[25]

The Clinton Administration meanwhile dedicated itself firmly to democracy, following prescriptions outlined by the *Washington Post* and *New York Times*.[26] The preferred solution, John Goshko explained in the *Post*, would "delay indefinitely" the return to Haiti of the "radical priest with anti-American leanings" whose "strident populism led the Haitian armed forces to seize power," and would "allow Bazin or some other prime minister to govern in his place." Bazin was then prime minister under army rule, but he posed one problem. Though he is "well-known and well-regarded in the United States," unfortunately "the masses in Haiti consider him a front man for military and business interests." So perhaps someone else will have to be selected to represent the interests of the moderates.

In the second national newspaper, Howard French indicated the scale of the required delay, quoting unidentified "diplomats," the usual device for presenting state propaganda while maintaining the fabled objectivity that is the pride of American journalism. "In the past," he wrote, "diplomats have said the Haitian President could return only after a substantial interim period during which the country's economy was revived and all its institutions, from the army itself to the judiciary to health care and education, were stabilized." That should overcome the danger of Aristide's "personalist and electoralist politics." But unfortunately, the troublesome priest has been recalcitrant: "Father Aristide and many of his supporters have held out for a quick return," undermining the moderate course.

As understood on all sides, the "delay" need not be too long. It is only necessary to dilly-dally until 1996, when Aristide's term ends (he is barred from running again). By then, military terror should have sufficiently intimidated the population and demolished popular organizations so that "free elections" can be run, as in Guatemala and El Salvador, without too much fear of any threat to "civil society" from the rabble. Even if Aristide is ultimately permitted to return, "he would have difficulty transforming his personal popularity into the organized support needed to exert civilian authority," Americas Watch observed as Clinton took office, quoting priests and others who fear that the destruction of the popular social organizations that "gave people hope" has undermined the great promise of Haiti's first democratic experiment.[27]

The basic idea was presented by Secretary of State Warren Christopher during his confirmation hearings. Christopher "expressed support for Father Aristide," Elaine Sciolino reported, "but stopped short of calling for his reinstatement as President. "There is no question in my mind that because of the election, he has to be part of the solution to this,' Mr. Christopher said. 'I don't have a precise system worked out in my mind as to how he would be part of the solution, but certainly he cannot be ignored in the matter'."[28] With this ringing endorsement of democracy, the Clinton Administration took charge.

To much acclaim, Washington finally succeeded in achieving the desired outcome—no great surprise. Under severe pressure, in July 1993 President Aristide accepted Washington's terms, which were theoretically to allow him to return four months later in a "compromise" with the gangsters who overthrew him and had been robbing and terrorizing at will since. Aristide agreed to dismiss his Prime Minister in favor of a businessman from the traditional mulatto elite, Robert Malval, who is "known to be opposed to the populist policies during Aristide's seven months in power," the press announced with relief, noting that Malval is "generally well regarded by the business community," "respected by many businessmen who supported the coup that ousted the President," and seen as "a reassuring choice" by coup-supporters.[29]

Expected to be a transition figure, Malval resigned at the year's end. His presence did, however, serve a useful role for Washington and its media, diverting attention to a "political settlement" while attacks on the popular organizations and general terror mounted, Aristide's promised return was blocked, and new initiatives were put forth to "broaden" the government to traditional power centers. Aristide's reluctance to accept arrangements that further marginalized the general population and undercut what remained of democracy also served a useful purpose, demonstrating even more clearly his extremism; the press never failed to note that he couldn't even agree with "his hand-picked Prime Minister," the phrase that ritually accompanied the name "Robert Malval," so that no reader would miss the point.

So matters continue to the time of writing, without essential change or any surprise. Under Clinton, the embargo became still more porous. The Dominican border became a complete joke, even noticed by the press. Meanwhile, U.S. companies continued to be exempted from the embargo—so as to ease its effects on the population, the Administration announced with a straight face; only exemptions for U.S. firms have this miraculous consequence. There were many heartfelt laments about the suffering of poor Haitians under the embargo, but one had to turn to the underground press in Haiti, the alternative media here, or an occasional letter to learn that the major peasant organization (MPP), church coalitions, labor organizations, and the National Federation of Haitian Students continued to call for a real embargo.[30] Curiously, those most distressed by the impact of the embargo on the Haitian poor were often among the most forceful advocates of a still harsher embargo on Cuba, notably liberal Democrat Robert Torricelli, author of the stepped-up embargo that the Bush Administration accepted under pressure from the Clintonites. Evidently, hunger causes no pain to Cuban children. The oddity passed unnoticed.

As did the impact of Clinton's tinkering with the embargo on Haiti. "U.S. imports from Haiti rose by more than half last year [1993]," the *Financial Times* reported, "thanks in part to an exemption granted by the U.S. Treasury for imports of goods assembled in Haiti from U.S. parts." U.S. exports to Haiti also rose in 1993. Exports from Haiti to the U.S. included food (fruits and nuts, citrus fruit or melons) from the starving country, which increased by a mere 3500% from January–July 1992 to January–July 1993. "The Clinton administration still formally declares its support for Mr Aristide, but scarcely disguises its wish for a leader more accommodating to the military," the world's leading business journal reported, while "European diplomats in Washington are scathing in their comments on what they see as the US's abdication of leadership over Haiti."[31]

By March 1994, Washington had succeeded in blocking efforts to impose a meaningful embargo or to punish the killers or their supporters. Its own plan "would leave the military largely in place," AP reported, though it "does not state a date for Father Aristide's return to Haiti and does not guarantee him a role in a proposed 'national unity' government that would include his enemies." The circle closes. Aristide's rejection of the plan merely demonstrates again his "intransigence" and "meager" democratic credentials.[32]

At the far right, the Haitian Chamber of Commerce could scarcely contain its delight as it debated measures to join army leaders in establishing a "new, broadly based government" with at most symbolic participation of the elected president, "with the assumption that nobody, including the Administration in Washington, wants Aristide back," a participant in the debate commented. A senior U.S. official quoted by the *Wall Street Journal* insisted that the U.S. was not backing away from Aristide, while noting that Washington "had never called for" his "immediate return" but rather "always preferred to have Haiti first build a functioning government" without him, after which he *might* return, though the Clinton Administration's current proposals "could possibly lead to a situation in which Mr. Aristide doesn't return" at all. Secretary of State Christopher reiterated that President Aristide "continues to be a major factor in the policy" the Administration is crafting, with an unknown role. Meanwhile, officials made it clear that any such role will be contingent on Aristide's agreement to extend the government to traditional power sectors while excluding the population ("broadening his political base") and to accept a merely symbolic presence. If only he can overcome his intransigence, we can proceed towards "democracy," meanwhile basking in glory as "the gatekeeper and the model" for a wondrous future.[33]

The sordid story easily fits with the reigning system of beliefs, on the principle, discussed earlier, that we are necessarily perfect, so that the course pursued by our leaders is one of moderation, set squarely between the extremists who fail to comprehend that we are right. In a typical effort, Howard French reports that legislators seeking to displace Aristide are "working very hard to build a center and construct a reasonable solution," though Aristide and equally recalcitrant elements in the military "are now taking actions that force things toward extremes," rejecting Washington's course of moderation. As moderates and pragmatists, the Americans seek to establish a "more broadly based governmment" that shifts power to the "moderate" elements of the military and the business community. Haitian moderates agree with Washington that the population should not be simply massacred and tortured. They have their place, not in the political arena to be sure, but seeking work for a few cents an hour in U.S.-owned assembly plants and exporting food to the United States while their children starve.

As usual, French quotes an unidentified "diplomat" to express required doctrine. We have to turn elsewhere to find the thoughts of a French military adviser, one of the last of the U.N.observers to remain after Aristide was barred from entry (alive) on October 31, 1993. "Do you know what the real problem is?," he asked Canadian reporter Linda Diebel: "The Americans don't want Aristide back, and they want the rest of us out"—"the rest of us" being Canada, France and Venezuela, the other three of "Aristide's so-called Four Friends."[34]

That this judgment is exactly right has been apparent throughout. It is necessary to add, however, that the issue is not specifically Aristide; rather, the forces he represents, the lively and vibrant popular movements that swept him into office, greatly alarming the rich and powerful in Haiti and their American counterparts.

Paul Farmer hopes that the stories he relates "will move readers to reject dominant readings of Haiti," and to respond to the Haitians who seek "to reach the hearts and minds of North Americans to change the policies" that have crushed them. Many others throughout the world join in that plea, including growing numbers in the desperate third world at home.

—Noam Chomsky
March 5, 1994

What's at Stake in Haiti

The pain in our shoulder comes
You say, from the damp; and this is also
*   the reason*
For the stain on the wall of our flat.
So tell us:
Where does the damp come from?

—Bertolt Brecht

Haiti may capture the headlines of the American popular press, but understanding of what is at stake here
remains, at best, persistently superficial. At worst, journalistic writing about Haiti distorts events and processes
in predictable ways, helping to perpetuate a series of
peculiarly potent myths about Haiti and Haitians. All of
this together—distortions, half-truths, myths, old and
new—leaves even people of good will and discernment
puzzled as to what is really happening in Haiti.

Yet the struggle of the Haitian poor—the vast majority of Haitians—has seldom been easier to decipher.
Events emblematic of both that struggle and misinforma-
tion about it were recently registered on the U.S. military
base on Guantánamo, Cuba, where 278 HIV-positive
Haitians were held against their will. These refugees were
among the thousands who had fled Haiti after the
September 30, 1991, coup that overthrew the country's
first popularly-elected government. Although *The New
York Times* claimed that this "U.S. Base Is an Oasis To
Haitians," the detainees I interviewed had a radically different view of Guantánamo. Shortly after speaking of
their plight at a conference on "AIDS and Its Unforeseen
Consequences," I was asked by one of the conference
organizers how, exactly, *he* could be seen to bear some

responsibility for these refugees: "Am I supposed to welcome these sick people into my country," he asked with some heat, "and to care for them? If so, am I not required to care for all the world's destitute sick?"

I did not expect, in the company of historians, to be confronted with such a question. The historical record is rich in incident and lays the groundwork for a resounding *yes* to at least the first part of this man's query. Neither the coup nor Guantánamo are comprehensible without an understanding of Haitian history, and this includes U.S. foreign policy towards Haiti. In few places in the world are the lineaments of responsibility so easily traced. In few places in the world have the actions of the powerful had such direct, if unanticipated, effects among the poor.

The United States and Haiti are something other than the richest and the poorest countries in the hemisphere; they are also its two oldest republics. Rarely, in fact, have two countries been as closely linked as the United States and Haiti. Haitians are, by and large, fully aware of this historical fact. But citizens of the United States are, by and large, oblivious to these links—ignorant, even, of the two-decade U.S. military occupation of Haiti earlier in this century.

This disparity of awareness has led Haitians to adopt a moral and analytic explanatory framework that differs substantially from that of Americans. U.S. journalists and even certain scholarly investigators, manifestly uninformed about the history of U.S.-Haitian relations, have mistaken this awareness as a Haitian tendency to paranoia. One *Washington Post* reporter commented on this tendency in an article entitled "Haitians Look for U.S. Hand in Whatever Befalls Their Nation." The journalist, Lee Hockstader, notes that:

> Throughout the world, it is common practice to ascribe dark motives to U.S. foreign policy, but in Haiti the practice often borders on the bizarre...In much of Latin America, Washington's machinations

are the subject of speculations and accusations. The hand of the CIA, real or imagined, is seen everywhere. And the long history of 20th-century U.S. intervention in the affairs of Caribbean countries is cited as evidence of present-day intrigue. But when it comes to divining obscure meanings in Washington's words and actions, no country can match Haiti.[1]

Hockstader cited as examples of this bizarre paranoia the suggestion that the Bush administration was somehow involved in Aristide's overthrow; Haitians' inclination to see the long arm of the CIA at work in their country; and the belief that the United States wished to establish a military base on the Môle St. Nicolas, across the Windward Passage from Guantánamo.

As we shall see, even cursory historical investigation of these allegations will show that each one has a basis in fact.

Gustavo Gutiérrez, the leading proponent of liberation theology, has long been among those who have called for careful investigations into the mechanisms by which the Latin American poor are oppressed:

> The situation of oppression and exploitation under which these people labor is well known. But it is known in general terms. It should now be subjected to a close examination in its precise, current forms. Nothing can replace a serious, scientific knowledge of the nature of the exploitation that the popular masses are suffering.[2]

The Uses of Haiti is offered as a close examination of the exploitation of the Haitian poor. Such an exercise calls for two complementary investigations. One examines the "large-scale" forces that have determined, to no small extent, the nature of the current crisis. These forces are chiefly economic and political and have evolved over time; this is thus necessarily a historical investigation—even though it purports to shed light on events as recent as the murder of Jean-Sony Philogène. The second part of this exercise seeks to discern these same large-scale forces at work in the experiences of individual Haitians I have known.[3]

Students of Haiti might well ask why another history of the country is warranted at this time. There have been several recent overviews of Haitian history; some would argue that they are perfectly adequate, and they are certainly more in-depth than my review. It is not my intention to try and upstage standard historical inquiries, although the coup of September 1991, deserves careful and prompt examination. Instead, Part I of *The Uses of Haiti* is an interpretive history of Haiti that attempts to capture some of the "affective tone" of Haitian readings of their trajectory as a people. History, it has often been remarked, varies according to winners and losers; this version is that of the self-described losers.

Such a rereading reflects a concern native to anthropology, which has tended to privilege informants' accounts of events. The importance of taking seriously the commentaries of my Haitian hosts was driven home in a previous investigation of "conspiracy theories" concerning AIDS. In 1985, a peasant from central Haiti asked, "You know, don't you, that the United States has a trade in Haitian blood?" Admiring the metaphoric connotations of a traffic in blood, which both history and poetic license would authorize as an apt description of three centuries of Haitian history, I did not take the accusation at face value.[4] After hearing this remark a second, then a third time, however, I looked into the matter.

Accusations of a traffic in Haitian blood are not mere poetic exaggerations. Precisely such a commerce was assured by the Hemo-Caribbean and Co., financed with U.S. and international capital and organized by cronies of the dictator-president François Duvalier. North American hemophiliacs, who needed factor VIII, a coagulant then distilled from the plasma of thousands of donors, were for years the indirect beneficiaries of the trade. Its direct beneficiary, however, was Miami-based stockbroker Joseph B. Gorinstein, who negotiated the traffic in blood with Papa Doc. The arrangements were made through Luckner Cambronne, one of the era's most notorious *macoutes*. In 1972, a journalist evoked the ambiance of the Hemo-Caribbean plasma center in downtown Port-au-Prince:

> The Haitians, many in rags and without shoes, crowd into Hemo Caribbean six days a week from 6:30 A.M. to 10 P.M. They spend about one hour and a half to two hours in screening and actually giving blood. They lie on 47 cots in the center's crowded second floor. A liter of blood is taken from then and the amber plasma is separated out. Then the blood is pumped back into the person who gave it. The plasma is frozen and shipped to the United States by Air Haiti....The donors receive $3 for a liter of plasma. If they have a series of tetanus shots, the plasma is more valuable...They then receive $5 a liter. Some sell their plasma once a week and earn $150 to $250 a year.[5]

It was estimated that, at the height of activity, some five tons of plasma were shipped each month to North American laboratories owned by Cutter Laboratories, Armour Pharmaceutical, Dade Reagent, and Dow Chemical. The plasma, some of which went to Sweden and to West Germany, was sold for seven times what it cost to collect. This brisk and profitable trade earned Cambronne the epithet "Vampire of the Caribbean."[6]

The tale proved lurid enough to merit a few stories in the international press. Biochemist Werner A. Thrill, technical supervisor of the operation, posed the following question to *L'Express*, the French weekly: "If the Haitians don't sell their blood, what do you want them to do with it?"[7]

Thrill's comment captures perfectly a common attitude regarding Haiti. Halfway through this book is a chapter called, "The Uses of Haiti (Reprise)." It examines continuity and change in the uses—pragmatic and symbolic—of this country. From the European "discovery" of Haiti in 1492 to the *coup d'état* of 1991, a pattern clearly emerges: Haiti and Haitians exist to serve the powerful. The chapter then asks how distinctively Haitian this pattern might be. Casting the net wider—over Guatemala and El Salvador, for example—we are forced to see that the plight of Haiti is emblematic of the plight of the poor elsewhere in Latin America.

Part II of *The Uses of Haiti* foregrounds the voices and experiences of the poor. The nature of their oppression is revealed in the stories of three young Haitians, whose trials bring into relief what might be called a "political economy of brutality." Their lives—and deaths—cannot be understood without an understanding of the large-scale forces described in the first half of the book. At the same time, their experiences speak to old and emerging myths perpetuated in American popular commentary about Haiti and Haitians. Throughout the book, we will examine the roles of certain academics and journalists in shoring up these myths.

It is the contention of this essay that Haiti, and U.S. foreign policy towards it, are best understood in a general Latin American context. Although Haiti is rarely considered to be a part of Latin America, it is in many respects the most representative of Latin American republics. This was true in the sixteenth century, when Haiti first took up its vocation as provider of services to the North; it was true in the nineteenth century, as Haiti struggled to remain independent; and it remained true during the Marine occupation of Haiti, one of several U.S. military adventures in Latin America.

It is still true now, after the overthrow of the government of Jean-Bertrand Aristide. In fact, the September 1991, *coup d'état* strongly supports the contention that the drama of Haiti continues to follow an essentially Latin American script:

> This consists of an underdeveloped country in a region traditionally viewed as vitally important to the United States, a nationalist and reformist political movement, the most powerful capitalist country in the world, and two administrations of that country whose overriding concern [is] to advance the capitalist system.[8]

This paragraph, though applicable, does not refer to Haiti, nor does it make reference to the administrations of Reagan and Bush. Rather, it is in reference to the Arbenz government in Guatemala, and to the administrations of Truman and Eisenhower, who planned Arbenz's 1954 overthrow through a covert CIA operation known in classified documents as "PBSUCCESS."

As in Guatemala, our foreign policy towards Haiti has not been honorable. *The Uses of Haiti* is addressed to an audience in the United States, the chief player in Latin American politics. Noam Chomsky, in introducing a recent study of U.S. intervention in Central America and the Caribbean, put it as follows: "There is no way to give a precise measure of the scale of our responsibility in each particular case, but whether we conclude that our share is 90 percent, or 40 percent, or 2 percent, it is that factor that should primarily concern us, since it is that factor that we can directly influence."[9]

In Haiti, our share is high indeed. Many Americans resist the idea that U.S. administrations have hastened the decline of this beleaguered little nation. This resistance is due to many factors, not the least of which is the discomfort born of facing ugly realities about the role of our government in the Third World. It is far more comforting to attribute the ongoing violence in Haiti (or Guatemala or El Salvador) to factors native to that setting. Among the most popular explanatory models are those invoking "cultural" factors; voodoo, in particular, is often evoked to "explain" Haiti (in previous generations, the concept of race was used with similar intent). The garish extremity of events in Haiti reinforces these erroneous notions: much that happens here—a hospital-room execution, for example—seems outlandish to North American audiences.

The gulf between these two settings, which are nonetheless intimately related, is indeed vast. But the gap is more economic than cultural. Chilean theologian Pablo Richard, noting the fall of the Berlin Wall, sounds a warning:

> We are aware that another gigantic wall is being constructed in the Third World, to hide the reality of the poor majorities. A wall between the rich and the poor is being built, so that poverty does not annoy the powerful and the poor are obliged to die in the silence of history...A wall of disinformation...is being built to casually pervert the reality of the Third World.[10]

As important purveyors of disinformation, many U.S. journalists are helping, even now, to pile ever higher this wall of disinformation. Representative contributors would include Lally Weymouth, writing in the *Washington Post* of the "extremely radical anti-American priest named Jean-Paul [sic] Aristide" who "showed brazen intolerance for those who didn't support him," who "condoned violence and mob terror."[11] How much higher did that wall go when, shortly after the coup, *The New York Times* could explain that "Aristide's Autocratic Ways Ended Haiti's Embrace of Democracy"?

Haiti's embrace of democracy, as we shall see, was swept away by old forces and new guns. It is my hope that *The Uses of Haiti* might play a role in countering the mystifications seen in the most influential forums of the United States. The reality of Haiti is the reality of Latin America at its most wretched. Time is running out if we are to help make sure that the Haitian poor do not "die in the silence of history."

PART I

The Uses of Haiti

*The time has come for postindustrial society to start reread-
ing the Caribbean...This second reading is not going to be easy
at all. The Caribbean space, remember, is saturated with messages.*

—Antonio Benítez-Rojo,
The Repeating Island

But rereading *history also means* remaking *history. It
means repairing it from the bottom up. And so it will be a subversive history. History must be turned upside-down from the bottom, not from the top.*

—Gustavo Gutiérrez,
The Power of the Poor in History

A little over ten years ago, anthropologist Eric Wolf
asked a question of particular significance to those who
wish to understand Haiti: "If there are connections everywhere, why do we persist in turning dynamic, intercon-
nected phenomena into static, disconnected things?
Some of this is owing, perhaps, to the way we have
learned our own history."[1] As recent surveys have
shown, journalistic and even scholarly commentary on
Haiti has tended to depict the country as isolated and
disconnected—a static country of backward peasants
caught in a time warp. To cite one of the leading texts
purporting to examine U.S.-Caribbean relations: "Haiti in
1950 was in general what it had been in 1900: a pre-
industrial society inhabited by ignorant, diseased peasants oblivious to the outside world."[2] But depicting Haiti
as divorced from "the outside world" turns out to be a

feat of Herculean oversight, given that Haiti is the creation of expansionist European empires—a quintessen-
tially Western entity. There is, simply, no other way to
understand Haiti.

What follows is a reading of Haitian history
informed, chiefly, by two complementary perspectives.
The first is a view of history as a dynamic and intercon-
nected process, and, accordingly, a view of Haiti as
enmeshed in a larger social and economic system. That
system's boundaries are ill-defined and shifting, certainly, but the whole is nonetheless subject to historical
analysis. Mine is an approach common enough in the
field of Caribbean studies, but the systematic perspective
is curiously absent, as we shall see, from much commentary on Haiti.

My second, and perhaps more controversial, decision
has been to privilege a "Haitian version" of the country's
history. Often, this has been less a question of choosing
one account over another, and more a question of choosing to amplify certain events in order to capture the
affective tone of commonly registered Haitian reactions to
events. By choosing to take seriously Haitians' readings
of their own history, it becomes easier to understand the
divergence between "inside" and "outside" readings of
what is happening, today, in Haiti—a task long overdue,
as all sides' perceptions of history inevitably direct their
actions in the present.

These two complementary readings of Haiti are important correctives, for well-entrenched modes of analysis
depict Haiti as somehow singular in its isolation from the
rest of the hemisphere. An article by Lawrence Harrison on
the current crisis in Haiti offers a classic example of this
way of thinking, and also of its political and moral consequences. Mr. Harrison, for years the director of the United
States Agency for International Development in Haiti, tells
the story of his 1991 trip to the town of Ouanaminthe,
where he met a group of "young followers" of the then-

president Jean-Bertrand Aristide.

"The discussion was supposed to give me an opportunity to learn what could be done to help promote democracy in Haiti," complained Harrison, "but it quickly degenerated into repeated, often vehement attacks on the United States for its 'exploitation' of Haiti, for its 'support' of the Duvaliers and the military, for the 'suppression' of the Haitian people." (The deft use of quotation marks is, of course, in the original.) When Harrison fired back that "the United States had never had any significant economic interests in Haiti and that we had cut off all aid to Papa Doc, they were incredulous."[3]

And well they might have been, along with the historians, anthropologists and political scientists who study Haiti. With brief exception, as we shall see, the United States and Haiti have been trading partners from the first decade of the nineteenth century, when they were the only independent republics in the hemisphere. That the United States did not officially recognize Haiti did little to alter the fact that, by 1851, the United States sold more goods to Haiti than it did to any other Latin American country, including Mexico. Trouillot reminds us that "well before 1900, the number of North American ships docking in [Haitian] ports exceeded the number reaching all of Europe."[4]

In Part I of this book, I hope to bring into relief the forces that have bound Haiti to the Western political and economic system in general, and in particular to the political economy of the United States. The exercise is not merely academic, as witness Mr. Harrison's further claims that "When, after the Spanish-American War, the United States acquired the base at Guantánamo Bay, in Cuba, Haiti was forgotten."[5] This, too, will come as news to historians of the period, who document an almost continual invasion of Haitian waters by U.S. gunboats throughout the period in question. In the two years prior to World War I, gunboats were maintained there almost without interruption.

If asked to signal the three chief events of the twentieth century in Haiti, many observers would point to the U.S. occupation of the country (1915–1934), the rise of the Duvalier family dictatorship (1957–1986), and the emerging popular movement that brought Jean-Bertrand Aristide to power (1986–1990). All of these seminal events took place against a backdrop of economic and ecological decline. What follows, then, is an attempt to summarize 502 years of history in a manner that will permit the reader to see where to place responsibility for the current crisis, the gravest in a long history of crises.

The Template of Colony

Let's be realistic: the Atlantic is the Atlantic (with all its port cities) because it was once engendered by the co-population of Europe—that insatiable solar bull—with the Caribbean archipelago; the Atlantic is today the Atlantic (the navel of capitalism) because Europe, in its mercantilist laboratory, conceived the project of inseminating the Caribbean womb with the blood of Africa; the Atlantic is today the Atlantic (NATO, World Bank, New York Stock Exchange, European Economic Community, etc.) because it was the painfully discovered child of the Caribbean, whose vagina was stretched between continental clamps, between the encomienda of Indians and the slave holding plantation, between the servitude of the coolie and the discrimination toward the criollo, between commercial monopoly and piracy, between the runaway slave settlement and the governor's palace; all Europe pulling on the forceps to help at the birth of the Atlantic: Columbus, Cabral, Cortes, de Soto, Hawkins, Drake, Hein, Rodney, Surcouf...After the blood and salt and water spurts, quickly sew up torn flesh and apply the antiseptic tinctures, the gauze and surgical plaster; then the febrile wait through the forming of a scar: suppurating, always suppurating.

—Antonio Benítez-Rojo,
The Repeating Island

For a Haitian people to be created anew, the original Haitians had to be effaced. This process took surprisingly little time, despite the island's large indigenous population. It started shortly after Christopher Columbus arrived in December of 1492, with the construction of the first European settlement in the New World. Columbus chose a bay on the northern end of an island called *Ayiti*, "high country," by the people who lived there. These Arawak-speaking natives warmly welcomed Columbus, but they did not survive long against a deadly admixture of imported infectious disease, slavery and outright slaughter.

The "lovable, tractable, peaceable, gentle, decorous Indians," as Columbus had described them in letters home, sickened and died at a rate that appalled even the Europeans. Estimates of their number at the close of the fifteenth century reach as high as eight million, but by 1510, only 50,000 natives remained on the island. Less than thirty years later, the native population could be counted in the hundreds, and the French chronicler Moreau de Saint-Méry would later note that, late in the seventeenth century, "there remained not a single Indian when the French came to wrest the island from the Spanish."[1]

With the rapid disappearance of the "Indians," Spanish settlers needed another source of expendable manpower with which to build forts, mine for gold, and clear and till the soil. Columbus had introduced sugar cane, an event that was to have enduring significance on this island, as elsewhere in the New World. Cultivation of this difficult crop required *slaves*, and for this, the enterprising colonists turned toward Africa. Transatlantic traffic in humans began in earnest in 1517; by 1540, some 30,000 Africans had been imported to Hispaniola. By then, many sugar plantations boasted more than 200 slaves. At the end of the century Spanish historian Antonio de Herrera observed, "There are so many Negroes in this island, as a result of the sugar factories, that the land seems an effigy or an image of Ethiopia itself."[2]

But these agricultural experiments did not last long. Sugar manufacturing declined with the progress of the sixteenth century. In its place arose cottage industries, chiefly leather making. Smuggling was also brisk, despite the brutal repression of these and other activities performed outside the Spanish crown's control.[3] The western part of the island slowly became a backwater frequented chiefly by buccaneers, many of them French. Some settled there and, starting from a tiny island off the northern coast, slowly spread south. By the middle of the seventeenth century, the French were definitively (if illegally) installed.

The newcomers were more interested in agriculture than in the quest for gold, and the slave trade, which had temporarily decreased in intensity, was stepped up after the western third of Hispaniola was officially ceded to France by the Treaty of Ryswick in 1697. The French colonialists called their territory "Saint-Domingue," and adopted a method of agriculture that required many able bodies. Thus began in earnest the era of sugar slavery, which had been foretold in the previous century but would in the 1700s become a malevolent machine—"a medieval vacuum cleaner," as Benítez-Rojo calls it.[4]

> It turned out that an entire kingdom, a mercantilist monarchy, would be needed to get the big machine going with its gears, its wheels, and its mills...Europeans finally controlled the construction, maintenance, technology, and proliferation of the plantation machines, especially those that produced sugar.[5]

The plantation machine established the Caribbean as "an important historico-economic sea." Soon, slave ships were running a triangular trade, exchanging manufactured goods from the European metropolises for slaves from the west coast of Africa, ferrying Africans to the Caribbean and bearing the sugar and spirits produced by slave labor back to Europe. This trade brought down kingdoms, African and European, accelerated the development of virtually all important European port cities, and changed forever the populations of the new world.

The trade's bookkeepers left precise records. One has only to compare annual "import" figures with the year-end census to see that slaves did not last long on the plantations of Saint-Domingue. One historian estimates that between 1766 and 1775, the quasi-totality of one sugar plantation's slaves were replaced by "new blood," most of it in newly arrived Africans.[6]

The slaves soon made the French traders and planters quite wealthy, and in the process generated enormous revenue for France. Late in the eighteenth cen-

tury, wrote Moreau de Saint-Méry, "the French part of
the island of Saint-Domingue is, of all French posses-
sions in the New World, the most significant in terms of
wealth procured for its metropolis and in terms of its
influence on agriculture and commerce."[7] As the plantation economy reached staggering proportions, so, too, did
the demand for chattel labor; Saint-Domingue became
the chief port-of-call for the slave trade. Between 1784
and 1791, the average annual import was 29,000 slaves.
The small territory was by then home to almost half of all
slaves held in the Caribbean colonies.

At one time or another, the colony was first in world
production of coffee, rum, cotton, and indigo. On the eve
of the American Revolution, Saint-Domingue—roughly
the size of the modern state of Maryland—generated
more revenue than all thirteen North American colonies
combined. By 1789, the colony supplied three-fourths of
the world's sugar. Saint-Domingue was, in fact, the
world's richest colony and the busiest trade center in the
New World. C.L.R. James wrote that the colony then
"received at its ports 1,597 ships, a greater number than
Marseilles, and France used for the San Domingo trade
alone 750 great vessels employing 24,000 sailors."[8]

These figures give some idea of the pace of the slave
economy at its height; they speak less clearly of the
immense suffering that underpinned that economy.
Published accounts of visitors to the territory show that
the planters of Saint-Domingue were notorious for their
abuse of the slaves. Although a French colonial observer
complained that the "Africans transplanted to Saint-
Domingue remain in general indolent and idle, quarrel-
some and talkative liars, and are addicted to stealing,"[9]
the pace on the plantations left little time for idleness:
"one of every three slaves died during his first three years
of intense exploitation."[10] Few slaves were able to put
their thoughts to paper, and so the words of the Baron
de Vastey, a Haitian who had grown up a slave, are
worth quoting at length:

Have they not hung up men with heads downward, drowned them in sacks, crucified them on planks, buried them alive, crushed them in mortars? Have they not forced them to eat shit? And, after having flayed them with the lash, have they not cast them alive to be devoured by worms, or onto anthills, or lashed them to stakes in the swamp to be devoured by mosquitoes? Have they not thrown them into boiling cauldrons of cane syrup?[11]

Colonial realities would forever mark Haitian understandings of social process. Modern-day Haitians are the descendants of kidnapped West Africans, and their collective identity today cannot be fathomed without an understanding of Saint-Domingue. Hailing from scores of tribes, speaking as many mutually unintelligible languages, the Africans of Saint-Domingue had nothing in common but their bondage and their hatred of their oppressors.

Anthropologist Karen McCarthy Brown observes that, for the early Haitians, "natural powers such as those of storm, drought, and disease paled before social powers such as those of the slave holder."[12] It may be argued that the tendency to see all actions as willed by powerful individuals or social interests has endured to the present day.

Modern Haitian social institutions have their origins in Saint-Domingue. To begin with language: it is clear from the historical record that Creole, termed by some a "language of survival," had taken on many of its present characteristics by the latter part of the eighteenth century. The pedigree of Haitian popular religion is similar. Many authors have offered histories of voodoo, most often focusing on African contributions. But, as anthropologist Alfred Métraux has noted, voodoo and its larger cultural systems were fundamentally the products of the plantation economy. "It is too often forgotten" he writes, "that voodoo, for all its African heritage, belongs to the modern world and is part of our civilization."[13] Métraux's seminal work on Haitian voodoo is too rarely consulted by those who freely comment on the much-maligned religion.

French cruelty and African servitude, the constant threat of revolt, the ever-present whip—all lent to Saint-Domingue an ambiance of dread. As the eighteenth century wore on, the population of what was soon to become Haiti came to be defined by rigid social categories, each with its own linguistic and religious practices, each with its own hatreds. The brittle status quo of the colony at the time of the French Revolution is sketched by Eric Williams, who writes of five classes:

> The first was the planters, the big whites...they were restless under the Exclusive [trade arrangements with France]. The second was the royal officials, the representatives of the Exclusive, the symbols of the denial of the self-governing institutions. Then came the poor whites, the overseers, artisans, professional men, hating the planters above, determined to maintain the bridge that separated them from the men of color below. The three groups of whites number 40,000. Below them came the fourth class, the mulattos and free Negroes, numbering 28,000, possessing one-third of the real estate and one-fourth of the personal property in the colony, but denied social and political equality with the whites. Finally, there were the 452,000 slaves, many of them only recently arrived from Africa, the foundation on which the prosperity and superiority of Saint-Domingue rested.[14]

These demographics, notable for the high proportion of enslaved labor, spelled trouble for the plantation owners. The latter decades of the 1700s were marked, increasingly, by scattered revolts and acts of resistance. Accusations of sorcery and poisoning of whites grew more and more frequent. Historian Pierre Pluchon writes that, with its "collective obsession with poison, its pitiless repression prompted by mere suspicion and by unshakable convictions, the North of Saint-Domingue drew itself into a hellish cycle and, attempting to snuff out crime, applied itself to torture."[15] As the eighteenth century drew to a close, it became clear to visitors that not even torture would permit such a tiny number of slave holders to control so many slaves. The cycle of repression, hysteria, and atrocities was spinning towards an inescapable finale: "This colony of slaves," observed the Marquis du Rouvray in 1783, "is like a city under the imminence of attack; we are treading on loaded barrels of gunpowder."[16]

The Haitian Revolution has been well chronicled by its partisans, and by many scholars. C.L.R. James entitled his classic study *The Black Jacobins*, for if Saint-Domingue might be likened to barrels of gunpowder, the French Revolution of 1789 was the spark that ignited them. In the confusion following the distant events in France, the white slave holders gained control of the new Colonial Assembly by excluding their economic competitors, the mulattos, and setting a property qualification that effectively excluded the "poor whites." The plantocracy envisioned a self-governing Saint-Domingue, one in which their power would be unchallenged. While favoring a nominal tie with France through allegiance to the (by then) powerless king, they rejected the authority of the National Assembly in Paris, and openly sought an end to the restrictive trade arrangements mandated by France.

Their ambitions were resisted by the new colonial authorities, by much of the rest of the white population, and by the mulattos. In the first months of 1791, a group of wealthy mulattos initiated an open revolt against the status quo. They found political support in a French abolitionist society, *les Amis des Noirs*. But, as Eric Williams tersely notes, "the issue involved was equality for the mulattos. No one mentioned the slaves."[17] In fact, the slaves *had* been mentioned in the debates of 1790, when mulatto spokesmen made it abundantly clear that they wanted full civil rights in order to stand on equal terms with the whites—as upholders of slavery. Though they rallied between 300 and 400 armed men to their cause, the mulattos in revolt were easily defeated by the colonial militia, and the movement's leaders were tortured and executed with the usual brutality in March of 1791.

Thus far, then, the slaves had served chiefly as pawns, with both white and mulatto factions recruiting slave armies-in-waiting. In August 1791, the slaves took matters into their own callused hands. Revolts, alleged poisonings of whites, arson, and the standard battery of slave abuse led slowly to the first explosion. The insurrection of 1791 is famous in Haiti as having been opened by a voodoo ceremony in Bois Caiman, in the north of the colony. On the night of August 22, under a lashing tropical storm, tens of thousands of slaves set forth to wreak vengeance. Armed with picks, machetes, clubs, and torches, they razed approximately 180 sugar plantations, and perhaps 900 plantations of coffee, cotton, and indigo. At least a thousand whites lost their lives; well over 10,000 slaves were killed outright, and up to 25,000 were thought to have taken to the hills.

Compared with previous slave revolts, this one was remarkable in both its scale and its degree of organization. Although the damage was restricted to the northern half of the island, its symbolic message was, of course, understood colony-wide. And, as a result of the merciless reprisals of the plantocracy, the numbers of rebels swelled considerably. The key figure emerging from the early revolts was Toussaint Louverture. Legally a slave until the age of 45, Toussaint is said to have introduced guerrilla tactics into the slave army. His organizational and military skills won him great acclaim, and he soon held sway over a majority of the island's inhabitants.

Reverberations from the 1791 revolt and the ensuing pandemonium were felt in both Europe and in the rest of the New World. The United States already had a booming business with the colony: by the time of the French

Revolution, some 500 U.S. ships sailed to Saint-Domingue's ports each year, more than one per day. In order to protect its investments, the young republic sent $750,000 in military aid, as well as troops, to defend the white colonists.

But attempts to prop up the status quo were foiled by the contingencies of history and by the ingenuity of Toussaint Louverture. In April of 1796, to the astonishment of European and New World observers, Toussaint named himself "Lieutenant Governor of a colonial state within the French Empire." Toussaint's goal was nothing less than the restoration of the colony's economic prosperity—without slavery. Somewhat surprisingly, his plans did *not* involve changing the plantation basis of production. Instead, he planned to replace slavery with a system of contract labor enforced by a *gendarmérie*. In one striking departure from the past, Toussaint broke the old exclusive trade agreements with France by signing trade agreements with Britain and the United States. This dismantling of "the Exclusive" did not sit well with the French, but, faced with a war in Europe, France was in no position to send a punitive force to Saint-Domingue. Delegates from Paris were expelled in 1797 and 1798. Even Napoléon, who came to power in 1799, was initially constrained to "offensives of charm towards Louverture, whom he could not yet overtly attack."[18]

On October 23, 1801, the French, victorious in Europe, became less charming. Napoléon ordered Captain-General Leclerc, his brother-in-law, to lead an expeditionary force, already gathering at Brest, to Saint-Domingue. Leclerc arrived in January, 1802, at the head of a formidable army of well over 20,000 men, one of the largest armadas ever to set sail for the New World; its numbers were later doubled. These troops were not exclusively French: the crusade to retake the colony brought together Polish, Dutch, German, and Swiss mercenaries. Napoléon's goal was to reestablish French rule and, it was rightly suspected, slavery. Through treachery—Toussaint was captured at a parley—the architect of Haitian independence was dispatched to a prison in a remote part of France, where he died, according to his biographer, a "slow death from cold and misery."[19]

After Toussaint's kidnapping, his military disciples, led by Jean-Jacques Dessalines, carried on an armed struggle against the French. Although it seemed otherwise at first, the ex-slaves and the inhospitable environment soon proved more than a match for Europe's best soldiers. Of the 28,000 regular troops initially dispatched to the colony, Leclerc was forced to announce, in a letter to Napoléon dated September 16, 1802, that 20,000 of them were dead. Many of these had succumbed to yellow fever; the remainder, to reckless but skillful ex-slaves who feared nothing so much as the reinstitution of bondage. Leclerc's final letter to Napoléon is both desperate and telling:

> Here is my opinion of this country. We must destroy all the negroes in the hills, men and women, sparing only children under twelve, destroy half of those living in the plains and leave behind not a single man of color who has worn a uniform—without this the colony will never have peace.[20]

But the colony was already lost to France. Two weeks later, Leclerc, besieged in Cap Français, himself fell ill with yellow fever. Ten days later, he was dead.

For Dessalines, considered by many Haiti's founding father, it had become clear that nothing short of total independence would suffice. Mistrustful of the French, he developed a scorched-earth approach to battle, which was rapidly successful. A decade of violence brought an end to almost three hundred years of foreign domination when the last of Napoléon's select forces were routed in November 1803. On the first of January 1804, the island's new leaders reclaimed its Indian name. "I have given the French cannibals blood for blood," proclaimed Dessalines. "I have avenged America."

The Republic of Haiti became the first independent nation in all of Latin America. In the hemisphere, only the United States is older. This point is overshadowed, however, by the overriding singularity of Haiti's birth: there exists outside Haiti no other case of an enslaved people breaking its own chains and using military might to defeat a powerful colonial power.

> Haiti was more than the New World's second oldest republic, more even than the first black republic of the modern world. Haiti was the first *free* nation of *free* men to arise within, and in resistance to, the emerging constellation of Western European empire.[21]

But, as we shall see in the following chapters, this victory has been a Pyrrhic one. The Haitians would never heal the wounds of colonialism, racism, and inequality. The ruins and contradictions of Saint-Domingue society, whether through prescription, reaction or deformation, have remained as the fixed template for contemporary Haiti. Perhaps it is ironic that Haiti, riddled with inequity, is considered by its people to be "the birthplace of freedom"—a heritage for which Haiti, and Haitians, would be repeatedly punished.

It was at the moment of independence, too, that the first major divergence of Haitian and non-Haitian readings of Haiti would be born. The locally prevalent notion of Haiti as a *singular place embedded in a system hostile to the ideal of equality* has flourished, even in a climate as inegalitarian as that of Haiti. This collective reading is quite different from dominant notions of Haiti as *singularly estranged* from the civilized world.

The revolution that ended in 1804 destroyed much of the agricultural infrastructure of Saint-Domingue. Contemporary British estimates suggest that, of the more than half million blacks and mulattos in Saint-Domingue in 1792, only 341,933 survived the revolution. Of these, a mere 170,000 were judged capable of field labor.

What is more, the Haitians found themselves in a world entirely hostile to the idea of self-governing blacks. Sidney Mintz puts it neatly when he suggests that the birth of Haiti was a "nightmare" for every country in which slavery endured.[22] The new nation was surrounded by islands ruled by slave-owners. A southerner from the United States commented on the decline of the plantations: "It was *French*—it is now *African*. This explains all."[23]

For several decades, at least, attempts by the subjugated people of other countries or colonies in the region to improve their condition were inevitably attributed to collusion with Haiti. The Haitian example was invoked, for example, during the 1843 uprisings in Cuba, where a group of planters called for an end to the slave trade—not on ethical grounds, but because census results suggested that slaves outnumbered whites and freedmen. "If only nearby Haiti did not present so horrifying an example," read one proclamation, "but one that should never be disregarded so that the second edition of the same book does not come to be."[24] One wealthy Cuban planter complained of his slaves' "stupidity and swagger," which he linked to the news from Haiti: "For the very reason that there are abolitionists, Haiti, and England in the world," he counseled, "it is necessary to correct [slaves] severely, to make them bend their backs, and to whip them, which is what truly tames them, and [the slave holders] are quite ready to work that way."[25]

The same paranoia invaded the southern plantations of the young United States. In 1793, "white refugees from Haiti came streaming into American ports, many bringing their slaves with them. That year saw the growth of a peculiar uneasiness, especially in Virginia, where many refugees had congregated."[26] From then on, any wayward behavior among slaves was likely to be attributed to the example set by Haiti:

As much as they were repelled by the events on the

island, America remained fascinated. The popular press regaled its readers with tales of horrible atrocities...St. Domingo assumed the character of a terrifying volcano of violence, liable to a new eruption at any moment. A single black rebellion was bad enough, but this was never-ending, a nightmare dragging on for years. Worst of all, the blacks were successful, and for the first time Americans could see what a community looked like upside down.[27]

There are indications that some Haitians did not discourage this image. Following the 1804 massacre of the French, Dessalines proclaimed, "Never again shall colonist or European set foot on this soil as master or landowner. This shall henceforward be the foundation of our constitution." The new constitution, drafted by Dessalines, was intended to mark Haiti's drastic departure from the regional status quo. Haiti was officially declared an asylum for escaped slaves, and for any person of either African of Amerindian descent.

Before long, such nationalist pronouncements were gradually toned down. Dessalines, an obstacle to international commerce, was assassinated in 1806. (The murderers of Haiti's first leader went unpunished. Thus began a long and thus far unfinished series of violent deaths for Haitian heads of state.) But a new tension had already developed, and it would forever mark Haiti. The new republic found itself divided according to the economic priority of its citizens. This division reintroduced the inequalities of the colonial system, replacing the gulf between master and slave with a gap between those whose interests led toward participation in the global economy and those who saw more advantage in keeping a safe distance from it. The new elite insisted that the emerging peasantry produce commodities for an international market, but the peasants—the former slaves—wished to be left alone to grow foodstuffs for themselves and for local markets.

Sidney Mintz has written of the formation of the

Haitian peasantry as a form of resistance, one in which "an entire nation turned its back upon the system of large estates, worked by forced labor."[28] But using a variety of coercive measures, the elite won the day. Haiti again began producing sugar and rum, and, as in the pre-independence era, became an important exporter of cotton, mahogany and other woods, cocoa, and—especially—coffee. "Thus the Plantation reorganized itself anew in Haiti," notes Benítez-Rojo, "although under other work and power relations."[29]

In the years following independence, the United States and allied European powers helped France to orchestrate a *diplomatic* quarantine of "the Black Republic," as the island's leaders dubbed their new country. France's foreign minister wrote to President Monroe that "the existence of a Negro people in arms, occupying a country it has soiled by the most criminal of acts, is a horrible spectacle for all white nations...There are no reasons...to grant support to these brigands who have declared themselves the enemies of all government."[30] The United States, having consolidated its holdings with the vast Louisiana purchase, was inclined to be placatory towards France:

> The United States blocked Haiti's invitation to the famous Western Hemisphere Panama Conference of 1825 and refused to recognize Haitian independence until 1862. This isolation was imposed on Haiti by a frightened white world, and Haiti became a test case, first, for those arguing about emancipation and then, after the end of slavery, for those arguing about the capacity of blacks for self-government. Great Britain was one of the few nations that had diplomatic relations with Haiti, and it was from the writings of English racists and antiabolitionists that Haiti began to get its widespread bad press.[31]

Haiti became the outcast of the international community. Though some have confused this status with economic and political isolation, a pariah nation may have many *uses*. It may be a source of raw materials and tropical produce, much as a colony; it may serve as a market for goods; it may serve as a cautionary tale. For the French, the uses of Haiti included all of these. As late as 1824, the French monarch Charles X pressed Haiti's President, Jean-Pierre Boyer for 150 million francs and the halving of customs charges for the French trade—all as indemnity for the losses of the plantation owners. These conditions, accepted in 1825, led to decades of French domination of Haitian finance, and had a catastrophic effect on the new nation's delicate economy. Despite its nominal independence, Haiti could not escape the shackles of foreign domination.

The very fact of a debt to France strikes the modern observer as odd. Why might a country of former slaves feel compelled to remunerate the plantocracy for losses incurred in a war of liberation? Why would a fragile—but balanced—young economy be thus jeopardized by its leaders? The legally anomalous indemnity is best thought of as a *business expense*. An elite who saw diplomatic recognition as essential to their own survival held the growth of the republic to be tied to continued export of subtropical commodities. It was for this reason that the "major, essential, primordial objective, pursued in diverse ways by all [Haitian] governments—from Dessalines to Geffrard—was, even when not explicitly announced, the recognition of our independence."[32]

The new pariah republic, desperately seeking trading partners, became the source of advantageous trade deals, particularly for the British. Shortly after the October 1806 assassination of Dessalines, his successor published, in London, a decree entitled *Adresse du Gouvernement d'Haïti au Commerce des Nations Neutres*. Henry Christophe, an anglophile autocrat who ruled the northern part of the then-divided country, demanded that his subjects turn all of their efforts to producing goods for export. Less than a decade after Christophe's proclamation, most of the foreign houses of commerce in Haiti were British, and Haiti was soon one of England's three most significant trading partners in Latin America.

But brisk trade by no means assured equal relations between Haiti and the developing imperial powers. As early as 1827, both France and Britain had taken to sending uninvited gunboats into Haitian waters. These surprise visits not only "served...to produce in the minds of the natives a favorable impression towards the whites," attested one British subject, "they also tended to ensure a continuance of their peaceful and respectful behavior."[33]

Production for a world market also necessitated relations with the other emerging societies of the Americas, and Haiti quickly sought diplomatic recognition from the one other independent nation in the hemisphere. Such recognition, however, was bitterly opposed by members of the U.S. Congress, especially those from slave-holding states. John W. Eppes of Virginia set the tone for Congressional debate: "Some gentlemen will declare St. Domingo free; if any gentleman harbors such sentiments let him come forward boldly and declare it. In such case, he will cover himself with detestation. A system that will bring immediate and horrible destruction on the fairest portion of America."[34]

During the first two years of Haiti's unrecognized sovereignty, however, the United States quickly consolidated its position as her chief trading partner. Within a decade of Haitian independence, many North American merchants had built up a Haitian trade. By 1821, almost 45 percent of imports to Haiti came from the United States; 30 percent were of British origin, and 21 percent were French.

A mere four decades after its own independence had been declared, the United States boasted one of the largest merchant marines in the world. It was not long before Haitians became the first Latin Americans to complain of Yankee imperialism. David Nicholls cites an editorial that appeared in the official *Gazette* of October 1805. "Owing to its proximity, as well as to the frequent visits of its citizens to the ports of [Haiti] and to 'the pretensions to which these might give birth', the USA [the writer] warned, might in the future be a greater threat to Haitian independence than were the countries of Europe."[35]

Much of the nationalist rhetoric of Haitian politicians was addressed to the United States. The hypocrisy of the North Americans was revealed, they noted, by their loud insistence that Britain and the other European powers recognize all the new American republics—all except Haiti, that is. "Our policy with regard to Hayti is plain," declared Senator Robert Hayne of South Carolina in 1824, a few months after President Monroe enunciated his famous Doctrine: "We never can acknowledge her independence. ...The peace and safety of a large portion of our union forbids us even to discuss [it]."[36] Some U.S. statesmen persisted in referring to the Haitians as "rebel slaves."

Many modern-day commentators on the fractious relations between Haiti and the United States point to the U.S. Occupation of 1915-1934 as the source of these misunderstandings. But the tone was set much earlier, as diplomatic commentary regarding Saint-Domingue reveals. After the 1810 collapse of the Spanish empire, the Haitians marched east. Although an independence movement seemed to be gathering force in Spanish-speaking reaches of the island, Haitian President Boyer sought to reunite the two factions under one Haitian flag. As historian Rayford Logan notes, "he met no opposition: indeed...he was received in an enthusiastic manner, and in February of 1822 was formally acknowledged as ruler of the entire island."[37]

This state of affairs prevailed until 1844, when the Dominican Republic declared its independence from Haiti. Again, a troubled interregnum followed; again, the British, French, Spanish and North Americans vied for influence and control. The diplomatic pronouncements of these powers were consistently cast in racist terms. Although the North Americans were informed by their agents that "only the United States could save the Dominican Republic from sinking 'into a Negro province under the Haytien constitution,'" the statesmen felt that there were "not enough 'white' Dominicans to warrant recognition of the republic." The British foreign secretary had soothed his own envoy, who feared that the United States would respond to Dominican calls for annexation, with the suggestion that the United States was not likely to "choose to take into their Union, even if it were disposed to join them, a State which like Haiti contains a population chiefly composed of free Blacks."[38]

More than one Haitian leader was alarmed by the calls of Dominicans for foreign, and especially U.S., annexation. What, asked a number of Haitians, might come of the annexation of the better part of the island by a slave-holding nation? Referring to the indivisibility of the island declared decades ago by Toussaint, Haitian armies invaded the eastern portion of Hispaniola during the reigns of Presidents Guerrier (1844-1845) and Soulouque (1847-1859). One North American diplomat reported that Soulouque's plan was to establish a nation of "pure black race," which would serve as the nucleus of a "black empire" encompassing all of the Antilles. An even more detailed (and impassioned) account of the strife of this period is given by Jean Price Mars, who concludes,

> The Haitian-Dominican dispute was invested with a significance far beyond the issue of the territorial indivisibility of the island or the Dominican community's right to national independence; it grew, taking on dramatic proportions as a racial antagonism that pitted the tiny group of some six or seven hundred thousand black and mulatto Haitians against hundreds of millions of white Europeans and Americans.[39]

That this "racial antagonism" was virulent and near-ly universal is suggested by the best-selling memoirs of Sir Spenser St. John, who in 1884 described Haitians as savages and cannibals. After long experience as the British Consul in Port-au-Prince, he had this to say about "the Negro":

> As long as he is influenced by contact with the white man, as in the southern portion of the United States, he gets on very well. But place him free from all such influence, as in Hayti, and he shows no signs of improvement; on the contrary, he is gradually retro-grading to the African tribal customs...If this were only my own opinion, I should hesitate to express it so positively, but I have found no dissident voice among experienced residents since I first went to Hayti in January, 1863.[40]

Given the fact that both Northern and Southern Haiti were still selling commodities on the world market, and were entangled in conquests and battles and inter-national intrigue, how were several leading scholars of the island's history led to speak of the 1800s as a "centu-ry of isolation?" One reason may have been that early legislation, while encouraging international trade, restricted the activities of foreign merchants to stipulated port cities. Most Haitian producers were linked to the world market by intermediaries who bulked and/or processed the produce of small landholders. The result of such restrictions was a spatial isolation of the peasantry, not just from the "outside world," but from the other classes inside Haiti as well. To cite the most incisive work treating these changes: "the economic structures, the very mechanisms of extracting this surplus, made it possible to bleed this peasantry without ever touching or seeing it."[41] These feudal structures have endured to the present day.

The chief bleeders of the peasantry, then as now,

were the State and the small commercial class it came to represent. Anthropologist Michel-Rolph Trouillot has referred to this partnership as "the Holy Alliance." Although the alliance relied heavily on indirect taxes that masked the extent to which the peasants were gouged, the small farmers could not have been unaware of the heavy price they paid for their participation in the export economy. Why, then, did those owning land not simply withdraw into subsistence farming? One reason was (and is) that many of the items long perceived as necessary to any rural household—soap, cooking oil, charcoal, and salt, for example—could only be acquired with cash. Further, peasant families regularly needed clothing, medicines, and money for children in school. The peasants could cut their losses by refusing to devote *all* their land to produce crops whose prices fluctuated wildly on the world market, but they were nonetheless fully enmeshed in a market economy increasingly centered in North America.

This is not to suggest that the United States began purchasing a greater percentage of Haitian exports. Instead, *imports to* Haiti were increasingly significant to the United States. By 1851, according to Trouillot, the North Americans sold more to Haiti than they did to most Latin American countries, including Mexico—this in spite of the fact that the United States still refused to recognize Haitian independence.

Shortly after it did recognize Haiti's sovereignty, the United States began showing great interest in the Môle St. Nicolas, a safe harbor across the Windward Passage from Cuba. In 1869, U.S. Minister Hollister paid a visit to the Môle:

> The harbor of St. Nicolas Môle is so out of the way of ordinary works of nature that words cannot do it justice. The môle proper must be more than three miles long, is almost of uniform height, and at a distance looks like some vast Roman wall. Cape St. Nicolas, on

your right...is magnificently bold and volcanic looking, and clouds always hide the summits...The cape
rises in a series of natural terraces, at proper dis-
tances for the mounting of guns. The first three seem
as level as a house floor, the others are more rugged.
I think there are six in all...The outer harbor is...pro-
tected from storms, and would hold all the fleets of
the world.[42]

Thus began a long series of international intrigues
regarding the Môle, which the United States tried to
obtain—through diplomacy and through force—on a
number of occasions. Haitian presidents knew that
access to the harbor was of interest, and dangled it
before the great powers.[43]

Haiti was troubled from within and without. By the
1860s, the Haitian economic system was bursting at the
seams. Dissatisfaction with the Geffrard government
(1859-1867) surged among the urban poor, the small-
scale merchants, the market women, the unemployed,
and the progressive sector of the middle class. In 1865,
the poor quarter of Cap Haïtien rioted, calling for an end
to the Geffrard government. When the business community later turned against the regime, the combined force
of the different factions allowed Cap Haïtien to successfully stave off government forces, which had laid siege to
the city. For six months, the revolt held strong, and it
was only by appealing to British naval power that
Geffrard was able to snuff out the insurrection. Citizens
of northern Haiti watched as three of Her Majesty's ships
bombarded the Cap and surrounding fortifications. The
event was a watershed: "The Geffrard government thus
became the first Haitian administration openly to obtain
foreign aid to remain in power."[44] It set a lamentable
precedent.

By 1870, the preceding decade could be assessed as
ruinous. Even the privileged classes, with notable exceptions, were brought low by the political crisis. The names
of the business establishments that survived and pros-

pered in this environment, and the products they marketed, speak both to the question of "isolation" and to the nature of the crisis: *Oliver Cutts*, military supplies and victuals; *Simmonds Brothers*, naval munitions; *White Hartmann*, munitions and paper money. These details, and the entire story they inform, also reveal the increasingly important roles played by foreigners in Haitian affairs of state. Not only did expatriates bankroll and arm opposing groups, but their governments directly intervened in Haitian politics. In 1888, U.S. Marines supported the military revolt against the Légitime government. Four years later, the German government openly supported the suppression of the movement led by Antenor Firmin. In 1912, Syrians residing in Haiti participated in an anti-Leconte government plot, during which the presidential palace was blown to bits. In January 1914, at the end of Haiti's short-lived first experiment in civilian rule, United States, British, and German forces entered Haiti to "protect their citizens."

By the close of the nineteenth century, then, it was clear even to charitable observers that the destiny of the Haitian people was under the jurisdiction of foreign powers. As Georges Adam would have it, "from 1879 to 1915, the striking feature of international developments in Haiti was without contest the battle between the four imperialist powers."[45] How had this come to be, given the fiercely nationalist intentions of the founding fathers? Clearly, what was visionary about the Haitian revolution—the struggle against slavery and racism in a monolithically racist world—was not accompanied by a new economic vision. Haiti became a dependent peripheral state, with the last decades of the century marked chiefly by the struggle between Britain, France, Germany and the United States for ascendancy in the Haitian economy.

As the nineteenth century gave way to the twentieth, the Republic of Haiti, like many of her Latin American neighbors, came increasingly to be linked to the United States. "Between 1870 and 1913," records political scientist Robert Rotberg, "the United States increased its share of the Haitian market from 30 to about 60 percent."[46] In the latter part of the nineteenth century and in the beginning of the twentieth, United States primacy in the Haitian marketplace was no longer seriously contested by Britain or France. Germany became its chief rival, controlling a significant portion of Haitian commerce by the outbreak of the world war.

Commercial primacy was not established merely through negotiating profitable trade agreements. Warships were called in by foreign merchants who claimed, often, that debts owed them by Haitians were unpaid. Two examples will illustrate. Although by no means the sole perpetrators of gunboat diplomacy, the Germans were, after their victory in the Franco-Prussian War, particularly heavy-handed in all that concerned Haiti. On the standard debt-collecting pretext, two German ships steamed into Haitian waters in June of 1872. The vessels were commanded by Captain Karl F. Batsch, who bypassed established diplomatic channels by dispatching a note directly to the Haitian government. Two German commercial establishments had been damaged during recent unrest (one, it should be noted, was bombarded by a British gunboat). Batsch demanded indemnities totaling $15,000—by sundown. The Haitian government, temporizing, replied that one case had already been fully assessed and payment was forthcoming, but the second claim had not yet been processed. Batsch thereupon seized two Haitian vessels—the bulk of the navy—anchored nearby. The government of President Nissage Saget wavered briefly, then agreed to pay the sum. With the help of the British consul (no stranger to this sort of diplomacy), the sum was raised and dispatched to the enterprising German captain.

In most respects, the "Batsch Affair" was nothing new. But national pride, reports Haitian historian Alain Turnier, was "murdered" by the German postscript to the affair. As the history textbook used in Haitian elementary schools explains: "our flag was spread over the ships' bridges and soiled in a foul manner." Two U.S. military historians capture the Germans' regard for Haitians as well as the ambiance of the gunboat era more explicitly:

> With the special finesse Hohenzollern diplomacy reserved for lesser breeds, the German boarding parties left calling cards. When the Haitians were allowed back, they found their cherished flag spread out on the bridge of each ship, smeared with shit. It was, remarked [Haitian statesman Antenor] Firmin, the republic's first contact with the methods of German diplomacy.[47]

The "Luders Affair," an even more flagrant example of imperialist diplomacy, is the story of one Émile Luders, who, born in Haiti of a Haitian mother and a German father, was by law a Haitian citizen. In September 1897, Luders was arrested for assaulting two police officers and sentenced to prison. The German emperor's *chargé d'affaires* set the cogs of imperial retribution in motion: although Luders had already been released from prison, in December a threat was published in a government newspaper in Berlin. Unsurprisingly, it went unread by any Haitians, and the emperor sent another of his warships to exact reparations. The Haitian Secretary of State received a "brutal, vulgar, and monstrous ultimatum," demanding an indemnity of $20,000, a letter of apology to His Majesty the Emperor, a twenty-cannon salute to the German flag then flapping above the bay, and a "gracious reception" for the German envoy by the Haitian president. The emperor himself publicly referred to Haiti as "a despicable band of negroes, lightly tinted by French civilization."[48] The Haitian statesmen were given four hours in which to consider these terms. They mulled it over. The stakes, it was concluded, were high: they were faced with the loss of the Haitian navy—both boats of it—as well as the country's coastal fortifications, much of which were over a century old. They knew also—from past experience—that cities built largely of wood burned quickly when bombarded. Four hours was not enough time in which to evacuate the civilian population. The Haitians capitulated.

Such "reclamations" were *au courant* in the German, French, British, and United States communities. In 1883, Haitian statesman Louis Joseph Janvier estimated that a total of 80 million francs had been drained from the national coffers in just this fashion, while the French debt had sucked up no less than 120 million francs. Between 1879 and 1902, one conservative estimate is that $2,500,000 were extorted from federal reserves in order to stave off gunboats. The perpetual draining of the state treasury was of a piece with the total failure to invest in agriculture. By the end of the century, 80 percent of national revenue—most of it derived directly from peasant labor—was earmarked to repay debts.[49] Before long, Haiti was unable to make payments: "The foreign debt had grown to the point of exceeding the nation's capacity to repay. In 1903, it was estimated at $33,121,999. In December, 1904, it was $40,891,394."[50]

In addition to these interventions by European powers, Haitian waters were violated by the United States no fewer than 15 times in that "century of isolation." In 1908, for example, the North American author of a popular travelogue suggested that "the United States should take this irresponsible island republic in hand and administer to it a salutary lesson."[51] The U.S. government was only too ready to comply. On more than one occasion, the U.S. Marines came calling and claimed from the vaults of the Banque Nationale d'Haïti large sums of money deemed to be owed to the United States. U.S. military historians assert that:

> The United States Navy had been compelled to send warships into Haitian waters to protect the lives and property of American citizens in 1849, 1851, 1857,

1858, 1865, 1866, 1867, 1868, 1869, 1876, 1888, 1891, 1892, 1902, 1903, 1904, 1905, 1906, 1907, 1908, 1909, 1911, 1912, 1913, and, during 1914, 1915, had maintained ships there almost without interruption.

They conclude, somewhat lamely: "If, as has truthfully been said, no American ever lost his life in any of these disturbances, possibly the nearly continual presence of the U.S. Navy may have been at least partly responsible."[52]

The issue was less one of protecting American lives than of enforcing the Monroe Doctrine. Access to the Panama Canal was through the Windward Passage, and the United States was increasingly strict in controlling Caribbean commercial traffic. In June 1913, Secretary of State William Jennings Bryan wrote to President Wilson that Môle St. Nicolas "will be of great value to us and even if it were not it is worth while to take it out of the market so that no other nation will attempt to secure a foothold there."[53]

Haiti's first century, then, was hardly one of "isolation," as some scholars have claimed; nor is "quarantine" the appropriate metaphor. Certainly, Haiti was ostracized, or diplomatically isolated. But the new republic became a useful—and much-used—pariah. Foreign involvement in Haiti was most often a predictable story of domination by the United States and European powers. The later U.S. occupation of 1915-1934 was not, as its apologists suggest, the sudden manifestation of a new U.S. interest in protecting the Haitians from their own corrupt rulers. It was rather the continuation of a pattern established in the nineteenth century, and in many ways the logical succession to a brand of imperialism that had already taken root throughout Latin America.

The United States Marine Corps invaded Haiti in 1915. To the student of Latin American history, it is hardly surprising that penetration of foreign capital, coupled with the almost continuous invasion by U.S. warships of Haitian waters, led to an armed occupation. In his study of the rise of the United States to world power, historian Foster Rhea Dulles does not mince words: "The virtual protectorates the United States set up over the Dominican Republic, Haiti, and Nicaragua, in conjunction with possession of Puerto Rico and the Canal Zone, and the semiprotectorate over Cuba, consequently transformed the Caribbean into a [North] American lake from which all trespassers were rigidly barred."[54] Colombia, Venezuela, Honduras and, especially, Panama would also be drawn ineluctably into the "back yard" of the United States. The decades of the "Big Stick" and "Dollar Diplomacy" would change the Caribbean basin forever.

As is often the case, the pretext for the U.S. intervention was "instability" in Haiti. There can be no denying that the political situation there was often anarchic. The majority of Haiti's chief executives had been deposed by revolution of one sort or another. The decade preceding the occupation was nothing if not "unstable," as the historian Brenda Plummer has noted: "Haitian political life had degenerated quickly between 1910 and 1915. The expatriation of resources and capital by the foreign and foreign-oriented enclaves intensified this deterioration. Exploitation had been proceeding for some time, but now crises followed one another in ever more rapid succession."[55]

These crises reached their apogee during the brief reign of General Vilbrun Guillaume Sam (March to July, 1915), whose jails overflowed with political detainees. When President Sam, beleaguered by forces from the north as well as another faction based in the capital, saw that his fall was imminent, he ordered the execution of the prisoners in the Pénitencier National. One hundred sixty-three of 173 prisoners were summarily executed. Meanwhile, the newly deposed president sought refuge in the French embassy. A mob including family members of the slaughtered prisoners formed outside the legation, stormed it, and brought President Sam to rude justice in the streets of Port-au-Prince.[56] The commander of the prison met a similar fate the same day.

The Marines landed near Port-au-Prince on July 28, 1915. The U.S. popular press, by and large, applauded the occupation or remained silent. On the day of the invasion, *The New York Times* served as a State Department mouthpiece, a role that it was to perfect in later years: "It was almost hopeless to expect an orderly government to be established without [military intervention] on the part of the United States."[57] On August 10, the *Times* noted that "All Haiti's Affairs Now in Our Hands...to guarantee the political and territorial integrity of the Haitian Republic."[58] No irony was intended.

The New York Times merely reflected the era's enlightened opinion. For example, the *National Geographic* ran a number of articles about Haiti during the occupation. In one of these, entitled "Haiti and its Regeneration by the United States," the editors of the august monthly warn that "It is difficult for an American to comprehend the situation which existed in Haiti when our troops first landed." Indeed, too frank discussion of the lives of the "unthinking black animals of [Haiti's] interior" might wound the sensibilities of its readers:

> Chaos reigned in all departments, and to all appearances the entire structure of life in Haiti was on the verge of dissolution. This is a true picture of conditions in Haiti when the United States forces first landed. It is not an exaggerated picture—in fact, many details are omitted which are not suitable for publication in the United States.[59]

Among those details, as we shall see, was the killing of peasants by U.S. Marines.

The "Convention haitiano-americaine," promulgated in 1915, granted the United States complete political and administrative control over Haiti. Of note, Article X of the treaty decreed the formation of a new *gendarmérie*, this one to be trained by and under control of the U.S. Marines. These arrangements were more stringent than the legal trappings of other Latin American occupations of the time, as they granted receivership not only of customs receipts—"control of the customs houses," observed President Woodrow Wilson, "constituted the essence of this whole affair"—but also of all governmental outlays. Furthermore, the Republic of Haiti could not undertake any foreign debt without the approval of the United States. The Convention was ratified by the U.S. Senate in February 1916. Other, more finely-tuned documents followed, culminating in the Constitution of 1918, which Franklin D. Roosevelt claimed to have written while Secretary of the Navy.

But there was resistance, even from the Haitian elite, to this new document. Many Haitian congressmen refused to sign. The occupying force solved this dilemma "by genuinely Marine Corps methods," to use the words of Major Smedley Butler: it dissolved parliament and put the question to plebiscite. The official announcement, signed by a Marine lieutenant, noted that all citizens were *invités à se présenter*, but added that "any abstention from such a solemn event would be regarded as an antipatriotic act." The voters were marched to voting stations and handed a white ballot marked *OUI*. The Marines noted that they could have asked for a pink ballot marked *NON*, but very few did.[60] In fact, 99.9 percent of the Haitians consulted approved of the arrangements, which abolished Dessalines' most famous law, that forbidding foreign ownership of land.

There was no outcry against these tactics in the United States, even though there was, curiously, a great hue and cry over the Russians' decision to rescind their own constitution. In January 1918, when the Soviets dissolved the Constituent Assembly, President Wilson responded angrily, historian George Kennan notes dutifully. The abrogation of the Russian charter at the menace of "the bayonets of the Red Guard" deeply offended his and his compatriots' "strong attachment to constitutionality."[61] Wilson, as Noam Chomsky notes in a commentary about the American occupation of Haiti, "is revered as a great moral teacher":

> Wilson's 'strong attachment to constitutionality' was unmoved by the sight of a government with no mandate beyond 'the bayonets of the Marine occupiers;' nor Kennan's. Quite the contrary. To this day the events figure in the amusing reconstructions entitled 'history' as an illustration of US 'humanitarian intervention,' and its difficulties (for us). Gone from the 'history' along with this episode is the restoration of virtual slavery, Marine Corps massacres and terror, the dismantling of the constitutional system, and the takeover of Haiti by US corporations, much as in the neighboring Dominican Republic, where Wilson's invading armies were only a shade less destructive, perhaps because their racist barbarism did not reach such extreme levels when confronting 'spics' instead of 'niggers.'[62]

Unshackled, many North American companies scouted Haiti for land for new plantations of rubber, bananas, sugar, sisal, mahogany and other tropical produce; many of these companies leased large tracts. Historian Suzy Castor has documented the concession to North American firms of 266,000 acres of Haitian soil.[63]

What happened to the peasants who farmed these tracts of land? Widely varying responses are offered to this question. The occupying force stated that no Haitians were displaced in these transactions, several of which did not lead to the establishment of new farms or plantings. Haitian historians tell a different story. Writing in a Haitian academic journal in 1929, Georges Sejourné estimated that *50,000* peasants were dispossessed in the North alone.[64] Augmenting the number of the landless and unemployed was not without benefits for investors. For many, the real draw was not land, but cheap labor.

"Haiti offers a marvelous opportunity for American investment," announced the New York daily *Financial America* on November 28, 1926. "The run-of-the-mill Haitian is handy, easily directed, and gives a hard day's labor for 20 cents, while in Panama the same day's work cost $3."

The decades of fierce infighting and resistance to foreign interference—Haiti's alleged period of "isolation"—might suggest that an invasion by U.S. Marines would be resisted; it was. The existence of a commercial class with scant national loyalty might also suggest that resistance would not spring from the urban bourgeoisie; it did not. The U.S. Marines, aided by the local police force of their own creation, set out to disarm a rural population that had kept its weapons from the days of the Revolution. Invoking a law ratified in 1916 by the U.S. Senate, the occupying force resurrected the hated institution of the *corvée*—the involuntary conscription of labor crews. The round-up of several thousand men by U.S. Marines did not sit well with Haitian memories of white domination from 125 years earlier, and resulted in the "Cacos Insurrection," which found its latter-day Toussaint Louverture in a former soldier named Charlemagne Péralte. The American press was unkind to this nationalist. To cite the *National Geographic*: "A man of considerable and unscrupulous cunning, Charlemagne exhibited much intelligence in securing supplies and ammunition from Germans and others interested in promoting disturbances."[65]

Peralte organized the resistance from his home town in the Central Plateau, where he found thousands of peasants who resented both U.S. appropriation of land and the creation of chain gangs to build roads. In contrast to the version offered by the *National Geographic*, there was never any evidence of foreign support of this peasant-based rebellion. Peralte's movement came to have a significant number of adherents before it was finally quelled. The Marines responded with machine guns and bombs, but the Cacos held them at bay until

Péralte's assassination in November 1919.

The significance of the Cacos Insurrection continues to be debated both inside and outside Haiti. Heinl and Heinl, U.S. Marine Corps historians, attempt to counter what they see as the "strident, unbridled, and ashamedly partisan" accounts offered by nationalist Haitians and their North American sympathizers. They insist that the "Caco rebellion at most involved no more than one quarter of Haiti and a fifth of its population."[66]

To appreciate the true meaning of the Caco rebellion—which received no outside funding—compare even these conservative figures to the more recent struggles in Nicaragua, where even hundreds of millions of dollars and the most modern weapons could not muster more than 10,000 *contras*.

Many Haitian lives were lost during the "pacification period," as the Marines termed their reaction to "the bandits." An in-house investigation of the rumors of "indiscriminate killings" was conducted, in 1920, by Brigadier General George Barnett, former Commandant General of the Marine Corps. He concluded that 3,250 "natives" had been killed. *The New York Times* of October 14, 1920 noted that

> On 2 September, 1919, [General Barnett] wrote a confidential letter to Colonel John H. Russell, commanding the Marine forces in Haiti, bringing to the latter's attention evidence that 'practically indiscriminate killings of natives had gone on for some time,' and calling for a thorough investigation...'I think,' General Barnett wrote to Colonel Russell, 'this is the most startling thing of its kind that has ever taken place in the Marine Corps, and I don't want anything of the kind to happen again.'[67]

In reviewing the records over fifty years later, Heinl and Heinl suggest that the "best evidence, which is not very satisfactory for either side, suggests that, in putting down the Cacos, Marines and Gendarmerie sustained 98 *killed and wounded*; and from 1915 through 1920 some 2250 Cacos were *killed*."[68] The authors do not cite their sources, nor do they offer the evidence rejected. Hans Schmidt, the North American authority on the occupation, suggests that 3250 peasants were killed in the 20 months of active resistance.[69] According to Haitian historians, however, the cost was far more dear. After exhibiting several of the figures most commonly cited, Roger Gaillard asks,

> if the total number of battle victims and casualties of repression and *consequences* of the war might not have reached, by the end of the pacification period, four or five times that—somewhere in the neighborhood of 15,000 persons. This figure is all the more impressive when it is compared to the 98 dead and wounded among the 'marines' and the American and Haitian constabulary. This war, in many instances, must have resembled a massacre.[70]

With peasant rebellion silenced, the occupying force went about its business. The United States began a process of fiscal and commercial centralization that continued the work of earlier Haitian administrations, undermining the coastal cities that had once collected the majority of the State's customs receipts. Although few of the commercial elite had protested the landing of the Marines, losing control of state wealth dealt them a heavy blow. The indiscriminate racism of the occupying force was also jarring for the elite, accustomed as they were to being the discriminators in a system based on both class and color.

It was further suggested, perhaps first by British diplomat R.S.F. Edwards, that many of the U.S. servicemen had been recruited from the southern states on the notion that southerners were better equipped to "handle colored people." This is hotly contested by Heinl and Heinl, who suggest this to be propaganda floated by non-Haitians, such as Edwards, who were hostile to the occupation. Regardless of the actual proportion of southerners in the occupying force, one notes that the Marines were first brought ashore by one Colonel Littleton W.T. Waller of Virginia. "I know the nigger and how to handle him," he wrote in 1916 to a superior officer. In another commentary, Colonel Waller qualifies the Haitians as "real niggers and no mistake—There are some very fine looking, well educated polished men here but they are real nigs beneath the surface."[71] Captain John Houston Craige, the Marine who served as Port-au-Prince chief of police, was slightly more philosophical about the matter: "I believe that the white man of western Europe is the most able and progressive of earth's types," wrote Craige in one of two memoirs of Haiti, "and that the men of the United States are the most able group of the western European stock. I believe that the yellow and red men are less able, and the black men least of all."[72]

But Haiti's "black men" were able to resist the vision of men like Captain Craige. In 1929, as world prices collapsed with the U.S. stock market, workers attempted to organize themselves in defiance of the Marines. Although such attempts were most visible in Port-au-Prince, they had repercussions elsewhere. The nation's students, too, became more militant, and a nationalist movement among university students culminated in a strike that, in the first days of December 1929, spread to parts of the business community. One of their slogans was "Down with Freeman!," in reference to an unpopular U.S. administrator. A few days later in the southern city of Cayes, stevedores, students, and peasants took up this refrain, adding À bas la misère! ("Down with poverty!").

The demonstrations clearly shook the Marines. On December 5, the soldiers responded with low-altitude bombing of the city's port, causing panic in a population unaccustomed to airplanes. On December 6, another demonstration began in Marchaterre at the edges of the city. A large group of peasants and local distillers were marching towards Cayes to protest the bombing and also a series of new taxes. In her study of the U.S. occupation of Haiti, historian Suzy Castor describes the confrontation between the peasants and the Marines:

> Hundreds of peasants and several dignitaries from the region of Torbeck, galvanized by news of the strike in Cayes, decided to go there for more information and to take part in the nationalist demonstrations. Peasants from Gauvin, Laborde and other villages swelled the ranks of the initial group. Thus a crowd of 1,300 men reached Marchaterre and the gates of Cayes with cries of 'Down with taxes!,' 'Down with poverty!' The peasants were unarmed.

> The 'marines,' under the direction of Roy C. Suring and first lieutenant Fitzgerald, proceeded to Marchaterre, taking up positions behind a large ravine with trucks, cars, machine guns, automatic rifles, etc. The demonstrators were barred from proceeding.[73]

What happened next is the subject of some debate. According to Castor, arrests were made and the grumbling peasants were dispersing "when they were surprised by a burst of gunfire." Within minutes, the fleeing crowd left behind 22 dead and 51 wounded.[74]

The Marchaterre killings led not only to renewed demonstrations elsewhere in Haiti, but also to a U.S. Congressional inquiry into the occupation. Specifically, the newly elected President Hoover sent his Forbes Commission to Port-au-Prince to "study the modalities of our withdrawal from Haiti." From May 1930, when a transitional president was chosen, until August 1934, when the last contingent of Marines pulled out of Haiti, the Americans reinforced structures designed to serve their interests. Although nominally "nationalist," the Haitian administrations installed in the final years of the occupation did little to upset U.S. enterprises, which were of course substantial.

What, then, is the economic verdict on the U.S.

occupation of Haiti? The *National Geographic* could be counted on for an evenhanded evaluation: "Peace and security of life and property have been given to this island republic, which before the American occupation had not known peace since the overthrow of the French, one hundred years ago."[75] Even in more recent assessments, the "peace" and "abundance" of the slave plantations could be evoked without irony. Heinl and Heinl thought it appropriate to compare Haiti at the close of the occupation with Haiti at the close of the Revolution: "In 1804 Haiti was wrecked and ravaged; in 1934, the country was modernized, solvent and thriving, with a national infrastructure passing anything in its history."[76]

No one, regardless of political persuasion, would wish to contest the assertion that post-occupation Haiti was in better shape than the smoking ruins of Saint-Domingue, and it is unlikely that the comparison occurred to anyone residing in Haiti. The question of solvency may, however, be disputed. The administration that took over in 1934 was propped up on shaky foundations: the country was heavily indebted, no longer to the French, but to the United States. It was still saddled with a 1922 loan—at $40,000,000, a record even for loan-happy Haiti—and both the "national" treasury and the Banque Nationale were owned by a New York bank. What is worse, the treasury was even more dependent on customs duties, especially from coffee, than before the occupation. In other words, the wealth of the State still derived largely from the extraction of a surplus from peasant production, and much of it was still owed to off-shore creditors.[77]

An equally damning evaluation has recently been advanced by anthropologist Michel Rolph Trouillot, who argues that the U.S. occupation "improved nothing and complicated almost everything."[78] He suggests that the racism of the U.S. stewards reinforced color prejudice in Haiti, paving the way for the *noiriste* rhetoric of François Duvalier.

And there were further, tragic consequences of the occupation. As an example of one of the forgotten consequences, consider the fallout from the establishment of a new frontier between Haiti and the Dominican Republic, also occupied (1916–1924) by the United States. These arrangements, made by the Marines, granted to Haiti a swath of disputed land far from both Port-au-Prince and the Dominican capital; some of northern Haiti's dispossessed peasants relocated there. In 1937, after the U.S. troops had left the island, Dominican strongman Rafael Trujillo, by way of redrawing the boundary, ordered the massacre of thousands of Haitians in the eastern reaches of their own country.

The number of people killed during a three-day, genocidal spree has been estimated at between 18,000 and 35,000. Although Trujillo's handlers subsequently denied the massacre, the future dictator did not bother to do so initially. He merely offered a justification: "Haitians are foreigners in our land. They are dirty, rustlers of cattle, and practitioners of Voodoo. Their presence within the territory of the Dominican Republic cannot but lead to the deterioration of the living conditions of our citizens."[79] The United States stepped in, arguing that some sort of acknowledgment and indemnity would calm tensions in the region.

> After prolonged negotiation Trujillo recognized the death of eighteen thousand Haitians on Dominican territory. According to him, the figure of twenty-five thousand victims, put forward by some sources, reflected the intention to manipulate the events dishonestly. Trujillo agreed to pay the government of Haiti, by way of indemnity, $522,000, or twenty-nine dollars for every officially recognized death.[80]

U.S. Secretary of State Cordell Hull subsequently declared that "President Trujillo is one of the greatest men in Central America and in most of South America."[81]

From Duvalierism to Duvalierism Without Duvalier

Our Doc, who are in the National Palace for life, hallowed be Thy name by present and future generations. Thy will be done in Port-au-Prince and in the countryside. Give us this day our new Haiti, and never forgive the trespasses of those traitors who spit on our country each day. Lead them into temptation, and poisoned by their own venom, deliver them from no evil.

—François Duvalier,
Catechism of the Revolution

Zombies—dead people who walk or live ones who have lost their souls—have a look of hopeless stupidity. But in no time they can escape and recover their lost lives, their stolen souls. One little grain of salt is enough to awaken them. And how could salt be lacking in the home of the slaves who defeated Napoleon and founded freedom in America?

—Eduardo Galeano,
Century of the Wind

If the departure of U.S. troops briefly diminished expressions of discontent, Haiti nonetheless continued her slow decline. As elsewhere in Latin America, the occupying forces left behind indigenous governments beholden to U.S. interests. The "friendly" regimes were, by and large, military or military-backed. With the possible exception of the reformist administration of Dumarsais Estimé (1946-1950), Haitian regimes after the U.S. occupation were intolerant of any dissent, despite clear signals of dissatisfaction among peasant groups, among students, and within the Catholic Church. The advent of the Second World War also seemed to lessen social tensions, as it meant increased world market prices for a number of goods that Haiti sold, including cotton, sisal hemp for rope, and tropical produce.

Shortly after the war, however, unrest among the urban and rural poor, two ever-expanding classes, led to the formation of parties such as the *Mouvement des Ouvriers et Paysans*. Founded by populist Daniel Fignolé, a schoolteacher and labor organizer, this party soon became a force to be reckoned with in Port-au-Prince. Although future President Jean-Bertrand Aristide would often be compared to Fignolé, the latter's devoted following remained chiefly urban, whereas Aristide enjoyed broad support in the countryside. During a troubled interregnum in which a military junta assumed power, Fignolé was briefly made Haiti's chief executive—an acknowledgment of what would have happened at the urns. But when Fignolé attempted, in 1957, to follow through on promised reforms, the military leaders promptly put him on a plane to New York.

The army recognized that a more pliant civilian facade than Fignolé was needed, and thought they had found their man in the person of an owlish doctor who dabbled in anthropology. François Duvalier had grown up during the U.S. occupation. Like many Haitian intellectuals who came of age at the time, Duvalier had been involved in the *mouvement indigéniste*, which attempted to elevate Haitian culture as a nationalist response to the cultural imperialism of the U.S. forces. At a time of extreme color consciousness, Duvalier declared himself a *noiriste* (a partisan of the blacker citizens, rather than the lighter urban elites), and exhorted rural people and the middle classes to support his bid for the presidency immediately after Fignolé's departure.

It has often been remarked that François Duvalier was elected in Haiti's first universal suffrage. This is incorrect. No official observers monitored the 1957 election. Had they been present, they might have wondered about army-organized elections that excluded the single most popular candidate—Fignolé—and featured such transparent anomalies as were registered on the small island of La Tortue, where 900 registered voters delivered 7,500 ballots for Duvalier. Similar irregularities were reported throughout the republic. Duvalier was, of course, the army's candidate, as well as that of a number of U.S. citizens influential in Haiti.

The major institutions of modern Haiti—the army, business, the Catholic Church—had seriously underestimated this unassuming doctor. An expert in both Haitian history and culture, Duvalier knew what he must do to acquire personal power. As a first step, Duvalier created his own personal security force, the Volunteers for National Security. A militia responsible only to Duvalier, the VSN effectively neutralized the might of the army, and were quick to carry out the new president's orders.

The VSN were soon dubbed *tontons macoutes*— mythical "bogeymen with sacks" into which sleeping children could be stuffed. The press, business, voodoo temples, labor unions, and especially the army rapidly became infiltrated with *macoutes*. And the freebooting *macoutes* carried more than sacks. They carried guns, as an ever-mounting body count attested. Within the space of a few years, it became clear that the best way of staying alive in Haiti was to have a powerful *macoute* as guardian angel.

The most handsomely rewarded of these "volunteers" were those charged with "disappearing" annoying individuals. Reports from this time are scarce, but most believe that Duvalier and his bogeymen killed tens of thousands. If Duvalier judged an enemy sufficiently annoying, he often had whole families wiped out. Graham Greene recalled in his memoirs that "Haiti really was the bad dream of the newspaper headlines,"[1] but Duvalier's crimes against his own people provoked relatively little international outcry. At crucial points in his tenure, Duvalier received the support of the U.S. government, an embarrassing fact often forgotten or obscured.[2] During his first four—and his bloodiest—years in power, Duvalier received $40.4 million from Washington, much of it in the form of outright gifts. "Papa Doc" took to appropriating USAID trucks to haul peasants to his rallies—an act betraying considerable assurance that the United States might be embarrassed, but would not cast him off.

Well after Duvalier had revealed himself as a cruel tyrant, the U.S. Marines landed in Haiti once more—but this time at Duvalier's invitation. According to the colonel who led the contingent in the 1960s, the only statement of mission they received was from a State Department undersecretary: "the most important way you can support our objectives in Haiti is to help keep Duvalier in power so he can serve out his full term in office, and maybe a little longer than that if everything works out."[3]

Why would the most powerful, the most wealthy country in the world prop up a small tyrant like Duvalier? In a sense, Papa Doc was a terrible Latin American reflection of the Cold War, which has always had the Third World as its hottest battlefield. Recently declassified U.S. documents written in the early 1960s, at the height of Duvalier's brutality, lend a certain credence to this hypothesis. U.S. policy objectives in relation to Haiti were then summarized as follows:

1. The overriding objective is to deny Haiti to the communists.
2. In short-term political terms, the U.S. desires to assure Haiti's support of the U.S. on matters of importance in the OAS, U.N., and other international organizations.
3. The U.S. has the continuing objective of protecting private American citizens and property interests in Haiti.[4]

But the Cold War, in reality, only reinforced a pattern well-established in the region. The United States supported a whole roster of tyrants like Papa Doc, and had done so well before the start of the U.S.-U.S.S.R rivalry. It is important to recall the consistency in U.S. foreign policy towards Haiti over the 100 years preceding the rise of Duvalier. A tyrant who would look out for U.S. interests was quite good enough to deserve Washington's support.

As pretext, however, the Cold War was perfect. A few years before Duvalier's ascent, President Eisenhower proclaimed that U.S. citizens were "professional patriots and Russian haters."[5] Like other U.S.-supported leaders, Duvalier protected himself by turning anti-communist hysteria to his advantage. He eventually formalized this hysteria in draconian laws, two articles of which read as follows:

> Article One: Communist activities are declared to be crimes against the security of the state, in whatsoever form: any profession of Communist faith, verbal or written, public or private, any propagation of Communist or anarchist doctrines through lectures, speeches, conversations, readings, public or private meetings, by way of pamphlets, posters, newspapers, books, and pictures; any oral or written correspondence with local or foreign associations, or with persons dedicated to the diffusion of Communist or anarchic ideas; and furthermore, the act of receiving, collecting or giving funds directly or indirectly destined for the propagation of said ideas.

> Article Two: The authors and accomplices of these crimes shall be sentenced to death. Their movable and immovable property shall be confiscated and sold for the benefit of the state.[6]

For the first time in decades, Haitians began to flee. In 1963, a small boat reached Florida's shores, and its occupants requested refugee status. "Perhaps as a deliberate signal of things to come, American authorities denied political asylum to all twenty-five passengers."[7]

Duvalier's struggle with the powerful Catholic

Church is emblematic of his dealings with all Haitian institutions. As early as 1959, Papa Doc staged such scenes as the beating and arrest of 60 individuals worshipping in the national Cathedral. Those present had bowed their heads in prayer for several priests who had been expelled. Duvalier later offered the following rather extraordinary justification for the brutality: "Even Christ went into the temple and chased out the evildoers." In 1960, the French-born Archbishop of Port-au-Prince was accused of participating in a "communist plot" and forced onto a flight for Miami in his cassock and underwear. Less than a year later, Duvalier turned to Monsignor Augustin, then the sole Haitian-born member of the Catholic hierarchy; he, too, was expelled. Expulsions of entire *orders* were soon to follow. For this series of spectacular offenses, Duvalier was excommunicated by Pope John XXIII in 1961.[8]

But the wily doctor would soon have his way with even the Holy See. The dictator later proposed to normalize relations with the Vatican on several non-negotiable conditions, including Papa Doc's right to fill vacant bishoprics with clerics of his own choice.[9] Rome protested, but in August, 1966, Duvalier signed an accord with the Holy See, which conceded him every important point. "An amazing document, all in all," wrote historian Elizabeth Abbott of the new Concordat, "and Duvalier was justly proud of it, though it must have given Paul VI some restless nights."[10]

It is not clear why the Vatican capitulated, but most underline the role of anti-communist hysteria, which swept the Church as well as the secular world. This decision, in any case, would have many repercussions. For one, it established the church in which future president Jean-Bertrand Aristide was raised: "Duvalier took himself to be the head of Haitian Church and he wanted his priests to obey him just like the *tontons macoutes*," wrote Father William Smarth, himself exiled in 1969.[11]

Many priests were only too happy to oblige. Monsignor Ligondé, the newly elevated Archbishop of Port-au-Prince, proved to be a faithful supporter of the dictatorship. "Excellency," he gravely informed Duvalier in one official address, "your authority partakes of the Divine."

The *macoutes en soutane*, as the obsequious priests were termed, participated in the anti-"communist" witch-hunt, which continued with more arrests, beatings, and executions. The entire Jesuit order was expelled in 1964 "for plotting against the government." In 1968, as noted, Duvalier's puppet Congress passed a law making the possession of "communist propaganda" a crime punishable by death. In 1969, nine Haitian priests were expelled. Shortly thereafter, the entire Holy Ghost and Immaculate Heart of Mary orders were expelled. Archbishop Ligondé, said to have been party to these decisions, simply replaced the management of the seminaries with more pliant administrators.

It was a dark time for the Catholic Church, and the people abandoned it, often for evangelical Protestantism, in droves. Haitian Catholics were scandalized and despondent as "the Church was silent before massacres committed in broad daylight, before disappearances that could no longer be counted, before the pillage of the public coffers and the shameless exploitation of the poor classes. The Haitian Church had no prophetic charism."[12]

All other institutions would be similarly cheapened under Duvalier. The modern Haitian Parliament, mistakenly thought by the foreign press to have been a force in the pro-democracy movement, took shape during Papa Doc's reign:

> [Duvalier] forced the Haitian Parliament to amend the Constitution to name him "President for Life." Duvalier went one step further, however, and forced Parliament to lower the minimum age for a President from forty to eighteen which conveniently qualified his son Jean-

Claude for the office. In a subsequent referendum in 1971 asking the Haitian people to approve his choice of Jean-Claude to succeed him as President for life, 2,391,916 voted in favor and no one opposed.[13]

After François Duvalier died in 1971, going, as he had promised, "from palace to cemetery," the Haitian people breathed somewhat easier. Some of those exiled by Papa Doc were confident that the Duvalier reign of terror was over. After all, how could his tubby 19-year-old son—nicknamed Baby Doc—possibly stay in power?

But Jean-Claude Duvalier remained in the palace, thanks largely to the ceaseless efforts of his father to crush all meaningful opposition before his death. The transfer of power went rather smoothly, by Haitian standards. But, as usual, the impression of a purely "national" event was misleading, as anthropologist Robert Lawless suggests:

> Apparently, the 1971 transition from Duvalier Senior to Duvalier Junior...was part of a deal worked out between François Duvalier and the Nixon administration during Vice President Nelson Rockefeller's trip there in 1970. The United States would support the continuation of the Duvalier dynasty, and Jean-Claude, when he came to power, would support a new economic program guided by the United States, a program featuring private investments from the United States that would be drawn to Haiti by such incentives as no customs taxes, a minimum wage kept very low, the suppression of labor unions, and the right of American companies to repatriate their profits.[14]

Although the junior dictator's advent is said to have marked a move towards liberalization, Duvalierism underwent no great change of heart with the passing of Papa Doc. Duvalier *père* had repressed dissenters heartily, but his son proved only too willing to continue the job. Unlike his father, however, Duvalier *fils* found it necessary to hire Madison Avenue public relations firms to clean up his image. For even more than his father, Jean-Claude Duvalier was dependent on U.S. largesse. As Michel Rolph Trouillot has argued:

> With the perspective gained from the passage of time, the two Duvalier regimes appear as two sides of the same coin. There are, of course, dissimilarities, but most of them are superficial. The greatest difference between the two regimes lay in the deepening of relations between the state and holders of capital at home and abroad, and in the increased support of the U.S. government. It was not, however, a difference in principle. On the contrary, the blueprint for the economic policies executed under Jean-Claude Duvalier...can be found in the speeches of François. In the late 1960s, Papa Doc...projected a vision of what may be described as a totalitarianism with a human face, one that rested on increased economic dependence, particularly on a subcontracting assembly industry heavily tied to the United States.[15]

A new phase in the history of the Haitian economy had been initiated in the last years of François Duvalier's tenure, when offshore assembly for U.S. corporations and markets was touted by both nations as "aid" to Haiti. The *assembly industry* is not really an industry, as it is inessential to the production of goods and services. Rather, it is a reflection of steep gradients between countries in the cost of labor. Materials produced in a well-to-do country are exported to a poor country to be assembled by the comparatively cheap and "disciplined" labor there. In this sense, the Duvaliers' Haiti offered enormous benefits for offshore assembly—generous tax holidays, a franchise granting tariff exemption, tame unions, a minimum wage that was but a tiny fraction of that in the United States. These advantages did not just descend from the heavens, as Papa Doc's 1969 welcome to Nelson Rockefeller notes: "Haiti could be a vast reservoir of manpower for Americans establishing re-exportation industries closer, safer, and more convenient than Hong Kong."

Haiti was not among the first countries favored by investors seeking conditions for optimum profit through offshore assembly. The trend, as Duvalier's comments suggest, began in Asia, and came to Latin America in the 1960s. The businesses set up in Mexico were referred to as "export platforms" or *maquiladores*:

> In 1973 there were some 448 *maquiladores* in Mexico, chiefly in electronics and the garment industry. But by this time Mexican workers had begun to organize, and companies began to look to Central America and the Caribbean for a cheaper and more docile labor force. They found what they were looking for in Haiti and El Salvador.[16]

In fact, Haiti and El Salvador in the 1970s and 1980s resembled each other more than the government of either would care to admit.[17] Each was poor, over-crowded, and ruled by a U.S.-backed, right-wing regime, factors all intimately related to the growth of the U.S.-backed assembly plants: "Largely because of its cheap labor force, extensive government repression, and denial of even minimal labor rights, Haiti is one of the most attractive countries for both the subcontractors and the *maquilas*."[18] The misery of the Haitian majority was not without certain benefits, according to a CIA document from the same period: "To some extent the incredibly low standard of living and the backwardness of the Haitian masses work against communist exploitation in that most Haitians are so completely downtrodden as to be politically inert."[19]

A mere decade after its arrival, the assembly sector claimed to be the "dynamic" part of the Haitian economy. Shortly before the fall of Jean-Claude Duvalier, Haiti was the world's ninth largest assembler of goods for U.S. consumption—the world's largest producer of baseballs—and ranked among the top three in the assembly of such diverse products as stuffed toys, dolls and apparel, especially brassieres. All told, the impact of international subcontracting was considerable: "Contributing more than half of the country's industrial exports, assembly production now earns almost one-quarter of Haiti's yearly foreign exchange receipts."[20] By 1978, "exports" from off-shore assembly operations had surpassed coffee as the number one export. In terms of employment, the World Bank and the United States Embassy estimate that, as of 1980, there were approximately 200 assembly plants employing 60,000 persons, a majority of whom were women. These factories were (and are) all located in the capital city of Port-au-Prince. "Assuming a dependency ratio of 4 to 1," add Grunwald, Delatour, and Voltaire, "this means that assembly operations supported about one-quarter of the population of Port-au-Prince in 1980."[21]

Unsurprisingly, this form of "industrialization," did little to arrest an economy in free fall, and Haiti was sinking deeper into debt. One Haitian economist reported that "in just seven years, Haiti's external public debt increased seven fold: from $53 million in 1973 to $366 million in 1980. This represents almost twice the rate of growth of external indebtedness in Latin America, as a whole, over the same period of time."[22]

In 1976, the World Bank fixed the threshold of absolute poverty at $140 per capita income *per year*. Even using this stringent criterion, fully 75 percent of all Haitians fell into this category. The need for drastic change was obvious, but each attempt by the Haitian poor—or their advocates in religious communities and the press—to improve their lot was met with arrests, disappearances, or expulsion. William O'Neill, former Deputy Director of the Lawyers Committee for Human Rights, put it this way: "Political dissent was forbidden, the *Macoutes* and the army arrested, extorted, tortured and sometimes killed anyone suspected of opposing the Duvalier regime. The erosion of the justice system continued."[23]

Thus ravaged, Haiti generated refugees by the thousands. The arrival of Haitian "boat people" to U.S. shores engendered a great deal of debate as to how to classify these refugees. While the Haitians and their advocates insisted that the boat people were political refugees, fleeing the consequences of political pillage, the Immigration and Naturalization Service (INS) termed them "economic refugees." For some years, anthropologist Alex Stepick has followed the vicissitudes of the Haitian refugees:

> Since 1972 national political authorities, goaded by local political groups, have attempted both to deter Haitian immigration and to deport those Haitians already in Florida. Members of southern Florida's political elite—including Democratic party members, elected officials, and some Cubans—believed that the boat people were a disruptive force, destroying the community and draining public resources. They appealed to their local Congressmen, who apparently pressured the INS into a response.[24]

Notes Robert Lawless: "The record of the INS since then has been strikingly repugnant."[25]

The stream of exiles persisted as Haiti continued to show no sign of improvement. Before long, Haitian emigrés became a presence in all the major cities along the U.S. eastern seaboard. Dominicans and Bahamians reserved their most unpleasant tasks for Haitian immigrants. It is estimated that as of 1990 between 700,000 and 1,500,000 Haitians lived outside the country, the majority of them in urban North America (New York, Miami, Montreal, and Boston) or in the Caribbean basin. The members of the "diaspora," as they called themselves, would play an important role in the coming years. In addition, future president Jean-Bertrand Aristide came of age in this setting: a country increasingly immiserated even as the false "industrialization" of offshore assembly grew; a country governed by one iron-fisted family; and a country increasingly inhospitable to its own people.

As late as the summer of 1985, after 14 years of rule, Baby Doc Duvalier still seemed permanently affixed to his presidential throne. Large segments of the population teetered on the edge of famine; thousands tried to flee the country in rickety boats. It had become a cliché, in some circles, to note that Haiti was "the poorest country in the hemisphere" and "one of the 25 poorest in the world." The visitor to rural Haiti was often struck by the aridity, the erosion, the limitless poverty. Haiti seemed to have been "used up." By the time Duvalier *fils* was firmly entrenched, the majority of Haitians had long since left behind even a peasant standard of living. Deforestation and concomitant erosion were each year washing thousands of acres of topsoil into the sea, and thousands more acres were being claimed by alkalinity:

> Haitian soil was so exhausted and poor, it could produce only .90 units of rice per hectare whereas the Dominican Republic produced 2.67, Mexico 3.28, the U.S. 5.04, and wonderfully fertile Spain 6.04. Haiti could grow .67 units of corn to the Dominican Republic's 2.10, Canada's 5.38, the U.S.'s 6.35. Its sugarcane grew at 49 units compared to the Dominican Republic's 62.35, the U.S.'s 80.51, and Spain's 100. And coffee, Haiti's chief export crop, grew only .25 units whereas the Dominican Republic grew .31, Guadeloupe .95, and Mexico .75, statistics as dry as the eroded land that was starving the Haitians.[26]

These sad figures were no news to the stomachs of the starving Haitian poor. In the summer of 1984, a series of food riots reflected the general despair and pervasive hunger.

Another anti-government riot—spurred by police brutality against a pregnant woman—was registered the following year in the provincial city of Gonaïves. While some foreign observers predicted this protest would spread from the provincial cities to the hinterlands, the peasants themselves seemed indifferent to the uprisings. Instead, they awaited the results of a July referendum on the Duvalier presidency. It was patently a sham ballot, engineered to lend the dictatorship the appearance of political pluralism, and the U.S. State Department, for which the referendum was staged, asked for little more. With the subtlety one had come to expect of the Duvaliers, who had no doubt taken their cues from the U.S. Marine plebiscite of 1918, the Ministry of Information announced that 99.8 percent of the voters had approved the referendum. It granted (among other things) continued carte blanche to the *president-à-vie.*

The referendum offered, as Minister of the Interior Roger Lafontant stated on the governmental radio, "a resounding lesson to all those who have not grasped the fact that Haiti belongs to Duvalier and Duvalier belongs to Haiti." Dr. Lafontant, head of the *tontons macoutes,* was considered by most to be the regime's strong man. (In more open times, the press would later label him "Haiti's Mengele.") During the last years of the regime,

> Lafontant had orchestrated a new reign of terror. Once again the prisons bulged, and new exiles swelled the Diaspora. Within Haiti the Macoutes swaggered with the confidence of those who know they are truly appreciated, and they had as tangible proof the envelopes Lafontant dispersed among them just as grandly as Papa Doc had.[27]

It was apparent to many observers that, even in a country long accustomed to such polarization, something had to snap in Haiti. It was at a tense moment, then, that Father Jean-Bertrand Aristide returned, in January 1985, from three years of graduate study in Montreal. It was the young priest's second return to Haiti. As a Salesian seminarian, the bookish son of a rural family had left Haiti to study biblical theology in Israel from 1979 to 1982. Returning home for his ordination in

1982, Aristide had expected to return to Israel to complete a doctorate, but instead was assigned to a parish in Port-au-Prince. The young priest soon became known for his incisive sermons, offensive to the Duvalier regime; Roger Lafontant himself is said to have demanded Aristide's expulsion. The Salesians dispatched him to Montreal, where he remained until his return in time to participate in the smoldering anti-Duvalier movement. In September, 1985, Aristide was assigned to Saint-Jean Bosco, a parish on the edge of a large slum near Port-au-Prince's waterfront.

Struck by the absence of young people in the church, Aristide set out to organize church youth. Together, they formed *Solidarité Ant Jen* (SAJ), "Solidarity Among Youth." The members of SAJ proclaimed their solidarity not only with youth in other towns, but with the *ti kominote legliz*, or "base ecclesial communities" that were then forming in rural Haiti. (The term and the practice of such communities derived from the tenets of liberation theology.) Aristide inaugurated a weekly participatory youth mass, and openly exhorted his growing audience to demand a say in Haiti's future.

Suddenly, a future loomed before them. Although there had been sporadic explosions of discontent in the years before 1985, it was not until autumn of that year that any coherent uprising emerged. Duvalier tried to appease his subjects by expelling Roger Lafontant, popularly associated with the regime's worst excesses, but it was too little and too late to save Baby Doc. In November, an obscure anti-government protest again in the city of Gonaïves became the focus of national rage when government forces shot and bayoneted three schoolboys. Over the protests of the children's families, their bodies were buried in an unmarked grave at an undisclosed time, as the regime wished to prevent the children's funerals from giving rise to popular demonstrations. It was the first of a series of miscalculations by Duvalier, who tried lamely to placate the families by sending them condolences and envelopes stuffed with money. "The mourners spat at one and refused the other," noted reporters. Students throughout the country "went on strike," and after Christmas vacation simply refused to return to school until Duvalier was gone.

Popular uprising spread throughout the provincial cities during the first week of January 1986, and finally to Port-au-Prince. One of the chief organizers of urban resistance was Father Aristide. Again, the priest attracted the attention of the now tottering and desperate regime. On January 31, Aristide was confronted by a would-be assassin, who fortunately lost his nerve once he entered Saint-Jean Bosco. The hit-man had received a fresh passport and a great deal of money from his superiors, and, as Aristide's parishioners observed, not many people in Haiti could issue valid passports. This narrow escape added to the persistence with which the priest denounced injustice in the face of threats—and led many to think of Aristide as an envoy from on high. The poor, especially, began to refer to the young Salesian as *mistik*—mystically protected against the bullets of his enemies.

Demonstrations grew; protest leapt from town to town. Haitian military and *macoute* forces fired on the crowds, who replied with rocks and flaming barricades. Work stoppages and school strikes continued. The disgruntled commercial sector joined the students, paralyzing the entire country. Duvalier declared a state of siege, suspending (gratuitously) all constitutional rights. The *macoutes* also responded with their expected virulence: in one village an hour south of the capital, a notorious *macoute* machine-gunned everyone in sight. A nationwide bloodbath seemed likely, but was averted by Duvalier's hasty departure, itself triggered, it appears, by both internal and external forces: on January 31, the United States announced that it was reducing its $56 million aid package to Haiti by $7 million. On February 3, Secretary of State George Shultz spoke of Haiti on national television:

> Appearing on the ABC television program 'Good Morn-
> ing America,' Mr. Shultz said there was 'not a great
> deal' that the United States [could] do in Haiti 'except
> to stand by our views and our principles and, of
> course, all of our instincts to help people in a humani-
> tarian way, and we do that.'[28]

The writing was on the wall. The baby dictator and
his family, carrying much of their ill-gotten wealth, left
battered Haiti in a U.S. cargo plane on February 7, 1986.

What had happened? Certainly, there had been a
popular rebellion. But as usual, what appeared to be a
"purely Haitian political event" was not so. The fall of
Duvalier was no more exclusively a consequence of
Haitian impulses than any of the other events and
processes in contemporary Haiti.

> Two series of events occurred on February 7, 1986:
> first, the departure of Duvalier; second, *the takeover
> of the state machinery by a group of apparently dis-
> parate individuals*: civilians and career army officers,
> Duvalierists and former opposition figures, past back-
> ers of repression and former human rights leaders.
> Missing from the dominant version, or at best viewed
> as secondary, are the negotiations—the tacit and
> explicit understandings between Haitian and U.S.
> politicians, in Haiti and the United States, local and
> foreign military and intelligence personnel, ambas-
> sadors, power brokers, and bureaucrats—that led to,
> and tied together, the two sets of events.[29]

This time, a new game was revealed in the pattern of
widespread North American ignorance of U.S. involvement in Haitian affairs, and widespread Haitian awareness of the same. The U.S. government claimed it had
played a major role in removing Duvalier; the leaders of
the rebellion claimed that the Reagan administration,
staunch supporters of Latin American tyranny, were simply grandstanding. Both sides were correct. The United
States had simply withdrawn its support for Duvalier

when it became clear that the government was going to fall. In this, they followed a pattern of opportunism expressed in Nicaragua in 1979 and in the Philippines in 1986. In addition to providing the Duvaliers with an airplane, U.S. representatives also helped to provide Haiti with a cosmetic change of leadership. It was not to be the last time.

The departure of the Duvaliers was marked by spontaneous street celebrations throughout the republic. In scores of churches, thanksgiving masses were offered. Haiti, went the saying, was liberated—*Ayiti libere*. Changes in the political culture of Haiti rapidly became evident. One of the first slogans to gain currency after Duvalier's fall was *baboukèt la tonbe*. A literal English equivalent would be "the bridle has fallen off," but the phrase is better rendered as "the muzzle is off." Journalist Amy Wilentz recalled "the feeling of a million people talking all at once and all of a sudden."[30] New (and sometimes short-lived) newspapers were peddled on the street corners of Port-au-Prince; banned radio stations were reopened, political tracts littered the streets, new labor unions began flexing their muscles.

One of the most striking things about post-Duvalier Haiti was the seeming unanimity with which the Haitians undertook the process they termed *dechoukaj*, "the uprooting." *Macoutes* were publicly persecuted and killed; Papa Doc's hated red-and-black flag was replaced with its blue-and-red predecessor; a statue of Christopher Columbus was uprooted and dumped into the Bay of Port-au-Prince, and the public square it had graced was rebaptized "Place Charlemagne Péralte," in reference to the leader of the armed resistance to the U.S. occupation. Furthermore, the cities and towns of Haiti were repainted and scrubbed as part of the clean sweep perceived to be integral to the uprooting:

> The operation termed *dechoukaj* was not merely the cleaning up or eradication of the *macoute* network, the nighttime eye of the terror infiltrating every cranny of this society. It was above all the expression of a desire to rebuild the nation on a foundation radically different from that of despotism.[31]

Surveying the destitute and dilapidated nation, it was apparent to all that a radical "uprooting" of the old institutions was necessary now that the dictator was gone. The new Haitian government, the Conseil National de Gouvernement, was led by General Henri Namphy, who had risen through the ranks of the army under two Duvaliers. Most Haitians were skeptical about his commitment to democracy, but the U.S. press seemed to love him. To cite an article that appeared in *Time* magazine shortly after the revolt:

> In his first meeting with the foreign press, the barrel-chested Namphy exhibited a whimsical personality. He spoke as he cut a zigzag path through a room in the palace filled with busts of past Haitian Presidents. When a woman reporter pressed for specific answers about his plans for the country, Namphy pinched her cheek. Said he: 'We have only been the government for three days, and those have been holidays. Give us a break.'[32]

Most of the foreign press were more than happy to give General Namphy a break. The *Times* of London credulously reported that the "Tontons macoute have been dissolved and their weapons surrendered, the general said. He added that they would remain only in the memories of the people."[33]

The United States government was also anxious to polish up the image of the junta. "The government is off to a good start," remarked State Department spokesman Charles Redman in mid-February, 1986. Other U.S. officials underlined the need for more aid: "Aid is intimately tied to stability. Many businessmen and their capital have left the country, army expenses are up, and expectations are raised."[34] The army was not to want for much in the coming years. One of their first gifts from the United States was $384,000 worth of riot control equipment. The population, as diplomats said in reports home, was getting carried away with its notion of *dechoukaj*.

The CNG, certainly, did not care for *dechoukaj*. Much of the activity was aimed at Duvalierists, and the CNG was becoming increasingly devoid of non-Duvalierists. Before long, the CNG was a military junta led by General Namphy and composed of the only kind of high-ranking officers in Haiti: Duvalierists. Expressions of popular discontent were soon met in proper Duvalierist fashion: the army shot demonstrators after dousing them in tear gas, a gift from the United States. The tone for the coming years was set on April 26, 1986, when the army opened fire on a crowd of unarmed demonstrators as they approached a notorious prison. The demonstrators, about 10,000 strong, had come from a memorial service for victims of the Duvalier regimes; it was led by a group of priests that included Jean-Bertrand Aristide. *The New York Times* cast the story in its own inimitable way: "An army officer said today that eight people were killed and dozens more wounded today when violence erupted between mourners and troops at a memorial service for 60,000 people said to have died as victims of the 29-year Duvalier regime."[35] The next day, the *Times* continued the story on the front page, under the headline "Haiti Backs Police on Deaths of 7, Saying Agitators Provoked Clash."

Although U.S. journalists had apparently not understood that the CNG (or, as the *Times* put it, "Haiti") and the police were one and the same, the Haitian people knew how much confidence to put in the government's exoneration of its troops. Noted a Haitian anthropologist: "By the end of its first year in office the CNG, generously helped by the U.S. taxpayers' money, had openly gunned down more civilians than Jean-Claude Duvalier's government had done in fifteen years."[36] "Duvalierism without Duvalier," as the policies of the CNG were termed, was outdoing its model.

The hopes of early 1986 quickly soured. What options remained for "hopeless Haiti," as the country was termed by international aid specialists? According to Father Aristide, there were many: national *reconciliation*, a code word for toleration of *macoutes*, was meaningless without justice, he warned. The Haitian people, and the poor in particular, needed to push for far-reaching, radical changes. According to Aristide, this could best be done by organizing the people, in large part desperately poor. And one of the best means of organizing the poor was in the grassroots ecclesial communities, *ti kominote legliz.*

As in the past, the established church cowered. The Episcopal Conference raised its voice against *dechoukaj.* Archbishop Ligondé, now covered with shame if unrepentant, was advised not to speak for the bishops, but other bishops called for reconciliation, and one warned obliquely against "the danger of communism." More than one observer noted with anxiety the adoption of Duvalier's tactic of evoking an irrelevant international specter. After years of crying wolf, conservative Haitians, in the Church and out of it, were losing their credibility in the international community. Within Haiti, they had lost it decades earlier.

These debates and changes, though centered in Port-au-Prince, were felt in small villages. Previously silent and (as one too easily supposed) uninformed villagers were astonishingly conversant with the slightest details of current national events. In March 1987, these villagers voted, in an unprecedented sense of the word. It was not, of course, the first time they had been called to the polls: the Duvaliers had regularly staged referenda to please their financial backers to the north. But this time, the Haitian people were called to approve or disapprove a new constitution, written in open sessions that had been broadcast—in Creole—on the airwaves.

The Constitution was distinctively the work of the democratic sector. In particular, it addressed the issue of the future composition of Haitian governments. It put the planning and execution of presidential elections in the hands of a provisional electoral council (Conseil Electoral Provisoire, CEP), to be composed of civilians. In addition, the controversial Article 291 of the Constitution barred from elections all "zealous partisans" of the Duvalier regimes. In both rural and urban Haiti, this single provision generated the most ardent discussion. The CNG disapproved of this article (and of many other aspects of the new Constitution), but when 98 percent of the voters approved it, most were expressing their approval of Article 291.

There was great enthusiasm for the Constitution, and a good deal of skepticism about the possibility of implementing it. "We'll wait and see," noted one villager from the Central Plateau. "Will it be that easy to get rid of the Duvalierists?"

The answer came less than four months later. In the summer of 1987, General Namphy's junta announced that it was dissolving a militant labor union and taking over the role of the CEP, and skepticism turned to angry cynicism. It was, most agreed, a veiled *coup d'état.* When a general strike was called by a hastily-formed opposition coalition, roadblocks were erected throughout the country. The strikers wanted the junta to *rache manyòk, bay tè a blanch*—"to pull up their maniocs, and leave the garden clean." They wanted, in short, the *dechoukaj* of the CNG.

These strikes, at first a huge success, eventually exhausted the rural population. Villagers heard, by *teledjòl* (word of mouth) and radio, that the army had taken to opening fire on demonstrators in Port-au-Prince: more than 50 were killed in a single month. Families with sons and daughters in the city begged them to be careful.

Even after the authority to supervise the elections was restored to the CEP and the banned labor union was reestablished, demonstrators continued to push for their ultimate objective, the resignation of the CNG, whose only non-Duvalierist member had long since resigned. The opposition pulled together a strong coalition of 57 democratic organizations. *Rache manyòk* was its slogan, as well. But this group proved impotent before the guns and money of the CNG.

As Haitians' demands for democracy were met by tear gas and bullets, feelings of frustration became entrenched; feelings of goodwill toward Americans evaporated. Many saw the junta's head, General Henri Namphy, as a reborn Duvalier. The more repressive the army became, the more aid the United States pumped into Haiti, much of it through the state apparatus:

> The junta stood tall amid the summer's carnage, and refused to *rache manyòk*. All the while, the U.S. government, though momentarily shaken by the strength of popular protest, remained steadfast at Namphy's side. The junta, said Elliott Abrams, then Assistant Secretary of State for Inter-American Affairs, represented 'Haiti's best chance for democracy.'[37]

In the 18 months after February 1986, Haiti was estimated to have received over $200 million in U.S. aid, some small portion of it in military and riot control aid. But that small part was of major symbolic significance. "More than any other single factor," said Haitians to one reporter, "the decision to send military assistance to the CNG has tarnished America's image in Haiti."[38]

The widespread hope that Haiti could change radically had been dealt a telling blow by the intransigent brutality of the CNG: "Despair vis-à-vis the State seemed to be at its height 16 months after the fall of the dictator. Is there, then, a way out of Duvalierism? This question was posed in examining the crisis shaking Haitian society, and the prime victim was the peasantry."[39] Chaos and confusion added to the despair. Lucid analyses, though by no means rare, were often drowned out by the "enemies of change," who controlled sectors of the press. From his pulpit, Father Aristide continued to preach against "Duvalierism without Duvalier." He passionately cried out for satisfaction of "popular demands." His was a voice in the wilderness, offering words of deliverance. Few then understood how many Haitians were listening to his message.

Just who is Aristide? In person, he is anything but imposing. A mere 32-years-old when Duvalier fell, Aristide gives the impression of a man who came of age in the midst of bitter struggle, a man rendered prematurely grave. Described by some as frail, he is really quite sturdy and strong. In conversation, he is often soft-spoken and attentive. He is, in any case, a far cry from the "radical firebrand" described in U.S. embassy cables of 1987.

Aristide is indeed a radical, but not in the sense of the dispatches to Washington: he is radically devoted to the poor. His political inspiration comes not from any manifesto or existing political system, but from the Bible and from theological documents elaborated in Puebla and Medellín—the wellsprings of liberation theology—as he has openly noted in his sermons.

Aristide's main inspiration comes directly from the poor themselves. He has worked with disaffected and unemployed urban youth, and with the street children and beggars and homeless inhabitants of a city of well over a million people. Reflecting the harsh conditions in which Haiti's poor live, Aristide's homilies have always been harshly and explicitly admonitory. Take, for example, a sermon delivered shortly before Easter of 1985, when sermons tended to be tame: "Today we can say that a Christian who wishes to grow in holiness must ask that the land be redistributed. He must ask that the big landholders give land to the poor, and that the poor work that land and make it fruitful."[40]

Through his preaching, Aristide became known not only for his militant stance, which he shares with other clerics, but for his bravery. In one celebrated act of defiance, Aristide continued a Radio Soleil broadcast from the midst of a demonstration on which the army had opened fire. Many remember this event, which took place in April of 1986 in front of Fort Dimanche, as one of the early manifestations both of Aristide's unwavering support for democracy and, some thought, of his invulnerability. Aristide is certainly tenacious. While the disappointments of the years after 1986 discouraged many in the vanguard of the splintered pro-democracy movement, Aristide himself never wavered. The higher the stakes, the more prophetic he became.

The massacre at Jean-Rabel illustrates just how high the stakes were and just how willing Aristide was to take risks. In an area of parched northwest Haiti, community organizers, including a number of progressive Catholics inspired by liberation theology, and led by Father Jean-Marie Vincent had for years pushed for meaningful land reform. On July 23, 1987, the struggle over land erupted around the town of Jean-Rabel. Hundreds of peasants were killed by thugs in the pay of local landowners, one of whom proudly boasted on television that they had "killed over 1,000 communists." Although no formal investigation of the murders was forthcoming, military complicity was reported by survivors and suggested by the few journalists who dared to report on the carnage.

The massacre occurred, reported Amy Wilentz, shortly after a visit to the region by General Namphy—"to reaffirm his bonds with the ruling families, the region's largest landholders. A visit by Namphy often signaled the beginning of a repressive wave." It was Aristide who both led the cry for justice for those killed in Jean-Rabel and unveiled the role of the military:

Aristide, perceiving what he took to be a new and tougher line among the junta and its supporters, was talking and preaching about Jean-Rabel, day after day. You couldn't listen to the radio without hearing his voice. While others in the opposition had gone into informal hiding after receiving multiple death threats, he remained adamantly visible.[41]

Namphy and his colleagues were enraged by Aristide's daring. Time and again, the Salesians were advised to muzzle the young priest, or at least to remove him from Port-au-Prince. He was a bad influence, clearly: under Aristide's leadership, youth involvement in Saint-Jean Bosco was at its peak, and SAJ, the Haitian youth group, could be depended on for regular commentary on all events of national importance.

The Salesians eventually caved in. In August 1987, Aristide received notice of his immediate assignment to a parish in the midst of the *macoute*-infested Cul-de-Sac Plain. But the youth of Saint-Jean Bosco, numbering in the thousands and coming from all parts of the capital, began a hunger strike when learned of Aristide's transfer. The strikers occupied the national Cathedral in dramatic fashion. The already skinny youths lay on straw mats before the massive altar. As the days went by, more and more people came to pray over the young men and women, who called upon the Episcopal Conference to state in unambiguous terms its support for the poor. Needless to say, they also called on the bishops "to stop their harassment of Father Aristide."

The strikers refused to budge, and soon all eyes were trained on the cathedral. People in the countryside listened to their radios to hear news of *ti moun k'ap fè grèv grangou*, the "kids on the hunger strike." The bishops were unable to call for their genteel removal by the police, and the church hierarchy—without Ligondé, who was nowhere in evidence—was at last forced to concede. Aristide, by now widely known as "The Prophet," joined three bishops and thousands of city-dwellers in an impromptu prayer of thanksgiving for the end to the crisis.

This triumph was to be fleeting, however. As Aristide's following grew, his threat to the status quo became apparent to all. Countless death threats had been leveled against him; I count at least four assassination attempts. The first, in Saint-Jean Bosco, was testimony to the newly-returned Aristide's place on the short list of Duvalier's enemies. Another occurred shortly after the hunger strike, at a mass commemorating the July massacre in Jean-Rabel. At a service held on August 23 near Pont-Sondé, another *macoute* stronghold, Aristide was speaking to a large crowd assembled in an abandoned cannery—the church was too small to contain the crowd—when shots rang through the building. After the screams died down and the dust settled, a lone gunman, his field of view unobstructed, stood a mere 20 paces from Aristide. His poor marksmanship was of little interest to those in attendance, who were fleeing, but it was later agreed that divine intervention had again spared the persecuted, *mistik* priest.

A third attempt came that very night. The Port-au-Prince contingent, several cars full of priests and nuns, had decided to risk returning to the capital, fearing another attack if they remained near Pont-Sonde. During an intense storm, at a town called Freycineau and in full view of a military post, the cortège was ambushed by a crowd of armed men. They were looking for "Aristide and the other communists." Aristide was hidden under a blanket in the back of one of the cars, shielded by his fellow priests. William Smarth, a priest expelled by Papa Doc in 1969, was forced out into the rain when his windshield was smashed. He found a machete poised above his head. "But brother," he said, "we are just four priests." His assailant wavered, but another threw a large rock at Father Smarth, wounding him in the groin (Father Jean-Marie Vincent was also wounded). The other passengers pulled Smarth back in as the car's driver accelerated through a hole that had opened in the barricade before them. They disappeared into the night, rain pouring in through the shattered windshield.

The following morning, the entire nation heard of the attacks on every radio and television in the country. Aristide and those with him—including William Smarth— were still missing. Since the hunger strike in the cathedral, Aristide had come to have a national, rather than a regional, following, and was arguably the most beloved figure in the country. The suspense was intolerable, and it was not until a day later when the nation learned that all had escaped the Freycineau ambush with minor injuries.

As Aristide's own account of the ambush suggests, his relationship with the church hierarchy became even more frosty: "And when the four Haitian priests who had been attacked at Freycineau asked the Haitian bishops to say a Mass of grace and thanksgiving with us, they refused. They refused!"[42]

As Aristide's relations with the hierarchy continued to deteriorate, his relations with the government—now a thinly disguised military dictatorship—were beyond repair. That the generals wanted Aristide dead was well-appreciated even before the Freycineau attack. But the regime was under tremendous international pressure to hold elections—they were scheduled for November—and further state-sponsored assassination attempts were likely to lead to an interruption of foreign aid, upon which Haitian governments have long depended. As the November elections approached, Aristide attacked the very notion of elections under a *macoute* regime. He predicted that any meaningful result would be negated and, further, that more blood would be spilled.

Spilling of blood was increasingly common in Haiti. In an incisive report filed on November 4, 1987 and published in the *New York Review of Books*, one journalist made the following observations:

Something strange and terrible is taking shape in

Haiti. In July hundreds of peasants agitating for land reform in a remote rural province were massacred by a ragtag force organized by a local landowner. The leader of one political party was hacked to death while addressing a crowd of peasants; another was murdered in full view of reporters while delivering a speech in front of police headquarters. At night, death squads roam the streets of Port-au-Prince, and bandits man roadblocks on rural thoroughfares. Haiti, preparing for elections this month, its first real elections in thirty years, is coming to resemble Central America at its most violent.[43]

As in Central America, elections were deemed absolutely necessary to lend the appearance of democracy. The "traditional politicians," such as former World Bank official Marc Bazin, continued a perfunctory campaign. (Bazin had been tagged the *kandida merikèn*—the Americans' candidate). At the eleventh hour, the left-leaning popular sector put up a candidate, human rights advocate Gérard Gourgue, who had discredited the CNG by resigning from it early in 1986. Needless to say, Gourgue was not a favorite of General Namphy.

The CNG, most assumed, was deeply embroiled in the daily escalations of violence. As Amy Wilentz noted, "The junta that Elliott Abrams had called Haiti's best chance for democracy was pleased by the attacks on the electoral process, and doubtless encouraged them."[44] Every morning, the streets of Port-au-Prince were littered with bodies:

Usually they were nobodies knocked off at random, perhaps killed to settle small scores. Sometimes, however, they were young members of opposition organizations, and the nightly murders, the daily cadavers in the street, the randomness, the unknown killers, the whole setup was a warning to everyone associated with the elections and with the opposition, and that included voters.[45]

The U.S. embassy was not interested either in investigating these killings or in protesting the assassinations of candidates. Kenneth Roth, then deputy director of Human Rights Watch, stated that "When we investigated political murders in Haiti, U.S. Ambassador McKinley refused all cooperation." When asked why the embassy failed to protest such killings, the envoy replied, "We have no proof of such killings." Roth and his co-workers offered to provide proof, at which point "Ambassador McKinley replied that he found protesting such things as political murders 'boring.'"[46]

The CEP, beleaguered by death threats and burned out of their offices on the day that they applied Article 291 to the Duvalierists, continued to insist that elections were possible. The United States, through its embassy, predicted that the elections would proceed as planned. "Of course we abhor all violence," said an embassy spokesman, "especially violence that is aimed at destabilizing a democratic election. But we are confident that the CNG will guarantee the safety of the voters and the honesty of the election."[47] Aristide continued to warn of a trap:

> Only if we elected a government would the cold country to our north, and its allies—other former colonizers—send us more money and food. Of course, that money and that food corrupt our society: the money helps to maintain an armed force against the people; the food helps to ruin our national economy; and both money and food keep Haiti in a situation of dependence on the former colonizers.[48]

As the elections approached, however, a great number of Haitians continued to hope that the vote might offer an end to the carnage. As if the public murders of two presidential candidates were not sufficient to shatter these hopes, a gruesome massacre of voters on November 29, 1987 once again proved Aristide chillingly prophetic. One Port-au-Prince polling place was in a school at the end of a cul-de-sac, and it was here that the most lurid of several massacres took place:

> A television journalist from the Dominican Republic was gunned down after he put his hands up over his head. Under an almond tree in the school's front yard, the attackers hacked a screaming woman to death. Two more women were killed in the bathroom. One family who came to vote, grandmother, daughter and granddaughter, were all killed. Voters who piled up in a corner of the classroom were massacred. The attackers left, then returned and bore down on the journalists who had come to record the results of the massacre.[49]

The army's involvement was witnessed by scores of foreign and local journalists, some of whom were injured or killed. The carnage at last forced the United States to cancel aid to the Haitian military.

Or so the White House said. In truth, the Haitian security forces continued to receive up to $1 million a year in equipment, training and financial support from the CIA. "The money may have sent a mixed message," observed *The New York Times* some years later, "for Congress was withholding about $1.5 million in aid for the Haitian military regime at the same time."[50] In the days after the voter massacre, however, the *Times* was not even willing to admit the slightest complicity on the part of the United States. On December 1st, an editorial noted that "It is Haitians...who are murdering other Haitians and trying to shove the country back into the perpetual nightmare of terror and despotism."[51]

The Power of the Poor in Haiti

To the extent that the exploited classes, poor peoples, and despised ethnic groups have been raising their consciousness of the oppression they have suffered for centuries, they have created a new historical situation. It is an ambivalent situation, as is everything historical. But at the same time it is a situation charged with promise—a promise that the lords of this world see rather as a menace.

—Gustavo Gutiérrez,
The Power of the Poor in History

The voter massacre of November 29, 1987 marked the end of the ratty veneer of democratic forms that the army had attempted to polish for its chief financial backer. Now, an overt military dictatorship was declared. General Namphy blustered that he would not allow "communists" (*viz.*, the centrist, Gourgue) to come to power to appease foreign interests. The major foreign interest in question, though now officially opposed to the junta, did not seem to have a radically different interpretation of events. A Democratic congressman was later informed by U.S. Ambassador McKinley that "the electoral council was being run by foreign leftists, and Gourgue was at least a Communist front man, if not a Communist himself."[1]

Against the protests of the CEP (in hiding), the army decided to sponsor its own elections. Although all the leading candidates from the previous race refused to participate and only a tiny fraction of the population—5% according to most estimates—could be coerced to vote, the army ordered people to the ballot on January 17, 1988. Amy Wilentz offers the following assessment:

> The January election had been one big joke. Manigat's voters were given rum and money; 'campaign' workers'

doled out dollars to voters from the back of a big black car outside Cité Soleil. A foreign journalist, a white man, was paid five dollars to vote for Manigat. The voters, ragtag groups in most places, toured the towns by tap-tap, voting—and then voting again.[2]

Professor Leslie Manigat, a long-winded political scientist who had exhorted his partisans to avoid the polls on November 29, was "selected President," as the Haitians put it. Manigat knew that he was obliged to form an allegiance with the army, or so he had written in 1964: "The support of the police-army is needed to overthrow a government, and police-army opposition makes the election of any candidate insecure. It makes and unmakes chiefs of state."[3]

Inaugurated on February 7, 1988, Manigat was regarded coolly by most politicians. Popular attitudes toward the rotund professor ran the gamut from apathy to frank hostility. Even the Haitian bishops were scandalized at his willingness to assume power under such conditions. Manigat's insight into the workings of military politics proved to be his only legacy. When the professor attempted to make modest changes in the army, Namphy responded by exiling him, on June 19. The general then dissolved the national assembly, suspended the Constitution, and declared himself president of the republic.

Fear was rampant in the summer of 1988, and it sometimes seemed that Aristide's was the sole voice raised against the army's excesses. As a reward for the priest's courage, Namphy and other close associates sponsored one of the most lurid crimes ever perpetrated against the church in Latin America. This incident occurred on September 11, 1988, when Father Aristide began a morning mass at his church, Saint-Jean Bosco. He had received death threats prior to the service, but this was nothing new and his parishioners, in any case, insisted that the mass be celebrated. The gates of the courtyard, which open onto the capital city's main thoroughfare, were closed and the liturgy began. Those inside Saint-Jean Bosco could not see that, a few blocks away, an armed gang was raucously approaching the church.

These thugs, well-armed and over one hundred strong, reached the gates as Aristide began the liturgy. Inside, the noise of stones against cement, of metal against metal, began to frighten the parishioners, who nonetheless continued singing. As Aristide shouted "Blessed be the Eternal!", the churchyard gates were broken down by the men, who sported red armbands. A murderous spree began:

> Everyone was running, trying to find a place to hide. One man was shot in the outside courtyard, with his Bible in his hand. Bullets were zinging left and right. I saw a pregnant woman screaming for help in the pews, and holding onto her stomach. A man had just speared her there, and she was bathed in red blood. Another priest was trying to organize people to give the woman first aid. I saw an American journalist running up and down the aisle with torn clothes; the men with red armbands had torn the clothing, trying to hurt the journalist. A group of young women were in the front courtyard and were attempting to resist the onslaught, attempting to resist, with our own kind of arms, the heavy weapons that the men were using against us from the street—this was a prophetic, historic resistance that we will never forget.[4]

Within an hour, at least a dozen parishioners were dead. The church was stripped of its valuables and then gutted by fire.

This time, though, the Haitian military had overstepped its wide bounds. The attack on Saint-Jean Bosco precipitated an unprecedented wave of anger against General Namphy and his acolytes, especially after they appeared on television to boast of their feat. The dictator was toppled by enlisted men only a few days later. In three months, Haiti had had as many presidents, not one of them chosen by the Haitian people.

Again the winds of *dechoukaj* whistled through the country. In town after town, the *ti solda* ("little soldiers") manacled their corrupt officers and led them to jail. A few *macoutes* were killed; a few officers went into retirement; there was a great deal of talk about the housecleaning that would be necessary before a popularly-elected government could come to power.

Although there were once again high hopes in early October, the little soldiers handed power over to a big soldier. Brigadier-General Prosper Avril had been the hard *éminence grise* of Jean-Claude Duvalier's soft state. A shadowy figure, Avril had been extremely familiar with state finances under the Duvaliers—one journalist termed him "Haiti's unofficial minister of corruption." As the weeks went by, Avril eliminated the *ti solda* who had foolishly passed him the reins.

Aristide, meanwhile, came under scrutiny, once again, by the Salesians. A communiqué from Rome, dated August 23 but reaching Aristide in early October, announced his imminent transfer abroad. He was ordered to leave Haiti no later than October 17.

The order was met with resistance—not from Aristide, but from his supporters. The radio stations of Port-au-Prince and elsewhere were full of people who wished to speak out against his transfer. Whether or not Aristide had resigned himself to leave Haiti is not clear. Furthermore, it was a moot point. For several days in a row, crowds of over 10,000 people blocked Aristide's access to the airport; banners were draped throughout the slums of the city, and also before the charred shell of Saint-Jean Bosco, saying: *Titid p'ap fè yon pa kita, yon pa nago*—Aristide isn't going anywhere.

On December 8, 1988, Father Aristide was expelled from the Salesian order. Among the offenses listed:

- Aristide's "choices" were fundamentally opposed to "community demands;"
- Aristide's political engagement was opposed

to the philosophy of the order's founder, and Aristide's ideological positions (termed "incitation to hate and violence, exaltation of class struggle") were contrary to the "magisterium of the Church;"

- Aristide put "the eucharist and the sacraments at the service of politics," and was thus guilty of "profaning the liturgy;"
- Aristide had "broken off communion" with the church hierarchy and thus "destabilized the faithful."

Aristide denied each of these charges, and in fact appealed the Salesians' decision. He had only been doing, he claimed, what the Gospel exhorted him to do: "The crime of which I stand accused," he stated, "is the crime of preaching food for all men and women."[5]

Many thought that Aristide would be ineffective without his pulpit. And indeed, in the months that followed the Salesians' decision, he seemed less present in the ongoing struggle of the Haitian poor. But Aristide was a product of the Haitian popular movement, and his persecution only enhanced his standing in the eyes of the poor majority. "Aristide himself, shorn of his church, had already become something much larger than a radical priest. White-robed, hands outstretched Christ-like as he preached, he had become pure symbol: the righteous leader in a nation shorn of them, the pure-hearted bringer of Justice."[6]

On the walls of the capital was sprayed the message *Aristide: pale sikile*—"Aristide: speak, move among us." He did not disappoint. He exhorted. He warned. He predicted. He exhorted the "little church" to continue the struggle. He warned the people not to be satisfied with cosmetic reform, such as that offered by the flight of yet another general. He predicted that elections under such conditions would be rigged in favor of "the enemies of change."

General Avril had certainly given every indication of

being one of those enemies. In January 1989, his Minister of Information publicly slandered leaders of the democratic sector, and deplored the *ti kominote legliz*. Avril called for the establishment of regional "offices of information" in order to watch over the population. In April, independent radio stations were sabotaged by the army. The death squads were more active than usual, and several leaders of the democratic sector were arrested. Tension peaked in the fall of 1989, when on Halloween Avril arrested three popular political activists, had them tortured, and then displayed them, bloodied, on television. It would later be revealed that Colonels Prudhomme and Clerjeune, the two officers who directed the torture, were then in the pay of the CIA.[7]

The grotesque display of the Halloween prisoners was followed by more repression, including that against the *Mouvman Peyizan Papay*, the major peasant movement in the Central Plateau. In January 1990, a wave of arrests and deportations knocked out the leadership of the center and left-leaning democratic sectors. A state of siege was declared. But the final affront came on March 5, 1990, when, in the course of attacking an anti-Avril demonstration in the town of Petit Goâve, the army killed Roseline Vaval, an 11-year-old schoolgirl who was reading her *Histoire d'Haïti*.

Haitians do not like it when their children are shot, and popular revolt once again spread throughout the country. Student demonstrations paralyzed the provincial cities. Thousands flocked to Petit Goâve for the funeral of Roseline Vaval. On the same day, progressive priests in other cities, including Fathers William Smarth and Antoine Adrien in Port-au-Prince, held symbolic funerals to express solidarity with the schoolgirl's family and friends. These services turned into anti-Avril demonstrations, and it was clear even to the army that Haiti was again "ungovernable." On March 10, following a closed-door conference with the U.S. ambassador, General Avril resigned, and he left Haiti two days later. Transportation was, once again, courtesy of the United States.

Following Avril's departure, a new executive had to be patched together, and the nearly forgotten constitution seemed to point to the Supreme Court. Ertha Pascal Trouillot, a previously unknown judge, was deemed the least offensive candidate. She signed an agreement to work with a "State Council" to be constituted by freely chosen representatives from "civil society." Political pundits began prematurely celebrating the advent of democracy. From the midst of celebration, though, Aristide called for calm reflection. "The driver's gone," he said in a taped message sent to radio stations. "But the truckload of death is still with us." When, in an address to the United Nations, Trouillot referred to "my spotless white dress" as a symbol of purity, Aristide observed that it was not so spotless, really: it was spattered with blood. On the day she named her cabinet, a massacre in the Artibonite Valley claimed 11 lives and 338 homes.

Trouillot showed little more inclination to share power than had her uniformed predecessors. On May 21, she named a notorious Duvalierist to be Minister of Finances, whose nomination was not submitted, as had been stipulated, to the State Council. Ten days later, yet another massacre occurred in the Artibonite Valley, this one in Pérodin. On June 21, four uniformed men burst into a meeting of the State Council, killing councilman Serge Villard and unionist Jean-Marie Montès.

A more disturbing development was the July 7 return to Haiti of Roger Lafontant, Baby Doc's henchman. The event seemed to confirm both Aristide's role as prophet and Trouillot's ineffectiveness. Although new elections were called for December 1990, Aristide reiterated his earlier concerns:

> The election drums are sounding, but for what kind of elections? Without judgment, many of the criminals will return to the polling place, even more demonic, to drink the people's blood, to kill people, to

burn, to empty guns into radio stations, to fire on rec-
tories, to hunt down priests, to hunt down lay people,
to persecute the organizations of the people.[8]

The democratic sector called a general strike protesting Lafontant's presence in Haiti and calling for his
arrest. The impotent and conciliatory new civilian government issued an arrest warrant, but the military police
simply refused to execute it. Don't stir up trouble now,
the army seemed to be muttering, or we'll never have
elections. Trouillot agreed, and decided to side with the
military. In early August, the State Council announced
that it could no longer work with Mme. Trouillot.

Once the arrest warrant ceased to rankle him, if
indeed it ever had, Lafontant announced the formation of
his own political party, the Union for National
Reconciliation (URN). He declared himself the party's presidential candidate. This moment may have had a comical
ring to those living outside of Haiti: after all, how could
the leader of the most despised group in the country, the
macoutes, declare himself a presidential candidate? But
Haitians did not laugh, and 1500 Duvalierists attended
the Lafontant rally. The activity of the death squads
markedly increased, and many anticipated the return of
unmitigated violence. Collective despair set in over Port-
au-Prince, and was reinforced in the moribund countryside. The passing euphoria of the preceding year was difficult to recall. It had all ended in tears, blood and ashes.

Throughout Haiti, people turned to Father Aristide
for comfort, counsel and hope. Having lost his parish,
Aristide seemed to have become the pastor of all of
Haiti's poor. Some community leaders openly encouraged
Aristide to run for president, although others countered
that Aristide would never participate in something as
irremediably filthy as Haitian politics. His dependable
detractors, now a small minority, spread rumors that
Aristide was mentally ill, had a brain tumor, was living in

Moscow, et cetera.

In truth, however, a very influential group of citizens *was* pressuring Aristide to run for president. These individuals were by no means radical; most were well-to-do residents of Port-au-Prince, and some were seasoned veterans of the progressive church. They saw in the young priest "the candidate of national unity." To the surprise of many Aristide-watchers, he assented, declaring his candidacy at the last moment. "If we're going to participate in elections," he said in a November press conference, "we must take them over entirely." Even the most doubtful progressives were eventually won over to *lavalas*, "the flood," as Aristide's campaign was termed. And Aristide repeatedly underlined the participatory nature of the experiment: He was not willing to be the president of Haiti unless the majority would be able, through him, to take over the machinery of state.

As the December 16 elections approached, the gamble seemed to be working. In the days following Aristide's announcement, hundreds of thousands of peasants and poor city-dwellers rushed to register to vote. Roger Lafontant was excluded from the race on technical grounds—he had not submitted his birth certificate to election officials—leaving bureaucrat Marc Bazin as the symbolic counterweight to Aristide.

If one were to choose symbolic associations to avoid in a popular Haitian election, one might consider those suggesting close affiliation with the U.S. government, foreign aid, toleration of *macoutes*, slow reform, and close association with the Catholic hierarchy. Marc Bazin, who could not shake his reputation as *kandida merikèn*, chose to underline his access to foreign aid, promising Haitians that he would find hundreds of millions of dollars if only they would elect him. He alone could deliver this aid, he said, because the international community would never trust a madman like Aristide. Bazin also made the error of attempting to placate the *macoutes*, promising "reconciliation," a term that most Haitians had come to despise. Bazin also hung out banners announcing that he, unlike Aristide, had no problems with Rome and the Catholic hierarchy.

What Bazin did not see was that the Haitian people had problems with the Catholic hierarchy; the Haitian people had problems with the U.S. government; and they wanted to punish the *macoutes* for their crimes. Perhaps Bazin did see this, but thought that the people's will was not relevant. After all, no one had ever consulted the people before.

As the brief, tense campaign unfolded, many felt the calm could not last, and it did not. On December 5, a grenade exploded in the thick of an Aristide rally immediately after a suspicious power outage plunged the area into darkness. Seven were killed and over 50 were severely maimed. Most believed that Lafontant was making good his promises to prevent the priest's election. Aristide, again unharmed, called for Lafontant's arrest.

Lafontant was not arrested, but *lavalas* continued to gather strength. In the only pre-election poll published in Haiti, Aristide was predicted to win 58 percent of the vote in a field of 11 candidates. Bazin, his closest competitor, had 12 percent. In rural Haiti, many with whom I spoke doubted these projections: "If everyone's for Aristide," noted one market woman, "why are they suggesting he'll win less than 60 percent of the vote?" The question seemed to be, just then, not who would win—Aristide was unbeatable—but rather how the military and Duvalierists might prevent, yet again, expression of the popular will.

The New York Times painted a rather different picture. On December 13, 1990, through the eyes of journalist Howard French, the "Front-Running Priest [was] a Shock to Haiti."[9] Mr. French's reporting on Haiti would have an important effect on the way developments in Haiti were viewed in North America, and this article displays the key ingredients of his commentaries. He described Aristide as a "maverick priest-politician...long known for his strident brand of liberation theology." There was no mention, in this report, of Aristide's work with orphans and youth groups, nor of his parish work. There was no mention, either, of five years of work in the democratic movement and the attendant attempts on his life.

Allowing that Aristide's most virulent detractors were from the right wing, French added that "many more mainstream Haitians who have long hoped for democratic change have scarcely been gentler in their appraisals." One example of a "mainstream Haitian," for Mr. French, was this businessman: "'He is a cross between Ayatollah and Fidel,' one downtown businessman said in a typical assessment of Father Aristide in the entrepreneurial class. 'If it comes to a choice between the ultra-left and the ultra-right, I'm ready to form an alliance with the ultra-right.'"

Mr. French's analysis further called into doubt the predictions of a landslide victory for Aristide. Admittedly, French noted, the priest's rallies had drawn "large groups of highly enthusiastic supporters wherever he appeared in public." But French felt that some of these supporters were young, "apparently under voting age...By contrast, Marc Bazin, a conservative former World Bank economist who is Father Aristide's main challenger, has drawn smaller, but older crowds in the countryside, where he maintains his support is strongest."

On December 16, the pre-election polls were proved incorrect: Aristide won even more handily than predicted. Voters turned out in huge numbers, and the election proceeded with surprising smoothness. As the Lawyers Committee for Human Rights would later observe, "despite the logistical problems, virtually all observers who monitored the voting, both international and domestic, attested that the elections were free and fair and that voters experienced no threats, intimidation or harassment."[10]

That night, the city's silence was broken not by gunfire, as in previous elections, but by shouts of joy welling up from the poor quarters sprawled throughout Port-au-Prince. The foreign press had begun predicting a landslide victory for Aristide, and the Haitians had heard this on the radio. December 17 brought an even larger explosion of joy as hundreds of thousands of Haitians—perhaps not the "mainstream Haitians" of whom Mr. French had written—took to the streets in the first unhindered celebration since Duvalier's fall.

The popular democracy symbolized by the election of Aristide was not at all the democracy expected by the powerful. "But democracy," as journalist Michael Kamber observed, "is a funny thing. Sometimes it gets away from its handlers. In Haiti, the hemisphere's poorest country where 80 percent of the people can't read and only a tiny elite have TVs, the skills of Roger Ailes and Lee Atwater are useless. The people vote with their hearts, they vote for justice, morality, and true democracy. It seems a uniquely modern idea."[11]

The elections of December 16 had given voice to the popular will, but had done little to allay the tensions between the Haitian people and the country's powerful. The army was restless, and the commercial elite had never masked its horror over Aristide. Lafontant was at large, as were other *macoute* heavies. But these groups remained silent, and the Christmas holiday was one of the most peaceful in recent memory.

The Catholic hierarchy was also silent. Days went by, and then weeks. Radio commentators asked why the "institutional Church" had said nothing of Aristide's election. True, Bishop Willy Romélus had termed the day "a marvel," but what about the rest of the Episcopal Conference? What about Rome? The hierarchy's silence was widely interpreted as yet another manifestation of its failure to support "the people," as the Haitian poor term themselves. The silence was also indicative of the forces arrayed against Aristide—now one of the most popular elected leaders in the world, in terms of the strength of his victory.

These tensions were overtly expressed at the year's outset. On January 1, 1991, Independence Day in Haiti, Archbishop Ligondé presided over a traditional *Te Deum* at the pink and yellow cathedral towering over the northern side of the capital. No one had spoken much of Ligondé in the preceding months. It was as if, in the excitement, the archbishop had been forgotten. In his homily for the heads of the army and government and foreign diplomats, he openly attacked Aristide as a "socio-bolshevik," and wondered whether or not 1991 would mean the "beginning of a dictatorship." The archbishop ended his sermon with a message of hope for those who shared his fears: Be not afraid. This too shall pass.

Reactions to Ligondé's homily came swift and furious. Bishop Romélus tactfully noted that, although he had not heard the address, he saw no reason to suspect that an Aristide government would show the tendencies predicted by the archbishop. SAJ, the large youth group initiated by Aristide in 1985, was especially scandalized by Ligondé's hypocrisy:

> Today, Monsignor, you deplore all provocation, revenge, hate. Monsignor, your memory is short: you have already forgotten the indoctrination of youth through Catholic schools, parishes, and chapels; you have already forgotten, Monsignor, the hope you crushed throughout the archdiocese; you have already forgotten, Monsignor, the host of brave clergy and lay persons you had arrested, tortured, killed, exiled. Your memory is short, Monsignor....Today, Monsignor, you are recognized as a pastor, a shepherd. We know you as the pastor of the exploiting classes; you're the shepherd of the *macoute* flock you've tended since

Duvalier made you a bishop. Monsignor the Archbishop, we have excellent memories.[12]

Father Joachim Samedi, a very popular young parish priest from southern Haiti, was even more acerbic. He remarked that Ligondé's attack was quite similar to that on the Aristide rally of December 5, "except this time Electricité d'Haïti *augmented* the current so that the verbal grenade would hit its mark." He closed with a Biblical allusion implying that the archbishop's attack was entirely predictable: "A pig that has been washed goes back to roll in the mud" (2 Peter 2:22). These denunciations and others were followed by rumors anticipating a Vatican-blessed coup against Aristide. As the rumors came from a newspaper in the Dominican Republic, many did not know what to make of them. But others suspected that Ligondé's bashing was the bowsprit for a return to Duvalierism.

Late on the night of January 6, word spread like wildfire: Roger Lafontant had toppled the provisional government. He soon appeared on state television. The horrible farce of December 16, he said, was over. The Haitian people would not have to endure a communist dictatorship. The army and police, who he claimed had supported his takeover, would help him to assure a peaceful transition....

As if in answer, the poor neighborhoods of Port-au-Prince erupted with cries towards the heavens. This time, they were screams of rage. Many were also beating on the tin roofs of their shacks, adding to the strange predawn din. Before sunrise, tens of thousands of people, the poor of Port-au-Prince, headed for the palace. They were armed with rocks, sticks and machetes. To those thinking of the tanks and Uzis awaiting the poorly-armed populace, it may have looked preposterous. But others knew it to be a sign that the people were ready to die to preserve nascent Haitian democracy. The radio stations made it clear that in cities and towns throughout the republic the citizens had also taken to the streets.

The Commander-in-Chief of the army said he knew nothing of the alleged coup until the morning of the 7th, and yet it seemed by dawn as if the entire country had revolted against Lafontant; the slightest sign of army complicity might mean that it would be the next target of popular fury. As armed *macoutes* were stalked by unarmed crowds, guns seemed less threatening than they had in years. The high command announced that the armed forces would put down "the mutiny" as soon as possible.

In some ways, reactions to the Lafontont coup were a denouement to the bitter, decades-long struggle traced in the preceding pages. When hundreds of thousands of angry Haitians took to the streets to *dechouke* Roger Lafontant, they cursed Archbishop Ligondé as well. The destruction in the days that followed was massive, but not random. In addition to the scores of *macoutes* killed outright, there were the "accomplices" who lost their homes and cars—Lafontant's lawyers, politicians who had supported him, merchants who had funded him. And every building associated with Ligondé—and some none too closely—was attacked and destroyed: the arch-bishop's residence, the eighteenth-century cathedral in Bel-Air, the headquarters of the Episcopal Conference, and the huge and lavish papal nunciature that once sat proudly atop a hill called "Morne Calvaire."

For those with the temerity to think of Lafontant's attempted coup as a political event, there was always the wisdom of the U.S. press. Under the title "Haitian masses exact savage revenge on Duvalierists after coup fails," the Associated Press wire service offered the following news analysis:

> Burned bodies, cannibalism and torched homes give an aura of madness to the capital, but the violence in Haiti this week was anything but random...

On Tuesday, two photographers took pictures of two men eating the flesh of a man who had been burned as hundreds of people looked on.

Haitian religious experts say cannibalism has seldom occurred in Haiti but is indirectly linked to voodoo, an African religion exported by slaves.

'To eat a piece of flesh means the soul of the burned person cannot return to life in any form,' said Laënnec Hurbon, a Haitian author and a renowned Caribbean religion expert. 'Burning the bodies is done as rapidly as possible to prevent the survival of the person.'[12]

The challenges that faced Aristide were perhaps the most difficult in the hemisphere. There was, first of all, an ongoing and unsubtle resistance to his inauguration, which was to take place on February 7, 1991. A few days before the event, Lafanmi Selavi, an orphanage Aristide had founded, was set on fire. Four children perished, including a teenager who had been trying to evacuate the younger children. The survivors stated that they had heard a bang and smelled gasoline.

But it seemed, just then, as if these acts were the pathetic spasms of a dying order. In the days prior to Aristide's inauguration, Haiti bustled with people sweeping, shoveling, scraping, painting. Neighborhood associations entered into friendly contests to see which area would be the most well-decorated. In Port-au-Prince, every square inch of road front was festooned in ribbons, flags, flowers, and palm branches. Plastic soft-drink bottles, which had previously littered the entire republic, were painted red and blue and hung across the streets like Chinese lanterns. Narrative murals, all of them political, covered the walls of the city. The ditches lining the major roads leading to the capital had become veritable works of art: cleaned of all debris, flattened and raked, they were then used as tableaux on which to write, with pastel-colored or white pebbles, a host of messages. Most were for Aristide—"Titid, We Love You," "Aristide, the Country is Behind You," "Titid, Liberate Haiti"—but others were directed at the *macoutes*. "The Rooster Pecks At the Guinea Fowl" was one popular phrase, usually accompanied by an image of Aristide's mascot triumphing over that of Papa Doc.

Inauguration day—five years to the day from Baby Doc's ouster—was to open, as usual, with a mass at the cathedral. But there was nothing usual about either the mass or the rest of the proceedings. The first reading, from the book of Isaiah, was chosen carefully:

> *The Sovereign Lord has filled me with his spirit.*
> *He has chosen me and sent me*
> *To bring good news to the poor,*
> *To heal the broken-hearted,*
> *To announce release to the captives*
> *And freedom to those in prison.*
> *He has sent me to proclaim*
> *That the time will come*
> *When the Lord will save his people*
> *And defeat their enemies.*
> *He has sent me to comfort all who mourn,*
> *To give to those who mourn in Zion*
> *Joy and gladness instead of grief,*
> *A song of praise instead of sorrow.*
> *They will be like trees*
> *That the Lord himself has planted.*
> *They will all do what is right,*
> *And God will be praised for what he has done.*
> *They will rebuild cities that have long been in ruins.*

"The Lord says," continued the passage, "I love justice and hate oppression and crime." The theme of justice was woven throughout the celebrations. Aristide promised, in his inaugural address, that *wòch nan dlo ap fin konnen doulè wòch nan soley*, "the rocks in the water are going to know the suffering of the rocks in the sun."

A few of the rocks in the water may have been alarmed, but most agreed that Aristide's speech was remarkably deft. Some dared to hope that the first sampling of his gifts as a statesman were to be found in a masterful neutralization of the army, the chief threat to his effectiveness. From the final days of his campaign until the day of his inauguration, Aristide had spoken of the army as "transformed, committed to democracy." He underlined the importance of the patriotic sector of the military, and declared its members the "fiancés of the people." Given the brutality of the army, its long allegiance with the *macoutes*, and its involvement in drug trafficking and contraband, many found Aristide's comments disturbing, especially given his previously uncompromising analysis of the problem. In a book published a mere month prior to his election, the priest had asked,

> Those who are at the table, from which social class do they come? We find the majority of them in the class called the bourgeoisie, and in the Army. Now the majority of soldiers are born under the table, but the system turns them into sycophants and flatterers and kept-boys who sit at the table next to their masters.[14]

In his inauguration speech, Aristide showed that his more recent treacle was to sweeten the harsh reform he knew to be necessary. February 7 was the wedding day, and "since those who love each other make sacrifices," added Aristide, "I'm going to ask you to make a few changes in the army." He promptly retired the entire high command, and even asked them to applaud him.

The rest of the address was both subtle and charming, and including full participation by those present. Most of the speech was in Creole. *Tim tim*?, Aristide asked, using the standard opening salvo of a Haitian riddle. *Bwa chèch*! came the response.

"Are there still people under the table?"

Yes!

"Are there still people on top of the table?"

Yes!

"Would you like everyone, brothers and sisters, to be seated at the table together?"

Yes!

"With each passing day, we will reach our goal of sitting together at the table."

The final "event" of the festivities involved sharing the table with the poor. Aristide's first breakfast in the palace was not for visiting dignitaries, nor was it for the members of the local Lions' Clubs: instead, he served breakfast to hundreds of street kids and homeless poor. "Do you feel at home?" asked Aristide, addressing himself to the large crowd. "Is the National Palace your home?"

> Today, I'm here to say to you that you are human beings just as important as anyone else. Rich and poor, we're all people, and we must love one another. If there's enough for the rich, then there must be enough for the poor, too. If the National Palace was formerly for the rich, today it's for the poor.

On February 8, Aristide, perennial victim and prophet, awoke as president of his country. The transition to ruler promised to be a difficult one, and it was. Unsurprisingly, his opening month was rich in rebuke. For starters, the new president declined his $10,000 monthly salary, terming it "scandalous in a country where most people go to bed hungry." He called on his congressional colleagues to do with $2,000 a month rather than the $7,000 they were requesting. Aristide was rebuffed coldly, even by members of the coalition with which he had been affiliated.

But Aristide was not undone, in spite of the fact that, although the majority of Haitians wanted him to succeed, his detractors in *la classe politique* made themselves readily available to the foreign press. Howard French of *The New York Times* continued to misrepresent Haitian reality in striking fashion, referring to industrial-

ist and perennial presidential candidate Louis Déjoie II
as "a veteran left-of-center politician who placed third in
the presidential race." (Mr. Déjoie, whose politcs vary with
the wind, received less than eight percent of the vote). "To
me it is unbelievable that Aristide has not even called me
to ask my opinion on how the country should be run,"
complained Déjoie on inauguration day.[15] Other members
of *la classe politque* were equally piqued. For example,
Bella Stumbo of the *Los Angeles Times* interviewed Leslie
Manigat ("I intend to remain quiet for a while, until
Haitians can see for themselves what they've done"). Her
favorite informant was the "idealist" Jean-Jacques
Honorat, who made it clear that Aristide was to blame for
the January violence—prior to his inauguration:

> 'He is inciting people to riot! We have all the ingredi-
> ents here for a new fascism. Human rights violations
> have been as severe in the last month as they were
> under Duvalier,' exploded Jean-Jacques Honorat,
> head of the Haitian Center for Human Rights, one of
> the few willing to go public with his complaints. 'As a
> Haitian, I am ashamed! We have political prisoners
> [Lafontant and others] who are being held incommu-
> nicado. Lawyers are afraid to defend them!
> Journalists are afraid to criticize. *Everybody* is
> afraid.'[16]

In fact, foreign journalists, though happy to continue
citing people like Honorat, were struck by the elation
that pervaded the country in the months after the inauguration. It was the traditional elite who were griping.
The rest of the country seemed to approve of the government's program.

Three organizing principles—justice, transparency
and participation—ran through the platform of the
Lavalas government that Aristide was attempting to constitute. The members of his new cabinet were largely
technocrats, more liberal than radical, and they had
quickly identified a series of priorities, including those
highlighted in Aristide's platform documents, *La chance*

qui passe and *La chance à prendre*. The new government proceeded to attack, as it had no choice but to do, the host of problems that defined Haiti: the worst health indices in the hemisphere, a moribund economy, widespread illiteracy, landlessness, the exploitation of workers, unemployment, ecological devastation, a bloated and ineffective public administration, and, most of all, the entrenched gangsterism and drug trafficking closely linked to the army.

A major adult literacy program, modeled to some extent on the one suppressed in 1986-87, was kicked off; a number of Haitians who had been living abroad returned, vowing to help remake the university and the rest of the public-education system. Public-health interventions included the restructuring of the country's major hospital and other facilities and, at the same time, the elevation of primary health care to be the top priority of the new Ministry of Health. Agrarian reform was a much more volatile subject, but by early summer, Aristide announced the distribution of fallow state lands to peasant farmers, and appointed official ombudsmen to oversee land disputes, which had previously cost so many lives. A program to increase small farmers' access to credit was launched at the same time as an effort to halt erosion and decertification.

Aristide's government pushed for the improvements of workers' rights and lobbied to increase the minimum wage from 15 to 25 gourdes per day—still less than $3.00. It announced a major public-works program to create more jobs through improvements to roads and other infrastructure. International aid agencies had promised hundreds of millions of dollars in assistance; Aristide hoped this would offset bitterness over his efforts to trim a bloated and corrupt public administration: in his first few months in office, over 2,000 federal jobs were eliminated. He eliminated the Bureau of Tourism and made deep cuts into such dubious endeavors as the "Ministry of Information," which was trimmed by almost

50 percent. In another celebrated instance, when state bookkeepers could not account for over one million dollars in ostensibly *collected* taxes, Aristide himself showed up unannounced in the office and politely but firmly asked to see the books. Throughout the country, various ministries and offices were "closed for restructuring."

Perhaps the most significant of Aristide's undertakings involved his anti-crime efforts. His government kept good its promises to fight the "insecurity" endemic in Haiti. By arresting key figures in a number of crime rings, the government was able to curb significantly the gangsterism that had made nights sleepless for so many Haitians. The separation of the police and army along the lines of the Constitution of 1987 was a more difficult process, but peasants throughout Haiti heaved a collective sigh of relief as the position of *chèf de section*, the pivotal representative of state power in village Haiti, was abolished. William O'Neill, former Deputy Director of the Lawyers Committee for Human Rights, signaled the importance of this move:

> Perhaps the most important step taken by the Aristide government to improve respect for the rule of law was the dissolution of the institution of rural section chiefs. Section chiefs have been at the center of human rights abuses in Haiti. Their unfettered authority over the lives of the peasants has led to a systematic disregard for individual liberties and fundamental rights.[17]

Aristide's anti-corruption campaign had promised not only to reform the state apparatus, but to halt drug trafficking and other smuggling. This had been the army's bailiwick, and some thought that Aristide was going too far. But here, too, real headway was made, and the U.S. Drug Enforcement Agency reported that the amount of cocaine passing through Haiti decreased under the new government.

Strong forces were opposing these efforts, although

the true dimensions of their strength would not be revealed until much later. But Aristide could, and did, point to some tangible improvements under six months of democratic rule. Insecurity had all but disappeared in the capital. There was a dramatic decrease in the number of Haitians attempting to leave Haiti by boat. For the first time in years, the Haitian treasury had a positive balance, and most trade indices were picking up.

Certainly, Aristide and his government spent a great deal of time putting out brushfires. Throughout the spring and summer of 1991, there were small "mutinies" in the army, usually against unpopular officers, and many demonstrations by peasant groups and other factions. Often the demonstrators demanded, through radio journalists, that "Titid" intercede personally on their behalf; they were visibly (or audibly) disappointed when a cabinet minister showed up instead of *ti pè a*, the little priest.

But these disturbances seemed less palpable than the hope that suffused the country in the first half of 1991. How long would hope have tided over a hungry people? Where, at the end of the summer, were the roads, the new jobs? These questions, curiously, were asked chiefly by members of the middle and lower-middle classes rather than by the hungry themselves. From rural Haiti, at least, it was striking to see the patient, expectant attitude of the poor. The peasantry was so accustomed to receiving much worse than nothing from the state that just being left alone (by the *chèfs de section*, for example) seemed an improvement.

Many of Aristide's more "empowered" interlocutors felt, however, that his government was not living up to its promises. Even those who refrained from attacking him insisted that Aristide was a "novice" who knew nothing of politics or how to run a government. He was, they said, vague:

> I was often criticized for the absence or the vagueness of my program. Lack of time? Poor excuse. *La chance*

qui passe and *La chance à prendre* are two key documents, long, interesting, but largely indigestible and inaccessible to 90% of all Haitians. The people had their program. No need for a seer to divine its outlines, after years of struggle against neo-duvalierism. A simple program: dignity, transparence, participation...Rarely had a candidate promised so little.[18]

Two Haitian intellectuals writing from Canada, responding to Aristide's observation that "rarely had a candidate promised so little," put it this way:

In spite of this vagueness, never had a candidate promised so much, given that the symbolic content of his own personality, in which were invested the people's hopes and the many demands coming from all segments of the population, announced a rupture. A rupture with a past of mismanagement, gangsterism, corruption and pillage...[19]

Eight months was little time in which to implement a progressive or even a reformist agenda, especially in a setting such as Haiti. One Haitian analyst acutely observed that, "What emerged was a beleaguered regime struggling, without the support of a strong institutional left, to enact popular reforms after almost 200 years of entrenched corruption and dictatorship, and facing the enmity of powerful ruling groups, as well as indifference and sabotage by international actors."[20]

The extent of sabotage by international actors is only now becoming known. There were covert operations to undermine Haitian democracy, but these were not exposed until long after Aristide was overthrown. The overt efforts, however, were not subtle. Aristide's attempt to raise the minimum daily wage to 25 gourdes a day—about $3.00—did not please the U.S. Agency for International Development, which had invested millions, according to a report by the National Labor Committee, in keeping Haitian wages low: "Though the new minimum wage under the Aristide government would have still been less than one-eleventh of the average U.S. apparel wage (50 cents versus $5.85 an hour), USAID opposed this increase and orchestrated opposition to it." The report continues:

> Three months before the coup d'état that toppled the democratically elected government, USAID was musing: 'If Haiti's investment climate can be returned to that which existed during the CNG or improved beyond that and the negative attitude toward Haiti appropriately countered, Haiti stands to experience significant growth.'[21]

Recreating the "investment climate" enjoyed under the CNG was not merely a business project, but part of a broader campaign to weaken Aristide's government and the democratic movement that had spawned it.

As one example, USAID's "democracy project" was initiated to "strengthen democratic institutions." Former USAID director Lawrence Harrison insists that "the United States gave full support to Aristide following his election, and my work on the democratization program was part of that support."[22] What, precisely, was this program? Amy Wilentz describes USAID's approach as "specifically designed to fund those sectors of the Haitian political spectrum where opposition to the Aristide government could be encouraged."[23] Kenneth Roth of Americas Watch concurs, noting that substantial aid was routed to conservative groups—such as the one run by Jean-Jacques Honorat—to serve "as an institutional check on Aristide," and "move the country in a rightward direction."[24] Similar "Democracy Enhancement" programs blossomed in Nicaragua after Somoza was overthrown.

As the summer progressed, Aristide stepped on more toes. He continued to press for an end to the drug trade, and appointed a commission to investigate the election-day massacre of 1987, the Jean-Rabel massacre, and the sack of Saint-Jean Bosco. No one had ever been tried for these crimes, much less punished, and people continued to cry for justice on these scores. The same was true for the case of Roger Lafontant, which turned out to be a spectacle, to say the least:

> The trial of Roger Lafontant and his accomplices on July 29, 1991 took place under conditions which can only be categorized as intimidating. Crowds ringed the courtroom and the courthouse, jeering at the defendants and calling for conviction and death. Many demonstrators carried tires, threatening to use them to 'necklace' the defendants and their advocates.[25]

Aristide's detractors insisted that he had planned these demonstrations.

The young president's opponents in the legislature became increasingly confrontational as well. This angered Aristide supporters, who saw the legislators as deeply opposed to any semblance of democracy. In early August 1991, when senators promised to make good on their threats to block Aristide's reforms, crowds again resorted to open intimidation, carrying tires to the Palais Législatif to make their point. "President Aristide failed to condemn the crowds," observed the Lawyers Committee for Human Rights, admitting in a footnote that Aristide's spokeswoman, Minister of Information Marie-Laurence Lassègue, "issued a statement the next day calling on the population to respect one another's rights."[26]

In fact, all of Aristide's detractors blamed him for this event, just as they had blamed him for the violence following an abortive coup attempt prior to his inauguration. The foreign press were quick to echo these accusations, as if the angry crowds—which Haitian journalists, in contrast, called *pèp souvren*, "the sovereign people"— were incapable of remembering the traditional role of *la classe politique*.[27]

After the subsequent coup against Aristide, what had actually happened during "the Aristide experiment"

proved, ultimately, to be less significant than the interpretations of the period. These varied, of course, according to the interpreter; for every script, there was a
counter-narrative. In some U.S. newspapers, one could
read of both the thuggery of the poor, who longed to
exact revenge, and of Aristide's anti-Americanism. But,
as one British journalist has recently noted, Aristide's
"fiery rhetoric" was hardly what it was painted to be:

> Instead of unleashing the vengeance of the poor, he
> spoke in parables at the Chamber of Commerce. He
> talked of love to contemptuous generals. He still
> believed that he talked to God and to the people, but
> he tried to tone down the fire. Where he used to
> denounce "the cold country to the north" as the
> source of all evil, he began to talk about the difference
> between capitalism in Haiti and capitalism in the
> United States. "I still think capitalism is a mortal sin,"
> he explained, "but the reality's different in the United
> States..."[28]

That President Aristide was "anti-business" was also
a staple of much U.S. press commentary. But there is, in
fact, little from his tenure to support this thesis. An article written in the month before Aristide was overthrown
cited the president of the Association of Industries:

> I am a businessman. I have to deal in facts. Aristide, I
> think, is a social man—not a socialist man, a social
> man. He understands the poor first. His speeches
> sometimes go on about anti-bourgeoisie and anti-
> elite, but as a businessman, I have to look at the
> facts. And the fact is, there is no new law to national-
> ize industry. The fact is, when we talk to cabinet min-
> isters, they don't try to control the market. There is
> no restriction on trade, no law changing the tax sys-
> tem. I don't see any battle between the business com-
> munity and this government.[29]

The public-relations war continued long after
Aristide was overthrown. On October 30, 1993, British

journalist Isabel Hilton noted that, "Today the little priest should have returned in triumph. But the miracle didn't happen." Writing from Haiti, she summarizes commentaries on Aristide's tenure as follows:

> On what had happened in between—in the eight months of Fr Aristide's rule—opinions divide. For those who share his faith, it was an age of miracles, the priest in the white palace was their man. For those whom one US ambassador called the "morally repugnant elite," it was a time of unsufferable humiliation."[30]

What, precisely, were these humiliations? The greatest humiliation for the Haitian elite was the insistence that the poor majority, previously so effectively silenced, should have some say in what was to happen in Haiti. There was, certainly, no *physical* assault: from the day that Aristide was inaugurated until the day he was overthrown, no members of the elite had their property confiscated or died violently. Why, then, was resistance to Aristide so implacable? Poet Jean-Claude Martineau recently attempted to address this question:

> And why do the elite hate him so much? All their traditional privileges have been questioned; the way that they make their money, most of the time illegally: drugs, and contraband, and abuse. All of these kinds of things have been questioned, with a very strong possibility of changing the way the country is run; changing the way people perceive power. Because in Haiti the power is an absolute power.[31]

The jury may still be out on whether or not Aristide "understands" politics. In an interview that appeared, curiously, on the day of the coup, he observed that, "Sometimes they say politics is money and guns. I believe it is force of spirit."[32] Some would argue that the little priest was dead wrong on that one.

The Coup of 1991

The Power of the Rich in Haiti

Crime once exposed has no refuge but in audacity.

—Tacitus

How long will we Haitians be obliged to leave our country against our will? We turn to the Dominican Republic with its cane-cutters' barracks and barely masked slavery; to the United States with its internment camps at Krome and Guantánamo for our boat people, who are returned by the boatload for the slaughter; we turn to the Bahamas with their periodic pogroms; to Guyana and its slums reserved for the 'Haïchiens'; to Canada, where the cold brings frozen tears and our cab drivers and school kids are each day reproached with their color. Foreigners, you don't want us in your country? At least let us live peacefully at home. Let us elect whom we want.

—Paul Anvers, *Rizières de sang*

Rumors of an impending coup have been a Port-au-Prince staple for decades. Since most Haitian administrations come to power through violent or otherwise extra-constitutional means, coup rumors are taken seriously, even though only a tiny percentage of them is ever borne out. Rumors of plots to overthrow Jean-Bertrand Aristide began, unsurprisingly, in the hours *preceding* his election in December 1990, and less than a month later they were proven to have a basis in fact. The January 7 attempt by die-hard Duvalierists to prevent Aristide's inauguration was a sobering reminder that the old order was not about to exit gracefully.

But the swiftness and fury with which Haitians responded to the Roger Lafontant coup attempt changed, at least slightly, the standard equation. The first popularly-elected Haitian leader, Aristide was different from all the presidents and presidents-for-life who had gone before.

The capital city, it seemed, was brimming with a response force that could be mobilized on the slightest provocation. Moreover, this force was loyal to the elected president, and would not tolerate his violent removal from office. Besides, Aristide, to many Haitians, was *mistik*—protected by eldritch forces beyond the ken of mere mortals like themselves. Or so it seemed until the following September.

Although retrospective assessments often emphasize Aristide's "increasingly hard-line" stances vis-à-vis the rich, the priest never had much of a honeymoon with any part of what some have called "the four-headed monster" of Haitian society. The army, the church hierarchy, the *macoutes*, and the wealthy may have felt constrained to temper their criticism of the intensely popular president, but there was little doubt as to their feelings on the matter. "Everyone who is anyone is against Aristide," quipped one well-to-do businessman, speaking to a reporter a couple of weeks before the coup. "Except the people." As elsewhere in Latin America, in Haiti the people are not considered to be "anyone."

Throughout the summer of 1991, Aristide continued to press for substantive land reform, an increased minimum wage, and a freeze on the prices of certain "products of first necessity," such as bread, rice, and flour. He pushed forward his anticorruption program, terminating "zombi" positions in every federal office, and vowed to stop drug transshipment through Haiti. Cabinet members with strong ties in the business sectors began whispering of increasingly menacing rumors in the mill: following the traditional formula, the elite would simply pay the army to unseat him. Plans were already underway, some said. Others felt that Aristide was making an error taking on the drug runners so early in his mandate. To those who had witnessed the pro-Aristide response of early January, however, these threats seemed hollow.

On September 23, 1991, after seven months in office, Aristide addressed the United Nations. The performance was classically Aristide, an expansive speech steeped in concern with social justice and a religiously-tinged progressivism. No address entitled "The Ten Commandments of Politics" could have been standard U.N.fare. Aristide did not seek to curry favor, as he underlined an accelerating transfer of resources from the poor countries to the rich. The globe's powerful few, he suggested, bore responsibility for the parlous state of the world. He offered, as an example, the narcotics trade, which imperiled the stability of democracy in Haiti and elsewhere in Latin America: "As regards the drug traffic itself, it is important to note that it is generated and sustained by the demand from the North. It is thus necessary to eliminate this demand for production, which comes from consumers in the industrialized countries."

Aristide's tenth commandment—"Everyone must have a place at the table"—made reference to his inaugural address, and to a small booklet that he had written in 1986. Haiti, he had written, was like a well-laid table at which a small number of persons were permitted to dine. The vast majority of Haitians were kept beneath the table, and it was their job to upset the table. In front of the United Nations, Aristide did not miss his opportunity to observe that the whole world could be viewed in precisely this way. He concluded his speech by saying "Yes to all *around* the table of democracy. No to a minority on top of the table; no to a majority under the table."

Back home, the speech did not sit well with the Haitian elite, including the military. While still in New York, Aristide was apprised of a plot to overthrow him upon his return. The rumored plan seemed unusually detailed; members of the delegation were skittish, and even Aristide was worried. Aristide responded by holding an impromptu preemptive rally upon his return to Haiti on September 27. He called on the wealthy to share their bounty, to reinvest profits locally rather than abroad, to pay taxes, to work to provide jobs for the unemployed and the hungry. Those on the side of social justice had, he said darkly, a tool to help ensure these goals were met. Although Aristide maintains that he was referring to the constitution, the only "tool" mentioned by name, his detractors insisted that he was referring to *pelebren*, as "necklacing" is termed here. This insinuation was quickly repeated and circulated by the foreign press.

Two days later, on the night of September 29, 1991, a group of Haitian soldiers attacked Aristide's residence, an unfortified house in a rural area to the north of the capital. Aristide watched with horror as "friends, militants who were there with me or who tried to reach the house, were massacred."[1] Aristide was whisked away by the French ambassador to the National Palace; en route they were attacked several times. Once at the palace, Aristide discovered that he had walked into a trap:

> The palace was surrounded. I had with me no more than a handful of sure friends. I tried, with them, to escape, to prevent a civil war. Objective: to discuss, talk things over, perhaps persuade. Across from us, bullets were singing. One of those standing next to me crumbled. I had been in similar situations: I threw myself to the ground.[2]

Aristide was handcuffed and taken to Brigadier General Raoul Cédras, then head of the army. "I'm the president now," said Cédras, smiling. "What should I do with the priest?"

"Kill him," jeered a group of soldiers, having done just that to Fritz Pierre-Louis, a soldier expressing loyalty to the president. Aristide later reported that only the interventions of the French ambassador and other diplomats prevented his own execution. He was escorted out of Haiti to Caracas on a plane dispatched by the Venezuelan president.

As these events transpired, the programming director of the state radio announced the beginnings of a *coup de force*, but he was quickly arrested, and a new version of the story was broadcast: Yes, there had been disturbances and automatic-weapons fire, that much was beyond dispute. But these represented isolated mutinies, and the army high command was again in complete control. It was not until very early on the morning of September 30 that it became clear that the attacks had been part of a centrally orchestrated *coup d'état*, and that a three-man military junta led by General Cédras had taken over the state apparatus.

One young physician, then a mid-level bureaucrat in the *lavalas* government, recalled the hours before dawn. Shortly after midnight, she and her brother-in-law struck out on foot for the palace:

> I said to myself, 'No way am I going to tolerate this coup,' and we snuck out of my mother-in-law's house and headed for the palace. When I reached the [park in front of the palace], it was chaos. There were large numbers of people there to protest, but the soldiers were firing on them. I couldn't believe it, seeing them mow down people like that. One group had foolishly climbed up on the pedestal of the statue of the Indian, and the soldiers were shooting them, picking them off! I threw myself to the ground, and heard my brother-in-law yelling at me to run. But it was those who were running who were being shot...It was really the first time I realized that people could be treated the same as animals.[3]

As news of Aristide's overthrow spread through the urban slums, the alleyways and passages of Port-au-Prince's poor quarters were quickly filled with angry citizens. But the security forces had learned their lesson from the abortive January coup. Troops were posted at strategic points around the city, and soldiers simply fired on residents who attempted to assemble. Bishop Willy Romélus, the one member of the Haitian Episcopal Conference identified with the democratic movement, later detailed the mechanisms of the initial carnage:

> There are reports that in the first few days after the coup that more than 1,500 people were killed. Yet no

one could find all the bodies, so a report got out that these figures had been exaggerated. Not at all. This is what took place: when those in the slums came out in great numbers after the coup, the Army descended on them and then shot into the crowds as people were running away from the soldiers. The Army used quick, high-powered guns. They loaded the bodies on trucks and hauled them away. After unloading the bodies, they drove back, loaded more bodies. They repeated this time after time until all the bodies had been removed.[4]

These actions were said to have been orchestrated by a certain Joseph Michel François, commander of the Port-au-Prince police precinct. Colonel François, the son of a member of François Duvalier's presidential guard, was strongly linked to the death squads that had become increasingly active under General Henri Namphy. Aristide's police chief had attempted, earlier in the month, to have François dismissed, but General Cédras had blocked this move.

On October 1, 1991, from Caracas, Aristide broadcast a message: "Hold strong! I have confidence that we as a people will resume the road to democracy. Hold strong, don't give up." But the death toll was mounting. There was the usual broad range of opinions as to just how many were dying. On October 1, Radio France Internationale reported that 130 had been killed, but a photographer who reached the morgue of the downtown general hospital, Haiti's sole tertiary-care facility, counted 140 bodies at that facility alone.

By the coup's second day, the hospital ground to a halt when physicians there, under threat, left the facility. The hospital remained shut down until a small group of nurses convinced a few surgical residents to return, forced open the doors of the pharmacy, and cared for the wounded. They did this at their own peril, as the head of the group later recalled:

A few hours into the coup, they stopped bringing in

the dead. Even living victims were not brought to medical attention. One reason is because soldiers kept breaking into the hospital and threatening us. They finished off one poor fellow after he'd been operated on. Perhaps he would not have survived, anyway, as we were short of antibiotics.

I would guess that the perioperative mortality rate in those first few days was close to 80%.

Most radio stations and newspapers were shut down by force or intimidation, but Radio Lumière carried a report of a massacre of 30 to 40 unarmed civilians in a poor suburb of Port-au-Prince.[5] The killings were in retaliation for the death of a soldier, who area residents said had in fact been killed by "friendly fire" from his own unit. *Washington Post* reporter Lee Hockstader—who would later have trouble understanding why Haitians were given to conspiracy theories—filed the following story on October 8:

The casualty figures reported by the residents of Lamentin were confirmed by the Haitian Center for the Defense of Human Rights, an independent monitoring group. Some Haitians and analysts said it was the worst spasm of killing in the nation in more than 30 years. As described by residents of Lamentin, 'it was a scene of unimaginable horror.' Two old men where shot at a table under a shady mango tree where they were playing dominoes. A dark patch is visible on the ground where the men bled. A pair of preschoolers, one boy and one girl, died in their house, which the troops then torched. A teenage boy called Ti Ati was shot in front of a cinderblock house, his body left to rot in the baking sun for two days. Estimates of the death toll vary from 250 to 600 or more. Much of the killing took place in the desperately poor slums such as this one on the outskirts of the capital and Cité Soleil near downtown Port-au-Prince, where Aristide is extremely popular. Some people said 250 people were slaughtered in Cité Soleil alone.

Condemnations of the coup were heard, initially, from all quarters. The Organization of American States convened the foreign ministers of its member states, and together they issued a statement calling for Aristide's prompt reinstatement. On October 4, an OAS delegation traveled to Port-au-Prince to "open dialogue" with the putschists. When the military and their civilian colleagues proved intransigent, the OAS called, on October 8, for a trade embargo against Haiti.

By then the Bush administration was initiating what would soon prove to be a veritable public-relations campaign *against* Aristide. If Aristide had been overthrown, went the new logic, it was his own fault. In an October 8 article entitled "The White House Refuses to Link Aristide's Return and Democracy," *New York Times* diplomatic correspondent Thomas Friedman wrote that,

> American officials...signaled privately that they were moving away from their unequivocal support of Father Aristide in light of concerns over his human rights record....Today, when the White House spokesman, Marlin Fitzwater, was asked if that was the case, he responded with a less than ringing endorsement for the Haitian president, and suggested that Washington was most interested in the restoration of constitutional democracy in Haiti, not a particular individual.[6]

Bolstered, the army decided that international opposition to the coup would dissolve more quickly if there were a civilian facade to the regime. The ever-pliant parliament vacated the presidency, appointing, on October 7, Supreme Court judge Joseph Nérette as provisional president and Jean-Jacques Honorat as prime minister.

Intimidation was required even among such willing tools as the members of parliament (there were, after all, a number of legislators who opposed the coup). There was significant variation in the way the story was reported in the U.S. press. A report in the *Philadelphia Inquirer* entitled "Interim Haiti President is Named, At Gunpoint" opened with the following line: "Enraged soldiers stormed Haiti's legislative palace yesterday and forced lawmakers at gunpoint to name a Supreme Court judge to replace exiled President Jean-Bertrand Aristide."[7] The article by Howard French of *The New York Times* ran under a more staid title: "Haitian Legislators Name a Judge to be President Until New Vote."[8]

The appointment of Jean-Jacques Honorat, the noisy detractor of Aristide so favored by the U.S. press in the early months of 1991, was proof, asserted some commentators, that opposition to Aristide was "broad-based" and not just "right-wing."[9]

And who is Mr. Honorat? He was commonly described in the U.S. press as a "human rights activist," or depicted as a man forced into exile in the United States during the Duvalier years. But Jean-Jacques Honorat was notable for his rise to prominence as a Duvalier appointee—he was Minister of Tourism, a plum job—at the height of state violence. It was no surprise to those who follow Haitian politics that Honorat would become prime minister in the days following a violent military coup. In an interview with Canadian journalist Francine Pelletier, Honorat stated that, were Aristide to return, "he will be executed." By whom?, Pelletier asked. "*Par n'importe qui,*" responded the human rights activist. "It's not important who." Mr. Honorat brazenly dismissed the allegations of killings by the army:

> Asked what he had done as Prime Minister to halt the massive human rights violations that followed the overthrow, Honorat huffed, "I don't have my files here." But he claimed supporters of the deposed President had exhumed cadavers from the potter's field of Port-au-Prince, sprayed the bodies with bullets and fresh animal blood, and then dragged out the corpses to stain the military's reputation.[10]

Honorat did not have his own files on hand, but he apparently carried with him a nicely bound compendium of Aristide's alleged human rights violations. This dossier was widely circulated. "According to journalists in Haiti, the U.S. Ambassador called in the correspondents of *The New York Times* and the *Washington Post* for a briefing on the 'dossier' that the army had compiled, perhaps with a little help from their friends."[11]

The *Times* and the *Post* certainly bought the story. In an early analysis of media coverage of the coup, David Peterson accurately discerned what would, in fact, become a major trend in U.S. reporting on the violence in Haiti:

> Once the *Times* had caught on to the [Bush] administration's desire to be rid of Aristide, Howard W. French, reporting from Port-au-Prince, went to work unearthing complaints against the ousted president for his "provocative and legally questionable behavior" ("Haiti's Democracy, Such as It Was, Is Swept Aside By a Chaotic Coup," October 6, p. E2). From October 4 on, French cited unnamed soldiers, diplomats, and the "traditionally influential sectors of Haitian society" ("Haitians Consider an Interim Leader," October 7, p. A8), who charged Aristide with condoning violence to attain his goal, with mistreatment of the army, and with what French called alarm due to "the arrival of Swiss police experts last week to accelerate the training of a presidential militia" ("In Haiti, Jumpy Soldiers Patrol the Streets of a Frightened Capital," October 4, p. A8).[12]

Such readings would prove tremendously valuable to those attempting to give the Cédras coup institutional respectability. If this has not yet come to pass, it is with no thanks, as we will see, to members of the U.S. press, who proved only too willing to devote space to Aristide's "provocative and legally questionable behavior"—even after such reports were revealed to be the crude agitprop of interests opposed to Haitian democracy.

It soon became clear that the coup against Aristide was unlike any of the dozens that had preceded it. In addition to being exceptionally violent, it also was not taking hold—as a rule, vigorous opposition to a Haitian coup can be expected to die down within days. Two weeks after Aristide's departure, however, the country remained paralyzed. The army found it necessary not only to continue its punishment of the poor, but also to harass or disappear the exiled president's more prominent supporters. Antoine Izméry, the democratically-minded businessman who had been a key financial supporter of Aristide, was arrested and threatened with summary execution on October 15. The next week, U.S. Ambassador Alvin Adams advised the 10,000 Americans resident in Haiti to "consider leaving at once."

Tales of horror filtered in from rural areas, where a vibrant press had been silenced. One young woman from the provincial city of Gonaïves reported that, on Wednesday, October 2, soldiers had entered her house and shot her three younger brothers, Pierrot (16), Joël (18), and Jean (20).[13] Her father, she reported, was in hiding, and, no, she had no idea why her brothers had been executed. She noted, however, that other members of student organizations had been killed and that "most young people have fled to the hills."

Because it targeted supporters of Aristide—to judge by the recent vote, the overwhelming majority of the population—post-coup repression generated huge numbers of refugees, creating a problem of unanticipated dimensions. Most of the refugees left urban areas for their home villages in the hills. Over 100,000 Haitians were believed to have crossed the Dominican border to the east; tens of thousands left the country by sea.

Throughout the month of November 1991, repression of Aristide supporters continued. Many local observers took the waffling of the Bush administration as something of a green light for the *de facto* regime, which took an increasingly hard line toward those within the diplomatic corps who opposed the coup. On November 16, for example, the junta declared the French ambassador "undesirable" and gave him until 5 p.m. the following day to leave the country.

The public-relations war against the deposed president was also taking its toll. "Aristide's Autocratic Ways Ended Haiti's Embrace of Democracy" was the title of an October 22 *New York Times* "news analysis" that was widely published. It was filed, of course, by Howard French:

> While Aristide performed as expected in combating the corrupt vestiges of the political class that flourished during the 29-year Duvalier family dictatorship, he also quickly froze out newly elected officials who had equally long records of fighting dictatorship.[14]

Amy Wilentz spoke of these same elected officials in less flattering terms: "the legislature, with its smaller, unmonitored elections, became the roosting place of a handful of Duvalierists, military puppets, discontented radicals, and presidential candidates manqués."[15]

French's *New York Times* story, resonating nicely with the Bush administration's line, took on a life of its own. Cited as contributing to the coup were a series of "increasingly strident statements by Aristide blaming the wealthier classes for the poverty of the masses." French further suggested that wealthy merchants were able to convince soldiers to overthrow Aristide by calling their attention to a speech made two days prior to the coup, a speech, said French, marked by laudatory reference to necklacing.

Suddenly, Aristide was on the defensive. "Reports that our Government incited the people to violence or revenge have no basis in reality," he replied from Caracas. "Not one political assassination occurred during our Administration. Not one political prisoner was jailed. No boat filled with frightened political refugees fled Haiti for U.S. shores."[16]

Drowned in the clamor about Aristide's shortcomings was a report in the *San Francisco Chronicle*, which detailed the planning and financing of the coup. Entitled "Haiti's Richest Families Financed Coup That Toppled Aristide," it ran the same day as Howard French's wire story:

> In what now appears to have been a well-coordinated
> operation, Haiti's small and wealthy elite provided
> money, food and transport to the rebellious soldiers
> who took over the country late last month in a bloody
> coup. Details have emerged of weapons shipments
> and payments to military units before the September
> 30 coup, and they implicate some of the richest and
> most reactionary families in Haiti.[17]

The story went on to document shipment of some 2,000
Israeli-made Uzi submachine guns and Galil assault
rifles, which arrived in Haiti almost a month prior to the
coup.

The you-got-what-you-had-coming explanation of
the coup was soon upstaged by an even more vulgar
attempt at character assassination, this one from the
CIA. In a document later denounced as a crude forgery,
the agency described Aristide as a manic-depressive who
had been prescribed lithium in the past. In testimony
solicited by Senator Jesse Helms, CIA analyst Brian
Latell went even further, referring to Aristide as "a murderer and a psychopath." General Cédras, Latell's report
continued, belonged to "the most promising group of
Haitian leaders to emerge since the Duvalier family."[18]

Although some U.S. statesmen were later said to be
scandalized by the report on Aristide, the endorsement of
Cédras seemed to cut across party lines. Representative
Robert Torricelli, a Democrat from New Jersey who sits of
the House Intelligence Committee observed that "the U.S.
Government develops relationships with ambitious and
bright young men at the beginning of their careers and
often follows them through their public service. It
includes people in sensitive positions in the current situation in Haiti."[19]

At the close of 1991, as the embargo began to bite,
what was at stake for the various parties involved came
more clearly into focus. The Bush administration could
hardly be termed a strong advocate of a left-leaning
priest who espoused liberation theology. But there were

other reasons for the U.S. government to want an end to the violence in Haiti: the "hordes" of refugees pouring out of Haiti in boats. The U.S. government—and perhaps its citizens, as well—simply did not want boat people washing up on the shores of south Florida. The Haitian army seemed strangely content with the status quo; gradually, it was becoming clear that the embargo did not affect their income. With no bothersome anti-corruption campaign to hinder their activities, the military was making a killing—this time, only figuratively—by permitting cocaine and other drugs to be stockpiled in Haiti for transshipment to North American consumers. Haitian businesses not involved in the drug trade were hurt to some extent by the embargo, but this particular blockade was leaky enough to permit those with capital and ingenuity to skirt and even profit from it.

And then there were the Haitian people themselves. While the army and the pro-coup elite fought for the spoils, the peasants and urban poor fought for their survival. They were hungrier and sicker than they had previously been; the dissolution of the weak public health sector would soon mean thousands of easily preventable deaths from measles, for example. Above all, they were cornered and frightened. Peasant movements, such as the *Mouvman Peyizan Papay* in the Central Plateau, were almost wiped out; soldiers and other representatives of the state killed key movement leaders, drove others underground, and destroyed tool banks, grain-storage facilities, and other modest infrastructures it had taken over two decades to build. Representatives from Americas Watch visited MPP headquarters ten months after the coup:

> When we visited the MPP headquarters on July 2, the buildings remained much as the army had left them the previous October. Not one door remained on its hinges, nor a piece of furniture in any room. Every building was littered with a three-inch layer of ripped papers, posters, books and files. The repression in the Central Plateau against people affiliated with the MPP

remained so severe that no one dared to clean up the mess, much less to resume using the buildings for fear of being labeled an MPP sympathizer and carted off to jail.[20]

In spite of repression of this magnitude, peasants and other poor people continued to tell American reporters that they supported the embargo:

The skyrocketing price of fuel, which peaked at $16 a gallon two weeks ago, has made it difficult for farmers to transport their rice and bananas to the capital or to obtain such needs as cooking oil and batteries.

Yet in village after village, people living virtually hand-to-mouth say they are determined to endure the embargo, without complaint, if it will bring back their president.[21]

Conflicting with the image of defiant peasants was one which had them increasingly passive and cowed. The image is not entirely false, but the processes used to intimidate the rural and urban poor almost inevitably involved physical force. Post-coup Haiti has been filled with stories detailing the pitiless and often arbitrary repression of perceived opposition. In one case, already cited, soldiers entered a young man's hospital room, asked his grandmother to leave, and then shot him; in another, an unknown number of young people were killed as they posted brightly colored flyers of Aristide to the city's walls. The directors of two radio stations were assassinated, and thereafter other journalists moved quickly into line.

The peasant movements suffered the most sustained repression. Rural Haiti was the theater of countless unwitnessed arrests; these were followed by beatings, torture, and then extortion—cash was required to end any imprisonment.[22] Dazed and bleeding peasants would lie in filthy cells until family members could cough up the money demanded by the local heavy. Add to this the "structurally given" repression of landlessness and sickness and it is a marvel, really, that the people fought back at all.

But there was resistance. There was, first, the "small arms fire in the class war," to use political scientist James Scott's apt phrase. He described everyday forms of resistance as

> the prosaic but constant struggle between the peasantry and those who seek to extract labor, food, taxes, rents, and interest from them. Most forms of the struggle stop well short of outright collective defiance. Here I have in mind the ordinary weapons of relatively powerless groups: foot dragging, dissimulation, desertion, false compliance, pilfering, feigned ignorance, slander, arson, sabotage, and so on.[23]

Each of these forms of resistance was engaged throughout rural Haiti. In the cities, students refused to return to school; when finally back in classrooms, they held demonstrations. Clandestine publications, usually short-lived, appeared in the mornings along with tracts demanding the return of Aristide. As the coup wore on, everything became, obliquely, a means of speaking out against it. People complained about the piles of garbage, the condition of the hospitals or roads, the insecurity—even the embargo, which they privately supported—and meant something quite different. But in more hardbitten moments, it seems only fair to ask what all this defiance amounted to in the face of Uzis and assault rifles.

The new guns were certainly put to use, primarily against the poor, but even members of the legislature were attacked. On December 15, 1991, pro-Aristide congressman Astrel Charles was casually shot dead as he emerged from a church service. Since his execution was public, everyone knew that he had been killed by a *chèf de section*. As military and paramilitary death squads continued to hunt down progressive activists, the OAS organized a series of meetings, culminating in talks between Aristide and a group of parliamentarians concerned to end the embargo. These talks, initiated in Cartagena, Colombia, continued in Caracas, Venezuela on January 7, 1992, when members of parliament proposed a plan for a return to constitutional order by replacing Aristide's prime minister with one of his long-time political adversaries, René Théodore (one persistent rumor had it that Théodore, a perennial presidential candidate, had been involved in plotting the coup). Aristide accepted this arrangement, perhaps to the surprise of those who proposed it: at the behest of the *de facto* regime, parliament later reneged on the deal.

Commentators from diplomatic circles soon began to refer to a *culturally-sanctioned* inability to negotiate. Speaking, in November 1991, to a *Washington Post* reporter, one State Department official opined that, "If this problem is not solved, it won't be because of a failure of the new world order or a lack of political commitment by the White House or the OAS. It will be because Haiti is Haiti."[24] The fact that an astounding majority of Haitians had recently managed to agree on who should lead their country—giving one candidate among a dozen almost 70 percent of the vote—was never mentioned in these discussions of the fractious ways of "the Haitians."

On January 18, 1992, the OAS Secretary General convened a meeting of all concerned parties in Washington. Aristide attended, reiterating his willingness to work with René Théodore in order to form a consensus government. Aristide was criticized, however, for suggesting that the Haitian military was negotiating in bad faith; Bush administration officials continued to depict the priest as a "radical firebrand," unstable and untrustworthy. Haitian security forces or their heavily-armed *attachés* responded to these diplomatic efforts on January 28, by attacking Théodore as he and his associates left a Port-au-Prince political meeting. A member of his entourage was killed. Shortly thereafter, U.S. ambassador Alvin Adams was recalled to Washington.

What did all this diplomacy mean? In Haiti, the bad faith of the army, the parliament, and the Bush administration was widely assumed. People used the word *dilatoire* as a code word for the filibustering designed to drag out negotiations. One also heard a number of oft-repeated questions. It seemed unthinkable to most Haitians that the United States had been oblivious to plottings for a coup. After all, weren't key army officers in the pay of the CIA? Had they not attended training programs at Fort Benning in Georgia? And if the U.S. truly wanted the negotiations to lead to restoration of Aristide, why had they advanced Théodore's name for prime minister? As the former head of the then-defunct Haitian Communist Party, he would be tolerated by neither the Haitian military nor the United States State Department. And, finally, how could an embargo fail so miserably if the world's only remaining superpower, which had just pulverized Iraq, was truly behind it?

These were hard questions, but they seemed, by some, to have been answered on February 4, when the Bush Administration announced that it would be "fine tuning" the embargo by allowing certain American companies to export materials to Haiti for assembly. The announcement was cheered by the *de facto* government, which predicted an end, and soon, to all sanctions. The U.S. National Labor Committee was later able to report that, "In 1992, despite the OAS international embargo, U.S. apparel firms and retailers—'under a loophole benefiting U.S.-owned exporters'—imported $67,629,000 worth of clothing sewn in Haiti."[25]

Nearly half a year after the coup, the *Boston Globe*, in an editorial, was able to complain of "six months of virtual inaction" from the Bush administration.[26] The Bush administration's footdragging was countered by a number of key members of Congress, including Senator Edward Kennedy and members of the Congressional

Black Caucus. These individuals pushed for stiffer sanctions, a move which may have forced their Haitian counterparts back to the bargaining table. The next round of negotiations took place in Washington, where on February 23 a plan for Aristide's return was announced. The U.S. ambassador was dispatched back to Haiti, but it was soon clear that the *de facto* government intended simply to ignore the agreement.

Another unusual phenomenon was widely noted in the spring of 1992. Even as the military and their civilian representatives expressed a willingness to negotiate, repression of popular movements continued unabated. Refugees continued to flee Haiti. The United States, acting unilaterally, announced that it would halt the influx of all refugees and return them *forcibly* to Haiti. As many in the pro-democracy movement noted, this plan revealed, to any doubters, that the real Bush policy was pro-putsch; administration lawyers were obliged to defend their policy by insisting lamely that there was no repression in Haiti. Journalists Rowland Evans and Robert Novak attested to Haitian stability in the *Washington Post*:

> The situation here is both better and worse than generally supposed. Visible firearms are few, police fewer and military presence limited. Even U.S. diplomats unfriendly to the provisional government concede it is hard to say physical danger is higher today than it was under Aristide. The business community, with good reason, feels incomparably safer.[27]

Some members of the business community would have disputed this report. On May 26, a month after Evans' and Novak's piece appeared, businessman Georges Izméry was walking across a major downtown intersection when he was mowed down by gunfire after being insulted by his assassin. Suddenly, soldiers appeared, forbidding Antoine Izméry to approach his younger brother and informing him that he should leave at once "if he did not wish to go to the same place." The soldiers then took Georges Izméry directly to the morgue of the University Hospital, intimidating physicians who attempted to evaluate him.

The problem was that Georges Izméry was not yet dead. In a report entitled "Black Day at the University Hospital" the residents and interns reported that Izméry still had a pulse when he was transferred to the morgue. They went on to complain of other summary executions that had taken place *within the hospital.*

Even Izméry's funeral, which was held in the Port-au-Prince cathedral, was marred by violence. During the mass, Antoine Izméry gave a brief funeral oration:

> Today, I speak in the name of all the disappeared, the disenfranchised, the students, journalists, peasants, workers, and peaceful citizens. Moving beyond pain and emotion, we must understand that these people want to transform our country into a vast prison, an immense cemetery....Today, it's Georges, a well known businessman in the capital. Whose turn will it be tomorrow? Who'll be next?

The question was anything but rhetorical. As the funeral *cortège* approached the city's chief cemetery, it was attacked by the police, who beat and arrested scores of mourners, including foreign journalists.

The Izmérys were not apolitical businessmen: they had criticized the U.S. embargo for its ineffectiveness. The U.S. government was sabotaging its own embargo, they had argued, fueling the conviction that U.S. support of Haitian democracy was, as they put it here, *blòf*—pure bluff. Fuel continued to reach Haiti from Europe, Africa, and even the neighboring Dominican Republic. In May, the foreign ministers of the OAS again met and called for broader enforcement of the sanctions. They further advised that prominent coup supporters' visas to enter the United States be revoked.

Many wealthy civilians were themselves dissatisfied with the results of the coup performed for their benefit, and traditional alliances between the oligarchy and the army began to fray. The upper echelons of the military, glutted on drug money, no longer cared much about the embargo. Since they effectively controlled the contraband market, it was an arrangement in which even lower-level officers found opportunities for profit.

The embargo's stalling of legal commerce affected much of the business community. A number of key coup supporters began, in the first months of the year, to pressure the regime to resume negotiations with the OAS. In response to these pressures, on June 19, 1992, Marc Bazin was sworn in as prime minister in a ceremony attended by the papal nuncio. An audience of silenced observers watched bitterly as Bazin—roundly rejected by plebiscite eighteen months earlier—pledged to "normalize the situation," and to "reintegrate Haiti into the international community."[28] Observers were both silenced and frightened, for any plans to "normalize the situation" implied entrenchment of both the *dilatoire* and the repression of the pro-democracy movement. Haitian scholar Yanique Joseph captured sentiments widespread in Haiti at the time of Bazin's investiture: "The stalemated negotiations have only given the army time to eliminate as many Aristide partisans as possible and are a clear signal to Aristide that, should he return, his safety is by no means assured."[29]

Two days after Bazin was sworn in as prime minister, 18 U.S. companies announced their willingness to pay Haitian taxes and customs duties. The embargo was easily skirted, it transpired, through an escrow account. These political and economic events were interpreted by pro-democracy Haitians as more evidence of the bad faith of the Bush administration: first, Bazin had been called "the American candidate" for as long as he had been involved in Haitian politics. To again cite Yanique Joseph: "Since Bazin had been the U.S. favorite, he also seemed to symbolize U.S. opposition to the return to power of Aristide and the Lavalas movement."[30] Second, if the United States was not winking complicitly at

Bazin's newly-minted civil-military government, why had the pro-American Vatican sent its ambassador to grace Bazin's swearing-in? Finally, U.S. companies were openly flouting the already sieve-like embargo.

By July 1992, some in the Aristide camp realized that they were losing the diplomatic battle, as they had lost the battle in the streets. New strategies were required. That month, the exiled leader called a meeting in Miami, where he formed the "Presidential Commission." The Commission would have the task of opening negotiations with Marc Bazin, a painful prospect for those who felt that Aristide's landslide victory had demonstrated the people's rejection of Bazin in particular.[31] The Presidential Commission included prominent laypeople and was led by Father Antoine Adrien, an eloquent and widely respected priest who had survived several decades of anti-Duvalier pro-democracy work. He and others pressed for increased OAS or U.N.involvement in order to attenuate the arbitrary brutality against the popular movement.

Some continued to deny the brutality. In July, Brian Latell, the CIA's leading analyst of Latin American affairs, traveled to Port-au-Prince and reported that he "saw no evidence of oppressive rule" there. "I do not wish to minimize the role the military plays in intimidating, and occasionally terrorizing real and suspected opponents, but there is no systematic or frequent lethal violence aimed at civilians."[32] Mr. Latell's brief on Haiti proved as accurate as the one that he had prepared on Aristide. On August 18, three young men were arrested by members of the Haitian security forces. Their offense: putting up posters of Aristide just prior to the arrival of an OAS delegation. On August 19, their bodies were found in the city morgue.[33]

In the end, however, Bazin's first summer as prime minister brought no significant change; it merely continued the *dilatoire* strategy designed to perpetuate a crisis painful for most but profitable for a few. It certainly did little to improve the human rights situation in Haiti, in spite of the fact that the *de facto* government agreed, on September 11, to an OAS observer mission to monitor human rights abuses.

On the first anniversary of the coup, Aristide again addressed the United Nations, taking on the Vatican for its recognition of the *de facto* regime: "What scandal is this? What would the attitude of Pope John Paul II have been if Haiti had been Poland?" Aristide concluded his address by calling for stronger sanctions. But in a United Nations that seemed suddenly to have rediscovered the notion of the Caribbean as back yard, it is unsurprising that the international body was no more eager to see Aristide's return than was the White House: "There was no indication that the United Nations intends to reverse its aloof stance towards Haiti's crisis," wrote a reporter from the *Boston Globe*, "and there are new signs that Washington and other regional governments are giving up on the embargo they imposed on Haiti last year." This article, like so many others, displays a habit of referring to Aristide and the putschists as equal and opposed forces: "privately American and other diplomats express frustration with both Aristide and his opponents, whom they accuse of being intransigent."[34]

Howard French, writing at the same time, echoed this speciously "reasonable" line: "Despite much blood on the army's hands, United States diplomats consider it a *vital counterweight* to Father Aristide, whose class-struggle rhetoric...threatened or antagonized traditional power centers at home and abroad."[35]

The belief, almost universal in Haiti, that the Bush administration did not want Aristide back in power began to appear in the U.S. press. "The Vatican may stand alone in its official recognition of Haiti's coup leaders," ran an editorial in the October 1, 1992, *Boston Globe*, "but the Bush administration's actions are no less appalling. By refusing to acknowledge the carnage taking place in Haiti, the administration has all but bestowed its blessings on the putschists." By this time, Aristide and his cabinet were merely biding their time, fearing that Bush's reelection would mean an end to attempts, diplomatic or otherwise, to restore democratic rule to Haiti.

According to data from the U.S. Department of Commerce, trade with Haiti amounted to $265 million during the first nine months of 1992.[36]

Many observers felt that Bill Clinton's election gave new hope to diplomatic efforts to restore constitutional democracy to Haiti. In December 1992, for example, the United Nations became more directly involved in the crisis by appointing Argentine diplomat Dante Caputo as special envoy to Haiti. The *de facto* regime announced that it would not permit more foreign observers on Haitian soil, and prevented 18 human rights monitors already on site from traveling outside of Port-au-Prince. At the New Year, as Clinton prepared to take office, General Cédras insisted that "Haiti's problems should be resolved by Haitians, and not by personalist and electoralist politics or by meddling from overseas."[37]

Clinton predicted, before his inauguration, that the coup leaders would fall into line or risk further punitive isolation. Clinton was expected to initiate an altogether different U.S. foreign policy towards Haiti. He had, after all, promised as much in his campaign. Such a change would not be universally welcomed in the United States. Several south Florida papers predicted a "massive tide" of Haitian refugees, publishing aerial photos suggesting that huge numbers of boats were being crafted all along the Haitian coastline in preparation for the Democrat's inauguration. Clinton, it was said, was too soft on boat people (whose zeal to leave Haiti, it was never pointed out, resulted from U.S. encouragement of the *de facto* government's thuggery). Florida officials, including the governor, spoke of "the Haitian peril." In response, on January 14, 1993, President-elect Clinton announced that he would maintain his predecessor's policy toward Haitian refugees. The next day, the U.S. Coast Guard surrounded the western part of the island in an effort to stave off the predicted tide of refugees. For obscure reasons, the exercise was termed "Operation Able Manner."

Clinton's flip-flop was greeted by most Haitians with dismay. Refugees held on the U.S. naval base at Guantánamo, led by Yolande Jean, began a hunger strike. But some active in the democratic movement found comfort in Clinton's promise to do "every thing in my power to see that Jean-Bertrand Aristide is restored to his rightful place." One Aristide cabinet member stated privately that, although they were outraged by the plan to continue Bush's treatment of the refugees, they were under "intense, intense pressure. If we can just hold on a bit longer, there would seem to be light, at last, at the end of the tunnel." He did add, however, that the light might well be from oncoming traffic.

The Clinton transition team announced that resolving Haiti's ongoing crisis would remain a top foreign policy priority. The cause of the refugee crisis, they acknowledged, was the Cédras *coup d'état* of September 1991. The team would work closely, it was announced, with Dante Caputo, and assigned high-level U.S. diplomats, including Lawrence Pezzullo, to help move the process forward. On February 9, under new pressure from abroad, the *de facto* regime announced that it would reconsider the OAS/U.N.observer mission proposed by Caputo and others. On March 16, Clinton met for the first time with Aristide and reiterated his support for the restoration of Haitian democracy. Although it is not clear what transpired at this meeting, the Haitian press in exile reported that Aristide was pressured to accept proposals of blanket amnesty for General Cédras and other coup leaders. Against the express counsel of several of his advisors, Aristide finally gave in to this demand.

But the military announced, on April 16, that amnesty was no longer enough. Close observers of

Haitian politics discerned a pattern: diplomats involved in the process would press Aristide for concessions. His advisors would advise him against compromising his pact with the Haitian people, and Aristide would underline the probability that the military and its representatives were acting in bad faith. The priest would then be depicted as intractable and rigid, even though he, in the end, acceded to key demands. The U.S. press would dutifully echo this depiction. And finally, the *de facto* regime would fail to live up to its end of the bargain, leaving Aristide with nothing to show for his concessions.

The more such machinations followed a tortuous path to nowhere, the more difficult it became, even for the U.S. press, to paint Aristide as the "difficult" party. And the more violent the military and their *attachés* became in Haiti, the more difficult it became to put Cédras and François in a favorable light, although some journalists were clearly determined to go on trying. Throughout the spring of 1993, the United Nations and the OAS had strengthened their presence in Haiti; their representatives were able to witness, often first-hand, the sometimes spectacular violence endemic to post-coup Haiti. Bishop Willy Romélus, by now an outspoken opponent of the regime, told of one incident in his diocese:

> On April 26, while priests were saying Mass in our Church of Ste. Hélène, soldiers came and surrounded the building....After the Mass, the soldiers demanded one of the priests, Father Samedi, but the congregation had hidden him in the back of the church before taking him away to the presbytery. When the soldiers realized that no priest was to be found, they proceeded to kill some of the worshippers and beat and arrest others.[38]

Such events, though commonplace, were rarely covered in the international press. Even as envoys from the UNDP, the World Bank, the International Monetary Fund (IMF), the IDB, and USAID traveled to Port-au-Prince to join the United Nations and OAS in elaborating a series of plans to "rebuild the shattered Haitian economy," it appeared to some that the pace of human rights abuses had only accelerated. Some felt that the more spectacular events were deliberate displays directed at the observers, although it must be noted that, in several cases, intervention by foreigners saved the lives of people detained by the armed forces. The army, in any event, was above the law; in some parts of the country, officers had created veritable fiefdoms, which they ruled, as the Haitians say, through "crush and break" principles. In May 1993, a report on the entrenchment of human rights abuses in Haiti was issued by the U.N.mission—and denounced by the Haitian military, which predictably rejected U.N.plans for an international police force to pave the way for Aristide's return.

U.N.envoy Dante Caputo announced that he was at the end of his patience. He gave a press conference following his sixth visit to Haiti, and this time he did not blame Aristide for stalled negotiations. "I will not return to Haiti," he stated from Washington, "until those in power there are serious about negotiating. And let us not fool ourselves: the Haitian people are living under the most ferocious repression in their entire history."

On June 4, 1993, Clinton announced that he favored sterner sanctions against the increasingly brazen *de facto* government. Oil and arms would not be permitted to reach Haiti, he warned; coup leaders' stateside assets would be frozen. Administration officials also made it clear, through other channels, that U.S. Drug Enforcement Agency officials would work, with or without cooperation, to halt the flood of cocaine pouring out of Haiti.[39] The United Nations agreed to these stiffer sanctions. Four days later, Marc Bazin, who had promised to serve as an effective bridge between the *bourgeoisie* and the army, stepped down. His resignation was something of a non-event in Haiti.

The newly stiffened embargo went into effect on

June 23. Now it took only days to draw the military to the bargaining table, situated this time on Governor's Island in New York. The new-and-improved plan for a return to constitutional rule once again granted blanket amnesty to the military high command upon its resignation. Aristide would name a new government, subject to approval by the Haitian parliament (or what was left of it). The plan was to culminate in the return of Aristide on October 30, 1993. The entire process would be monitored by a U.N.-sponsored team of "military experts" who would also supervise the "professionalization" of the Haitian armed forces. Both Aristide and Cédras—ensconced in separate buildings—signed these principles into the Governor's Island Accord on July 3, 1993.

Having watched these developments from Haiti, I can relate that any satisfaction people may have felt about this apparent triumph of diplomacy was tempered by what we witnessed all around us. Those with radios were privy to the uninterrupted stories of arbitrary arrests and beatings and killings; those with the stomach for such things could count the bodies that greeted residents of the capital most mornings as they opened their doors. Those with televisions could watch other instructive spectacles:

> Even on the very day late in June when Aristide and his associates and Cédras and his officers began working out their accord in New York, in Port-au-Prince heavily armed police were invading a church during mass and beating up parishioners who had shouted the deposed president's name—a scene broadcast live on the state television network.[40]

Haitian social reality, always tense, split into an increasingly surreal juxtaposition of diplomatic pronouncements and acts of unrestrained barbarity by the men with the guns. The divide between actions and words yawned ever wider as the members of the U.N./OAS team were obliged to witness the military's violence against the poor.

General Cédras and his associates had come to
Governor's Island with a number of pressing concerns, to
which U.S. newspapers gave ample play. The soldiers,
including Cédras and François, were frightened, they
said, of popular retribution. They feared that Aristide's
return would trigger a blood bath. Unfortunately, there
were no Haitian cartoonists left to depict ironically the
terror of Uzi-toting soldiers being manhandled by school-
children or gaunt peasants. Previous media coverage,
with its sophistic commitment to presenting "equally critical views of both parties," had moved the margins of
acceptable discourse: it was thus no longer absurd—
indeed for some it was pleasingly symmetrical—to have
heavily armed aggressors asking for protection from
unarmed victims. Yet no one in the Aristide camp could
mention the thousands of deaths since the coup without
being denounced for obstructionism by those managing
the parleys. As media critic Catherine Orenstein notes,
"the accords legitimized the *de facto* rulers by recognizing
Cédras as equal in standing with the democratically
elected president, who, according to the [*New York*]
Times, 'grated on the nerves of many diplomats' during
the negotiation process on Governor's Island."[41]

This was Aristide's quandary: If he wanted the help
of the powerful, he would have to play by their rules.
Mark Danner, writing for the *New York Review of Books*,
correctly saw the Governor's Island Accord as something
of a Faustian bargain: "In order to attain international
support to return to the Palace, he essentially agreed to
treat the *coup d'état* and the killing that followed it as if
they had never happened."[42]

It seemed a far cry from his prophetic anger of previous years, when Aristide would have derided attempts to
bargain with thugs like Cédras. Members of the
Presidential Commission privately pointed both to
Aristide's desire to stop the killing in Haiti and also to

the intense pressures placed on him by members of the diplomatic community. These pressures, apparently, had not been subtle. One reporter, writing for *Boston Globe*, noted that the message presented to Aristide was tantamount to: "Sign the agreement or return to Washington and begin applying for a green card."[43]

So Aristide signed. Instead of putting an end to the killing, however, the Governor's Island agreement seemed only to trigger a rash of disappearances and summary executions as the military took advantage of their newfound legitimacy. The U.N./OAS mission again acknowledged its impotence before the surge of violence, which was as usual directed chiefly against the poor. But Aristide's more prominent supporters were not spared. On August 17, Antoine Izméry and Father Yvon Massacre were roughed up by police for putting up posters of Aristide; the portly, white-bearded priest went to jail on charges of "terrorism."

On August 25, Aristide nominated Haitian businessman Robert Malval as prime minister. Malval, though a friend of Aristide's, was pro-business and had opposed a number of Aristide's initial policies during his seven months in power. In naming Malval, Aristide put forth an olive branch not to the military high command, happily glutted on drug money, but rather to the bourgeoisie, discontented and discomfited by the embargo on legal trade. The new cabinet was by and large devoid of progressives, although its members had given their loyalty to Aristide as the choice of the Haitian people. This transitional government won parliamentary approval on August 27, and the U.N.Security Council immediately suspended, as agreed, the oil embargo. A few days later, on September 2, the transitional government's ministers were invested, and all sanctions were lifted.

Typically, this step, too, was accompanied by paroxysms of violence. The new minister of foreign affairs, Claudette Werleigh, a Catholic social activist, was threatened at gun point during her first *hour* in office. Evans Paul, elected Mayor of Port-au-Prince in 1990 with over 90 percent of the vote, was attacked as he attempted to resume his post; five people were killed, although Paul escaped unharmed. One student bled to death over the course of four hours, pleading for assistance until the end.

These events were interpreted differently by Haitian and American diplomats. Lawrence Pezzullo, U.S. special envoy to Haiti, was interviewed the following day by "Frontline" reporters:

> The great suspicion you find within Haiti still leads to disturbances. Even yesterday in the return of the mayor to Port-au-Prince to his office, there was resistance. It was overcome. I think it was one of the great success stories of the new administration asserting itself, demanding its rights, putting itself back in power. But on the other hand it was marred by some violence—not terrible, but there was violence.[44]

Pezzullo's vagueness, his reluctance to assign responsibility for the killings, typified the U.S. approach to the intractable island republic. These attacks—qualified as "not terrible"—were perpetrated in the usual, public fashion by the military's *attachés*, who, under the new label "FRAPH", appeared to have closer ties to Port-au-Prince police chief Michel François than to General Cédras. Antoine Izméry and others denounced the new rash of violence. They suggested that the Governor's Island accords had been conducted in bad faith.

Izméry further announced that, on September 11, a mass would be held in honor of the memory of all those who died through military repression. Although he surely had his own brother in mind, the date was that of the 1988 sack of Saint-Jean Bosco. Five long and brutal years had elapsed. On the morning of the mass, in the Église Sacré-Coeur in Port-au-Prince, Izméry and his family—including members of his brother Georges' family—were putting the finishing touches on the program.

Izméry granted interviews to a number of journalists, and chatted amiably with members of the U.N./OAS team of observers. A truckload of almost 50 soldiers patrolled the neighborhood throughout the service; they must have been interested in the disturbance created when, in the middle of the mass, Izméry was dragged at gun point from the church into the busy street. He was executed with bullets to the head at point-blank range. Unlike his brother, Antoine Izméry died quickly.

Reactions to the murder of Antoine Izméry were swift and unusually candid. Dante Caputo, back in Haiti, openly linked the murder to Michel François.[45] Many called for the resumption of sanctions, but the situation was a delicate one—Malval, not Bazin, was prime minister. Aristide, who counted Izméry as one of his closest friends, pointed accusingly at both Cédras and François. He nonetheless repeated his intention to comply with the terms of the Governor's Island Accord, which would result in his return to Haiti in less than three weeks. Members of the international community began to express doubts about the feasibility of meeting the terms of the agreement, but announced that "the timetable for the restoration of democracy will proceed as planned."

Port-au-Prince became the theater of an increasingly grisly spectacle as the activities of the death squads and *attachés* picked up throughout the rest of September—whether to settle accounts with partisans of democracy before Aristide's return, or to make that return impossible. An example of the impunity with which they carried out their business was offered on October 5, when *attachés* fired on a political meeting, wounding a United Nations security officer. The U.N./OAS mission reported that "death lists" were being drawn up throughout the country; those found on these lists were to be executed if the terms of the Governor's Island Accord, meaning Aristide's return, were met. *Attachés* were kind enough to type and then fax copies of these lists to many of the concerned parties.

On October 6, the first members of the international police force arrived, and on October 7 and 8, Port-au-Prince was paralyzed by a military-backed strike. Several merchants were wounded as they attempted to open their businesses in defiance of the *attachés*. "The gunmen collaborated openly with uniformed Haitian police, the very forces who are supposed to be retrained by international police experts as part of the diplomatic settlement of Haiti's political crisis."[46] *Attachés* announced that they had every intention of "killing foreigners who intervened in Haiti's affairs."

On October 11, the USS *Harlan County* attempted to dock in Port-au-Prince. The ship carried 218 American troops, many of them technicians; they were to join other members of a multinational force that was expected to swell to 1300 in the days prior to Aristide's scheduled return. As promised, a group of heavily armed *attachés* crowded the docks, firing their weapons in the air and attacking the cars of the U.S. diplomats who had come to welcome the soldiers. The *Harlan County*, for hours stalled in the middle of the harbor, eventually pulled out of Haitian waters and steamed toward Guantánamo. Prime Minister Malval went into hiding as diplomats went on talking and *attachés* went on shooting.

The United States and the U.N.reimposed economic sanctions the next day. On October 14, Clinton's warning that the Haitian military would be held accountable for the safety of Malval and his cabinet was widely broadcast on Haitian radio. "I want to send a clear signal today, too, that the United States is very concerned about [Malval's] ability to function and his personal safety and the safety of his government."[47] Hours later, the *attachés* sent their own clear signal: Justice Minister Guy Malary and his entourage were gunned down in downtown Port-au-Prince. A wealthy lawyer with strong ties to business, Malary had been assigned the task of "retraining" the army. In an interview days prior to his assassination, Malary spoke of the threats he had been receiving: "I have come not to work with the justice establishment I've found on the ground. I've come with the intention of building something new that this country can be proud of."[48] Newspapers carried photos of Malary's pregnant wife weeping over his bullet-ridden body.

Another group of *attachés* concurrently occupied the National Assembly, taking hostages and vowing that they were planning to "cut off heads and burn down houses." They again referred to their death lists of Aristide supporters, both Haitian and foreign, to be executed as plans to restore the deposed president were advanced. Shortly thereafter, 51 Canadian troops left the country; Clinton announced that the 46 U.S. troops remaining in Haiti would also be withdrawn if the Haitian security forces would not guarantee their safety.

Meanwhile, the worst Duvalierist torturers were returning to Haiti. At the close of October, 1993, Franck Romain, the mastermind behind the Saint-Jean Bosco massacre, showed up for breakfast at the Oloffson Hotel, where journalists were free to hear of his plans for Haiti's future.[49]

The team of U.N.and OAS observers, already frightened by Malary's execution, had their radio system and telephone lines cut in a single day. Shortly thereafter, the Security Council ordered their removal to the Dominican Republic. Well before the targeted return date of October 30, the Clinton-U.N.attempts to restore democracy to Haiti were in tatters—rent, it would seem, by a small number of men willing to go to great lengths to protect their privilege and by a great number of international power-brokers who had consented to treat that privilege as a legitimate diplomatic interest.

Official responses to the scrapping of the Governor's Island Accord were Olympian. Pentagon officials responded to the latest turn of events by saying, in diplomatic language, "I told you so." By echoing—for the first time—what Aristide and his advisors had been saying all along, the Pentagon was credited with a sort of intelligence scoop:

> While the State Department has held out hope that the Haiti military would go along with a peace accord to restore President Jean-Bertrand Aristide to power, Pentagon officials believed the junta was never serious and has now proved its bad faith.[50]

What accounts for the Pentagon's astonishing prescience? When Aristide had made similar observations, the same press referred to him as "obstructionist," "difficult," and "paranoid," accusations that doubtless had their sources among the brokers of the Governor's Island accords.

Other dark hints regarding the nature of U.S.-Haitian relations came into light during the last weeks of 1993. A number of key Haitian officers were discovered to be in the pay of the CIA. On November 14, 1993, *The New York Times* reported that the "the agency paid key members of the junta now in power for political and military information up until the ouster of Father Aristide in 1991." These payments were part of a significant CIA operation in Haiti, which had trained a secret intelligence unit unbeknownst to the elected government. "The unit evolved into an instrument of political terror whose officers at times engaged in drug trafficking, American and Haitian officials say."[51] One of those officers was Raoul Cédras.

The Haitian National Intelligence Service unit, which went under the sublime acronym SIN, received up to one million dollars per year from U.S. coffers—the exact figures are unavailable, as the CIA is not obliged to report them to Congress—nominally to investigate the drug trade. *The New York Times* points out that, although SIN had its shortcomings, it had certain successes as well:

> The unit produced little narcotics intelligence. Senior

members committed acts of political terror against Aristide supporters, including interrogations and torture, and threatened last year to kill the local chief of the United States Drug Enforcement Administration.

On the other hand, United States officials said, one senior Haitian intelligence officer dissuaded soldiers from killing President Aristide during the 1991 coup. The CIA also helped to save the lives of at least six Aristide supporters after the coup, evacuating them in a late-night rescue that involved the Navy's elite SEAL unit, officials said.[52]

This report confirmed Haitian suspicions, although such fears had been chalked up to the paranoia supposedly native to the culture. To cite, once again, a rather unself-conscious commentary on the Haitian bent for conspiracy theories: "Throughout the world, it is common practice to ascribe dark motives to U.S. foreign policy, but in Haiti the practice often borders on the bizarre."[53]

One man's bizarre, clearly, is another man's explanation. How else would one account for the regularly floated stories about Aristide's supposed history of mental illness? Initially advanced in a CIA report (whose author branded Aristide as a "murderer and psychopath"), the theory that Aristide is mentally unstable has received a good deal of press at a time when the Haitian military—the initial source of the rumor—was busy sabotaging diplomatic efforts to return the deposed president. The CIA report stated that Aristide had been prescribed lithium by a Dr. "Harvé Martin" of Canada. Canada's national medical association has denied the existence of such a physician. That should have put an end to the story, especially when joined to the CIA's subsequent admission that the document was probably forged.[54] But U.S. network television jumped into the fray, with the CBS evening news offering an unflattering profile of Aristide in October of 1993; again, its source was the CIA report. As James Carroll noted on the editorial page of the *Boston Globe* of October 26, "The main purpose of attacks on Aristide at this crucial moment, of course, is to distract from the character of the real murderers and psychopaths who refuse to yield power in Haiti."

Although it is difficult to assign to the media—which consist, of course, of journalists and other commentators writing from a variety of positions—an inordinate role in shaping public perceptions of current events, there can be little doubt that readings of the Haitian coup were strongly shaped by key stories. What representational work is done by titles such as, "Haiti's Democracy, Such as It Was, Is Swept Aside By a Chaotic Coup"? Or by "Aristide's Autocratic Ways Ended Haiti's Embrace of Democracy"?

The issue is not one of titles alone. In a widely read, in-depth essay appearing in the *Atlantic Monthly*, Lawrence Harrison, the former head of USAID in Haiti, offered the following portrait of General Cédras: "Contrary to his U.S. media image as a bloodthirsty brute, Cédras conducted himself professionally and flexibly during our four-month mission."[55] Perhaps the general's bearing during meetings with an agent of his chief patron was "professional." But to judge the general by the behavior of the men under his command, "bloodthirsty" and "brute" seem apposite enough terms.

The second error, Harrison's purported correction of Cédras' "U.S. media image," is far more insidious. In Aristide's seven months in office, Amnesty International documented 26 human-rights violations—the majority of these committed by the anti-Aristide army. In contrast, Boston Media Action, citing the Haitian Platform for Human Rights, recently reported "1867 executions, 5096 illegal and arbitrary arrests, and 2171 cases of beatings and shootings under the *coup* government." Thus, during 1991 and 1992, the coup government presided over 99.8 percent of recent, documented human rights abuses, while the Aristide government presided over 0.2 percent of these abuses.[56] In spite of these figures, Harrison commandeered several pages of a national journal of opinion to describe General Cédras as a "professional," "flexible" moderate. Aristide, in these pages, is portrayed as a bloodthirsty extremist.

But the problem is far more systemic, for a similar picture has been painted in much of the U.S. media. Boston Media Action analyzed 415 articles on Haiti taken from the *New York Times*, the *Washington Post*, the *Miami Herald*, and the *Boston Globe*: "For the period from September 30 to October 14, 1991, the papers we studied devoted 60 percent of all paragraphs on human rights abuses to Aristide, and 40 percent to the coup government."

Social scientists of various persuasions have written tomes about the "politics of representation," but the mechanisms used by the Haitian elite would not defy even the most superficial analyses. Baby Doc Duvalier hired a Madison Avenue public-relations firm and a Washington law firm to polish his image, and soon thereafter he had the symbolic capital of a kinder, gentler dictatorship. In the 1980s, for example, Ron Brown—now Clinton's secretary of commerce—represented the Haitian government through Patton, Boggs & Blow. Although Brown insisted in a 1989 news conference that he "never had any involvement either on a client basis or any other basis with the [Duvalier] family," his November, 1983 memorandum to Baby Doc suggests otherwise. The memo was a progress report on his lobbying on behalf of the Haitian government:

> My current role as deputy chairman of the Democratic National Committee has served us well in these efforts, while my contacts with my counterparts in the Republican Party assure continued access and excellent relations with the government of President Reagan.[57]

More recently, members of the military and business elite have also hired U.S.-based lawyers to defend their interests.[58]

Today's Haitian army, we learn, has retained Lynn Garrison, a former Canadian fighter pilot who now divides his time between Haitian military headquarters and a home in Los Angeles. In an interview given to a *Boston Globe* reporter, Garrison stated that he was "asked by the plotters of the September 1991 coup against Aristide to search the National Palace for any damaging information that could be used against Haiti's first democratically elected president." Garrison reached Haiti the day before the putsch, and shortly thereafter produced materials—Aristide's diary, some paintings, and a "statement" from a psychiatrist who had allegedly prescribed anti-depressants for Aristide—that were then used to good effect by the CIA and others. Garrison "was pleased with the CIA's profile on Aristide's mental state, adding, 'The truth is finally out about this supposed lover of democracy.'"[59]

No one paid much attention to Garrison's detective work in Haiti, as Aristide had clearly won the struggle for the hearts of the Haitians, and not through any such crude chicanery. But the point of these antics was not to sway Haitian popular opinion—newspaper reports noted that Lynn Garrison speaks neither French nor Creole.[60] Stories about Aristide's mental instability were directed to the people who read *The New York Times* and the *Atlantic*, and those who watch CBS and CNN. When Lynn Garrison complains that the "the international media have been unfair to the Haitian military," it is in order to have his words echoed in the North American press, not in Haiti.

If the delicate sympathies of the Haitian high command are to find such an audience in the North American press, it is because ideological blinkers are in place. These will prevent us from noting that certain constructions—for example, the suggestion from an already hemorrhaging Haiti that Aristide's return will trigger a blood bath—simply do not make sense.

The Uses of Haiti

(Reprise)

Haiti has generally failed to elicit much scholarly interest abroad, save for a titillating exoticism which led to the image of the country as being an isolated, unique, or extreme case.

—Patrick Bellegarde-Smith,
"Haitian Foreign Policy and Relations," 1984

Haiti is not simply one more of those tropical dictatorships where to rule is to steal, and headless bodies are found by the road. Haiti contorts time; it convolutes reason if you are lucky—and obliterates it if you are not. Haiti is to this hemisphere what black holes are to outer space. Venture there and you cross an event horizon.

—T.D. Allman,
"After Baby Doc," 1989

It's hard to sell Haiti as a tourist paradise when popular perceptions of the place make a visit fall into the category of 'Holidays in Hell.' Dire poverty, AIDS, child slavery, zombies, voodoo animal sacrifices and political violence are just some of the negative images facing tour operators. A U.S. government travel warning 'strongly advises' Americans to avoid Haiti.

—San Francisco Chronicle Sunday Punch,
March 31, 1991

From the arrival of Columbus to the coup of 1991, Haiti has had many uses. Some of these are obvious. Certainly, the plantations established by the French, the great extractive machines that transformed sweat and blood into sugar and gold, did little but turn chattel labor into exportable wealth. "Rich as a Creole" was a common expression in the capitals of eighteenth-century Europe.

Independence changed much, but not all. The land itself, the poor who tilled it, continued to yield the same bounty, and if the profits were not as great, they were hardly shared in a more equitable manner within Haiti.

As seen from the outside, however, Haiti had become a completely different sort of symbol after 1804. In a monolithically racist world, Haiti was "the nightmare republic." Throughout the nineteenth century, European and American visitors to Haiti culled material for best-selling texts that told readers what they most wanted to hear. The hypothesis to be confirmed, invariably, was that blacks were incapable of self-rule. Haitians had been quick to understand that the country would be punished for daring to suggest otherwise: "To fully appreciate the origin of the unceasing and persistent calumnies of which Haiti has been made the target," observed one Haitian diplomat in 1907, "one must go back to the very first days of her existence and call to mind the circumstances under which she started life as an independent country."[1]

Haitian statesmen at the turn of the century would continue to present their country as an inspiration for enslaved people even as it became increasingly difficult to link present-day Haiti to its origins in the struggle against slavery. Two Caribbeanists aptly summarize the Haitian elites' message to the rest of the world:

> The Haitian elites viewed their country as a beacon of freedom for the colonized of the world and as a black republic carrying the traditions of France into the New World. Thus, they supported the Greek independence movement. They supported Simón Bolívar who took refuge in Haiti, and they expressed their enthusiasm in 1898 for the freedom movement in Cuba while expressing their fears of U.S. intervention which might abort it. Dantès Bellegarde and Nemours Auguste denounced white South Africa and Fascist Italy in the League of Nations.[2]

But because these elites, on the inside, were often the very persons who profited from the feudal structures that so oppressed Haiti's peasantry, more mundane matters often preoccupied them. Their rhetoric of freedom was for export.

Further, the country *was* a mess, if for reasons quite different than those adduced by its foreign detractors.

Haiti *was* marked by violence, much of it externally funded. The majority of Haitians *were* desperately poor, and becoming poorer; they *were* sick and had no access to modern conveniences such as clean water. And Haitian elites were embarrassed by popular culture—voodoo and the Creole language with its supposed "deformations" of French. Some of these prejudices wore thin in the course of the twentieth century, but in 1990 the Haitian anthropologist Michel Rolph Trouillot could still bemoan "the middle-class contempt that most urban liberals feel toward the common people of Haiti."[3] For these reasons, perhaps, Haitian elites were always unconvincing nationalists and even more unconvincing progressives.

Throughout the nineteenth century, Haiti took on greater and greater symbolic functions. As the fruits of independence rotted on the vine, Haiti became a cautionary tale of great relevance to all colonial powers with holdings in the New World. British envoy Sir Spenser St. John set the tone in his memoir of *Hayti or the Black Republic*:

> I know what the black man is, and I have no hesitation in declaring that he is incapable of the art of government, and that to entrust him with framing and working the laws for our islands is to condemn them to inevitable ruin. What the negro may become after centuries of civilized education I cannot tell, but what I know is that he is not fit to govern now.[4]

St. John delighted his audience with tales of voodoo and cannibalism, including the "practice of eating young children and digging up freshly buried corpses for brutal ceremonies or food."[5] Soon translated into French, the book became a bestseller in England, the United States, and France. In Haiti, the section on voodoo provoked outrage, causing St. John to reconsider some of his arguments as he was preparing a second edition of the book from Mexico, his next post: "The result has been to convince me that I *underrated* its fearful manifestations; I have therefore rewritten these chapters, and introduced many new facts which have come to my knowledge."[6]

St. John's words seem harsh, but the commentary of Americans during the occupation was scarcely any kinder. The *National Geographic*, for example, was able to refer to Haiti's peasants as the "unthinking black animals of the interior."[7] St. John's accusations of cannibalism would continue to be taken as gospel, as the work of the staff writers of the *National Geographic* attests:

> In this carnival of barbarism religion also had its place. Cannibalism and the black rites of voodoo magic of the African jungles were revived in all their horror, and the sacrifice of children and of animals to the mumbo jumbos of the local wizard was practiced in the appropriate seasons. Poisoning and praying to death became the mode, and missionaries to the island report that fully four-fifths of all the population are either active believers in or hold in fear the spell of the witch doctors.[8]

Associations between Haitians and infectious disease are currently particularly strong in the U.S. popular press. This, too, is nothing new. Writing in 1920, *National Geographic* journalists noted that "it is estimated that 87 percent of the entire population were infected with contagious diseases."[9] AIDS is merely the most recent in a long series of plagues attributed to Haiti. In the sixteenth century, Europeans insisted that syphilis originated in Haiti, and was brought back by Columbus's sailors. (The converse now appears to have been the case.)

In fact, Haiti has never shaken these and other fraudulent accusations, which are sure to resurface whenever editors and publishers send their writers to the island. Throughout the twentieth century, Haiti kept its reputation of being an isolated and barbaric country, quite immune to the civilizing influence of American occupiers. In a book-length review of *Haiti's Bad Press*, anthropologist Robert Lawless has concluded that "there is a continuity in thematic biases that spans almost two centuries."[10] Haiti's "bad press" is bad indeed—not merely because it is defamatory, but also, as I have argued here, because it obscures Haiti's real problems, their causes and their possible cures.

Most commentary on Haiti is inescapably racist. Lawless quotes a twentieth-century traveler's account of Haitians, impressed that their "dazzling white suits, dark heads and hands resemble a photographic negative...This negative to the white world, this proliferation of black," he surmises, "is the negation of what the white world most fervently wants to believe in, that is, the good will of whites in an essentially black world."[11]

From the time of slavery, racism has been used to justify the *economic* exploitation of the Haitian poor. Racist bias, in this analysis, serves economic ends; and to concentrate on racism without noticing exploitation would be to take an absurdly ideology-driven approach to Haitian history. For almost a century, the (largely American) owners of the vast sugar plantations of Cuba and the Dominican Republic had counted on Haitian labor. More recently, Haitians in Haiti have been used for cheap labor by a generation of U.S.-based businessmen, and the Caribbean Basin Initiative advanced by the Reagan administration promised to make Haiti the "Taiwan of the Caribbean."[12] The off-shore assembly industry makes cunningly efficient use of the high-repression, low-wage setting that Haiti offers investors. For those who objected to this system on moral grounds, the architects of the plan merely pointed at the country's staggering unemployment figures. Yes, the Haitians who flocked to these plants wanted jobs. No, they had no choice.

At the close of the twentieth century, Haiti's symbolic value continues to amaze. Its symbolic uses are often as important as the more pragmatic ones, but the uses of Haiti are unlikely to ever be purely symbolic, as the Caribbean Basin Initiative suggests. In the end, Haiti's tragedy is less about race, more about the right of investors to determine the living conditions of the poor. As Amy Wilentz has noted, "By tradition, the country was the private property of whoever ruled it; its coffers and customs were their source of revenue; its airstrips, ports, boats and planes theirs to use to ship whatever was most profitable: in our day cocaine."[13]

Drug transshipment became big business under Baby Doc; during his tenure, the trade was said to be linked to his wife's family (her brother was jailed in the United States on related charges). After February 1986, the trade was assured by Casernes Dessalines, as military headquarters are termed. One South American diplomat explained that the military have an airstrip on a ranch by the Dominican border. "It works like this: The big planes fly up from Colombia, unload there, and fly back. The stuff's then put in the little planes, and goes on its way. The fee is $30,000 a cargo. Of course, the whole operation is run out of Casernes Dessalines."[14]

Aristide's anti-drug campaign thus threatened a very lucrative enterprise. Small wonder, then, that those new Uzis and assault rifles are said to have been paid for with drug money.

What, exactly, does the most recent chapter of Haitian political history say about the country's uses? We have seen that the uses of Haiti have always included its symbolic value—Haiti as source of infection or boat people, Haiti as stereotypical other, Haiti as confirmation of one's worst racist theories, Haiti as exemplifying a "cultural problem," Haiti as all-around whipping boy—and this function is changing in interesting ways. In recent years, Haiti's sticky symbolic web has gathered new meanings without shedding the old myths, such as those regarding cannibalism.

The Cédras *coup d'état* is also of great symbolic value; in the larger scheme of things, this may be its true significance. In addition to obvious interpretations assigned to the coup—its convenient casting of Haiti as cash cow for the army, the Haitian elite, for foreign investors; Haiti as depot for international drug lords;

Haiti as "basket case" in need of international assistance; Haitians as just plain incapable of self-rule—it is possible to expose a number of less obvious parallel narratives.

In terms of mechanics, the coup of 1991 was and is a simple affair, really, but media constructions would suggest otherwise. In its July 12, 1993 edition, *Newsweek* offered an official version of reality in a news analysis entitled "When Elections Aren't Democracy." We read that, in Haiti, "elections brought to power an unstable populist....who was tossed by the military after he threatened to 'necklace' his opponents." Less than a month later, *The New York Times* spoke of Aristide as being marked "with some of the same thuggish tendencies as the military junta."[15] As media critic Catherine Orenstein has noted, Howard French, who wrote most of the *Times* post-coup copy, received a hero's welcome on Governor's Island: "During two years of stalled negotiations to restore democracy, the *Times* so eroded Aristide's stature that Serge Beaulieu, spokesman for the military at U.N.talks this year in New York, greeted *Times* correspondent Howard French on June 30 with, 'Our foreign minister! Welcome!'"[16]

Even if Howard French could write that "Aristide's Autocratic Ways Ended Haiti's Embrace of Democracy," Haiti's experiment with democracy was in fact ended by soldiers with new Uzis and assault rifles. This should not be forgotten. The junta's apologists needed to obscure this obvious fact; exploiting the rich vein of myths and half-truths at their disposal, establishment journalists and publishers have made the work of men such as Brian Latell, Jesse Helms, and Lynn Garrison that much easier. When the reporting wasn't right, they could always open editorial space to interested speculation. On December 3, 1993, the *Miami Herald*, perhaps Latin America's most influential daily, allowed Mr. Garrison to inveigh at some length against the embargo, the alleged source of all of Haiti's problems. After recounting the death of an entire Haitian family from starvation,

Garrison concludes: "These people have done nothing to us. Most have never managed the long trip to Port-au-Prince (120 miles) and have no concept of what democracy is, nor do they really care."[17]

Certainly, the Haitian poor know from long experience that they are not *supposed* to care about democracy. Perhaps post-coup Haiti's symbolic utility is chiefly as a warning to those who dare to care what democracy is. The coup is a warning to those who think that a country's wealth ought to be equitably shared among the people who live there.

Such was the plan of the Aristide government. From the perspective of the Haitian poor, the Aristide presidency, and not the coup, was a rupture with the past. Throughout his adult life, Aristide has made it clear that he thought the uses of Haiti should be altered in radical ways. Inspired by the idea of "an option for the poor," Aristide wanted, at a minimum, to provide a "decent poverty" for the majority of Haitians. This would require, he felt, greater popular input into decision making; it would require an end to the most flagrant injustices and the redistribution of some of Haiti's wealth. The Council on Hemispheric Affairs, noting that Aristide's victory "represented more than a decade of civic engagement and education on his part," heralded *lavalas* as "a textbook example of participatory, 'bottom-up' and democratic political development."[18]

Constrained by a new world order that was more concerned about making an option for the rich, and constrained, too, by his cabinet of moderates, Aristide's government was less about socialism or anti-imperialism than it was about a modest, reformist nationalism. His eight months in office saw significant reforms against tremendous odds. But, as Noam Chomsky has noted, it is precisely such dangerous notions as reform that are most likely to bring down the wrath of the international elite. Mimicking the jargon of the sort of editorials that damaged Aristide's reputation abroad, he writes: "An 'ultranationalist' regime becomes an even greater threat if it appears to be succeeding in ways that might be meaningful to other poor and oppressed people. In that case it is a 'virus' that might 'infect' others, a 'rotten apple' that might 'spoil the barrel.' It is a threat to 'stability.'"[19] Echoes of the nineteenth century allusions to the dangerous Black Republic resound.

Aristide's ascent, then, was a message of international currency. For the first time since 1804, the symbolic uses of Haiti included its value as a model of justice. Aristide's election was watched with interest throughout the rest of Latin America, as the comments of Msgr. Jacques Gaillot, the Bishop of Évreux, France, suggest:

> Aristide's inauguration represents immense hope, not only for the Haitian people, but also, I believe, for the people of the Dominican Republic and all the other peoples of Latin America. The beacon is no longer Nicaragua, it is now Haiti, and Haiti truly has the duty and the right to succeed on behalf of all people who desire this experience of liberation.[20]

It is for this reason, surely, that so much was invested in containing Aristide's ideas. Assembly plants can be moved, hastily if need be, but it is far more difficult to quash ideas such as the one so eloquently embedded in the notion of an "option for the poor." And so, conservative "counterweights" to Aristide were glutted with money from the National Endowment for Democracy, USAID and the CIA. Did the CIA fund or encourage the coup, as has happened elsewhere in Latin America when progressive governments came to power? The point may be moot:

> There need not be evidence the CIA egged on the military for this episode to inspire a re-evaluation of how the agency does overseas business. Merely by paying thuggish military leaders to be intelligence assets, the CIA might have caused coup plotters to believe their assault against Aristide would not upset their generous American friends. Predictably, with NED and CIA

money, Washington endowed not forces of democracy but of murderous oppression.[21]

How distinctively Haitian is all this? Certainly, the Haitian revolution of 1804 has no parallel in modern world history, nor did the ostracism that greeted the globe's only independent black republic. But as the symbolic and pragmatic uses of Haiti change over time, so, too, do the terms of its singularity. In the nineteenth century, Haiti was "the Black Republic." Haiti is now the poor, the violent republic. Haiti is now singular largely in the *degree* of its poverty and the *extent* of repression.

If the rise of Jean-Bertrand Aristide was in many ways unique, what happened on September 30, 1991, was not. The overthrow of progressive governments has been a staple of contemporary Latin American history. Since the Monroe Doctrine, the military and profiteering status quo in these countries has been maintained with the assistance, whether overt or covert, of the United States.

Recent history is rich in parallels between Haiti and Central America. As just one example, it is worth stepping away from Haiti for a moment and reviewing in some detail the CIA-funded overthrow of Jacobo Arbenz Guzmán, democratically-elected president of Guatemala, in 1954—a coup not often evoked in discussions of the Cédras coup.

In a scholarly assessment of the Guatemalan coup, historian Richard Immerman describes the philosophies of Arbenz and his predecessor, Juan Arévalo. Arbenz was a talented young military officer; Arévalo, a major figure in Guatemalan political and educational thought. Through them, "'Arévalism,' a romantic, pragmatic, and neo-idealist movement that rejected historical materialism and communism, guided Guatemala for almost a decade."[22]

On several points, Arévalo and Arbenz resemble the young Aristide who tried to assemble a coalition in 1991:

Each was a nationalist, somewhat of an eclectic idealist whose philosophy could best be characterized as an amalgam of liberal reformism, democratic socialism, and a certain tinge of anti-Yankee sentiment. As mandated by the 1944 revolution, they vowed to modernize Guatemala, to create the conditions necessary for the country's self-sufficiency, and to increase the standard of living for the majority of the population. Each outlined his programs during his campaign for the presidency, and each adhered to his platform.[23]

Another assessment, by historian Sheldon Liss, notes that Arbenz was dedicated to "converting the backward economy into a modern capitalist one, and elevating the living standards of the masses."[24] Although these philosophies and platforms were far from radical, they enraged the local oligarchy, which wished to maintain the feudal structures that guaranteed their privileges: "Condemning government officials as inexperienced, incompetent, and easily corrupted (and, of course, Communist), they predicted widespread looting, rampant inflation, and social and political chaos."[25]

As specious as such projections were, the Guatemalan elite knew that it could count on the supportive echo of the government of the United States. Communism was defined, then as now, as opposition to U.S. interests, and U.S. interests in Guatemala were defined by the mammoth United Fruit Company (UFCO). This was not subtle, as the remarks of President Eisenhower suggest: Arbenz "created the strong suspicion that he was merely a puppet manipulated by the communists. For example on February 24, 1953, the Arbenz government announced its intention, under an agrarian reform law, to seize unused United Fruit Company land."[26]

The UFCO had been in Guatemala a long time, and got on cozily with the men in uniform. During the 1940s, the Ubico dictatorship had granted UFCO "a ninety-nine-year lease on more land on both coasts, bringing its total property to more than the combined holdings of half of

Guatemala's landholding population. The contract specifically exempted United Fruit from virtually all taxes and duties."[27] It was estimated that UFCO used no more than 15 percent of that land. The Arévalo and Arbenz governments wished to grant the Guatemalan poor access to fallow land, as they had promised in their presidential campaigns. Both leaders had the support of the Guatemalan left, including its small communist-inspired Labor Party. Perhaps because UFCO and the Guatemalan oligarchy had reacted so virulently to his attempts to advance land reform, Arévalo had proceeded slowly. The Latin America Bureau states that "Arévalo was unwilling to introduce a land reform of any significance. But for the first time legislation was passed to improve the conditions of the labor force, and workers on the foreign-owned plantations and railways were allowed to organize to defend their rights."[28]

Arbenz, elected in 1950 in the first democratic elections that Guatemala had known, felt he had a strong mandate to come through on promised reforms:

> The agrarian reform program began in earnest in 1952, as the Arbenz government moved to bring the peasants more fully into the Revolution. Although the government concentrated on the vast foreign holdings of the lowlands rather than on the native-owned coffee fincas in the populous highlands, the concept of land redistribution struck fear into landlords all across Central America and caused intensification of the movement to terminate the Guatemalan regime.[29]

The land reform of 1952 affected about 1,000 plantations, but involved only "16 percent of the country's total idle cultivable lands in private hands."[30] Arbenz even confiscated and redistributed property belonging to his wife. Approximately 100,000 peasants received land through the reform.

Like the oligarchy, UFCO was furious, even though it was compensated for confiscated holdings. Clearly, Arbenz would have to go. His government, according to UFCO lobbyists, was riddled with communists and was serving as a "beachhead" for Soviet expansion. Arbenz declared that he was not a communist, but the U.S. ambassador to Guatemala, who did not speak Spanish, had a different assessment: "Arbenz thought like a communist and talked like a communist and if not actually one would do until one came along."[31] This line of thinking led Juan Arévalo to compare John Foster Dulles, Eisenhower's Secretary of State, to Joseph Goebbels, Hitler's propaganda minister: "How could the United States refer to a nation of 3 million people as a Soviet satellite when only seven Communists had positions of visibility there?"[32]

But the vast majority of American journalists reporting from Guatemala—many of them on UFCO-funded junkets—would somehow discover the vast power of the communists and, through them, that of the Soviet Union. In a dissenting and more accurate view, the publisher of the *Laredo Times* noted that, "Yes, Guatemala has a very small community of Communists, but not as many as San Francisco."[33]

The presence or absence of communists was not really the point. Members of the U.S. government proceeded to hatch PBSUCCESS, the covert plan to overthrow the government of Arbenz. Although attributed to the CIA, PBSUCCESS was in fact the outcome of close cooperation between the agency, the executive, and the State Department.

Not surprisingly, the entire project could be closely linked to United Fruit. John Foster Dulles, one of the masterminds of PBSUCCESS, was an executive partner of Sullivan and Cromwell, the law firm representing UFCO. This was not mere happenstance. A sort of early twentieth-century Bechtel Corporation, UFCO had just about everyone in its pocket. Secretary of State Dulles' brother Allen had also done legal work for UFCO; after he became director of the CIA, he would do illegal work for the company. Among UFCO's lobbyists, counsels, directors, or shareholders figured Assistant Secretary for Inter-American Affairs Spruille Braden, an important

UFCO lobbyist. Braden's successor, Edward Miller, was also recruited to Washington from Sullivan and Cromwell. Thomas Dudley Cabot, a director and president of UFCO, also served as director of the State Department's Office of International Security Affairs; his brother, John Moors Cabot, served also as Secretary of State for Inter-American Affairs. Walter Bedell Smith, as Undersecretary of State a key cog in the machinery of PBSUCCESS, would later join the board of UFCO. Senator Henry Cabot Lodge of Massachusetts was an UFCO shareholder.

As if these connections were insufficient, UFCO also employed Edward Bernays, later anointed "the father of public relations." Bernays led a campaign, said to cost $500,000 yearly, to publicize the communist menace in Guatemala: "He was extremely successful and, in reality, accomplished for the State Department the propaganda component of its own Guatemalan strategy."[34] Bernays had the help of numerous publishers, including his friend Arthur Hays Sulzberger of *The New York Times*. Publishers and journalists he knew less well were invited to Guatemala as guests of UFCO, with the desired results: "The alleged activities of Communists and mistreatment of United Fruit also received continuous coverage in such prestigious publications as the *Chicago Tribune*, *Time*, *Newsweek*, *U.S. News & World Report*, the *Atlantic Monthly*, and the *Saturday Evening Post*."[35]

Small wonder, then, that, as Richard Immerman notes, "their view was the majority view, accepted by both liberals and conservatives within the government, journalistic, and academic communities."[36] Parallels with the process of reporting on Haiti 40 years later are hardly subtle.

The CIA selected their man. Colonel Carlos Enrique Castillo Armas would lead the invasion from Honduras, which, along with Somoza's Nicaragua, was only too happy to help. Planning for the coup was in essence complete by the time that the *Alfhem*, a Swedish ship carrying arms destined for the Arbenz government, reached Guatemala in May 1954. The United States, increasingly belligerent about the "red peril" in Guatemala, had placed the country under an informal arms embargo—even though its own military advisors to the Guatemalan armed forces remained in place. In addition to the public-relations counsel of UFCO, the U.S. government was also creating the right climate of opinion with the help of the United States Information Agency:

> Despite the lack of lead time, the USIA boasted that, during the month after the *Alfhem*'s arrival, it prepared two hundred articles and backgrounders, designed some twenty-seven thousand anti-Communist cartoons and posters, and developed both films and scripts for media outlets. By means of wireless file, cable, and fast pouch, this propaganda blitz expeditiously reached all parts of the globe. The CIA worked closely with the USIA, pointing out areas where reports criticizing the United States for overreacting had to be countered. Action against Arbenz required a conducive international climate, and the State Department succeeded in establishing it.[37]

On June 18, Castillo Armas's small force crossed the border into Guatemala from Honduras, where it had been encamped on a United Fruit plantation. Although in reality the invaders could not have taken on the Guatemalan armed forces, the CIA had helped to create a different impression with the help of a radio transmitter and also by using U.S. planes to bombard the capital city. Though the ordnance dropped was not significant, the sorties had the intended effect. By June 27, Arbenz was forced to resign, and Castillo Armas was soon installed as president. PBSUCCESS had lived up to its name.

Eisenhower (who according to Dulles "abhor[red] all forms of imperialism") asked his Secretary of State to address the nation on the major television networks. Dulles, notes Immerman, "was at his rhetorical best."

> For this 'new and glorious chapter' in the 'already

great tradition of the American States,' Dulles thanked the OAS, the United Nations Security Council, and, above all, the 'loyal citizens of Guatemala who, in the face of terrorism and violence and against what seemed insuperable odds, had the courage and the will to eliminate the traitorous tools of foreign despots.' He did not thank the CIA.[38]

Arbenz later drowned in his bathtub in Mexico City. Castillo Armas received a ticker-tape parade in New York City, and honorary degrees from Columbia and Fordham universities.

A subsequent Congressional investigation had to prove two things: that there was no U.S. complicity in the coup and that the Arbenz administration had been dominated by communists. This proved easy enough: "Their findings totally exonerated the United States from any charges of complicity and left no room for any interpretation regarding the extent of the Communist threat in Guatemala."[39] In spite of obvious U.S. involvement in the overthrow, U.S. journalists saw no evil, heard no evil: "PBSUCCESS remained one of the administration's best-kept secrets."[40]

Journalistic silence on the CIA's role in the coup could not be attributed to a lack of attention to what was happening in Guatemala. As before the event, there was a great deal of press attention. As Uruguayan writer Eduardo Galeano has noted, shortly after the adventure, *Time* magazine published a poem by the wife of the U.S. Ambassador to Guatemala. "The poem says that Mr. and Mrs. Peurifoy are *optimistic* because Guatemala is no longer *communistic*."[41]

Of the policies of Castillo Armas, much is known. Guided by his mentors from the north, he reinstituted the policies of the predecessors of Arévalo and Arbenz. By 1956, 99.6 percent of the land redistributed in Arbenz's land reform was returned to its original owners.[42] And, as in Haiti, the coup made rich men of the military high command. As historian Ralph Woodward reports,

The military elite began to enter the economy in a major way. Not only did the Generals receive enormous salaries when they served as President (Ydígoras reportedly received $650,000 per year), but they were able to use their positions to acquire private companies, large land holdings, and monopolistic concessions, amassing fortunes in the process. They established their own banks as a further institutional base for their economic interests. The corruption associated with this economic expansion and the wealth of these military officers reached obscene proportions in a country beset with staggering poverty among the majority of its population.[43]

In addition, Castillo Armas outlawed the communist party, several trade unions, and the peasant organizations that had flourished under Arévalo and Arbenz. There were numerous executions and expulsions. "By the end of the decade, Guatemala's union membership had fallen to ten thousand, one-tenth of the total during Arbenz's last year in office. In all of Latin America, only Haiti had fewer organized workers."[44]

The effects of the repression and of the reinstitution of feudalism on the population are also well known: civil war eventually broke out. "Guatemala today resembles an occupied country," observes Immerman. "Government troops, in full battle gear, patrol both the city and the countryside."[45] The troops were doing more than patrolling: in 1982 alone, notes historian Sheldon Liss, in the Quiché Department, the "Indian pacification program accounted for sixty-nine massacres and the destruction of twenty-two Indian villages."[46]

When in January 1980 Maya-Quiché leaders from these communities pacifically invested the Spanish embassy in order to bring attention to these atrocities, General Romeo Lucas García, president of Guatemala, had the embassy burned to the ground. Thirty-nine persons were "roasted alive by the police bombs."[47] The Spanish ambassador had asked the police not to intervene.

As usual, the quasi totality of violence was committed by military or paramilitary forces against civilians. In rural areas, the violence was naked, often involving public executions. In Guatemala City, death squads were preferred. Fred Sherwood, the former president of the American Chamber of Commerce in Guatemala, offered the following comments in September 1980: "Why should we worry about the death squads? They're bumping off the commies, our enemies. I'd give them more power. Hell, I'd give them some cartridges if I could, and everyone else would too...Why should we criticize them? The death squad—I'm for it."[48]

Few could argue that Guatemala has long been a country riddled with inequity. "Arévalo and Arbenz sought to end this injustice through moderate reforms," concludes Immerman. "The CIA's 1954 coup made this moderation impossible."[49] It would appear that even the State Department would have to agree. "If only we had an Arbenz now," sighed one U.S. official in the 1980s. "We are going to have to invent one, but all the candidates are dead."[50]

U.S. foreign policy in Guatemala is no isolated case; similar stories make up the recent history of Chile, the Dominican Republic, Honduras, Nicaragua, Cuba, and Colombia. The zealous transfer of funds to Latin American militaries that torture their own people is by now well-documented. Even more disturbing, perhaps, has been the complicity of the U.S. press in this transfer, a complicity borne out by much current reporting on Haiti.

The experience of El Salvador serves as another case in point. Perhaps no country receiving overt military aid resembles Haiti more than does El Salvador. Both countries are small and agrarian; both are extremely inegalitarian and dependent upon the United States, their chief trading partner. Although Haiti is significantly poorer than El Salvador, most Salvadorans live in poverty. In 1980, as a guerrilla movement arose in response to these features of Salvadoran society, the United States increased its support of that country's army. Our aid was to "professionalize" that army as it sought to suppress the rebel movement. Over the next 12 years, U.S. taxpayers would fund this professionalization and civil war to the tune of $4 billion.[51]

When in 1987 journalists could refer to the "salvadorization" of Haiti, what they had in mind was military complicity in the many massacres and in the organization of death squads. In Haiti, the paramilitary groups' latest moniker is *attachés*—individuals attached, that is, to the army. As elsewhere in Latin America, this link is apparent to all, even though it has often been denied by U.S. administrations. For example, on the eve of the abortive 1987 elections, the following exchange took place between the public-affairs officer of the U.S. embassy and a group of journalists, most of them from the United States or Europe. After the spectacular murders of two presidential candidates, after the civilian electoral council was burned out of its downtown headquarters at midday, the U.S. press almost had to acknowledge what all Haitians knew:

"Who do you think is behind the violence?"

"That would be speculation, wouldn't it?" replied the public-affairs officer. "But obviously there are certain forces who have not been permitted to participate in the elections who may not be happy with that decision."

"You mean the Duvalierists?"

"I mean what I said."

"Then you don't think Namphy is involved in these activities?"

"As I said, we believe that the CNG will guarantee the safety of the these elections."[52]

Precisely this fiction was maintained in El Salvador as well. "There was no secret about who was doing the killing," remarked one public-affairs officer, recalling his stint at the U.S. embassy in San Salvador in the early 1980s. "I mean, you formed that view within forty-eight hours after arriving in the country, and there was no secret at all about it—except maybe in the White House."[53]

"In public," as journalist Mark Danner reveals, "the fiction was resolutely maintained that the identity of the killers was a mystery—that the corpses were the work of 'rightist vigilantes.'"[54] Jeane Kirkpatrick, Reagan's ambassador to the U.N., was downright indignant about the "allegation" that the Salvadoran government was "implicated" in the killings: "And I think its a terrible injustice to the Government and the military when you suggest that they were somehow responsible for terrorism and assassination."[55]

There is troubling resonance, too, between the 1987 killings in Jean Rabel and the 1981 massacre of civilians at El Mozote, a Salvadoran village on the edge of a zone controlled by FMLN forces. Colonel Domingo Monterrosa, who ordered the killing, ran the army's U.S.-trained Atlacatl battalion. Monterrosa was evidently a charismatic figure: "The press loved him," notes Danner. "And, of course, the Americans loved him as well."[56] The battalion was later to distinguish itself by murdering the Jesuit priests who ran the University of Central America, but the slaughter in the remote village of El Mozote was far worse.

The story of El Mozote is at last well-documented. There were, at the time of the killing, at least ten U.S. military advisers working with the Atlacatl, and Danner, writing for the *New Yorker*, interviewed one of them. The soldier spoke of the Salvadoran army's challenge in the area around El Mozote:

> You try to dry those areas up. You know you're not going to be able to work with the civilian population up there, you're never going to get a permanent base there. So you just decide to kill everybody. That'll scare everybody else out of the zone. It's done more out of frustration than anything else.[57]

On December 11, 1981, the soldiers of the Atlacatl Battalion worked out these frustrations on the over 700 villagers who had come to cower in El Mozote from surrounding hamlets. Danner has recounted the whole horrifying tale: summary executions would not suffice; rape and torture punctuated an arduous day of butchery. In El Mozote, only one woman, Rufina Amaya, survived; her husband and children, including a breast-feeding eight-month-old, were shot or bayoneted as they pleaded for mercy. "Though she had told her story again and again," writes Danner, "much of the world had refused to believe her."

Three American journalists, one of them a photojournalist with a camera, came to believe Rufina Amaya. Approximately five weeks after the event, Alma Guillermoprieto of the *Washington Post* traveled to El Mozote in the company of rebel forces. There she found "a stupefying number of bones" in the sacristy of the village church. Most were clearly the bones of children. The gutted houses of the hamlet were full of bodies, as were the surrounding fields. "The most traumatizing thing," said Guillermoprieto in an interview, "was looking at these little houses where whole families had been blown away—these recognizable human beings in their little dresses, just lying there mummifying in the sun."[58]

Raymond Bonner of *The New York Times* preceded Guillermoprieto by a couple of days, but their accounts appeared almost simultaneously. Both reported a massacre of hundreds of civilians by the Salvadoran army's Atlacatl battalion. Photographs by Susan Meiselas accompanied the *Post* story, which included testimony from Rufina Amaya, who, as noted, had seen her husband shot and heard her children killed. She had survived by hiding in undergrowth just a few yards from the carnage.

El Mozote made the front pages of the nation's most influential newspapers just as the Reagan administration was attempting to prove to Congress that the Salvadoran government was making a "concerted and significant effort to comply with internationally recognized human rights." Thomas O. Enders, the Assistant Secretary of State for Inter-American Affairs observed that "Coming on top of everything else, El Mozote, if true, might have destroyed the entire effort."[59] It is not clear if there was any hope of stopping U.S. military aid to the Salvadoran army—the murders of Archbishop Romero and a group of American nuns did not impact U.S. patterns of giving, nor had the deaths of thousands of civilians—but Americas Watch and other human rights groups were doing their best to do so.[60]

Elliott Abrams, at the time U.S. Assistant Secretary of State for Human Rights and Humanitarian Affairs, looked to the embassy in San Salvador for a report to gainsay the embarrassing accounts published in the *Times* and the *Post*. The first author of the embassy's report was a 28-year-old junior reporting officer. In January 1982, he traveled in the company of the Salvadoran army to the area around El Mozote. The soldiers, clearly hiding something, simply refused to take him to the village itself. "People were freaked out and pretty scared about talking, and stuff," commented the official, now at the Nicaragua desk of the State Department. But even these limited exchanges with the villagers "convinced me that there probably had been a massacre, that they lined up people and shot them."[61]

His report, in the form of a lengthy cable over Ambassador Deane Hinton's name, would say otherwise: "Civilians did die during Operation Rescate but no evidence could be found to confirm that Government forces systematically massacred civilians in the operation zone, nor that the number of civilians killed even remotely approached numbers being cited in other reports circulating internationally."[62] The cable offered information to further undermine the press reports, including the observation that El Mozote's population in December was only 300: how, then, could the army have killed between 700 and 1,000 civilians there, as Bonner and

Guillermoprieto had suggested?

This was all that Washington required. Elliott Abrams, after castigating both Bonner and Guillermoprieto, asserted that El Mozote was proof of the manipulation of the U.S. press by the rebels. The case of El Mozote, he said in testimony, "is a very interesting one in a sense, because we found, for example, that the numbers, first of all, were not credible, because, as Secretary Enders notes, our information was there were only three hundred people in the canton."[63]

The Senate Foreign Relations Committee seemed to find Abrams' arguments persuasive, for they immediately "certified" El Salvador's progress in human rights and substantially increased military aid to its army. *The New York Times* recalled Bonner from El Salvador. By 1992, when a peace agreement between the guerrillas and the government was signed, 75,000 Salvadorans had died over the preceding 12 years, the vast majority of them at the hands of their own army.

Not until March 1993, did *The New York Times* see fit to print more about El Mozote. It was then that the United Nations made public the report of its "Truth Commission." Among the many massacres and assassinations investigated was that in El Mozote, where forensic evidence incontrovertibly showed that "more than 500 identified victims" perished on December 11, 1981. The report noted that "many other" victims could not be positively identified. As Mark Danner notes,

> the analysis of the evidence was there, laid out for the reader in clear, precise language, each successive sentence demolishing one or another of the myths put forward during the previous twelve years....

> Finally, of the two hundred and forty-five cartridge cases that were studied—all but one from American M16 rifles—184 had discernible headstamps, identifying the ammunition as having been manufactured for the United States Government at Lake City, Missouri.[64]

The killing of peasants is of a piece with the larger project of the U.S.-backed juntas, the destruction of Salvadoran civil society. Our policies, initiated under Carter and stepped up by Reagan in 1981, permitted the destruction of the non-violent popular movement, the independent press, the labor and peasant movements, and human rights organizations. The student movement was decimated. The U.S.-funded military physically destroyed El Salvador's major public university in June 1980, killing its rector and several faculty members in the process; nine years later it would be the turn of the country's major private university, and its Jesuit leadership would be assassinated in the process. As in Haiti, progressive leaders of the Catholic Church were singled out for special punishment, including the assassination, midmass, of the Salvadoran archbishop. Other priests and religious would also be killed, often after torture and rape.

Sadly, there was nothing unique about El Mozote: "with the popular organizations effectively demolished, the war shifted to direct attacks against the civilian population in guerrilla-controlled areas, including ground sweeps and massacres by U.S.-trained elite units and an expanded air war."[65] Air raids against civilian villages, using U.S.-donated helicopters, introduced napalm, white phosphorus, and other incendiary bombs—with great effect.[66] The long litany of state terror would begin at Río Sumpul—where President Duarte admitted that 300 were killed, "all of them 'Communist guerrillas'—including, presumably, the infants sliced to pieces with machetes"[67]—and continue with the massacres at Río Lempa, Las Vueltas, Los Llanitos, Río Gualsing, La Cayetana, and countless others.

Equally disturbing—and resonant with coverage of Haiti—has been the complicity of the U.S. press. In Danner's account, American journalists, vindicated by the U.N. Truth Commission, emerge as heroes. But a careful review of reporting on El Salvador reveals a consistent pattern of news suppression and of editorial support for U.S. policy in El Salvador. It may be argued that the worst atrocities of this war—including the massacre at Río Sumpul—have not yet been "discovered" by the mainstream U.S. press. Writing of Río Sumpul, where human rights experts suggest that 600 were killed, Chomsky suggests how pervasive such biases were:

> The massacre is not mentioned in the State Department *Country Reports on Human Rights Practices* produced by the Carter Administration and was suppressed by the media for over a year, and then only barely noted, though the facts had been reported shortly after the events in the foreign press and the Church-based press in the U.S. This was just one example of news suppression so extreme that reporting of El Salvador was selected as 'Top Censored Story of 1980' by an annual media research project, and not because there were no reports, but because they were so biased and inadequate.[68]

The experience of Guatemala and El Salvador show that the tumult and pain of contemporary Haiti, though dramatic, are not unprecedented. Some stations of the Haitian poor down their *Via Dolorosa* are distinctive, but others, sadly, are evidenced throughout Latin America. Gunboat diplomacy, military occupation, massacres of the poor and their advocates, violent coups, entrenched feudalism—these are the common leitmotivs of the history of almost all Latin American republics.

Haiti, like other small and dependent nations in the Southern Hemisphere, has long existed to serve the wealthy—if not the wealthy of Haiti, then those of Europe or North America. Haiti exists to provide its clients with tropical produce, raw materials, or cheap labor. Outside of their country, Haitians are useful for cutting cane, cleaning buildings, or driving cabs. Of all the uses of Haiti, these have been the most constant. Similarly, for five centuries now, the poor of Guatemala, El Salvador,

Nicaragua, Bolivia, Peru, and Chiapas have been allowed to survive only so that they may serve the wealthy.

In Haiti, the advent of a popular democracy threatened to interrupt this service function. It did so timidly, certainly, but not timidly enough, to judge by the events of September 1991. What happened then is no great mystery; it has happened again and again elsewhere in the hemisphere. As Father Gustavo Gutiérrez would have it, "The hand of the dominator reaches out ruthlessly to castigate any protest on the part of the oppressed, any attempt at altering a social order that routinely manufactures a poor class."[69]

Perhaps it is dangerous to attempt to embed the brutal events of New World history in any war other than that waged by the rich against the poor. The valuable accounts of the CIA-directed coup in Guatemala and the El Mozote massacre in El Salvador sound a false note in this respect. For example, it's a matter of faith that the CIA-backed overthrow of the Arbenz government is only comprehensible in light of "the cold war ethos," according to Immerman. The massacre of El Mozote, Danner repeatedly informs us, was "a central parable of the Cold War"—just as we were informed that the U.S. funding of the Nicaraguan *contras* was to be understood as part of the Soviet-containment policies of the Reagan and Bush administrations. The 1987 massacre in Jean-Rabel was similarly linked, by its perpetrators, to the struggle between the Russians and the Americans. Progressive commentators and the minions of United Fruit thus tell the *same* story—only the roster of heroes and villains differs.

But the problem with such a historical consensus is that it does not explain the many massacres that took place, in Haiti and in each of these countries, *long before* the Cold War ever began and in the absence of any credible Soviet threat after it had begun. It will not illuminate the massacres that occur even now and will continue to occur in the future, even though the Cold War, we're told, is over.

PART II

A User's Guide to Haiti

We have for once learnt to see the great events of world history from below, from the perspective of the outcast, the suspects, the maltreated, the powerless, the oppressed, the reviled—in short, from the perspective of those who suffer.

—Dietrich Bonhoeffer
Letters and Papers from Prison

Although the privileged of this world can accept the existence of poverty on a massive scale and not be overawed by it (after all, it is something that cannot be hidden away in our time), problems begin when the causes of this poverty are pointed out to them. Once causes are determined, then there is talk of 'social injustice,' and the privileged begin to resist. This is especially true when to structural analysis there is added a concrete historical perspective in which personal responsibilities come to light. But it is the conscientization and resultant organization of poor sectors that rouse the greatest fears and the strongest resistance.

—Gustavo Gutiérrez,
A Theology of Liberation

Since before its war of independence at the end of the eighteenth century, Haiti has been depicted as a singular and isolated place where strange, often bad, things happen. In the first half of this essay, I have attempted to lay the groundwork for a different view of events and processes involving Haiti and Haitians. Bad things certainly happen, and frequently, in Haiti—but rarely in isolation from an international social and economic system of which Haiti is a part. It is impossible, as I have argued, to understand events such as the 1991 coup without a geographically far-ranging and historically deep knowledge of Haiti.

Such perspectives are no less useful in examining the fates of individuals, an exercise to which the rest of this book will be devoted. In fact, the case-history approach confirms that the fates of Haiti and the United States are intertwined in unique and persistent ways. As a physician-anthropologist, I have found this to be true in both the clinic and the field.

The three chapters that follow all start with the experiences of Haitians I have known.[1] My analytic and narrative task is to expose the mechanisms by which abstract and large-scale forces—U.S. intervention, for example—become manifest in the lives of individuals. In starting with the story of Yolande Jean, a political refugee who was detained for a year on Guantánamo, I am in a sense taking the easiest case first. Without doubt, her fate has been affected by U.S. policies; she has been a prisoner on a U.S. military base and describes in harrowing detail her treatment there. But there is much more to the story of Guantánamo than the simple violation of a refugee's rights by a powerful state. Yolande's story speaks directly to an ongoing "debate" about Haitian asylum-seekers.

The second story concerns Chouchou Louis, a young man from central Haiti who was tortured to death a few months after the 1991 coup. Unlike on Guantánamo, these were not U.S. soldiers restraining Chouchou as he was beaten; there had been, at the time of his death, no U.S. military presence in the region in decades. But it is not difficult to expose the effects of U.S. aid to the Haitian army, and these soldiers had received aid aplenty. Chouchou's death is in many ways the direct result of U.S. policies in Latin America—policies that took shape well before the Cold War.

The third chapter tells of Acéphie Joseph's battle

with AIDS, which ended in the spring of 1992. Her case would seem to be a more difficult one to make: the daughter of a poor peasant family, she might appear to have lived in even greater isolation from the international system limned in the previous chapters. But the more one probes, the easier it becomes to see that Acéphie, like Yolande and Chouchou, was fully enmeshed in this system. Shortly before her birth, Acéphie's parents lost their land to a U.S.-financed hydroelectric dam; they were not compensated for their losses, and Acéphie grew up in the abject poverty that resulted, I believe, in her ordeal with HIV. For doubters, there are many other aspects of the story that lend credence to the theses advanced here.

These are three very different cases, but the conclusions to be drawn are quite similar. Poor Haitians all too easily become pawns in a match that has been increasingly open and brutal. The stakes are life and death, but mostly death.

I hope that the personal detail of these chapters—the stories of Yolande and Chouchou and Acéphie—will move readers to reject dominant readings of Haiti. Sadly, the Haitian people find themselves in a position of needing to reach the hearts and minds of North Americans and to persuade them to change the policies that affect Haitians so directly. Such a change will not happen unless *we* ask questions about those modes of seeing that depict the detention of refugees on Guantánamo as a "humanitarian gesture," modes of seeing that might read the story of a young man's torture as having nothing to do with U.S. foreign policy. We should question modes of seeing that depict AIDS as having come *from* Haiti rather than *to* Haiti. All of these notions are expedient, predictable, and quite false. Their success speaks volumes, however, about the power of those who have a stake in perpetuating such chicanery.

On Guantánamo

The awkward fact with which U.S. policy wrestles is that people flee the world's Haitis for a combination of motives. All are deserving of some compassion, but how much?

—*Newsweek,*
December 1, 1991

Haitians are the immigrants that Americans love to fear and hate.

—Robert Lawless,
Haiti's Bad Press

In a situation of occupation or domination, the occupier, the dominant power, has to justify what it's doing. There is only one way to do it—become a racist. You have to blame the victim. Once you've become a raving racist in self-defense, you've lost your capacity to understand what's happening.

—Noam Chomsky,
The Prosperous Few and the Restless Many

More than any convulsion preceding it, the coup of 1991 generated refugees. The fleeing Haitians, mostly young people active in the pro-democracy movement, collided with a series of structures and opinions long in the making. Those who fled Haiti by sea would collide with U.S. immigration policy. At the same time, Haitian boat people would also come up against a host of preexisting notions about Haiti and Haitians—a widely held U.S. "folk model" of Haiti that is clearly reflected in American popular commentary on Haiti from its independence in 1804 to the days of the current crisis.

Perhaps nowhere has this model had greater effect than in the lives of a few hundred HIV-positive Haitians detained for up to two years on the U.S. naval base at Guantánamo Bay, Cuba. "U.S. Base Is an Oasis To Haitians," reads the headline of a November 28, 1991, article in *The New York Times*, often termed our national paper of record. The perspective of Yolande Jean, interned there for eleven months, is somewhat different from that of the *Times*:

> We were in a space cordoned off with barbed wire. Wherever they put you, you were meant to stay right there; there was no place to move. The latrines were brimming over. There was never any cool water to drink, to wet our lips. There was only water in a cistern, boiling in the hot sun. When you drank it, it gave you diarrhea...Rats crawled over us at night...When we saw all these things, we thought, it's not possible, it can't go on like this. We're humans, just like everyone else.[1]

It is first necessary to step back and examine the origins of this "oasis." Guantánamo, an otherwise full-fledged U.S. military base, is located roughly a third of the way between Haiti and Florida on the island of Cuba. In 1903, Guantánamo was leased "indefinitely" to the United States for $2,000 per year, and, by the terms of the lease, is not subject to Cuban laws.[2] Had Yolande Jean been on the other side of the fence separating the base from Cuba, she would not have been expelled, as Cuba does not restrict immigration or entry to those who are HIV-negative. Instead, she might have been placed in an AIDS sanitorium. A recent article from the *New England Journal of Medicine* (which might be termed medicine's journal of record), describes one of these sanitoriums:

> Located in a suburb of Havana, Cuba's main quarantine facility is largely fenced in and is composed of barracks housing hundreds of people. Since inspectors from other nations have not been permitted to report on conditions in the quarantine facility, it is impossible to know how much better or worse they are than those at Guantánamo.[3]

In reality, it is not "impossible to know how much better or worse are conditions than those at Guantánamo." First, it *has* been possible to visit these facilities and to interview HIV-positive persons living there. The Cuban AIDS program has hosted a number of visitors from North America and elsewhere. Most have been highly critical of the sanitoriums, but none of their reports have described conditions as bad as those depicted by the Haitians on Guantánamo. In 1991, anthropologist Nancy Scheper-Hughes interviewed a number of internees in the Santiago de las Vegas sanitorium. The comments of Patricia, the wife of a soldier who contracted HIV infection while doing military service in Africa, were not atypical. Like Yolande Jean, Patricia was asymptomatic and found to be HIV-positive through mass screening. Like Yolande Jean, Patricia was separated from her children. But the tenor of her comments is strikingly different:

> Naturally, one feels homesick. You miss your children a great deal. But our needs and the needs of our children are taken care of and we have to accept our situation with as much good will as we can.

> We celebrate Mother's Day, we go out on excursions to the movies, to the beach, to watch baseball games. And, of course, those of us who are responsible may go home on the weekends or, if you live far away as we do, on a longer visit. Now I feel like I am a stranger when I am away from the sanitorium and walk down the street in my own community.[4]

The above scenarios—that on Guantánamo and that on the outskirts of Havana—would seem to describe settings that are phenomenologically quite distinct. Both, certainly, are found on the same Caribbean island. In both cases, individuals find themselves restrained against their will by a state that uses force in the name of public health. The architects of these policies cannot look to the historical record for support for these approaches, for quarantine has never been shown to be an effective measure in containing sexually transmitted diseases. In short, both Guantánamo and the Cuban

AIDS Program are misguided public health initiatives.

But the similarities evaporate rather quickly upon closer examination of Guantánamo and Santiago de las Vegas. If these two settings are so different, what would lead commentators to suggest that they are similar? In what cultural and political contexts are these commentaries embedded? How are the events on Guantánamo linked to the very logic of quarantine that underlies such responses to HIV infection? What symbolic work do they perform?

The rest of this chapter will attempt to answer these questions by examining the experience of Yolande Jean and other Haitians detained on Guantánamo. As has been the case in previous chapters, there are conflicting accounts, even by eye-witnesses, as to what happened there. But one constant remains: many journalists have distorted this story in predictable ways.

Although Cuba is the stage on which were played out the contrapuntal dramas of Yolande and Patricia, Haiti and the United States are the nations most centrally concerned in the intersection of events and processes that led to Yolande Jean's detention.

The U.S. Immigration and Naturalization Service (INS) has long argued that Haitians are "economic refugees," fleeing poverty. For ten years, including the last four of the Duvalier dictatorship and six years of military juntas, the United States, in defiance of international law, forcibly returned Haitian refugees to their country. This process was the result of an arrangement, brokered in 1981, by which the government of Jean-Claude Duvalier permitted U.S. authorities to board Haitian vessels and to return to Haiti any passengers determined to have violated the laws of Haiti. The United States granted asylum to exactly eight of 24,559 Haitian refugees applying for political asylum during that period.

In the two weeks after the coup of 1991, with the attention of the world press fixed on Haiti, the United

States suspended this practice. As the military continued to arrest and execute partisans of the overthrown President Aristide, refugees streamed out of Haiti, both by sea, to the United States, and by land, to the Dominican Republic. The number displaced in the first three months after the coup has been conservatively estimated at 200,000.

On November 18, 1991, with an estimated 1,500 Haitians already dead in six weeks and military repression churning full throttle, the administration of George Bush announced that it was resuming forced repatriation; those intercepted would be returned to Haiti without being interviewed. The United Nations High Commissioner for Refugees expressed, the following day, his "regrets that the U.S. Government has decided to proceed unilaterally and return a number of asylum-seekers to Haiti."[5] The process was also denounced by human rights organizations, several of which sued the Bush administration when the first groups of refugees were returned to Haiti. The case eventually ended up before the U.S. Supreme Court, which ruled in favor of the U.S. government. Professor Kevin Johnson of the University of California writes of the high court's shameful acquiescence to the Bush administration:

> The courts were the last constitutionally viable means by which to halt the Executive Branch's unlawful treatment of the Haitians. As the constitution mandates, the Judiciary must check the excesses of the Executive. The Rehnquist Court, however, consistently deferred to the Executive Branch on immigration matters and refused to assert the Judiciary's constitutional role in reviewing challenges to the interdiction program. The Haitians, in this instance, suffered from that abdication.[6]

There was little other public outcry about the matter, but human rights advocates were able to force a compromise: the refugees would be brought to the naval base at Guantánamo. Shortly thereafter, scores of canvas tents were erected within the confines of the base. "The military and Coast Guard emphasize that theirs is a humanitarian mission," explained *The New York Times*.[7]

In the eight months following the coup, 34,000 Haitians were intercepted on the high seas by the U.S. Coast Guard; the majority of these refugees were transported to Guantánamo. Conditions in the camp were grim: the inmates lived in tents and other makeshift shelters on a landing strip, surrounded by barbed wire. These shelters, according to the Haitians, were infested with rats, scorpions and snakes. The lodgings let in the rain, and there were no adequate sanitary facilities. Yet, grim though these conditions assuredly were, the detainees' chief complaint concerned mistreatment by their American hosts.

Shortly after the arrival of the first refugees, rumors of mistreatment, including beatings and arbitrary detention, began to filter through Haitian advocacy organizations based in the United States. It was difficult to confirm the rumors, as the U.S. military restricted access to the base. Even as uncritical stories based upon military briefings appeared in the mainstream press, a group of journalists sued the U.S. government for access to the base. Ingrid Arnesen of *The Nation* filed one of the first stories upon visiting Guantánamo. One of the detainees, who had been on the base for over a year, spoke to Arnesen in no uncertain terms:

> Since we left Haiti last December we've been treated like animals. When we protested about the camp back then, the military beat us up. I was beaten, handcuffed and they spat in my face. I was chained, made to sleep on the ground. July, that was the worst time. We were treated like animals, like dogs, not like humans.[8]

In short, the Haitians and their advocates soon failed to see the human aspect of this "humanitarian mission." By the middle of 1992, there were the usual divergent readings of what was happening on the base.

Stories in the mainstream U.S. media continued to portray Guantánamo as a haven for refugees. Haitians, including the Haitian print and radio media, tended to refer to the base as a "concentration camp," a "prison," or, at best, "a detention facility."

Curiously enough, the Bush administration's reading seemed to be more in line with that popular among Haitians. They realized that refugees were being detained on the base for long periods of time—some almost two years—without a meaningful hearing. In response, the administration gathered some of the nation's leading legal talent, not to end but to justify this practice. Since Guantánamo is not technically on U.S. soil, the Bush administration lawyers developed the following rationale:

> While conceding that the Haitians are treated differently from other national groups who seek asylum in the U.S., the Government claimed that the U.S. Constitution and other sources of U.S. and international law do not apply to Guantánamo—this despite the fact that the U.S. military base at Guantánamo is under the exclusive jurisdiction and control of the U.S. Government.[9]

Most Haitians listen to radio; anyone who did so in the early months of 1992 came to know Guantánamo as a place best avoided. Meanwhile, military repression of the Haitian popular movement continued apace: anyone associated with community organizing or the democratic movement was branded as subversive. Yolande Jean's case is instructive. Both Yolande and her husband Athenor were members of *Komite Inite Demokratik*, a democratic organization founded shortly after Duvalier's departure; Yolande was heavily involved in adult literacy projects. After the coup, both Yolande and Athénor were subjected to many threats. On April 27, 1992, Yolande was arrested and taken to Recherches Criminelles, the police station that serves as the headquarters of Colonel Michel François, with whom Haiti's death squads are so intimately associated. The interview was something more than perfunctory; during the course of her torture, Yolande, visibly pregnant with her third child, began to bleed. On her second day in prison, she miscarried.

Yolande decided at that moment that, were she to survive detention, she would flee the country. Perhaps because there was, at the time, a movement among the business elite to resume negotiations to end the embargo, Yolande was released from prison the following day. Shortly thereafter, she stowed her sons with a kinswoman and headed for northern Haiti. Her husband remained in hiding. She would not see him again.

> I took the boat on May 12, and on the 14th, they came to get us. They did not say where they were taking us. We were still in Haitian waters at the time...We hadn't even reached the Windward Passage, when American soldiers came for us. But we thought they might be coming to help us...there were sick children on board. On the 14th, we reached the base at Guantánamo.

Yolande's initial instinct—that the U.S. soldiers "might be coming to help us"—was soon subject to revision: "They burned all of our clothes, everything we had, the boat, our luggage, all the documents we were carrying." U.S. television had displayed images of Haitian boats burning, but the process was described by both the Coast Guard and the media as the destruction of unseaworthy vessels. There was no mention of personal items. When asked what reasons the U.S. soldiers gave for burning the refugees' effects, Yolande replied,

> They gave us none. They just started towing our belongings, and the next thing we know, the boat was in flames. Photos, documents. If you didn't have pockets in which to put things, you lost them. The reason that I came through with some of my documents is because I had a backpack and was wearing pants with pockets. They went through my bag, and took some of my documents. Even my important

papers they took. American soldiers did this. Fortunately, I had hidden some papers in my pockets.

Haiti, as we have seen, was full to overflowing with others just like Yolande Jean. Soon, Guantánamo was full to overflowing as well. On May 24, 1992, President Bush issued executive order number 12,807 from his summer home in Kennebunkport: referring to the Haitian boats, he said that the Coast Guard was "to return the vessel and its passengers to the country from which it came...provided, however, that the Attorney General, in his unreviewable discretion, may decide that a person who is a refugee will not be returned without his consent." As attorney Andrew Schoenholtz of the Lawyers Committee for Human Rights wryly observed, "Grace did not abound; all Haitians have been returned under the new order."[10]

The bottom line: all Haitians leaving Haiti by sea would be intercepted and returned to Haiti without processing by the INS. This was broadcast, in Creole, by the Voice of America affiliates in Haiti. By the summer of 1992, Haitians under the gun understood that they would find no safe haven outside of the country. Haiti resembled more and more a burning building with no exits. The Bush administration's actions—denying to the refugees legal counsel or a hearing, preventing press coverage of the conditions of the detainees—served to reinforce widely-held beliefs that Haitians had been singled out for racist and exclusionary treatment.

In spite of the odds against all Haitians seeking asylum, Yolande Jean's case for refugee status would seem to have been airtight. She was a long-standing member of an organization targeted for political repression; she and her husband had been arrested and tortured; and she had managed to preserve key documents proving this. In fact, Yolande Jean *was* one of those few refugees who passed scrutiny. As a bona fide political refugee, U.S. law provided her safe haven. There was one problem: Yolande, like all the refugees, had been tested for HIV, the virus that causes AIDS.

It was inevitable, really, that AIDS, or fear of it, would figure in the course of the Haitian refugee crisis. In the 1990s, at least one case of HIV infection is certain to be present in any group of over 30,000 young adults from anywhere in the Caribbean. The flow of people and goods and capital through the socioeconomic system described in the first half of this book has always been subject to turbulence, usually introduced at borders. U.S. legislators at state and federal levels have introduced enormous numbers of bills regarding HIV, most of them punitive or restrictive. Although immigration law is in principle strictly separate from laws regarding political refugees, anyone familiar with INS policies toward Haitians could have predicted that screening for HIV would be made mandatory. By the time mass screening of all refugees was completed, the United States government had identified 268 HIV-positive refugees.

Although Yolande and many others had already passed the stringent requirements for refugee status and were thus guaranteed asylum, U.S. immigration law was invoked to keep these Haitians out. In contrast, Cubans who hijack planes to Miami or who appear on U.S. soil through other means are not even tested for HIV. Haitians were quick to point this out.

Immigration legislation regarding HIV has a short and undistinguished history. Although legislation designed to exclude or otherwise punish those with AIDS was introduced shortly after the syndrome was recognized, it was not until 1986 that the Department of Health and Human Services (HHS) was asked to draft laws requiring that aliens seeking to immigrate be tested for and found free of HIV. This legislation was sponsored in the Senate by Senator Jesse Helms and was approved—unanimously—in June, 1987. "This Senate action was extraordinary," notes a legal opinion, "in that it assumed a responsibility, previously entrusted exclusively to the HHS, to determine which communicable diseases would be grounds for excluding aliens."[11]

Public health specialists spoke out against this policy, which they regarded as unwarranted. Debate around this issue led, in fact, to a reconsideration of several other disorders on the list. The U.S. Centers for Disease Control came to argue, by 1990, that HIV and all other sexually transmitted pathogens should not be grounds for exclusion. They recommended that only active pulmonary tuberculosis remain on the list, and a second bill, reflecting their expert opinion, was introduced to congress. Notes lawyer Elizabeth McCormick:

> Opposition to the [second] bill was led by Sen. Jesse Helms, who considered the proposal an attempt to appease the AIDS lobby and the 'homosexual rights movement which fuels it.' Sen. Helms claimed that HHS was not acting in the interest of the public health but was 'promoting an agenda skewed to placate the appetite of a radical and repugnant political movement.'[12]

These debates played themselves out on Guantánamo. Again, the experience of Yolande Jean is instructive, for it reveals the repercussions of both arbitrary laws and arbitrary proceedings:

> They sent me to Camp Number 3, to have a blood test. They didn't specify what test they were doing, but everyone had one. The others [who had been classed as bona fide political refugees] were authorized to leave for the United States. There I was, and they didn't call me...I was the last person left in the Camp. After three days of waiting, they called me. They told me, 'You have a little problem.' They asked my age, they asked for a photo ID. They told me I had a little problem, but they'd send me to see a doctor...and he'd resolve everything for me. After 22 days, they said, you'll be fine, you'll go to the United States. I asked what sort of problem they were referring to. They said 'It's a little virus you have.' I replied there's no such thing as a 'little virus,' speak clearly

so that I can understand. They put me in a small room, and 8 soldiers surrounded me...I told them not to touch me. Don't worry, they said, you'll be cured. I told them to speak clearly so that I could understand. Even the interpreter couldn't explain. Tell me! I see what you're saying—that I have AIDS. Fine, I have AIDS. Don't tell me, then, that you'll cure me. That in 22 days I'll be fine! At that point, two military police turned me around, grabbed me by both arms in order to put me on the bus for [Camp] Bulkeley.

Out of encounters such as this was born the "HIV detention camp" on Guantánamo, Camp Bulkeley. Inmates were given new bracelets identifying them as HIV-positive. Yolande Jean insists that, "They were even harsher with us than with the others," and a group of American lawyers concurred: "[starting] in February 1992 those testing positive were interviewed and required to meet a higher standard to establish that they had a 'well-founded fear' of persecution. The Immigration and Naturalization Service denied requests by the refugees' attorneys to be present at these interviews."[13]

In the spring of 1993, Judge Sterling Johnson, a Bush appointee who years earlier had himself been an officer on Guantánamo, heard the case brought against the U.S. government by the Haitians and their advocates. The more depositions he heard, the more convinced he became that the detentions of the HIV-positive Haitians represented "cruel and unusual punishment" in violation of the Eighth Amendment of the U.S. Constitution. In his 1993 ruling on the case, the judge described Camp Bulkeley as follows:

They live in camps surrounded by razor barbed wire. They tie plastic garbage bags to the sides of the building to keep the rain out. They sleep on cots and hang sheets to create some semblance of privacy. They are guarded by the military and are not permitted to leave the camp, except under military escort. The Haitian detainees have been subjected to pre-dawn military sweeps as they sleep by as many as 400 soldiers dressed in full riot gear. They are confined like prisoners and are subject to detention in the brig without hearing for camp rule infractions."[14]

As terrible as this sounds, the stories told by the Haitians interned there are even worse. While U.S. press wrote of the detainees as unfortunates caught in a bureaucratic limbo, the Haitians spoke of more active processes. Yolande Jean recalled the events of July 18, 1992:

> We had been asking them to remove the barbed wire; the children were playing near it, they were falling and injuring themselves. The food they were serving us, including canned chicken, had maggots in it. And yet they insisted that we eat it. Because you've got no choice. And it was for these reasons that we started holding demonstrations.

> In response, they began to beat us. On July 18th, they surrounded us, arrested some of us, and put us in prison, in Camp Number 7... Camp 7 was a little space on a hill. They put up a tent, but when it rained, you got wet. The sun came up, we were baking in it. We slept on the rocks; there were no beds. And each little space was separated by barbed wire. We couldn't even turn around without being injured by the barbed wire.

For the Haitian refugees, then, Guantánamo represented a health hazard rather than an oasis. Even without subjecting the detainees to privations such as those described, it was unsafe to keep over 200 HIV-positive persons cramped together in such close quarters. This brings to the fore the question of medical care for the HIV-positive refugees and their dependents: Who was providing it, and how?

The camp was served by a Battalion Aid Station clinic staffed by two military physicians, one specializing in infectious disease and another in family practice. Again, commentary on this version of the doctor-patient relationship tends to appear as positioned rhetoric. To quote the *New England Journal of Medicine*:

> That the military physicians worked hard to treat the Haitians at the camp was not in dispute. Nonetheless, Judge Johnson concluded that 'the doctor-patient relationship has been frustrated.' The Haitians believed that the military physicians were involved in their continued detention, and there were also great cultural differences between the physicians and the Haitian patients. As a result, the patients did not trust either their diagnosis or the medications pre-scribed for them.[15]

In all that regards Haiti, as we have noted, attributing diverging interpretations of a situation to "great cultural differences" has been a recurrent theme. But Yolande Jean did not refer, even once, to cultural differences as an explanation of the substandard medical care:

> They gave me two pills and an injection. I asked them, why the injection? Because you have a little cold, they replied. But it wasn't a vaccine, it was an injection in the buttocks. And if you didn't want it, you had no choice: they simply said, it's for your own good, you have to accept it, or they call soldiers to come and hold you, force you to take it or they put you in the brig and bring your pills to you there. There were people who refused to have their blood drawn; soldiers came to handcuff them, tie them up in order to draw their blood.
>
> I learned that the injection the doctor had given me was Depo-Provera.[16] I began having heavy bleeding, I bled for three months, lost weight. There were other women who'd had the injection before me, but I didn't know that. If I'd learned of this ahead of time, I would've tried to warn the others and prevent their receiving it...When I learned this, I tried to stop them. No, I said, you will not commit this crime.

The degree to which cultural difference is invoked serves as a marker, it seems, for the degree to which commentators are uncomfortable with full exposure of what happened on Guantánamo. It never figured in the commentaries of the Haitians, even though the concept of cultural distinctness is widely deployed in Haiti. The refugees interviewed spoke of forced blood draws and forced medication; they spoke of the brig, of solitary confinement, of barbed wire. And yet, even the Haitians' advocates—their lawyers— failed to capture the refugees' outrage over this treatment. To quote one of the Haitians' lawyers:

> The military doctors are probably moved by humanitarian and population control objectives. On the one hand, the doctors may be concerned that HIV+ refugee women who get pregnant pose a serious health risk to themselves and their babies. On the other hand, the doctors are also undoubtedly eager to limit the growth rate of the refugee population on Guantánamo, particularly because it is a population which has a high prevalence of HIV infection.[17]

In June 1992, the prisoners, organized by, among others, Yolande Jean, began holding peaceful demonstrations. These were met, according to those interviewed, with intimidation, open threats, and detention in the brig. In July, the prisoners rioted, and responded to the soldiers' dogs and aluminum batons with rocks. About 20 inmates were arrested and placed in Camp 7, in near-solitary confinement.

Outcry over Guantánamo came late, but it eventually became an issue in the 1992 U.S. presidential election. Prior to the adoption of the cynical *Realpolitik* of President Clinton, the official platform of the Clinton-Gore ticket qualified George Bush's treatment of the Haitian refugees as "inhuman." One of the planks, called simply, "Stop the Forced Repatriation of Haitian Refugees," read as follows:

- Reverse Bush Administration policy, and oppose repatriation.

- Give fleeing Haitians refuge and consideration

for political asylum until democracy is restored
to Haiti. Provide them with safe haven, and
encourage other nations to do the same.[18]

Elsewhere, the platform also quite specifically
promised to "Stop the cynical politicization of federal
immigration policies. Direct the Justice Department to
follow the Department of Health and Human Services'
recommendation that HIV be removed from the immigration restrictions list."[19]

As the presidential campaign heated up, it became
clear that Clinton's proposed policy toward Haitian
refugees would not be his most popular one. The cover of
the September 1992, edition of *USA Today* carried a photograph of a huddled mass of Haitian refugees, some of
them children, on the decks of a Coast Guard cutter. "As
compassionate as Americans try to be," asked the cap-
tion, "can we realistically afford an open border policy?"[20]
One read, in some newspapers, of "the outrage over treatment of the Haitian refugees," but this outrage was
strangely absent from other manifestations of public opinion, which may have been more accurately reflected in the
comments of immigration officials. One Associated Press
reporter interviewed Duke Austin, special assistant to the
director of congressional and public affairs at the INS. Mr.
Austin could not understand all the fuss about the HIV-
positive internees: "They're gonna die anyway, right?"[21]

In the same edition announcing "Boat with 396
Haitians Missing; Cuba reports 8 survivors," the *Orlando
Sentinel* wrote of "what could be a huge problem for the
state: An explosion of Haitian migrants to South Florida."
The story, which ran on the front page, continued by noting that "Many fear that tens of thousands of refugees
could sail for Miami around Inauguration Day, Jan. 20,
because of President-elect Bill Clinton's pledge to give
Haitians a fair hearing for political asylum in the United
States."[22] On January 28, however, Clinton began
backpedaling, stating that he would be continuing his

predecessor's policies. Hearing of this, a number of refugees began a hunger strike. Yolande Jean was the leader of this movement:

> Before the strike, I'd been in prison, a tiny little cell, but crammed in with many others, men, women, and children. There was no privacy. Snakes would come in; we were lying on the ground and lizards were climbing over us. One of us was bitten by a scorpion...there were spiders. Bees were stinging the children, and there were flies everywhere: whenever you tried to eat something, flies would fly into your mouth. Because of all this, I just got to the point, sometime in January, I said to myself, come what may, I might well die, but we can't continue in this fashion. We called together the committee, and decided to have a hunger strike. Children, pregnant women, everyone was lying outside, rain or shine, day and night. After 15 days without food, people began to faint, the colonel called us together and warned us, and me particularly, to call off the strike. We said no. At four in the morning, as we were lying on the ground, the colonel came with many soldiers. They began to beat us—I still bear a scar from this—and to strike us with nightsticks...True, we threw rocks back at them, but they outnumbered us and they were armed. They then used big tractors to back us against the shelter, and they barred our escape with barbed wire.

Yolande Jean was arrested and placed in solitary confinement. This version did not make it into *The New York Times*, which reported only that "at least seven Haitian refugees protesting their detention here by refusing food have lost consciousness."[23] No mention was made of any retribution on the part of the strikers' wardens.

Even the Haitians' lawyers, who reached the base in the middle of the strike, seemed a bit annoyed by their actions. "The hunger strike took us all by surprise, especially given the fact that the litigation team is in the middle of settlement negotiations with the Department of

Justice."[24] The Haitians, it seems, were no longer impressed by bureaucratic efforts to have them released. They continued what they termed "active, non-violent resistance." On March 11, eleven prisoners attempted to escape to Cuba, but were recaptured. Two of the detainees tried to commit suicide, one by hanging. A letter from Yolande Jean to her family was widely circulated in the community of concern taking shape in response to the situation on Guantánamo:

> To my family:
>
> Don't count on me anymore, because I have lost in the struggle for life. Thus, there is nothing left of me. Take care of my children, so they have strength to continue my struggle, because it is our duty.
>
> As for me, my obligation ends here. Hill and Jeff, you have to continue with the struggle so that you may become men of the future. I have lost hope; I am alone in my distress. I know you will understand my situation, but do not worry about me because I have made my own decision. I am alone in life and will remain so. Life is no longer worth living to me.
>
> Hill and Jeff, you no longer have a mother. Realize that you don't have a bad mother, it is simply that circumstances have taken me to where I am at this moment. I am sending you two pictures so you can look at me for a last time. Goodbye my children. Goodbye my family. We will meet again in another world.

The Haitians' advocates, including Haitian refugee groups in the eastern United States, stepped up their pressure. On March 26, 1993, Judge Johnson of New York again ruled against the administration. He ordered that all detainees with fewer than 200 total T-lymphocytes be transferred to the United States. It was the first time that T-cell subsets were mentioned in a judicial order.[25]

Finally released from internment by the direct order of a federal judge, the refugees came in small groups,

Yolande almost directly from solitary confinement, arriving on the American mainland before dawn on April 8, 1993. At the beginning of the summer, over 150 Haitians still remained on the base, and a second hunger strike was initiated. Eventually, these actions, in concert with the legal and moral pressures brought to bear on the U.S. government, led to the closing of what Judge Johnson would call "the only known refugee camp in the world composed entirely of HIV-positive refugees." Like its predecessor, the Clinton administration had failed to prove that Haitians like Yolande Jean warranted "the kind of indefinite detention usually reserved for spies and murderers."[26]

What of the Cuban AIDS sanitoriums with which Camp Bulkeley was so often compared? The first case of AIDS registered in Cuba was reported in 1986. By the time a tourism worker who made frequent trips to New York fell ill with infections suggestive of the syndrome, a Cuban plan to quarantine people with HIV infection was already being elaborated. Millions of Cuban citizens were screened, and all seropositive persons were expected to accept internment (although an exception was made for one young mother of several young children).[27]

The sanitoriums visited by Dr. Scheper-Hughes—which have been described in similar terms by U.S. journalists—are said to resemble modern apartment complexes.

> The sanitorium was a large, enclosed community of several acres with modern, two-story apartment duplexes surrounded by lush vegetation, palm trees, and small gardens. Some of the apartments and structures were similar to ones we had visited earlier in the week that were being constructed for foreign athletes in preparation for the Pan-American Games in late summer. The AIDS complex resembled, in fact, many of the suburban, middle class housing developments one sees in Mexico and Brazil. The main difference, of course, was that *this* community was encircled by a gate.[28]

In the facility found in Santiago de las Vegas, where Patricia, the HIV-positive soldier's wife, was interned, all apartments were equipped with color televisions and air conditioning. The inmates were cared for by a team of specialists, including a number of HIV-positive physicians and nurses who were themselves "patients" in the sanitorium. Multi-pronged treatment plans were elaborated, with antiviral medications universally available. Dr. Julie Feinsilver, professor of politics at Oberlin College, describes the AIDS sanitoriums in her recent book on the Cuban health care system:

> ...patients confined to the sanitorium are paid their normal salary even though they can no longer work, and they do not have to pay for either residency or treatment. When possible, they work or study within the confines of the sanitorium, but many have no occupation other than recreational handicrafts. Many Cubans oppose quarantine simply because they resent what they perceive to be the "good life" of those in the sanitoriums who are not yet symptomatic.[29]

In July 1993, the Cuban Ministry of Health announced a change in its AIDS policy. People diagnosed with HIV infection would come to a designated facility for treatment and counseling. Afterwards, they would be permitted to return to their home communities. When current residents were offered the option of leaving, most declined to do so. Two recent books about Cuba document the refusal of inmates to leave and even the bizarre practice of auto-injecting contaminated blood. French journalists Jean-François Fogel and Bertrand Rosenthal interviewed a number of young people, some of whom claimed to have intentionally infected themselves:

> E.L and his friends injected themselves with the virus in order to live in a 'sidatorium'[30] (room, board, laundry, color television, allowance of 110 pesos per month). They had heard, who knows where, that the life expectancy of a seropositive [person] is seven

years. Between now and then, they thought, an anti-
dote or a treatment would be discovered. In the interim, they would enjoy a tranquil life and find some
affection or at least the attention of the medical staff.[31]

This anecdote certainly speaks eloquently to the alien-
ation of certain young people in Cuba today. But the curious comparison of Guantánamo to the Cuban AIDS program is equally evocative. The use of sanitoriums may be a
misguided public health intervention, as might be contact-
tracing, but these are not perforce crimes against humanity. Detaining the sick in concentration camps where they
are denied effective care, however, is a crime. Drawing
blood and giving injections against the expressed wishes of
the imprisoned, and using force to do so, are usually
classed as violations of human rights, as are beating and
imprisoning persons because they are HIV-positive.

A glance at history reminds us that there is nothing
unusual about the use of quarantine to contain diseases,
even those that are not easily transmitted to others.
What I would like to explore, then, is less the state's use
of force and more the nature of the social responses to
that restraint. Again, I will focus on the case of
Guantánamo. But it is important to note, in passing,
that Cubans and Haitians have very different ways of
seeing medicine. Authors such as Yale University's David
Apter have noted that, in Cuba, an "exceptionally high
level of medical research and health care has become the
central focus of the regime."[32] Visitors to Cuba are often
struck by the population's fascination with and faith in
medical science. To again cite Scheper-Hughes, speaking
of one of the patients in the Santiago de las Vegas sanitorium: "Like most Cubans we met, Jose's faith in science
and biotechnology was, to say the least, awesome."[33]

Yolande Jean and her fellow inmates on
Guantánamo, in stark contrast, felt that Haitians were
the preferred guinea pigs of the United States: "As if we
were monkeys, they try out medications on us to see if
they're effective. If they work, great; if not, we're dead."

Such "conspiracy theories" have been well documented in the ethnographic literature on AIDS.[34]

In attempting to understand the differences between U.S. and Cuban responses to AIDS, anthropologist Scheper-Hughes discerns

> two competing and perhaps incompatible political-moral systems, one (the U.S.) characterized by a cultural and political ethos and a bioethical position that privileges *individual rights* above all else, and the other (Cuba) characterized by a cultural and political ethos and a bioethical position that privileges *social responsibility* and some notion of the 'common good' above all else.[35]

But the Haitian story complicates the picture significantly, raising a host of questions regarding a complex symbolic web linking xenophobia, racism, and a surprisingly coherent "folk model" of Haitians held by many North Americans. For certain individuals—and nearly all Haitians fall into this category—the American bioethical obsession with individual rights is easily waived.

In analyzing these issues one by one, it is useful to examine the use of the U.S. legal system to buttress an illegal policy towards Haitians. The policies elaborated by the Bush administration invoke the rule of law more often than moral principles, but they violate a number of preexisting laws. Among the many U.S. and international laws violated by the forced repatriation of self-proclaimed refugees are the Immigration and Nationality Act and the United Nations Convention Relating to the Status of Refugees. An American human rights lawyer summarizes the legal case to be made against his government's policy:

> The U.S. policy of forced repatriation violated international legal obligations of the United States under Article 33 of the Protocol relating to the status of Refugees and undermines the credibility of the U.S. commitment to international law in the eyes of the rest of the world. The United States correctly con-

demned the forced repatriation of Vietnamese asylum-seekers from Hong Kong following flawed screening procedures and also criticized the Malaysian and
Thai governments for pushing back boats filled with
Vietnamese asylum-seekers. The horrific human
rights violations since the September 1991 coup render especially cruel the U.S. practice of forcibly repa-
triating all Haitians without even attempting to determine who among them might fear persecution at the
very hands of the Haitian armed forces waiting for
them at the dock in Port-au-Prince.[36]

Another lawyer puts it succinctly: "By treating
Haitians differently than any other refugee group, the
U.S. government has created a two-track asylum
process—one for Haitians and one for everyone else."[37]

With legal opinions such as these, how, precisely,
did two consecutive U.S. administrations manage to
detain people like Yolande Jean? Certainly, U.S. lawmakers seem to support the exclusion of HIV-positive
entrants: A February 1993 vote on a proposal to remove
HIV infection from the list of diseases for which an immi-
grant may be excluded failed in the Senate by a vote of
76 to 23. Not surprisingly, opposition to the bill was led
by Senator Jesse Helms.

But popular support for these policies is also disturbingly strong. When public health officials recommended that HIV be removed from the list of diseases for
which entrants could be excluded, there was a brisk
response: "During a thirty day public comment period following the issuance of Dr. Sullivan's proposal, the HHS
received 40,000 letters in opposition to the elimination of
HIV infection as a ground for exclusion of aliens."[38]

The persistent notion of Haitians as infected and,
more importantly, *infecting*, has clearly underpinned
much of the American response. One does not need to be
an anthropologist to notice the easy dominance of folk
categories and prejudices over facts and notions of equi-
ty. Another lawyer has acutely observed that "The exclu-

sion of HIV-infected Haitian refugees flows from the once firmly held perceptions that Haiti is the birthplace and primary source of that HIV virus and that most Haitian refugees are fleeing economic hardship rather than political persecution."[39]

With or without HIV, Haitians are not welcome, it would seem. As mentioned earlier, South Florida newspapers were full of alarmist headlines, such as that from the January 11, 1991, *Orlando Sentinel*: "South Florida braces for Haitian time bomb." More recently, the August 9, 1993 edition of *Newsweek* consecrated its cover story to the "Immigration Backlash." "A Newsweek Poll: 60% of Americans Say Immigration is 'Bad for the Country.'" Haitians fared especially poorly in the sympathy sweepstakes. *Newsweek* pollsters asked, "Should it be easier or more difficult for people from the following places to immigrate to the U.S.?," and offered respondents a list of regions or continents. Only Haiti and China were singled out by name; Haiti fared poorly. Contrary to the rumor of a "ground swell of revulsion" over ill-begotten policy towards Haitians, 20 percent of those polled said Haitian immigration should be made easier, while 55 percent said it should be more difficult. After a decade during which less than half of one percent of applicants were granted asylum, one wonders how much more difficult it could be.

It is clear that both Bush and Clinton administration officials were aware of these sentiments. One of the lawyers for the Haitian group made the following observation:

> [Department of Justice] officials indicated that they still had no position as to whether the [Clinton] Administration would be defending the Guantánamo policy in the trial scheduled for March. However, they made it clear that if they decide to defend it, they believe they would be on the right side of public opinion because the public doesn't care about Haitians with HIV.[40]

I think they were dead right.

Indeed, the "HIV Prison" on Guantánamo is not the first Haitian concentration camp. In the late 1970s, well before AIDS was first described, Haitian refugees were denied welcome into the United States, and many were detained by the U.S. Immigration and Naturalization Service:

> Although the seventies were a time when immigrants in general came under attack, immigrants other than Haitians were not detained simply because of their nationality; Haitians, however, were rounded up and placed in federal "detention centers" that were in fact concentration camps. Haitians were portrayed as ragged, wretched, and pathetic and were said to be illiterate, superstitious, disease-ridden and backward peasants.[41]

Any discussion of Guantánamo must necessarily lead to a number of "moral" considerations, but these can be left to other forums. Here it is more imperative to examine the mechanisms by which certain accounts, such as the one that depicts Guantánamo as "an oasis for Haitians," become *dominant*. Our inquiry into the case of Yolande Jean leads us rather easily toward theoretical questions, which concern, by and large, the modes of analysis best used to examine Guantánamo and the nature of symbolic production. The workings of the symbolic code are easily discerned in the various commentaries about Guantánamo; all of these commentaries, it would seem, are not of equal weight.

In writing of competing versions, Jean Baudrillard has claimed that "one is not the simulacrum and the other the reality: there are only simulacra...What we have now is the disappearance of the referent."[42] Baudrillard suggests that a discernible reality is lost in the recapitulation of events; but the referent on Guantánamo is not so obliterated that the ethnographer

cannot question such constructions as the "public outrage" narrative described above. Yolande Jean's account
of Guantánamo gives the lie to such constructions. The
trickle of public outrage against the U.S.-sponsored violation of Haitian detainees' rights paled in comparison to
the 40,000 postage stamps worth of outrage against liberal lawmakers who wished to allow HIV-positive
refugees into this country.

How does Yolande Jean's experience speak to the
central theses of this book? As reflected in the life of
Yolande Jean, Washington, Guantánamo and Port-au-
Prince are all part of the same civilization. The very existence of Guantánamo—a U.S. military base in the middle
of a small country supposedly hostile, a threat, to the
United States—reminds us that the real unit of analysis
required to understand processes taking place in the
Caribbean and in Latin America is not the nation-state,
but, rather, complex systems tied intimately to an international capitalism dominated, at the moment, by U.S.
capital and U.S. policies.

There are other obvious conclusions, such as the
importance, to any but the most superficial symbolic
analyses, of history and political economy. How are we to
make sense of these curious processes without some
understanding of the past century's history of U.S.-
Haitian relations? Of the push-pull forces that move both
people and viruses throughout an international web of
social and economic relations? But even more pressing
are questions of representation and interpretation of the
events and processes that have marked the lives of
Yolande Jean and many other Haitians.

That there will be dominant and oppositional
accounts of what has happened on Guantánamo is self-
evident; that the accounts of the powerful will be under-
girt by solid institutional supports, by those who control
the chief modes of symbolic production, is equally unsurprising. But there are interesting and unexpected twists.
On Guantánamo, the so-called "oppositional" voices,

when coming from the advocates of the Haitians rather than the Haitians themselves, are strikingly similar to the dominant voices more intimately linked to state power. The narrative structure is similar, even if the conclusions reached are ostensibly different. Much of the oppositional criticism of Guantánamo leaves the reader with the impression that the U.S. military, including their doctors, were themselves frustrated victims of bureaucratic snarls. The image offered is of unfortunates languishing on a base, and not that of active, malignant harassment.

For example, medico-legal specialist George Annas offers the following assessment in the *New England Journal of Medicine*: "That the military physicians worked hard to treat the Haitians at the camp was not in dispute."[43] But in fact this *was* in dispute, as Yolande's account reveals. The detainees themselves have an altogether different version of what transpired on Guantánamo, a version that is all too often lost in journalistic and scholarly accounts.

Narratives from the powerful, including their journalistic versions, inevitably reveal what Noam Chomsky has called "necessary illusions"; to partake fully in the "system" as a professional of any sort is to remain to some extent accountable to it. And so the conclusion of one of the Haitians' lawyers is not surprising: "We need to convince the Clinton people that what we want is reasonable and cost-effective."[44] No point, apparently, in convincing the Clinton people that the events on Guantánamo are an abomination and a crime. Journalists know this; lawyers know this.

In their earnest efforts to convince the empowered that their solution was "reasonable and cost-effective," the Haitians' advocates are misrepresenting Guantánamo. They are making the naval base resemble a sanatorium—a misguided public health intervention—when in fact it represents a much more malignant expression of our long-standing policies toward Haitians.

Chouchou Louis and the Political Economy of Brutality

Violent deaths are natural deaths here. He died of his environment.

—Dr. Magiot,
in Graham Greene's *The Comedians*

Well before the USS *Harlan County* retreated from Haitian waters on October 11, 1993, local Haitian newspapers and radio were buzzing with rumors of an imminent military occupation. Rumors contended that the "Americans" (or "the United Nations") were soon to send in an armed force. Some observed that the troops were meant to protect deposed president Jean-Bertrand Aristide when he was restored to his elected duties; others believed that these soldiers would protect the entrenched Haitian military from the alleged "mob vengeance" they said would occur if Aristide returned.

Many diplomatic observers noted that the U.N.-brokered action would represent the first time an international peacekeeping force was dispatched to a country not in the midst of a civil war. But as anyone familiar with Caribbean history was aware, the assignment of foreign military personnel to Haiti was in no real way unprecedented. In addition, a few would even pose the question of whether the situation in Haiti in the early 1990s represented a civil war—a war in which only one side was armed. International human rights groups estimate that, since the Cédras coup, more than 3,000 Haitians have died, all but a tiny number of them civilians killed by military or paramilitary forces. This number does not include those killed in rural areas, where no journalist or observer has been permitted to work since the coup. I doubt, for example, that this figure includes Chouchou Louis, a Haitian peasant who coughed up a great deal of blood on the morning of January 26, 1992.

Others should tell Chouchou's story, as I did not know the young man well. But since Chouchou was killed in a country where 80 percent of the peasantry are kept illiterate, he knew no one else who could put his story to paper. There were, when he died, no U.N.or OAS observers present, nor have they or anyone else investigated his murder. And since Chouchou was tortured to death in a country where a once-vibrant press is now silent, I take it upon myself to lay out the facts as I see them.

Chouchou's common-law wife, Chantal, is my patient. Like far too many poor women in rural Haiti, Chantal has pulmonary tuberculosis, and my colleagues and I have been treating her at a village clinic for the past several years. She had been doing well until the father of her baby died slowly in their two-room hut, situated in a village not too far from the clinic, leaving Chantal with the unpleasant task of raising their infant daughter alone.

Chantal later filled me in on her husband's life story. Chouchou Louis grew up in a small village in the Central Plateau's *mòn*, as the steep and infertile highlands in Haiti are termed. Chouchou attended primary school for a couple of years, but was obliged to drop out when his mother died. At that time, Chantal guesses, he was in his early teens; he joined his father and an older sister in tending their hillside gardens. In short, there was nothing remarkable about Chouchou's childhood; it was short and harsh, like most of them, and all too soon he found himself weeding at his father's side.

Throughout the 1980s, church activities formed Chouchou's sole distraction. He must have been about 20 years old when Duvalier fell, and Chantal recalls that he acquired a small radio shortly thereafter. Like many other area youth, Chouchou became a news junkie. "All he did," recalls Chantal, "was work the land, listen to the radio, and go to church. I met him when he came to [her home village] on a church outing." In early 1989, Chouchou moved in with Chantal, who was pregnant.

Like most rural Haitians, Chouchou and Chantal Louis welcomed the election of Aristide with great joy. The young man, especially, was familiar with the details of Haitian politics, as he had for years followed Aristide's trajectory. Chouchou regarded the priest as something of a prophet, and was sure that, as president, he would be Haiti's savior.

These are the very reasons why the coup of September 1991, stirred great anger in the countryside. Anger soon gave way to sadness, and then fear, as the repressive machinery of rural Haiti, dismantled under Aristide, was hastily reassembled under the patronage of the army.

In the month after the coup, Chouchou was sitting in a truck en route to the town of Hinche. Chouchou offered for the consideration of his fellow passengers what Haitians call a *pwen*, a pointed remark intended to say something other than what it literally means. As they bounced along, he began complaining about the conditions of the roads, stating that "if things were as they should be, these roads would have been repaired already." One eyewitness later told me that at no point in the commentary was Aristide's name invoked. But Chouchou's complaints were recognized by his fellow passengers as veiled language deploring the coup. Unfortunately for Chouchou, one of the passengers was an out-of-uniform soldier.

Military checkpoints are scattered throughout Haiti. State power is made manifest in the lives of the peasantry in many ways, but especially vividly and predictably at these checkpoints. In times of relative peace, it is here that "taxes" may be levied on whatever produce or goods peasants carry to market. In times of unrest, such as now, military checkpoints are centers of brutali-

ty. On this particular day in October 1991, Chouchou
had no idea what was coming when, at the next checkpoint, the out-of-uniform soldier had him seized and
dragged out of the truck.

Other soldiers and their *attachés* immediately began
beating Chouchou, in front of the other passengers, and
they continued to beat him as they brought him to the
military barracks in Hinche. The Hinche barracks, and
indeed all soldiers and *attachés* in the Central Plateau,
fall under the jurisdiction of Major Charles Josel, known
locally as *Zed*: "Commander Z is perhaps the most notorious provincial military chief in Haiti. Promoted from
captain to major several months after the coup, he gave
himself the nickname 'Z'; like the last letter of the alpha-
bet, nothing is needed after him—he is the final authority."[1] Commander Z's job, after the coup, was to extirpate
pro-Aristide sentiment, which would prove a Herculean
task. With Chouchou, the approach was torture. A scar
on his right temple was a souvenir of his stay in Hinche,
which lasted several days.

Perhaps the worst after-effect of episodes of brutality
is that, in general, they mark the beginning of persecution, not the end. In rural Haiti, any scrape with the law
(i.e., the military) leads to a certain blacklisting. If the section chief is not the person who makes an arrest, as is
usually the case, then he is certainly charged with subsequent surveillance of the offender. Their duties are officially listed as follows: (1) the protection of people and
property of their communal section; (2) the guarding of
livestock and gardens; (3) the maintenance of order and
public peace. Over the years, the section chiefs have of
course taken on an altogether different portfolio:

> In fact, a section chief has life and death power over
> the residents of his section. He often serves as *de
> facto* executive, legislature and judiciary to the popu-
> lation under his command. Section chiefs do not refer
> cases to the judicial system; rather, they make

arrests, detain prisoners, conduct trials and settle disputes. According to a former U.S. embassy official in Port-au-Prince, 'section chiefs are at the heart of the human rights violations in Haiti.'"[2]

For men like Chouchou, remaining out of jail often involves keeping the local section chief happy, and he did this by avoiding his home village. But Chouchou lived in fear of a second arrest, Chantal later told me, fears that proved to be well-founded.

He did not have long to worry. On January 22, 1992 Chouchou was visiting his sister in his home village when he was arrested by the section chief and an *attaché*. No reason for the arrest was given, and Chouchou's sister regarded as ominous the seizure of the young man's watch and radio. Chouchou was roughly marched to the nearest military *avant poste*, where he was tortured by soldiers and the section chief. One area resident later told Chantal that the prisoner's screams made her children weep with terror.

The army, which "released" the moribund man on January 25, scarcely took the trouble to circulate a rumor that he had stolen some bananas. Although Chantal qualified this accusation as complete fiction, this was the version we expected to hear on the radio. But since the Haitian press was by then so thoroughly muzzled, not even a false version was broadcast.

On January 26, Chouchou, a handsome man in his mid-twenties, was scarcely recognizable. His face, and especially his left temple, was misshapen, swollen and lacerated; his right temple was also scarred, although this was clearly an older wound. Chouchou's mouth was a coagulated pool of dark blood; he coughed up more than a liter of blood in his agonal moments. Lower down, his neck was peculiarly swollen, his throat collared in bruises, the traces of a gun butt. His chest and sides were badly bruised, and he had several fractured ribs. His genitals had been mutilated.

That was his front side; presumably, the brunt of the beatings came from behind. Chouchou's back and thighs were striped with deep lash marks. His buttocks were hideously macerated, his skin flayed down to the exposed gluteal muscles. Many of these stigmata appeared to be infected.

I am not a forensic pathologist, but since Chouchou will never have an autopsy, my guess is that the proximate cause of his death was pulmonary hemorrhage. Given his respiratory difficulties and the amount of blood he coughed up, it is likely that the beatings caused him to bleed, slowly at first, and then catastrophically, into his lungs. His head injuries, though severe, had not robbed him of his faculties, although it might have been better for him had they done so. It took Chouchou three days to die.

Who knows how many more Chouchous have died since the coup? Throughout Haiti, countless peasants are arrested for minor infractions. What happens after their arrest is entirely up to the man in charge. In some parts of Haiti, a beating is more likely than torture, or death; in other regions, the chances seem to be reversed. Arrests are a money-making proposition in the hinterlands, where local *chèfs de section* work with soldiers to extort money from anxious families, whose loved ones may be released on the payment of cold, hard cash.

Although the army is now enjoying a heyday of brutality, it has had years of practice. "The problem with the Haitian armed forces," observed the Lawyers Committee for Human Rights in October 1993, "is that they are unreconstructed thugs."[3] Their killing of Chouchou Louis will never be investigated, much less punished. This simple formula—repress with impunity—has always been a successful one for the army. In its long history, the only time the army has not reigned supreme was when it was out-repressed by François Duvalier and his *tontons macoutes*.

International power-brokers have sanctimoniously urged Aristide to make more concessions to this army, to "co-exist" with the generals who orchestrated both his exile and Chouchou's death. They have asked Aristide to grant continued immunity to the military. Haitians, however, elected Aristide precisely because they wanted desperately an end to despotic and arbitrary rule. As Aristide has commented, he made very few campaign promises, in contrast to Marc Bazin and many others. He did promise to work towards the creation of a meaningful system of justice and an end to the blind repression such as that which snuffed out a young father's life. His first step: to dismantle the entire network of section chiefs by terminating that position altogether.

The story of Chouchou's death is not primarily a tale of courage, even though he bore his suffering bravely, and Chantal is courageous enough. The story is, rather, one of unmitigated brutality. Although Chouchou's death, like so many others, went unreported, brutality generally *does* surface in the U.S. newspapers. Yet, even when reports include commentary on the scope of torture and killings in Haiti and elsewhere, inevitably missing from such accounts is any historical analysis of the forces promoting or suppressing the brutality—unless the repression happens to take place under the auspices of an officially designated enemy.[4] In much foreign coverage of stories like Chouchou's, his lot is held to be reflective of little more than the bizarre cruelty of his torturers.

Brutality is insidious. For example, Chouchou's murder resonates with recent events in California, where some U.S. citizens became outraged over a beating. Imagine, some say, what might have happened had motorist Rodney King been truncheoned to death. The furor over the initial King verdict, ironically, restored some people's faith in the fundamental decency of U.S. citizens. We could never sink into a barbarism that would permit the sort of torture that killed Chouchou Louis, goes this line of thinking. At the very least, we would never grant impunity to such fiends.

But there is more to these stories. It is important to discern what might well be termed a "political economy of brutality." In seeking to outline it, one need only recall the story, told in Chapter 3, of the sack of Saint-Jean Bosco, the Port-au-Prince parish where Aristide rose to prominence. Everyone came to know—indeed, most Haitians felt they knew immediately—who ordered the martyrdom of these people and the desecration of the church. But who actually swung the machetes, pulled the triggers? Who impaled a pregnant woman? Who doused a church altar with gasoline and tossed on the match? Survivors described the crime's perpetrators as *brasa wouj*, young men sporting red armbands. "According to all accounts," Amy Wilentz reports, "the men with the red armbands were paid seven dollars each plus a bottle of Barbancourt rum worth three dollars to do their damage."[5]

There has been a great deal of confusion regarding the nature of Saint-Jean Bosco and a litany of similar acts. In a recent interview, the poet Jean-Claude Martineau felt compelled to insist that "We are not a violent people. We are suffering violence."[6] Despite the strength of popular American myths to the contrary, Haitians are no more brutal than are U.S. citizens. And yet it would be very difficult to travel, say, to Los Angeles and induce a score of young men to burn down an occupied church for seven dollars and a bottle of rum each.

Attempting to trace the chain of command is essential in any exercise seeking to understand the political economy of brutality. The men sporting the red armbands had been organized, it appears, by Franck Romain, longtime mayor of Port-au-Prince, who rose to prominence as a Duvalier loyalist in the army. Most believe that Romain's orders came from General Henri

Namphy, the man so favored by U.S. diplomats through-out the violent interregnum after 1986.

Namphy, as noted, was a direct beneficiary of U.S. aid to Haiti after Duvalier's fall. Against the advice of those friendly to the Haitian democratic movement, Namphy's CNG had been the conduit for huge sums of American money. Although the vast majority of those funds were earmarked for non-military uses, they had the inevitable benefit of strengthening the hand of the Haitian army. And that, as so many had feared, was not an outcome to be desired. After worldwide attention was brought to bear on the desecration of Saint-Jean Bosco, the State Department, forgetting its unstinting praise for the "great democrat," later "deplored this brutal act."

"One of the great advantages of being rich and pow-erful," Noam Chomsky has noted, "is that you never have to say: 'I'm sorry.'"[7] As the attack on Saint-Jean Bosco and the murder of Chouchou Louis suggest, the world's privileged are protected from suffering violence, they are protected from having to perpetrate it—directly—and they are protected from having to apologize for it.[8] This, then, is the political economy of brutality. Just as the violence of the poor must be understood as embedded in their poverty—the structural violence done to them—so, too, must the "goodness" of the rich be measured against their power and privilege. When this exercise is per-formed, the privileged do not emerge so decent. To judge by the social explosion that greeted the Rodney King ver-dict, some citizens of Los Angeles sensed this as well.

There is more to this exercise than a mere shifting of responsibility among local actors. Historical investigation finds us, the American people, at fault, even and espe-cially in our ignorance. Earlier in this century—within the memory of the elders in Chouchou Louis's home vil-lage—similar acts of cruelty were perpetrated on local peasants. The construction of the road criticized by

Chouchou, the same road into which he was tossed to die, was a veritable Calvary for area peasants. The following vignette is drawn from Roger Gaillard's seven-volume study of the U.S. occupation, *Les Blancs Débarquent*. In an interview granted to Professor Gaillard in 1981, M. Saint-Aulème Saint-Pré, a peasant from the town of Maïssade, recalled "an unfortunate incident" that he witnessed as the road was being built in 1918, at a point not far from where Chouchou died:

> The forced-labor gang (*la corvée*) had arrived and William had come to evaluate the work. I had just given him some coconuts, so that he could refresh himself, when he espied a laborer displaying negligence in his work. William called out to him, ordered him to step forward, and, when he was close, ordered him to remove his hat and drop it. He did so. Then William said to him firmly: "Bend over and pick it up." The man bent over, exposing his neck. Then William drew a military knife that he carried in his bandoleer and drove it into the man's neck. The worker crumbled and died instantly. In silence, the other laborers dug a hole and buried him there.[9]

In the case of both Chouchou Louis and the laborer, the murderers acted with complete impunity, fearing no punishment. In both cases, the victims were poor peasants. In both cases, their grieving families had no recourse; even public displays of sympathy had to be silenced for fear of repercussions. There are, in fact, few important differences between the experience of Chouchou in 1991 and the murdered laborer of 1918, other than that the former was tortured and suffered horribly before he died, while the latter was dispatched quickly.

How do we examine the issue of U.S. complicity in the murder of these men? Chouchou was killed by an army with which the United States has claimed to have no ties. But even the declarations of members of the U.S. Congress belie this blandishment: "The military thugs down there understand," remarked Representative John Conyers in 1992, "that they have got a nod and a wink from the U.S. government." At key points in its recent history, the Haitian military benefited from direct aid paid for by U.S. tax dollars. The U.S. government provided riot gear—such as that used to truncheon Chouchou—and offered helpful training courses on crowd management and on the rights of detainees.

Doubtless the State Department would like to deny any complicity in the 1918 laborer's murder, as well. This is even more difficult, as the labor gangs were the creation of the U.S. Marines, who also created and armed the *gendarmérie* that now rules Haiti. As described in Chapter 2, the "Convention haitiano-américaine," written in the first months after the takeover, granted the occupying forces complete political and administrative control over Haiti. Of the various articles in this and subsequent documents, one appears to be most relevant to the fate of Chouchou Louis. Article X of the treaty decreed the formation of a new *gendarmérie*, to be trained by and at the orders of the U.S. Marines. It is this paternity that led one Haitian journalist, also a physician, to describe the current Haitian army as "the product of a forceps delivery in 1915," adding that the soldiers "grew up to become scoundrels, assassins, whose sole job is to repress Haitians."

The sight of a Haitian constabulary under foreign supervision, the brutality of the occupying force, the appropriation of land, the seizure of arms—all of this stirred significant resentment against the Marines. But the final blow, it seems, was the building of the road through central Haiti. In a December 27, 1917 letter from Major Smedley Butler to Secretary of the Navy Franklin D. Roosevelt, the Marine wrote that the roads would be completed as promised. But, he added, "it would not do to ask too many questions as to how we accomplish this work." Invoking a law ratified in 1916 by the U.S. Senate, the occupying force resurrected the *corvée*—the involuntary conscription of labor crews.

Elderly people living in central Haiti still recall images of "strings of peasants," bound to each other with rope as they headed for the infernal road.

There was minimal armed resistance to the occupation during its first year. But by 1917, scattered revolts gathered momentum and came to be termed the "Cacos Insurrection." This resistance to the occupation was based in the Central Plateau; it was led, initially, by Charlemagne Péralte of Hinche. The movement's soldiers, the Cacos, were almost all peasant farmers, many of whom had been seized in their gardens and dragged off in chains to join the *corvée*.

Many Haitian lives were lost during the "pacification period," as the Marines termed their quelling of the Cacos. Just how many lives has been, as we have seen, the subject of some disagreement— numbers range from 2,250 to 15,000. Even if we take the Marines' very low figure for "native" deaths, it is the disproportion between that figure and the 98 killed or wounded on the side of the United States that stamps the operation a massacre.[10]

It was a massacre that drew little attention in the U.S. press. The sparse coverage of U.S. military activities in Haiti tended to be strongly supportive of our objectives there. "Through the bloodiest years of the occupation," observed Noam Chomsky, "the media were silent or supportive. *The New York Times* index has no entries for Haiti for 1917–1918. In a press survey, John Blassingame found 'widespread editorial support' for the repeated interventions in Haiti and the Dominican Republic."[11]

In such a climate, the peasant revolt against the U.S.-led forces was doomed to failure. The Marines had at their disposal machine guns and aerial bombardment—a great novelty, at the time—and it is remarkable that the Cacos were able to hold the *gendarmérie* at bay at all. Charlemagne Péralte was assassinated in November 1919, and, shortly thereafter, the poorly equipped Cacos were wiped out:

> Major Smedley Butler recalled that his troops 'hunted the Cacos like pigs.' His exploits impressed FDR, who ordered that he be awarded the Congressional Medal of Honor for an engagement in which 200 Cacos were killed and no prisoners taken, while one Marine was struck by a rock and lost two teeth.[12]

With rebellion silenced, the occupying force went about its business, which was to control the Haitian economy. The Americans' economic policies—promotion of export of crops such as coffee, fiscal and commercial centralization—increased the state's stranglehold, through indirect taxes, on the peasants:

> The Occupation worsened the economic crisis by augmenting the peasantry's forced contribution to the maintenance of the State and of the urban parasites. It worsened the crisis of power by centralizing the Haitian army and disarming [citizens in] the provinces. Of course, by putting in place the structures of military, fiscal, and commercial centralization, the Occupation postponed judgment day for thirty years; but it also guaranteed that the finale would be bloody.[13]

And bloody it has been. Many have argued that the racism of U.S. stewards, who worked primarily through the mulatto elite, reinforced color prejudice in Haiti. This prejudice later paved the way for its symmetrical counterpart, the *noiriste* rhetoric of François Duvalier.

Whether U.S. foreign policy spawned Duvalierism may be debatable, but the army that put Chouchou Louis to death is the direct descendant of the *gendarmérie* of the occupation. Many Haitian intellectuals, such as poet Jean-Claude Martineau, have come to see the Haitian army as an indigenous occupying force:

> We are in a position where Haiti is occupied. Haiti is occupied, and no matter who the occupiers are, they are acting worse than a foreign force. They are maintaining their power by terror. This is the situation of

Haiti. Forget that they were born in Haiti. This is an
army of occupation that we have in Haiti, that we
have always had in Haiti.[14]

A strong Haitian military serves the ends of many
"occupiers," native and foreign. Certainly South
American drug traffickers would like to keep Haiti as a
convenient transshipment point. And although the CIA-
trained Haitian drug unit has been documented to be a
major player in both drug trafficking and political terror,
the U.S. Drug Enforcement Agency continues to share
narcotics intelligence with Haitian military authorities.[15]

Until very recently, in fact, the CIA *and* State
Department officials continued to argue that the Army
generals, even the most hardened Duvalierists, were
"Haiti's best bet for democracy."[16] It is hardly surprising,
then, that U.S. officials have demanded that the military
be seen as equal partners in negotiations with the democratically elected Aristide government.

Arguments against Latin American armies have traditionally fallen on deaf ears, at least in Washington's
corridors of power. That is because Washington has long
trained the very military officers most closely linked to
the death squads that liquidate people like Chouchou
Louis. Boston-based writer James Carroll recently wrote
an editorial about the U.S. Army's School of the
Americas, in Fort Benning, Georgia. It is, he wrote, the
"U.S. School That Teaches Militaries How to Torture."
Among the renowned alumni of the school are various
Latin American strongmen, including dictators in Bolivia,
Argentina (the chief architect of the "dirty war" there was
an alumnus), El Salvador and Panama.

But the lineaments of responsibility are much more
direct. In Peru, for example, six of the army officers
charged with the recent murders of nine students were
School of the Americas graduates. In Honduras, four of

the high-ranking officers who helped to create the "Battalion 316" death squad had been awarded diplomas. In Colombia, the list of officers designated by human rights organizations as the worst offenders reads like a Fort Benning honor roll. In El Salvador, two of the three officers cited in the assassination of Archbishop Romero, three of the five convicted of killing three Maryknoll nuns and their lay associate, and 19 of the 26 officers implicated by the United Nations' "Truth Commission" investigation of the murder of the Jesuits, their housekeeper and her daughter—all were graduates of the School of the Americas. "For decades," writes Carroll, "alumni of the School of the Americas have helped fill the morgues and mass graves of an entire continent."[17]

It should come as no surprise, then, that Haiti, the most Latin American of countries, should follow this pattern. As many now know, the *attachés* and death squads of post-coup Haiti appear to be under the control of the army high command. Colonel Michel François, head of the Port-au-Prince police and paladin of the Cédras regime, has been most closely linked to the squads; unsurprisingly, Colonel François is an alumnus of the School of the Americas at Fort Benning.

It is not, then, that Rodney King is "our" Chouchou Louis. It is, rather, that Chouchou Louis is our Chouchou Louis. If the above analysis of Chouchou's death is at all accurate, how do U.S. journalists manage to depict such events as unrelated to our foreign policy, which has been so consistent over the past century? Let us examine a recent "news analysis" by Howard French. "Haiti's Curse—Power Means Brutality; Practice Makes Perfect" was prominently displayed in the Sunday *New York Times* of October 17, 1993. On first blush, the story is an unstinting condemnation of the Haitian army. "Haiti's power equation," French notes, "has become even more brutally elementary." The embargo, he argues, has weakened the "potentially modernizing influence" of the traditional economic elite, and the army has emerged in recent years as the sole power in Haiti:

> Fed by its control of the country's ports and landing strips, and emboldened by an unfettered ability to cow a population with bullets, the Haitian military has become at once the new elite, the traditional nationalist dictatorship and even the Tontons Macoute—the Duvaliers' fearsome private militia—all wrapped into one.[18]

French's commentary is detailed. The leaders of today's army, he notes, "are descendants of prominent Duvalierists and were raised with a disdain of democracy." They make their money through the transshipment of drugs (a story which, to be fair, French has been careful, in recent months, to cover), and through control of monopolies over utilities and staples. French admits, too, that the U.S. occupation "merely strengthened the Haitian Army." For these and other reasons, efforts to "professionalize" the army are likely to fail.

There is much, as usual, that is missing from French's analysis. Nowhere is there mention of our own government's active and ongoing support for this manifestly corrupt and violent institution created, in essence, during the occupation. Nowhere is there mention of foreign aid being run through juntas after the fall of Duvalier. Nowhere is there mention of CIA agents who are officers in the Haitian army, and nowhere do we learn that men like Colonel François are *already* graduates of our training programs. By giving them a Duvalierist ancestry, French manages, ironically, to obscure the fact that Cédras, François, and company are, in truth, our own offspring.[19]

Certainly, the essay by Howard French is well-written. Following an apt turn of phrase by Graham Greene, French refers to Haiti as evoking corrupt and debauched Rome. But French is not a novelist, and he knows that such a metaphor only makes sense if the United States, and not one of its peripheral dependencies, represents the Roman Empire. Haiti and its rapacious army could then stand for some small and wayward satrap, whose actions are, as best, a source of amusement, a sort of circus.

It is difficult to believe that U.S. foreign policy could be unswervingly on the side of Haitian democracy—unless, of course, there *have* been truly significant changes in Washington. But evidence for a change of direction in U.S. foreign policy is scant. A move by Congressman Joe Kennedy to close down the School of the Americas was quite handily defeated in Congress in 1993. Alexander Cockburn summarized the foreign policy achievements of the Clinton administration in its first 100 days:

> [Clinton] sold out the Haitian refugees...let a Bush appointee, Herman Cohen, run Africa policy, essentially giving a green light to Savimbi in Angola to butcher thousands; put Israel's lobbyists in charge of Mideast policy; bolstered the arms industry with a budget in which projected spending for '93 is higher in constant dollars than the average spending during the cold war from 1950; increased intelligence spending..."[20]

It is less surprising, then, that the new U.S. administration is having a hard time letting go of the Haitian army. If top U.S. military officials can continue to praise the Haitian army's "professionalism" right through the recent killings of hundreds of pro-democracy figures in Haiti, using this expression even on the day before the Justice Minister was assassinated with obvious military complicity, it is because a pro-military bias has been central to *both* Bush and Clinton foreign policy towards Haiti. It has been central to U.S. foreign policy in Haiti for decades. The current crisis in Haiti proves yet again that it is less a question of new personalities in Washington and more a question of seemingly immutable institutions.

Shortly before he was killed, Antoine Izméry had the

temerity to ask why a small, poor country without imperial ambitions needed any army at all. Such questions were inadmissible, to judge from the fatal reply. In U.S. eyes, if longtime USAID director Lawrence Harrison can be said to see through them, one of Aristide's major flaws is his anti-military tendency: "Some of the military believed that [Aristide] was out to destroy their institution—as did some in the judiciary."[21] That the "destruction" of the army and the Duvalier-appointed judiciary as currently constituted would be applauded by the majority of poor Haitians—which is to say, of course, the majority of Haitians—is beside the point. Aristide was, if anything, imprudently moderate; he repeatedly counseled patience and reform even though he knew that these institutions were rotten to the core.

Other Haitians who maintain some faith in the diplomatic process are clinging to the possibility of a new attitude in U.S. foreign policy. It is for this reason that some progressives, including Aristide, have invited a multinational force into their country. Jean-Claude Martineau, a forward-thinking intellectual who terms himself "firmly anti-intervention," has nonetheless come down on behalf of sending in a U.N.-sponsored force:

> What we are trying to do is something monumental in the history of Haiti and Latin America. Putting the army under the command of a civilian government is not a joke; this is not something that is going to be easy. We need help. The Haitian people know that. They are not considering these technicians coming to Haiti to professionalize the army, to separate the army from the police, to be an occupying force. The occupying force that we have is the present army. The Haitian people have voiced their opinion about that.[22]

It is true that support for this plan is widespread among the poor, but one wonders if, here again, a Faustian bargain has not been struck. How can we further "professionalize" a Colonel François when he has already been through our training program and is performing as expected?

It would be naive to expect repentance and conversion from any U.S. administration, just as it is naive to believe that the Haitian military can now be dislodged without force. It is naive, too, to believe that unarmed Haitians are capable of taking on the Uzis and assault rifles of the army. As progressives debate the relative merits of various plans, another Chouchou is killed every day. Perhaps more than one a day: "some observers say the figure may be as high as five a day in the capital," wrote Nancy Nusser of the *Palm Beach Post*, reporting in October 1993, from the edge of a mass grave north of Port-au-Prince. "And this does not include the many others that are reportedly occurring in rural areas and distant cities."[23] According to Juan Mendez, director of Americas Watch, "There is no human rights situation that is more of an emergency than Haiti. We consider it a human rights disaster."[24]

This, then, is the fundamental sadness of the political economy of brutality. People like Chouchou Louis are in a mess, and this mess is not of their own making. The Haitian elites, military and civilian, and their foreign partners, most notably those in the United States, have created this crisis. People like Chouchou Louis are trying to get out of this mess by themselves, but decades of repression and hunger have taken their toll. There is little room for romanticism about the supporters of democracy taking to the streets in brave displays of non-violence. Haiti is not the Philippines, and we know from experience what the military will do to protesters. It will shoot them.

Acéphie

The people who criticize us, who say that we've done something wrong, they don't know what we've gone through. They know nothing of the pain of rocks in the sun. I would like, before I die, to show them this pain...not to make them feel pain, but to make them understand how life made us take risks we didn't fully understand.

—Marie-Andrée Louhis,
1955–1992

A small and wretchedly poor village, "Kay" is a community of approximately 1,000 people. The village is stretched out along an unpaved road that cuts north and east into Haiti's Central Plateau. During the rainy season, the road from Port-au-Prince can take several hours to traverse, adding to the impression of isolation. As elsewhere in Haiti, the impression is misleading: the village owes its existence to a project conceived in the Haitian capital and drafted in Washington, D.C. Kay is a settlement of refugees composed substantially of peasant farmers displaced almost four decades ago by Haiti's largest dam.

Before 1956, the village of Kay was situated in a fertile valley, near the banks of the Rivière Artibonite. For generations, these families had farmed the broad and gently sloping banks of the river, selling rice, bananas, millet, corn, and sugar cane in regional markets. Harvests were, by all reports, bountiful; life there is now recalled as idyllic.

Progress came in the form of a dam. During the U.S. occupation, inspired by the example of the Tennessee Valley Authority, military engineers proposed damming the Artibonite in order to better control irrigation in the valleys closer to the coast. It was not until 1948, however, that the Export-Import Bank, a U.S. federal agency, granted the loans necessary to launch a large development project, the centerpiece of which was the massive hydroelectric dam at Péligre. The project was costly and, ultimately, a failure, and it caused untold suffering in the now-inundated valleys behind the dam.

When the valley was flooded, the majority of the local population was forced up into the hills on either side of the new reservoir. Kay became divided into "Do" (those who settled on the stony backs of the hills) and "Ba" (those who remained down near the new waterline). By all the standard measures, both parts of Kay are now exceedingly poor; its older inhabitants often blame their poverty on the dam a few miles away, and bitterly note that it brought them neither electricity nor water.

When I began working in Kay, in May of 1983, the word *sida*, signifying AIDS, was just beginning to work its way into the rural Haitian lexicon. Although AIDS was already afflicting an ever-increasing number of city-dwellers, it was unknown in most areas as rural as Kay. Bent under the burdens of increasing political violence and unremitting poverty, the people of the region were uninterested in the new illness. But interest in *sida* became almost universal less than three years later, around the time that Acéphie Joseph contracted HIV.

When she died in 1992, Acéphie was 27-years-old. I visited her many times in the course of her illness, but I now most easily remember her as she was a couple of months before her death. Plagued in recent years with numerous skin infections, her face was nonetheless smooth and clear, and she punctuated her commentary, when appropriate, with an easy smile. Acéphie then weighed less than 80 pounds, and talking seemed, at times, to exhaust her, but she remained animated and engaging until only days before her death.

Ophilia, Acéphie's daughter, is also easily called to mind. By the time her mother was terminally ill, Ophilia was herself already small and spindly; though two, she looked like a scrawny one-year-old. But her peculiarly shrill cries reminded me that Acéphie had been sick for exactly two and one half years, as it was in the final trimester of her only pregnancy that she first fell ill with what would prove to be AIDS.

Acéphie's parents, also gaunt, were inhabited with a permanent worry that broke through their ready friendliness. I have known this elderly couple since 1983, when they were both much more robust. Mme. Joseph, a tall and wearily elegant woman who is younger than she looks, was then struggling along as a "Madame Sarah," a market woman. Madame Sarahs are the backbone of the rural economy, which, long tottering, has been prevented from total collapse only by the industry and strength of these women. In 1983, Mme. Joseph would purchase produce in rural areas like Kay and then sell it in Croix Bossale, a market area along the muddy border of one of Port-au-Prince's densest slums. Even by then she was beginning to give up: business had been bad throughout the '70s, she complained, and she no longer had enough capital to make ends meet. Her arthritis was acting up; her oldest son had given her a grandson. Someone responsible needed to take care of the baby, she said, threatening to abandon her no-longer profitable profession. Mme. Joseph finally stopped traveling to the city in the mid-1980s, and since then has held steady against a long stream of minor and major tragedies.

The greatest of these, clearly, has been the sickness and death of her daughter. Acéphie was known in Kay as a great beauty; she could "sign her name," as the saying goes, and then some; she could cook, and, for a poor girl, she dressed smartly. Acéphie was always thought of as a pleasant person with a ready smile. Witnessing her slow and inevitable decline was a source of pain for her family and for many of the villagers who had watched her grow up.

In 1992, Acéphie's sickness was merely the latest in a series of tragedies that she and her parents readily strung together in a long jeremiad, by now familiar to those who serve the poor in this region of rural Haiti. The litany begins, usually, down in the valley hidden beneath the murky surface of the lake. Acéphie's father never smiled when recounting their story. He and his future spouse were from Kalwas and Petit-Fond, respectively. Both came from families who made a decent living by farming fertile tracts of land—their "ancestors' gardens"—and selling much of their produce. "If it weren't for the dam," he would say, fixing his good eye on me, "we'd be just fine now. Acéphie, too."

Two of Acéphie's siblings were born in Kalwas, a sparsely wooded strip of land that is now largely submerged. Their house was drowned along with most of their belongings, their crops and the graves of their ancestors. Mme. Joseph says she may have been pregnant with Acéphie and her twin brother when, refugees from the rising water, they built a miserable lean-to on a knoll of high land jutting into the new reservoir. A bit of addition and subtraction (at which every market woman is accomplished) leads her to add, "No, I had a stillbirth that year." She pauses for effect, and repeats: "Had a stillbirth that year."

The Joseph family remained poised on their knoll for some years; Acéphie and two more children were born there. I asked them what induced them to move to Do Kay, to build a house on the hard stone embankment of a dusty road. "Our hut was too near the water," replied M. Joseph. "I was afraid one of the children would fall into the lake and drown. Their mother had to be away selling; I was trying to make a garden in this terrible soil. There was no one to keep an eye on them."

The elder Josephs guess that they moved up to Do Kay in the late '60s. A priest was then working with the children, they remind me, and they sent their offspring to his school. Times were hard, both agree, but it was somehow feasible then, "because we were younger and our joints didn't complain so." Acéphie attended primary school in Kay—not the big cement version that was built in 1981, but the banana-thatched, open shelter in which children and young adults learned the rudiments of literacy.

I spoke with several of Acéphie's childhood friends and classmates. "She knew how to talk with everyone," recalled one. "She was the nicest of the Joseph sisters. And she was as pretty as she was nice." Her beauty and her vulnerability may have sealed her fate as early as 1984. Although Acéphie was still in primary school, she was already 19 years old; it was time for her to help generate income for her family, which was sinking deeper and deeper into poverty. Hunger was a near-daily occurrence for the Joseph family; the times were as bad as those right after the flooding of the valley. So Acéphie would help her mother by carrying produce to a local market on Friday mornings.

On foot or with a donkey, it takes over an hour and a half to reach the market, and the road leads right through Péligre, site of the dam and a military barracks. The soldiers like to watch the parade of women on Friday mornings. Sometimes they tax them with haphazardly imposed fines; sometimes they tax them with flirtatious banter.

Such flirtation is seldom unwelcome, at least on the surface of things. In rural Haiti, entrenched poverty makes the salaried man ever so much more attractive. When Acéphie's striking looks caught the eye of Raoul Honorat, a native of Belladère formerly stationed in Port-au-Prince, she returned his gaze. Acéphie knew, as did everyone in the area, that Honorat had a wife and children. In fact, he was known to have more than one regular partner. But Acéphie was taken in by his persistence, she recalled, and when he went to speak to her parents, a long-term liaison was likely:

> What would you have me do? I could tell that the old people were uncomfortable, worried; but they didn't say no. They didn't tell me to stay away from him. I wish they had, but how could they have known? ...I knew it was a bad idea then, but I just didn't know

why. I never dreamed he would give me a bad illness,
never! I looked around and saw how poor we all were,
how the old people were finished...What would you
have me do? It was a way out, that's how I saw it.

Acéphie and Honorat were sexual partners only
briefly—less than a month, according to Acéphie. Shortly
thereafter, Honorat fell ill and kept to the company of his
wife in Péligre.

As Honorat got sicker, rumors abounded. Eventually
it was widely agreed that he was the victim of sorcery, a
"sent sickness." "Expedition of the dead" is a model of illness causation well-documented in the scholarly literature on voodoo, the much-maligned popular religion of
Haiti. Alfred Métraux refers to the sending of the dead as
"the most fearful practice in the black arts." The symptoms of "expedited" illness, in his description, resemble
those of untreated pulmonary tuberculosis:

> Whoever has become the prey of one or more dead
> people sent against him begins to grow thin, spit
> blood and is soon dead. The laying on of this spell is
> always attended by fatal results unless it is diagnosed
> in time and a capable *houngan* succeeds in making
> the dead let go.[1]

Sent sickness is thought to be best treated by a
houngan, who might be termed a "voodoo priest."
Honorat spent his last penny, it is said, attempting to
discover who had sent the dead to him. Some suggested
it had been his jealous wife; others were sure that the
perpetrators were the family of a young man who had
been beaten to death in military custody.

As Acéphie searched for a *moun prensipal*—a "main
man"—she tried to forget about the soldier. Still, it was
shocking to hear, a few months after they parted, that he
was dead. Acéphie was then at a crucial juncture in her
life. Returning to primary school was out of the question.
She wasn't making much progress, and she was much

older than most of the children. After some casting about, she went to Mirebalais, the nearest town, and began a course in what she euphemistically termed a "cooking school." The school—really just an ambitious woman's courtyard—prepared poor girls like Acéphie for their turn as servants in the city. Life as a maid was fast becoming one of the only growth industries in Haiti, and as much as Acéphie's proud mother hated to think of her daughter reduced to servitude, she could offer no viable alternative. "So I learned to cook and embroider and sew," recalled Acéphie. "It was something, at least, and I thought I could help my family."

At 22, Acéphie went to Port-au-Prince, where she had heard of an opening in a middle-class neighborhood. It was 1987, a time of great political upheaval in Haiti. And although these dislocations may have hastened the decline of many Haitian industries, the immediate post-Duvalier years were ones in which the U.S. government sought to reaffirm its preeminence in Haitian politics. Acéphie found a job as a housekeeper for a middle-class Haitian woman working for the U.S. Embassy. Acéphie's good looks and good manners kept her out of the backyard, the traditional milieu of Haitian servants. She was designated as the maid who answered the door and the phone. She did a fair amount of ironing and cleaning, but cooked only irregularly; there was another, full-time cook in the house.

What did Acéphie's employer do? "She worked for the American Embassy," repeated Acéphie, as if that were answer enough. When asked what, specifically, the woman did, Acéphie looked puzzled. "I guess I have no idea what she was doing. New York used to call all the time; I would answer the phone and it would be New York on the line." Although Acéphie admits that she was not paid well—she received $30 each month—she feels that her employer treated her fairly: the backyards of her neighborhood were full of the bitter complaints of men and women, also from decaying villages like Kay, who were treated badly by their bosses.

With hunger ever-present in her home village, Acéphie tried to save a bit of money for her parents and siblings. Still looking for a *moun prensipal*, she began seeing Blanco Nerette, a young man with origins identical to her own: Blanco's parents were also "water refugees" and Acéphie had known him when they were both attending the priest's school. Blanco had done well for himself, by Kay standards—he chauffeured a small bus between Mirebalais and Port-au-Prince. Amidst an unemployment rate of greater than 60 percent, Blanco could command considerable respect. He focused his attentions on Acéphie, stopping by to see her when Madame was out, or when she was on the phone with New York. They planned to marry, Acéphie later noted with some bitterness, and had even started pooling their resources.

Acéphie remained at the "embassy woman's" house for over three years, learning a bit of English ("Hold on; I'll get her") and spending her spare time with Blanco. She stayed, in fact, until she discovered that she was pregnant. As soon as she told Blanco, she sensed him becoming skittish. Her employer was not pleased, either. The woman noted that her job at the embassy was no longer sure, given the political situation, and that perhaps it would be safer if Acéphie were to return to her parents' home; although New York and other telephone callers could not have minded, it is considered unsightly to have a pregnant servant.

So Acéphie returned to Kay, where she had a difficult pregnancy. Blanco came to see her once or twice. They had a spat, and then she heard nothing from him. Following the birth of Ophilia, Acéphie was sapped by repeated infections, each one diagnosed by the staff of the clinic in Kay. As she became more and more gaunt, some villagers began to think that Acéphie was the victim of sorcery, of "sent sickness." In years past, they might have worried about a sorcery-induced death from tuberculosis. But by 1991, Kay had already experienced its first cases of AIDS, and villagers were quick to recognize the new syndrome; most people on Do Kay now believe that Acéphie died of AIDS. Acéphie herself knew that she had AIDS, although she was more apt to refer to herself as suffering from a disorder brought on by her work as a servant: "All that ironing, and then opening a refrigerator."

Acéphie continued to deteriorate throughout the early part of 1992 and died that May. Although this ended Acéphie's story, there has been no end to the grim and steady march of HIV. First it wasted Ophilia. Now, Raoul Honorat's wife from Péligre is much thinner than last year; she has already had a case of herpes zoster, indicating immune deficiency in a woman her age. This woman, whom we know well at the clinic, is no longer a widow; once again, she is the partner of a military man. After Honorat's death, she found herself desperate, with no means of feeding her five hungry children. Two of them are also HIV-positive.

Raoul Honorat had at least two other partners, both of them poor peasant women, in the Central Plateau. One is HIV-positive and has two sickly children. Blanco, the father of Acéphie's only child, is still a handsome young man, apparently in good health. He is still plying the roads from Mirebalais to Port-au-Prince. Who knows if he carries the virus? As a chauffeur, he has plenty of girlfriends. And so the sad cycle continues.

It is the thesis of this book that people like Yolande Jean and Chouchou Louis are caught up in systems that link them to far-off places. Their lives have been altered by often unseen forces that must be brought into relief if we are to understand their lot. Such is also the case with Acéphie Joseph. In Haiti, at least, any approach that does not employ such an analysis will leave unanswered many of the questions central to an understanding of

AIDS: Was Acéphie a representative victim of AIDS in Haiti? If so, how did she come to be at risk for exposure to HIV? If not, how did she differ from the majority of HIV-infected persons? Also left unanswered are the perennial "why" questions: Why might poor Haitians have been particularly vulnerable to an epidemic of a new infectious disease? Why did the people of Do Kay respond to AIDS in the way that they did? Why do they speak of AIDS in the way that they do, as a sickness that may either be sent by enemies or acquired sexually?

In order to address these questions, it is necessary, I believe, to leave ethnography behind. To fill these explanatory lacunae, we must turn to other disciplines: epidemiology, history, and political economy. Cautious recourse to these disciplines is part of the "responsible materialism" of anyone who would study an infectious disease that runs along the fault lines of our international order. Elsewhere, I have attempted to reconstruct a socioepidemiological history of HIV in Haiti, and to answer the following questions: How did HIV come to Haiti, and when did it arrive? How did AIDS come to be one of the leading causes of death among urban Haitian adults? How far has HIV spread within the country? How is the virus transmitted in Haiti? Who is at-risk for acquiring HIV infection? Why are sex differences in the incidence of AIDS diminishing, and why are "accepted risk factors" denied by more and more patients, even as the quality of epidemiological research improves? Why are other patterns of risk changing? What is the future likely to bring?[2]

To briefly summarize my review, research, and inferences: heterosexual transmission of HIV now accounts for the vast majority of Haitian AIDS cases, and cases associated with perinatal transmission, from mother to child, are increasing at a rate greater than that of the epidemic in general. In Haiti, AIDS is afflicting increasing numbers of women, and especially poor women like Acéphie Joseph.

But the history of the Haitian epidemic, and its relation to the larger pandemic, is of interest for other reasons. In the early 1980s, the first years of the epidemic, Haitians with AIDS were largely men, though increasing numbers of women reported to the urban clinics caring for these patients; the rate of transfusion-associated transmission was then higher in Haiti than in the United States; the microbial agent that led to AIDS was probably new to Haiti, as no one could report cases predating the much larger North American epidemic, and Haitian blood stored in the late 1970s was subsequently found to be free of HIV; there was an epicenter of the Haitian epidemic in the city of Carrefour, a center of prostitution bordering the south side of Port-au-Prince.

A significant percentage of the early cases had been linked to homosexual contact, some of it with North Americans. In a key paper published in 1984, Jean Guérin and coworkers from Haiti, the United States, and Canada stated that "17% of our patients had sexual contact with American tourists."[3]

This revelation stimulated a fair amount of controversy. The Haitian government, such as it was, reacted as usual, with guns, arrests and persecution. The gay community in North America, or its scholarly wing, responded with a good deal of doubt. One journalist writing for the *Advocate* quoted Dr. Guérin as saying "All of my patients denied having sex with Americans."[4]

When the dust settled a bit, the cluster-study data held firm—at least I believe they did. These studies are entirely unsurprising to those who knew something about Haitian tourism, which mushroomed in the 1970s, as it did elsewhere in much of the Caribbean. Tourism brought in more than just foreign exchange; it reinforced institutionalized prostitution. Although many commentaries on prostitution in Haiti are retrospective assessments made in light of the AIDS crisis, most agree that economic desperation gave the possessors of even modest sums of

money access to a sexual-services marketplace uncon-
scionably tilted in their favor. "Fantasies came true" raved
one promotion, on payment of what was, for the fortunate
outsider, "a nominal charge." What options—let alone fantasies—were left to the Haitian poor? Not many. There
were few avenues of escape for those caught in the web of
urban migration, severe unemployment and extreme
poverty. This combination, added to the marked dependency of the Haitian economy on the United States, set
the stage for a devastating epidemic.

What do we know about the contours of the larger
Caribbean pandemic? All of what are termed "the
Caribbean basin countries" have reported AIDS cases to
the Pan American Health Organization (PAHO). Among the
islands, Haiti, the Dominican Republic, Trinidad and
Tobago, and the Bahamas account for 82 percent of all
cases reported to PAHO between the recognized onset of
the epidemic and September 1987. Haiti had reported the
largest number of cases in the Caribbean region, lending
credence to the widely-shared but misguided belief that
citizens of that nation are somehow uniquely susceptible
to AIDS. Haiti is a populous country, and when the number of cases was standardized to reflect per capita case-
load, the uniqueness of Haiti disappeared: the attack rate
in Haiti was actually lower than that in several other countries in the region.

What is the nature of HIV transmission in these
countries? Many public health specialists, including
those from the World Health Organization (WHO), speak
of the entire Caribbean basin as demonstrating "Pattern
II," which differs from Pattern I "in that heterosexual
intercourse has been the dominant mode of HIV transmission *from the start*...homosexuality generally plays a
minor role in this pattern."[5] The above review of the data
from Haiti suggests that the WHO terminology obscures
more than it illuminates, for at least three reasons. First,
although "the start" was never accurately documented, it
is clear that same-sex relations between men played a

crucial role in the Haitian epidemic. Data from other Caribbean countries suggest that the WHO terminology is equally inappropriate there, and that the patterns seen in Haiti are suggestive of what has occurred in other countries in the region. Second, the WHO scheme underlines similarities between the Caribbean and Africa, drawing attention away from the history of the Caribbean pandemic, which is in fact, causally speaking, far more intimately related to the North American epidemic. Third, the WHO scheme is static, whereas the Caribbean epidemics are rapidly changing.

What studies allow such conclusions? The first case of AIDS in the West Indies was reported on Trinidad in February 1983. Since then, the number of cases has risen steadily, leaving Trinidad with one of the highest attack rates in the Americas. In an important study published in 1987, Bartholemew and coworkers compared the epidemiological correlates of infection with two retroviruses: HTLV and HIV. Infection with the former virus, thought to be long endemic in the Caribbean, was significantly associated with age, African descent, number of lifetime sexual partners, and "duration of homosexuality," that is, length of time as a sexually active gay man. In sharp contrast, "Age and race were not associated with HIV seropositivity. The major risk factor for HIV seropositivity was homosexual contact with a partner from a foreign country, primarily the United States. Duration of homosexuality and number of lifetime partners were not significantly associated with HIV seropositivity."[6] The same risk factors were documented in Jamaica, the Dominican Republic, and Colombia, also a Caribbean-basin country.[7] The Haitian experience would suggest that these countries can expect the relative significance of sexual contact with a North American gay man to decrease, as other risk factors—most notably, high turnover among partners—become preeminent.

The existence of tourism, some of it gay, does not of course prove that such commerce was "the cause" of the

Haitian AIDS epidemic, nor is it my intention to argue that it does. Such commerce does, however, throw into relief the ties between Haiti and nearby North America, ties not mentioned in early discussions of AIDS among Haitians, which often posited "isolated Haiti" as the *source* of the pandemic. As discussed in the first half of this book, a review of the pre-AIDS scholarly literature on Haiti would leave the impression that the country has been the most "isolated" or "insular" of Caribbean countries.

A more attentive study of Haiti's economy reveals that the nation has long been closely tied to the United States. In fact, the Caribbean nations with high attack rates of AIDS are all part of a U.S.-based socioeconomic system. A relation between the degree of "insertion" in this network and prevalence of AIDS is suggested by the following exercise. Excluding Puerto Rico, which is not an independent country, the five Caribbean basin nations with the largest number of cases by 1986 were as follows: the Dominican Republic, the Bahamas, Trinidad and Tobago, Mexico, and Haiti. In terms of trade, which are the five countries most dependent upon the United States? Export indices offer a convenient marker of involvement in the West Atlantic system. In both 1983 and 1977, the years for which such data are available, the same five countries were most linked to the United States economically—and they are precisely those countries with the largest *number* of AIDS cases.[8] The country with the largest number of AIDS cases, Haiti, was also the country most dependent on U.S. exports. In all the Caribbean basin, only Puerto Rico is more economically dependent upon the United States. And only Puerto Rico has reported more cases of AIDS to the Pan American Health Organization.

To understand the American AIDS pandemic, a historical understanding of the worldwide spread of HIV is crucial. The thesis that evolving economic forces run parallel to the lineaments of the American epidemics is confirmed by comparing Haiti with a neighboring island,

Cuba, the sole country in the region not enmeshed in the U.S.-centered socioeconomic system. In Haiti, in 1986 and 1987, several epidemiological studies of asymptomatic city dwellers revealed HIV seroprevalence rates of approximately nine percent. In 1986 in Cuba, only 0.01 percent of 1,000,000 persons tested were found to have antibodies to HIV.[9] Had the pandemic begun a few decades earlier, the epidemiology of HIV infection in the Caribbean might well be different. Havana, once the "tropical playground of the Americas," might have been as much an epicenter of the pandemic as Port-au-Prince.

The experience of Acéphie Joseph is not divorced from that of Yolande Jean, for each may be seen to "fit" into the social and economic nexus whose contours were defined in the first half of this book. This is no less true now that Ms. Jean has moved from her confinement on Guantánamo to New York City. And it has been true since the AIDS pandemic was first recognized. Take, for example, the experience of the first Haitians diagnosed with AIDS in the United States. Unlike other U.S. patients meeting diagnostic criteria for AIDS, the Haitian immigrants denied that they had engaged in homosexual activity or intravenous drug use. Most had never had a blood transfusion. In 1982, almost all other cases of the syndrome known at the time implicated one or more of these risk factors. Although the CDC had previously released data concerning AIDS in heterosexuals, epidemiologist Gerald Oppenheimer observes that "the [1982] article on Haitians constituted the first complete report focusing directly on persons outside the 'homosexual' category."[10] "The Haitians," noted another review of early AIDS epidemiology, "remained the wild cards."[11]

AIDS among Haitians was, in the words of many researchers, "a complete mystery."[12] Linguist Paula Treichler has observed that, "when one aspect of the AIDS story is declared impenetrably mysterious, reason and control must be elsewhere recuperated."[13] Indeed, U.S. public health officials were faced with the task of tidying up the non-groupable cases. In order to accurately assess risk among Haitian immigrants, a sound knowledge of the size of this population was necessary. However, no such data were available. Instead of acknowledging its inability to make an assessment of risk, the official—and spuriously low—figure of 200,000 recent Haitian entrants was initially used as the denominator. The resulting conceptual round-up officially brought *all* Haitians together in a "risk group." Soon, voodoo was invoked, along with monkeys, and cannibalism, and a whole panoply of fantastic theorizing that purported to explain the high rates of AIDS among Haitians.

But the best was yet to come. In a calculus of blame that surprised few Haitians, the disease was said to have *come from Haiti.* Some medical researchers flatly stated that Haiti was the source of the American epidemic. Others, favoring an African origin for AIDS, assumed that it was nonetheless via that "little Africa-off-the-Coast-of-Florida."

What might explain the profusion of theories about a Haitian origin of AIDS? Why was so much attention paid to voodoo? Why were such theories so widely and uncritically accepted? What might explain their resonance among North Americans in the popular *and* scientific sectors? In a review of the response of the U.S. press to the AIDS epidemic, one media analyst notes that Haitian-Americans "present pre-existing characteristics of an already non-normative character. They are black, tend to be poor, are recent immigrants, and the association of Haiti with cult-religious practices fuels the current tendency to see deviance in groups at-risk for AIDS."[14] In other words, the Haitian cases fit the already established script: the incidence of AIDS in Haitians served to *reinforce* the stigma experienced by gay men. For this to be so, there must have been strong, preexisting "folk models" of Haitians.

In fact, the press drew upon readily available images of filthy squalor, voodoo, and boatloads of "disease-ridden" or "economic" refugees. Several articles even made oblique or direct references to cannibalism. Dr. Jeffrey Viera, the senior author of the 1983 paper that helped to put Haitians on the risk list, later remarked,

> The original reports of AIDS among Haitian immigrants were sensationalized and misrepresented in the popular press. Some news broadcasts pictured scantily clad black natives dancing frenetically about ritual fires, while others caricatured Haitians with AIDS as illegal aliens interned in detention camps. The fact that the majority of the Haitian AIDS victims fit neither of these stereotypes was ignored. The impression left with the public in many instances was that AIDS was pervasive throughout the Haitian community. Unlike the homosexual or drug addict, the Haitian was a highly visible victim of the epidemic who could be singled out by virtue of his ethnic and cultural features.[15]

Dr. Viera was joined by many other researchers in pinning the blame on the media. But the popular press was in many ways upstaged by the medical-scientific community, whose members had long been the preferred sources of the popular press when writing about AIDS. In a letter published in the February 28, 1983 edition of *New York Daily News*, Dr. Viera admits that, in the course of an interview he accorded a wire service, "references to voodoo were made in the context of a discussion of theoretical means of transmission of a putative infectious agent among susceptible individuals." Dr. Viera also observed that "magic rituals sometimes transfer blood and secretions from person to person. Women have been known to add menstrual blood to the food and drink of partners to prevent them from 'straying.'"[16] Similar theories were floated by several other prominent members of the scientific community.

Social scientists were equally quick to grant voodoo a role in disease transmission. One essay attempting to make "The Case for a Haitian Origin of the AIDS Epidemic" manages to accommodate all of the exotic furbelows available in the American folk model of Haitians. The following scene is depicted by anthropologists Moore and LeBaron: "In frenzied trance, the priest lets blood: mammal's [sic] throats are cut; typically, chicken's [sic] heads are torn off their necks. The priest bites out the chicken's tongue with his teeth and may suck on the bloody stump of the neck." These sacrificial offerings, "infected with one of the Type C oncogenic retroviruses, which is closely related to HTLV," are "repeatedly sacrificed [sic] in voodoo ceremonies, and their blood is directly ingested by priests and their assistants." The model is completed with the assertion that "many voodoo priests are homosexual men" who are "certainly in a position to satisfy their sexual desires, especially in urban areas."[17]

This brand of theorizing may justly be termed "armchair anthropology," and it fits quite neatly into a symbolic network that stressed exoticism and the endemicity of disease. But there was never any evidence that the organism causing AIDS was endemic to Haiti, nor has there ever been the slightest evidence to back the idea that voodoo practices played a role in transmission of an infectious agent. On the contrary, the evidence suggests that the syndrome was new to Haiti, that it had been brought to the island by North Americans or by Haitians returning from North America, and that sexual transmission and contaminated blood transfusions accounted for most of the early cases.

Exoticism was only one possible form of commentary on Haiti and AIDS. There was another, more virulent strain of speculation that resonated with a symbolic web built around *race*. Racism may be overt or subtle, cloaked in biologic and evolutionary parlance. The racism network was of course related to that of cultural difference, but offered a coherence and discursive traditions of its own. One such tradition tapped into a well-entrenched mythology of venereal disease. The historian Elizabeth Fee recounts how syphilis came to be construed, in early twentieth-century Baltimore, as a "black disease." She underlines the role of "white doctors [who] saw blacks as 'diseased, debilitated and debauched,' the victims of their own uncontrolled or uncontrollable sexual instincts and impulses."[18]

Although the exoticism/racism symbolic webs are not entirely separate, it is possible to suggest that North American *experts* tended to rely on the former, whereas the latter was more often deployed in the popular sector. Quite frequently, however, these two symbolic systems were melded together into a comprehensive model that embraced both racist and exotic qualifiers.

For those who believe that the falsehoods spun around Haitians and disease have been decisively refuted, let me offer a letter received by *Boston Globe* editorialist Derrick Jackson, who has consistently deplored the racism inherent in mistreatment of Haitians in this country. In April 1992, he ran a piece about the hate mail he received for his efforts:

> One Florida letter, in response to a recent column criticizing the United States' rejection of thousands of Haitians who tried to flee on tiny boats to Miami, said: "Thank God there are men like President Bush who have the moral strength to take a stand. Haitians are worthless, genetically inferior scum...The elimination of the nigger with the AIDS virus is the greatest thing that has happened to the world...The U.S. Navy should use the Haitian boats for target practice."[19]

One of the people in those boats, at about that time, was Yolande Jean. Prior to her arrival on Guantánamo, she had been unwilling to believe that North Americans felt this way about Haitians. The young activists she worked with in Haiti were always attributing unsavory motives to U.S. governments:

> Everyone in Haiti was always criticizing the American government, and I'd say 'You're not there, so how do you know they really wish us harm?'...My experience on Guantánamo allowed me to discover that it was true—these things *are* their doing. I have no idea what we are to them—their *bêtes noires*, or perhaps devils. We're not human to them, but I don't know what we are.

The study of AIDS in Haiti and among Haitian-Americans reminds us that the ties that bind Haiti to urban North America are historically given, and they continue to change. These connections are economic and affective; they are political and personal. The AIDS pandemic is a striking reminder that even a village as seemingly remote as Kay is caught up in a network that embraces Port-au-Prince and Brooklyn, voodoo and chemotherapy, divination and serology, poverty and plenty. Indeed, the sexual transmission of HIV is as eloquent a testimony as any to the salience—and complicated intimacy—of these links.

In conclusion, the story of Acéphie Joseph confirms the basic thesis of this book: AIDS in Haiti fits neatly into an established political and economic crisis. Patterns of risk and disease distribution, social responses to illness, and prospectives for the near future are all illuminated by a mode of analysis that links the ethnographically-observed detail to historically-given structures. This analysis shows us that the social and economic forces that have helped to shape the world pandemic of HIV disease are those that drove Yolande Jean to Guantánamo and then structured her experience there. These are, in every sense, the same forces that led to Chouchou's death and to the larger repression in which it was eclipsed.

New Myths for Old

The conscious and intelligent manipulation of the organized habits of the masses is an important element in democratic society. Those who manipulate this unseen mechanism of society constitute an invisible government which is the true ruling power in our country.

—Edward Bernays,
Propaganda, 1928

I tremble for my country when I reflect that God is just.
—Thomas Jefferson

At the close of 1993, the lives of most Haitians, including the individual actors mentioned in these pages, remain bleak. President Aristide remains an exile in Washington, where he must ask himself whether further faith in diplomacy makes much sense. Certainly, the moral high ground is his. But even if Aristide believes that the United States no longer wishes to fund, overtly or covertly, the men who overthrew him, he must wonder if his most powerful enemies are to be found in Haiti or outside it. The ability of his U.S. detractors to keep alive a rumor such as that regarding his supposed mental illness should give him pause as he reflects on his chances of returning to his country and office.

Back in Haiti, General Raoul Cédras and Colonel Michel François run their small, ragged army with a certain economy. After all, even *The New York Times* has been willing to go on record suggesting that the high command's dealings with the South American drug lords have made certain officers fabulously wealthy. Like their predecessors, the new military elite has discovered that, in dirt-poor Haiti, it takes only modest emoluments to keep their political economy of brutality lurching forward. Cédras and company have now joined the traditional elite, whose lives have always been protected from the blood and tears beyond their villa walls.

The starkest sequels are to be found, of course, in this other Haiti. Yolande Jean now works in New York City for the Coalition for Haitian Refugees. But her husband, we hear, has been assassinated in Haiti. Details are not forthcoming, as his death occurred after the pullout of the U.N.and OAS forces charged with monitoring human rights abuses. Yolande Jean knows, simply, that he was killed in late October 1993. At this writing, she is working to retrieve her two young sons. They are currently living in one of Haiti's most notorious slums.

In central Haiti, Chantal Louis struggles to raise her daughter, who is now over two years old. Chantal seems to have been cured of tuberculosis, but she remains undernourished, unemployed, and frightened of further repression. She relates frequent nightmares. But Chantal is not completely cowed, and remains convinced that *ti pè a*, the little priest, will return to Haiti. She would like to see Chouchou's torturers brought to justice, although she allows that this is highly unlikely, regardless of what the coming years may bring.

Acéphie Joseph's family has suffered further blows. Her father hanged himself shortly after her death. Her daughter Ophilia, the sole comfort of Acéphie's mother, is gravely ill and will soon die as well. So many deaths have scarred this small village, already embittered by its displacement years ago, that one wonders, at times, what propels its inhabitants through another day.

Such harsh outcomes force a question that occurs in both waking and in sleep: What are the grounds for hope for the Haitian poor, who suffer defeat after defeat? On one score, at least, Howard French has it right: "Thus have those who have imagined that this country could fall no lower than it did under the Duvaliers been awakened to a much more frightening nightmare."[1]

How, then, did Haiti come to be such a nightmare? There is a large literature on this subject, and the first half of this book attempts a synthesis of some of these studies. But it only is fitting to regard ourselves as mere impotent scholars—academic Cassandras whose works are not often read, much less heeded. How else might we explain the influence of such theoretically shaky and historically inaccurate accounts as that offered by Lawrence Harrison in the *Atlantic Monthly*?

Mr. Harrison's central question is this: "If Haiti is not a victim of imperialism, how can its tragic history be explained?" But if Haiti is not a victim of imperialism, one might incredulously counter, what country has *ever* been the victim of imperialism? Does imperialism really exist, or is it simply the invention of paranoid Haitians and liberation theologians?

Lawrence Harrison's answer to his question is that *Haitian culture* is to blame for all the country's woes: "I believe that culture is the only possible explanation for Haiti's unending tragedy."[2] This has been Mr. Harrison's refrain in every one of the Latin American countries in which he has worked as a USAID official; it is the thesis of his books, *Underdevelopment is a State of Mind* and *Who Prospers?*.

To shore up his position, Harrison refers to a number of "authorities" on Haitian culture. It is difficult to know whether to class the resulting assertions under the rubric of factual errors or as mere errors of interpretation. I think that, for most anthropologists, they would fit rather neatly in the former category. For Harrison, "the stultifying peasant world view" predominant in Haiti is the product of "Africanisms" such as voodoo. Voodoo, he writes, "is not a religion that concerns itself with ethical issues."[3] In fact, most serious students of Haitian religion—from Alfred Métraux to Karen McCarthy Brown—conclude that it is *primarily* with ethical and moral issues that voodoo is concerned. But Harrison does not cite these studies. His source is a Baptist missionary—which might have given watchful editors pause even if they were unaware that this particular missionary is well-known in Haiti for his virulent hatred of voodoo.

Mr. Harrison dabbles in developmental psychology, as well, and links Haitians' child-rearing practices with their manifestly defective culture. Harrison ostensibly cites, as his source, the political scientist Robert Rotberg, who has never himself conducted ethnographic fieldwork in Haiti. But even this is misleading, for those who know Rotberg's study of Haiti know what *he* consulted for information on Haitian childrearing practices: a Yale undergraduate's unpublished paper on "spirit possession," which relies, evidently, on Freudian psychodynamic theory to explain Haitian culture. "In several senses," informs Rotberg, "we may say that Haitian young adults remain hostages of the guilt of the unresolved oedipal phase." Rotberg's conclusion, however, is stripped free of psycho-babble: "Haiti is not ready for representative government."[4]

Readings of Haiti have for more than 200 years been invested with peculiarly strong emotions, most of them negative. Both the historian Brenda Plummer and the anthropologist Robert Lawless have offered important analyses of this "literature of condemnation." Haitian intellectuals have for generations complained about the racism of their international interlocutors. A good deal of Haiti's bad press would seem to be linked to "schemata" that generate, year after year, a small number of scripts about what is wrong with Haiti and Haitians. These scripts emerge with surprising regularity in most popular commentary on Haiti and, indeed, in much scholarly analysis as well.

Many of these ready-made narratives have taken on the status of full-blown myths—stories more powerful than any mere fact. In the nineteenth century, when the uses of Haiti included the continued production of tropical produce and raw materials, Haiti's prime symbolic function was to serve as a model of "anti-civilization." Accordingly, the scripts generated in that era usually included voodoo, zombies, cannibalism, and savage misrule. The master myth of the era—that blacks were incapable of self-rule—was held to be reinforced principally by Haiti.

These myths were strong throughout the U.S. occupation of Haiti, and they continue to exert their pull even today. But there are new myths, minor and major, in the making. Some of the emerging myths come immediately to mind:

a. Haiti as the source of AIDS.

Among the most tenacious new myths regarding Haiti is one that paints it as the source of HIV. Although it will always be a tragedy that the virus reached Haiti at a time of great social upheaval, irrevocably hampering effective preventive efforts, there are no data to suggest that even the American pandemic originated in Haiti. What data do exist suggest that HIV reached Haiti, and most other Caribbean nations, from North America. AIDS-related myths have always served punitive purposes, and their scapegoats are people like Yolande Jean and countless other Haitians who may not even suffer from HIV disease.

b. Haitian boat people as economic, not political refugees.

As noted in Chapter 3, the refusal to see Haitian asylum seekers as political refugees has its roots in U.S. foreign policy, which for decades decreed that only "communist" nations could generate bona fide political refugees. Racism also played a role in the sorry welcome accorded the Haitians. Even the spectacular brutality of the 1991 coup has not stopped government insiders from claiming that the fleeing Haitians are "mere economic refugees." For example, Lawrence Harrison has much to say about the 40,000-odd people who fled the island in boats following the September 1991 *coup d'état*. He "feel[s] sure that the vast majority of the boat people are motivated by Haiti's grinding poverty."

Let us assume that Harrison knows more about the refugees' motivations than they do—for they all claimed, like Yolande Jean, to be the victims of persecution—or that they are all lying. What evidence does Harrison adduce to support his charge? "During my stint as director of the USAID mission in Haiti from 1977 to 1979 (fairly stable and prosperous years by Haitian standards), an anthropologist friend asked 200 Haitian villagers one question: 'If you could migrate to the United States, would you?' All responded yes."[5] The unanimous desire to leave the "fairly stable" Haiti of Jean-Claude Duvalier is thus *prima facie* proof that Haitians are really "mere economic refugees." In 1978, smack in the middle of Harrison's fairly stable years, Amnesty International reported that the mortality rate of Haitian political prisoners was the highest in the world.

c. Aristide as fomenter of class struggle, promoter of mob violence, lunatic, etc.

Aristide has regularly been portrayed in the U.S. press as a "radical firebrand" who "promotes class struggle and mob violence." Most political scientists would argue that class struggle is inevitably produced by extremely inegalitarian societies, regardless of what a priest might say about the matter. The accusation that Aristide ordered the execution of Roger Lafontant, who died in a military prison in the midst of a military coup, would seem to be so silly that it hardly merits response. Yet Rowland Evans and Robert Novak could present this conjecture as fact in the *Washington Post*.[6] Perhaps only

Aristide can take such calumny as this in stride. He must be accustomed to it by now. In 1988, Amy Wilentz documented a spate of very similar rumors about the priest:

> As Namphy's regime became weaker and more violent, such groundless rumors against Aristide—which you could hear from the mouths of bishops and ambassadors...grew wilder and more fantastic. Eventually, whisperers would accuse him of involvement in the attack on the [1987] presidential elections, would say that he had invented out of whole cloth various Church orders against himself, would even go so far as to claim that Aristide himself had paid a band of men to feign an assassination attempt against him. In other words, every action of the right-wing forces was accompanied by a rumor blaming Aristide for the thing. The campaign seemed organized—each rumor popped up whole and was reiterated each time by the same bunch of people.[7]

The game is crude, and has long been so. But not so crude that the world's editors would refuse to run story after story about Aristide's "mental instability," even after the Canadian Medical Association denied the existence of the psychiatrist said to have treated Aristide. And even after the CIA acknowledged that the document "proving" the allegation was most likely forged, Senator Jesse Helms could still muster a few more stories in the major U.S. media.

d. The Haitian crisis as the confrontation of two equal and opposed forces unable to resolve their differences.

This surprisingly potent myth, purveyed chiefly by U.S. journalists, has had obvious ramifications in diplomatic circles. If Aristide and the army are regarded as equal and opposed forces—rather than, say, a legitimate government and an illegitimate, *de facto* junta—the purpose of international negotiations is to cobble together a deal satisfactory to both parties. This means that the Haitian people, who chose Aristide and not the army, will have little say in the substance of these parleys. Nowhere was the impact of this myth, which was linked to sloppy notions of "neutrality," more evident than on Governor's Island, as media critic Catherine Orenstein has noted: "By undercutting Aristide, elevating Cédras, and downplaying the terror of the military regime, the media suggested that a settlement which left the police and the military largely intact was not unreasonable and set the stage for U.N.-sponsored negotiations."[8]

Every attempt by the "Aristide camp" to reiterate the fact that only the constitutional and elected government had any legitimate claim to power was met with stiff resistance from U.S. and U.N.diplomats. The message for the "intransigent Aristide," according to journalists, was straightforward: "Sign the agreement or return to Washington and begin applying for a green card."[9]

e. Our aid to Haiti as well-intentioned, but ineffective.

Throughout their tenures, the Duvaliers cynically promoted the idea of Haiti as a diseased polity that demanded rapid infusions of international aid. They appealed to every imaginable source of aid, but especially to USAID, which some in Haiti have termed "a state within the state." The Duvaliers also turned to Canada, France, West Germany, and to the World Bank and International Monetary Fund, to UNICEF and the United Nations Development Program, and to the World Health Organization. One recent study estimated that, during the 1970s and 1980s, such aid financed two-thirds of government investment and covered fully half of Haitian import expenditures. Despite obvious evidence of massive fraud, these organizations happily pumped money into the Duvalier kleptocracy:

While AID was being so charmingly credulous, the US Department of Commerce produced figures to show that no less than 63 per cent of all recorded government revenue in Haiti was being "misappropriated" each year. Not long afterwards—and just before he was dismissed by Duvalier—Haiti's Finance Minister, Marc Bazin, revealed that a monthly average of $15 million was being diverted from public funds to meet "extra-budgetary expenses" that included regular deposits into the President's private Swiss bank account. Most of the "public funds" had, of course, arrived in Haiti in the form of "development assistance."[10]

But graft and thievery are only part of the story. Several studies have shown that the effects of such international largesse as has actually reached its intended beneficiaries have often been highly deleterious to the local economy. For example, cereals donated under the PL 480 program have been found for sale in virtually every Haitian marketplace, thereby undercutting locally produced grains.[11] In an important study of the effects of international aid to Haiti, social analysts DeWind and Kinley conclude that the chief effects of such aid have been further immiseration of the poor (by now the vast majority of Haitians) and massive emigration.[12] Another book-length study of foreign assistance examines aid to Haiti and asks, "Did the ruin of the Haitian poor occur *in spite* of foreign aid, or *because* of it?"[13]

These patterns of giving have persisted in post-Duvalier Haiti. In June 1993, the National Labor Committee published an important report, *Haiti After the Coup: Sweatshop or Real Development?* The brief not only notes that U.S. companies in Haiti are paying wages of 14 cents an hour, it also implicates USAID in organizing and financing opposition to the Aristide government. Its conclusions are timely: "If USAID is allowed to pursue its failed policies of the past, we will be using massive amounts of U.S. tax money to bankroll a tiny and corrupt business elite in Haiti, thus recreating the very conditions which led to the violent September 1991 coup d'état."

f. Our foreign policy toward Haiti as well-intentioned, but ineffective.

One of the primary aims of this essay has been to show that our foreign policy towards Haiti has been remarkably consistent over the past 100 years or so. Surely U.S. positions were clear by the close of the nineteenth century, when our gunboats enforced the "dollar diplomacy" of the day. President Wilson stated, at the outset of the ccupation, that our goals in Haiti would be to "pacify" the peasants, control the customs houses, and diminish European influence in Haiti. I have also cited declassified documents written by the CIA during the time of Papa Doc which state the geopolitical rationale for U.S. support of that capricious regime.

In short, U.S. policies in Haiti bear a striking resemblance to those formulated for El Salvador, Guatemala, Honduras and other countries—small republics with a reserve army of dissatisfied poor people who want genuine change. Writing of El Salvador, Father Ignacio Martín-Baró has observed that the most significant form of terrorism is that sponsored by the government—"terrorizing the whole population through systematic actions carried out by the forces of the state."[14] Lucid analyses are often not tolerated in such settings; Father Martín-Baró was one of the Jesuits assassinated in November 1989, by U.S.-trained Salvadoran soldiers.

A second point raised by Martín-Baró, in a talk given a few months before his murder, was that such terrorism is an elementary part of the Salvadoran "government-imposed sociopolitical project." Noam Chomsky continues the analysis:

> Martín-Baró only alludes to a third point, which is the most important one for a Western audience: the sociopolitical project and the state terrorism that

helps to implement it are not specific to El Salvador, but are common features of the Third World domains of the United States, for reasons deeply rooted in Western culture, institutions, and policy planning, and fully in accord with the values of enlightened opinion.[15]

In Haiti, as in El Salvador, state terrorism has long had the support of the U.S. government, and much "enlightened opinion" has either denied or minimized our links to state terrorism—or baldly endorsed terrorism as preferable to some supposed greater threat.

From the point of view of the Haitian poor, then, U.S. foreign policy towards Haiti has never been well-intentioned. But with the possible exception of the refugee crisis, it may be said to have been quite effective. This remains true unless, of course, one believes that Clinton's foreign policy objectives are radically different from those so clearly stated by the preceding two administrations. Such views are widespread, even among European journalists. At the close of October 1993, one British reporter filed an interesting report from Port-au-Prince:

> ...had it not been for the campaign against Father Aristide by the CIA, busily briefing congressmen on what they claim is Father Aristide's mental instability, perhaps Bill Clinton would not have lost his courage, too. Had it not been for Elliott Abrams, once the key official on Haiti in the Reagan administration, whispering in the ear of General Cédras, perhaps the waters would be less muddy. But all these things happened.[16]

There are many reasons to believe that the views of Mr. Abrams, the effects of which have been experienced throughout Latin America, continue to determine policy towards Haiti. There is, for example, the ongoing campaign of the CIA to discredit Aristide. The Clinton administration is said to be embarrassed by the actions of the rogue agency, but no one there has lost a job. And are CIA agents really loose cannons, beyond the control of the executive branch? Perhaps no more than are the supposedly uncontrollable *attachés* in the pay of the Haitian regular army. In the overthrow of Guatemala's Arbenz, according to a leading student of the event, "a crucial component of the United States plan was the teamwork that existed between the State Department and the CIA."[17] Why should the present be any different?

Doubtless there are other important myths, new and old, that shape our ways of seeing Haiti. The key lesson is that these tenacious scripts help to generate the discourses by which we hide the world. A desire to understand the genesis of such discourse brings us to another myth—that U.S. journalists do not actively support the status quo. This myth is by no means specific to Haiti, and merits more extensive consideration. It becomes uninteresting, in the face of so much incontrovertible evidence, to argue about whether or not Haitian refugees are bona fide political refugees. It is much more instructive to ask how and why such debates are sustained. Why would we discuss, any further, the question of Aristide's mental health when we should attempt to discern the mechanisms by which such a canard takes on a life of its own? Similarly, if there is no clear evidence linking Aristide to human rights abuses, and if human rights observers across the board have written of thousands of executions by the army and their *attachés*, why, *how*, could more than half of all U.S. press stories about human rights abuses in Haiti focus on Aristide?

In 1968, Noam Chomsky wrote an essay on "Objectivity and Liberal Scholarship." In this and other works, he has detailed the role of the "new mandarins," the intellectual and cultural elite who serve as props to state power and corporate privilege. As such, they have, quite naturally, an almost innate hostility to popular movements:

> If it is plausible that ideology will in general serve as a
> mask for self-interest, then it is a natural presump-
> tion that intellectuals, in interpreting history or for-
> mulating policy, will tend to adopt an elitist position,
> condemning popular movements and mass participa-
> tion in decision-making, and emphasizing rather the
> necessity for supervision by those who possess the
> knowledge and understanding that is required (so
> they claim) to manage society and control social
> change.[18]

In the essay cited, most of Chomsky's illustrations
were from "scholarly" commentary on the Spanish Civil
War, but the arguments were intended to be generaliz-
able to other times and places, notably Southeast Asia.
Lawrence Harrison has been cited a number of times in
these pages as a purveyor of this sort of commentary,
but there are many other intellectuals, inside academia
and out of it, who fill similar roles with regards to Haiti.

But it is *journalists* who do much of this "work of
representation." In examining U.S. press commentary on
Haiti, we can easily discern three broad trends. First,
there is the atrophied independent press. Those few journalists who have written lucidly about Haiti are more
likely to represent the *National Catholic Reporter* or *The
Nation* than the major dailies of North America. There
are, of course, exceptions to these generalizations—independent journalist Amy Wilentz, Liz Balmaseda from the
Miami Herald, Linda Diebel from the *Toronto Star*, and a
significant number of editorialists writing in many
papers. Sadly, their influence is scarcely discernible in
popular commentary on Haiti.

A second trend in journalistic writing is openly hostile to the Haitian popular movement and aligned with
the right wing of the U.S. Republican Party. For example,
Rowland Evans and Robert Novak informed us in April
1992, that "Haiti bleeds for the sake of restoring a demagogue whose brief tenure was marked by violent class
warfare." Their sources are unnamed embassy

spokespersons, who inevitably confirm the columnists' prejudices, and also such luminaries as Leslie Manigat, who briefly rose to power under the sponsorship of the military: "'Aristide is not a democrat but a social revolutionary,' former president Leslie Manigat, a genuine democrat, told us." The genuine democrat further opined that "the military was the last institution keeping Haiti from leftist dictatorship and was in jeopardy before Aristide was overthrown."[19]

Then there is the establishment press, which presents itself as markedly different from the conservative press. It is "neutral," "balanced," and "dispassionate." It has been the goal of this essay to show that organs such as *The New York Times* and the *Washington Post*—in which, incidentally, the vitriol of Evans and Novak appeared—have distorted Haitian reality in predictable ways. These distortions have elided the role of the United States in creating the crisis, they have maligned the Haitian democratic movement, and thus given the appearance of fact, generally, to the fantasies of the more openly right-wing press.

Howard French of *The New York Times* is so associated with uncharitable interpretations of the democratic movement that he has been picketed by Haitians in New York on more than one occasion. On Governor's Island, coup leaders greeted him as "our foreign minister." To those unfamiliar with Haiti, French's slant has seemed, at times, subtle. To those who study popular commentary on the country, his reports and "news analyses" have merely reproduced the tales told by U.S. officials and by sectors of the Haitian elite.

Mr. French's indebtedness to this small group of sources is made plain by his recent stories about the effects of the embargo. One, published on November 9, 1993, ostensibly summarizes the report of a group of public health specialists affiliated with Harvard:

The study, titled 'Sanctions in Haiti: Crisis in

Humanitarian Action,' reports that although the international attention has focused largely on killings and political terrorism in Haiti since the September 1991 coup that deposed President Jean-Bertrand Aristide, 'the human toll from the silent tragedy of humanitarian neglect has been far greater than either the violence or human rights abuses.'[20]

French's story is illustrated with images of litter-strewn streets, soaring unemployment, lack of electricity, lack of access to anti-tuberculous medications. One is tempted to put aside the obvious observations (e.g., that litter was strewn in the streets of Port-au-Prince long before the embargo, that unemployment in Haiti had already "soared" to 70 percent by the late 1980s and could hardly go much higher, that over 95 percent of all Haitians have never had access to regular electricity, and that, as most studies of the subject show, most Haitians with tuberculosis have always been obliged to abandon treatment well before their course is completed) and also the obvious critiques to which the study itself is vulnerable (notably, the theoretical impossibility of attributing poor vaccine coverage and other health disasters to an embargo rather than to the post-coup collapse of the public-health system) in order to focus on the symbolic point of the story—its opposition, and moral counterbalancing, of the junta's rule of terror and the effects of the embargo (here blamed on Aristide's intransigence).[21]

The headline of the story tells us a great deal about the role of the establishment press. Although "the Harvard report" admits that "the September 1991 Coup is primarily responsible for the subsequent human damage inflicted during the crisis," the title of Mr. French's story, which ran at the top of the front page, was "Study Says Haiti Sanctions Kill Up to 1,000 Children a Month."

For those too busy to read the story, a sub-header in large type announced that "The embargo is said to take a greater toll than the violence."

The study's authors suggest the establishment of a "humanitarian corridor," a plan one can only applaud. But the distortions of *The New York Times* and other establishment media were entirely predictable. The utility of such misreadings was presaged, in fact, by the uses the *de facto* government had made of a draft of the report leaked earlier in the summer. In Haiti, the army-controlled media announce, simply enough, that the embargo kills 1,000 children a month; Aristide calls for a strengthened embargo. By the transitive power of propaganda, Aristide asks that children be sacrificed so that he can return to power.

The effects of the Harvard report were far-reaching. On November 24, 1993, the *Boston Globe* announced that the report "has contributed to the Clinton administration's reluctance to impose further sanctions on the Caribbean nation as part of efforts to restore democracy." But the article further cited an evaluation of the report by Physicians for Human Rights, which argued that "years of repressive rule in Haiti are responsible for Haiti's devastating health status." Referring to the dramatic rise in deaths due to measles, the physicians' group continued by noting that "the near elimination of the vaccination program has not been caused by the international embargo but has occurred because the Health Ministry, like many other parts of the Haitian government, has virtually ceased functioning."[22] The community organization which had collected much of the data used in the Harvard study issued a statement denying any formal connection with it.

Elsewhere in the establishment press, journalists who see themselves as neutral or even sympathetic to the democratic movement have seemed, at times, equally wedded to these ready-made scripts. Pamela Constable of the *Boston Globe*, for example, wrote as late as October 1993, that Aristide's "seven-month tenure was plagued by incidents of mob violence and frosty relations with Congress and the army."[23] As someone who has worked in Haiti for well over a decade, it is astounding to me that these seven months—the only relatively violence-free period in recent Haitian history—could be so qualified by a discerning, "neutral" observer of Haitian reality.

It is instructive to reexamine, after this review of both Haitian history and foreign commentary on it, the observations of the *Washington Post* reporter cited at the outset of this book:

> In much of Latin America, Washington's machinations are the subject of speculations and accusations. The hand of the CIA, real or imagined, is seen everywhere. And the long history of 20th-century U.S. intervention in the affairs of Caribbean countries is cited as evidence of present-day intrigue. But when it comes to divining obscure meanings in Washington's words and actions, no country can match Haiti.[24]

Surely Haitians have a right, after all they have endured at the hands of CIA-funded and U.S.-trained soldiers, to divine "obscure meanings" in U.S. policy toward Haiti? It is my hope that this essay might make a few journalists a bit more self-conscious, at least, about dismissive comments such as those offered by Mr. Hockstader.

But there is still the question of why, precisely, it is in the interest of reporters to obscure realities in the ways described here. In addition to the myths and ready-made scripts mentioned above, there are, certainly, the limitations of the medium itself—the lack of space necessary for responsible analysis, the need to produce printed "sound bites," hence some Haitian intellectuals' chronic vexation with North American journalists. Paul Déjean, an educator trained in philosophy and theology, closes his recent account of the violence in Haiti with the following acerbic comment:

> The visiting journalist, peremptory, wants an answer. Answer with a simple yes or no. No long sentences.

No disquisitions. No analysis. The question: 'if the work of the [U.N./OAS] civilian mission fails, will there be a revolutionary explosion? Answer yes or no!'[25]

Dejean responds with some heat and asks his own question, "the question people in resistance continue to throw in your face: yes or no, do we have a right to exist? To exist as human beings? Answer with a simple yes or no!"

There are other, darker reasons why the establishment press serves the interests of the powerful. Over the course of the past two decades, Noam Chomsky has compiled a great deal of evidence to support the thesis that "the major media and other ideological institutions will generally reflect the perspectives and interests of established power." After noting the influence of corporations who pay for advertising, he goes on to note that

Many other factors induce the media to conform to the requirements of the state-corporate nexus. To confront power is costly and difficult; high standards of evidence and argument are imposed, and critical analysis is naturally not welcomed by those who are in a position to react vigorously and to determine the array of rewards and punishments. Conformity to a 'patriotic agenda,' in contrast, imposes no such costs.[26]

Press coverage of the U.S.-funded civil war in El Salvador offers an interesting example. The establishment press rarely deviated from its uncritical stance regarding our policy there, relying, as usual, on U.S. and Salvadoran government officials as the key sources for most stories.[27] An exception arose in reporting on the 1981 El Mozote massacre, which came to light just as Congress was voting on increasing its aid to the Salvadoran military, the authors of the massacre. When reporters from both *The New York Times* and the *Washington Post* traveled to the village and reported what they had seen, Reagan Administration officials, furious, complained that "the media" were "unfair" in their cover-age of the war against the "rebels."[28] The *Wall Street Journal* devoted a 16-paragraph editorial to echoing the State Department:

> Take the recent controversy over charges of a 'mas-sacre' by an elite battalion of the El Salvadoran army. On January 27, Raymond Bonner of *The New York Times* and Alma Guillermoprieto of the *Washington Post* simultaneously reported on a visit to rebel terri-tory, repeating interviews in which they were told that hundreds of civilians were killed in the village of Mozote in December. Thomas O. Enders, assistant secretary of state for Inter-American affairs, later cast doubt on these reports. There had been a military operation but no systematic killing of civilians, he said, and anyway the population of the village was only 300 before the attack in which 926 people sup-posedly died.

> When a correspondent is offered a chance to tour rebel territory, he certainly ought to accept, and to report what he sees and hears. But there is such a thing as being overly credulous.[29]

The editorial went on to chastise the *Times* for "clos-ing ranks behind a reporter out on a limb," but, in fact, this the *Times* did not do. Raymond Bonner, once the most influential foreign reporter in El Salvador, was within months recalled to the Metro desk in New York. "The *Times*' decision to remove a correspondent who had been the focus of an aggressive campaign of Administration criticism no doubt had a significant effect on reporting from El Salvador," observed journalist Mark Danner. "The *New York Times* editors appeared to have 'caved in' to government pressure." The newspaper, of course, denied any punitive intent in this transfer, but it was an open secret, according to Danner, that executive editor A.M. Rosenthal was angry about the story.

Other, similar examples abound. Some journalists would be quick to agree, perhaps even proudly, with

Chomsky's thesis regarding the role of the establishment press. In the *Washington Post* of October 29, 1993, a journalist named Richard Harwood ran a column entitled "Ruling Class Journalists." He wrote of journalists' "active and important role in public affairs and of their ascension into the American ruling class." He closed the column with a question and an answer. "Is there something unethical in these new relationships, some great danger that conflicts of interest are bound to arise when journalists get cheek and jowl with the establishment?" Mr. Harwood's answer? "Probably not."

There is certainly no danger to the establishment. As part of his well-heeled campaign to expose the communist menace in Arbenz's Guatemala, United Fruit's Edward Bernays invited a group of journalists and publishers on a "fact-finding" junket to Guatemala. They were to be the guests of United Fruit:

> Among those who accepted were William Bowen, contributing editor for *Time*; Ludwell Denny, Scripps-Howard foreign editor; James G. Stahlman, *Nashville Banner* publisher; Gene Gillete, UPI day manager; Roger Ferger, *Cinncinati Enquirer* publisher; *Newsweek* publisher Theodore F. Mueller and his Latin American associate editor, Harry B. Murkland; Scott Newhall, *San Francisco Chronicle* Sunday editor; John D. Pennekamp, *Miami Herald* associate editor; J. David Stern III, *New Orleans Item* publisher; and William Stringer of the *Christian Science Monitor*. United Fruit's hospitality paid large dividends.[30]

The journalists relied on United Fruit officials as both their informants and guides. Bernays was delighted by the results, which he termed "masterpieces of objective reporting." Herbert Matthews of *The New York Times* later admitted that the press "saw and wrote exactly what the State Department wanted to see."[31] Dissenting views, offered by one or two journalists who had actually spent time in Guatemala were rejected by the establishment press.

There are always costs "when journalists get cheek and jowl with the establishment," regardless of what Mr. Harwood may say, and these costs may be disturbingly high. Bernays' "masterpieces of objective reporting" propped up myths about Guatemala that endure to this day and rendered toothless any investigative reporting about the 1954 *coup d'état*, which had been planned, funded and directed by the CIA:

> Except for a few leftist journalists, the press concurred that this was a successful anti-Communist uprising. In the absence of investigative reporting, United States participation remained secret. The numerous books appearing within the next few years supported this account. Most were written by the same journalists who covered the initial story and accepted the official interpretation, while the more scholarly studies drew their conclusions from documents supplied by the United States or the Guatemalan government.[32]

It is impossible not to ask, in closing this book, What is to be done? It strikes me, now, that many of the Haitians I have known—children, especially, but also young adults at the height of their powers—are now dead. The situation in Haiti is disastrous. When in 1991 health and population experts devised a "human suffering index" by examining several measures of human welfare ranging from life expectancy to political freedom, 27 of 141 countries were characterized by "extreme human suffering." Only one of them, Haiti, was located in the Western Hemisphere. In only three countries on the earth was suffering judged to be more extreme than that endured in Haiti; each of these three countries is in the midst of a recognized civil war. And the situation in Haiti has only worsened since this index was published. Against such odds, what could (say) a physician ever hope to do?

None of this is to say that it is time to adopt the cynical bookkeeping of the International Monetary Fund; none of this is to say that, because it is now clear that working in Haiti is neither "reasonable nor cost-effective," we should abandon this work. In making common cause with the poor of Haiti, we must, in the words of Sister Mary Lou Kownacki, learn how to "detach ourselves from results."[33]

But if this is a time for stocktaking, it would be wise to note that the enemies of democracy *have* succeeded in beating down the popular movement. That is a result, indeed. In a country as small as Haiti, there are not (romantic notions to the contrary) plenty of Jean-Bertrand Aristides among the clergy. There is not another Antoine Izméry among well-to-do businessmen; there are not scores of Yolande Jeans waiting to move center stage. There *are* plenty of democratically-minded peasants, but they face, at birth, a life expectancy of less than 50 years. The rural poor not only lack access to land, food and water, they are also prevented from organizing their communities in order to improve their lives. If it is true that one goal of U.S. foreign policy was to render the Haitian poor "politically inert," then even this cynical gambit may at last be succeeding.

At this writing, however, the majority of Haitians continue to offer obvious resistance to a coup that just won't take. But how long can their resistance endure? What means are left to those who envision an alternative to the bleakness depicted in these pages? There has been much talk of the embargo, which, at this point, has become the subject of great division in Haiti. The poor, it must be observed, have been under what amounts to an embargo of goods and services for years. If the embargo rankles Haiti's new masters, it also saps the strength of some in the middle classes who are hospitable to democracy.

In this war of attrition, who will be the first to cry "Uncle"? Looking elsewhere in Latin America, it is difficult to find consolation. In Nicaragua, a population weary from a war planned and funded by Washington finally acceded to the demands of the Reagan-Bush administrations. El Salvador offers an even more discouraging parallel. At Governor's Island, Aristide balked at one term of the proposed accord. Delaying his return until late October would only give the military more time to crush his supporters, he argued. As noted, international diplomats were quick to label Aristide "intransigent," "difficult" (epithets dutifully adopted by the U.S. press). But Aristide's doubts were soon proven accurate, and spectacularly so. When the killings do subside, it may be only once the army's task is done and the possibility of democracy has finally been eliminated. The analysis of Father Ignacio Martín-Baró is again instructive: In El Salvador, after a few years of U.S. military aid, "there was less need for extraordinary events, because people were so terrorized, so paralyzed."[34]

This essay has summarized a host of unpleasant realities, and my interpretation of U.S.-Haiti relations is sure to trigger denials. Such was also the case with early denunciations of our policy towards El Salvador. But the case against U.S. foreign policy, always compelling, is by now quite airtight. In November 1993, for example, some 12,000 documents regarding U.S. activities in El Salvador were declassified:

> The thousands of State Department, Defense Department and CIA documents demanded by Congress show that the Reagan White House was fully aware of who ran, funded and protected the El Salvador death squads of the 1980s, and planned the 1980 death of San Salvador Archbishop Oscar Arnulfo Romero. The documents were turned over the first week in November by a reluctant Clinton White House under pressure from Congressman Joe Moakley, D-Mass., and Lee Hamilton, D-Ind., and other congressional signatories.[35]

Of course, religious and human rights communities working in El Salvador had been making these arguments for years, and nothing reported in the U.N.Truth Commission report, issued in March 1993, was really news. For some reason, however, it was suddenly deemed fit to print.

In Haiti, similarly, the facts "now coming to light" were pointed out years ago by those in solidarity with the Haitian poor—many of whom understand quite clearly the mechanisms of their own oppression. The significance of the Salvadoran experience is not lost on those interested in the Haitian struggle for democracy.

Throughout North America, people of good will are horrified by the repercussions of our foreign policy in Haiti and elsewhere in Latin America. Even greater numbers are dismayed by the images of suffering that reach them via televisions and newspapers. What is to be done? Does the Haitian crisis call for more international aid? Certainly, any physician would be quick to underline the need for medications, vaccines, and the other tools of the trade. But it is important to see that the Haitian people are asking for more than humanitarian assistance, which does little in the long term. Aristide put it this way:

> In Haiti, it is not enough to heal wounds, for every day another wound opens up. It is not enough to give the poor food for one day, to buy them antibiotics one day, to teach them to read a few sentences or to write a few words. Hypocrisy. The next day they will be starving again, feverish again, and they will never be able to buy the books that hold the words that might deliver them.[36]

One is also reminded of a humbling song by Manno Charlemagne, a Haitian folksinger who has, himself, been a victim of the Haitian army. The lyrics to the title cut of *Oganizasyon Mondyal*—"International Organizations"—contain the following lines: *Oganizasyon*

*mondyal, se pa pou nou yo ye. Sa la pou ede piyè piye,
devore....Medsin entenasyonal mete kò-l sou kote.*
"International organizations are not on our side. They're
there to help the thieves rob and devour...International
health stays on the sidelines of our struggle."

One approach, the standard one in development circles, is simply to dismiss these critiques. How could international health, of all things, come to be perceived as
working *against* the interests of the Haitian poor? The
answer to this question is to be found in an analysis of
the ways in which international aid has too often served
to prop up the interests of an entrenched elite as well as
the interests of those in charge of the "new world order."
Medicine must pick its way through this morally treacherous terrain just as surely as must any other profession.

What, then, is to be done? Speaking of events since
the 1991 coup, Noam Chomsky has noted that "honest
commentary would place all of this in the context of our
unwavering opposition to freedom and human rights in
Haiti for no less than 200 years."[37] The first order of
business, for citizens of the United States, might be a
candid and careful assessment of our ruinous policies
towards Haiti. Remorse is not a very fashionable sentiment. But for many, old-fashioned penitence might be
the first step towards a new solidarity, a pragmatic solidarity that could supplant both our malignant policies of
the past and the well-meaning but unfocused charity
that does not respond to Haitian aspirations. The Haitian
people are asking not for charity, but for justice.

Epilogue to the New Edition*

The Oppressor as Savior

❖ ❖ ❖

In April, 1994, as the first edition of *The Uses of Haiti* went to press, refugees again began streaming out of Haiti.[1] The U.S. Coast Guard was intercepting over 1,000 Haitians each day, and the internment center at Guantánamo was soon full to bursting. Members of the Congressional Black Caucus decried the racism implicit in the treatment accorded the Haitian refugees, insisting that the only way to stanch the flow of asylum-seekers would be to restore democracy to Haiti. The governor of Florida, who had threatened to sue the federal government in order to recover monies spent, he said, in caring for the refugees, made a trip to Haiti; he was not well received. Escorted, simmering, to the Dominican border, the governor was expelled. Certain foreign journalists were also ejected by the *de facto* authorities.

The Haitian people continued to resist the coup by whatever means were available. Soldiers could not prevent refugees from fleeing, although they tried to: in one coastal city, boats were burned and refugees shot as they attempted to flee. In a sense, then, the coup had failed; the naked violence required to keep the lid on was proof of this. "That the junta felt it had to continuously use terror," remarked Laënnec Hurbon recently, "showed its failure to establish rule definitively."[2] Or, as the Haitians would have it, *tout bèt jenen mode*—it's the cornered beast that bites.

In May, President Bill Clinton appointed William

---

*Written December 1994.

Gray as special envoy to Haiti, replacing Lawrence Pezzullo, a man widely seen as opposing Aristide's return. Under Gray, there was at least a cosmetic strengthening of the embargo. New restrictions were placed on the transfer of cash from the United States to Haiti, and almost all international flights into the country were stopped. But rather than straightjacket the junta, both of these moves inconvenienced many middle-class and poor Haitians, who relied on small remittances from kin living abroad. It was more difficult to discern their effects on the wealthy, who had always found the embargo, such as it was, easy to circumnavigate. The Mevs family, one of Haiti's wealthiest and linked through Beltway lobbyists to the U.S. Congress, continued building their private oil storage facility (on which more later) as official talk of a tougher embargo emanated from Washington.

There was also tough talk about the need to end the stalemate in Haiti. In June, the U.N.Security Council passed Resolution Number 940, granting the United States the authority to craft an authoritative response to the crisis, and further entrenching the sphere-of-influence ideology that has characterized recent multinational "peacekeeping" missions. Although this did not please U.N.envoy Dante Caputo, who resigned citing "the total absence of consultation and information from the United States government," few others objected to the unilateral cast of the resolution. Indeed, the Clinton administration began leaking detailed invasion plans early in the summer. Troops were mobilized in the Caribbean. A clock labeled "Port-au-Prince" was placed in the State Department's strategic command center—a somewhat superfluous gesture, given that the capitals of Haiti and the United States are in the same time zone.

Despite the façade of toughness, Washington's statements about the Haitian military remained mixed. The language used in official pronouncements was often harsh, but high-ranking Democrats close to the White

House travelled to Haiti and had congenial meetings with Cédras and his colleagues. Relations with Aristide were often less chummy: one U.S. official with "extensive experience of Haiti," speaking to the *Boston Globe*, observed that "Aristide—slum priest, grass-roots activist, exponent of Liberation Theology—represents everything that the CIA, DOD and FBI think they have been trying to protect this country against for the past 50 years."[3]

By mid-summer, Beltway battle lines were somewhat more clearly drawn. Republican opponents of Clinton marshalled two reasons, both of them specious, to oppose an invasion to "restore democracy" in Haiti. The United States, they declared, had no interests there. In addition, Aristide was a lunatic, and no different from— indeed *worse* than—the military leaders. In June, Senator Robert Dole was able to argue, with no sign of irony, that the problem with U.S. Haiti policy was that it was "too closely tied to Aristide."

Dole also proposed that Congress should demand a 45-day "study period" during which our Haitian policy could be reviewed—a stall tactic (*dilatoire*, as the Haitians on the street would put it) to maintain the status quo. His utterances, applauded chiefly by Cédras and company, had their dutiful echoes elsewhere in the Grand Old Party. Senator Phil Gramm reflected the opinion of many when he called Aristide an "anti-American Marxist demagogue." In early August, 1994, Congressman John Myers of Indiana was quoted in one of his hometown papers as maintaining that "restoring former Haitian president Jean-Bertrand Aristide, whom [sic] he said tortured and killed hundreds of Haitian civilians, is not worth the life of one American soldier."[4]

No one quite matched the factuality and depth of analysis of the Louisiana congressman who noted that the problem with Aristide was that he was "un-American."

So much for the Republican view. How different was that of the Democrats? On the administration's side, Secretary of State Warren Christopher suggested that

Aristide need not be an indispensable part of a "democratic solution," alarming those close to the exiled president. The administration also conceded that "any effort to persuade Congress and the public that a relatively insignificant country like Haiti was worth American blood and dollars was bound to be an uphill struggle."[5] Together with the bipartisan derision of Washington's power elite, these official commentaries pressured Aristide to play by the rules—the American rules.

Over the course of the summer, in spite of statements to the contrary in late June, it became increasingly clear that Aristide was prepared to comply fully with the plans being elaborated in Washington, even if they involved military force. There was remarkably little opposition to this decision in the Haitian diaspora, even after the outlines of what many Haitians called the "American Plan" drifted into public view.

With little room to maneuver, Aristide continued to make concessions. Some of the largest of these were made in a series of agreements brokered in Paris in August. Through these agreements, the Aristide government put its name to a "structural adjustment plan" of the sort usually advanced by the World Bank and the International Monetary Fund—namely, the cutting of government bureaucracies and public programs, the privatization of publicly-owned utilities, the promotion of exports, and an "open-investment policy" that would slash tariffs and eliminate any import restrictions that might trammel investors, especially those of the foreign variety. Haitian-American scholar Patrick Bellegarde-Smith, speaking of the Paris agreements, complained that "the Haitian delegation to the World Bank signed away the economic independence of the country."[6] "Aristide Banks on Austerity," wrote Allan Nairn in the *Multinational Monitor*:

Axel Peuker, a World Bank desk officer, says Aristide's advisers 'did consult with relevant donors' as the plan was being written, and the final product was 'well received.' He added that 'there is this tension between the public image of Aristide' and the 'rather conservative approach, financial and otherwise' adopted by his Ministers when his government was still in Haiti. Peuker noted that the new plan 'goes a step further in this direction.'[7]

Aristide's economic advisers included Leslie Delatour, a Chicago-inspired economist who had been one of the chief cheerleaders for the offshore assembly plants under Baby Doc Duvalier. Delatour also served briefly as Commerce Minister under the first post-Duvalier junta, but was forced out of office by demonstrations against his policies. Little wonder, then, that the plan presented to the World Bank looked very much like the standard structural adjustment plan favored by the the Bank, the IMF, and by the governments of Japan, Korea, various European countries, and the United States—all of which sent delegations to the Paris meetings held to decide Haiti's fate. Aristide's 1991 plan to raise the minimum *daily* factory wage from about $2 to $4 was, according to Peuker, a "non-issue." World Bank representatives were a bit resentful of criticism, stating that the plan "is not going to hurt the poor to the extent that it had in other countries."

Why not? The Haitian poor, observed the Bank's Haiti desk officer, have so much less to lose.

Implementation of these plans required changes in Port-au-Prince—presumably, with Aristide as the IMF's interlocutor, including a change of personnel. Thus the overriding question became: would the United States really invade Haiti? And if so, with what intent? Clinton seemed to be drawing closer to the position of the Congressional Black Caucus, which favored the use of force to restore Aristide—sufficiently chastened—to office.

By late summer, the suspense was deadly—quite literally so in Haiti, where many of those living in the slums, emboldened by the sabre-rattling in Washington, began to show their support for the forcible removal of the Haitian military. Nonetheless, the Clinton administration continued to waver. In the United States, the invasion plans encountered significant public opposition—some of it, it should be noted, echoing the Republican position that Haitians were not worth the effort and risk, while a minority took a principled position against it. Simultaneously, refugee Cuban "rafters" created anxiety and hesitation in Washington, raising the stakes.

On August 4, 1994, the *Boston Globe* ran a story entitled "Haiti policy appears to lose momentum." The policy on the wane was the pro-Aristide shift that had allegedly gathered force among administration officials in recent months. Its loss of momentum was attributed to the work of Senator Dole, to conflicting statements from congressmen much closer to Clinton, and to a drop in the number of refugees.

This loss of momentum was further attributed to several U.S.-based groups pushing for a decent—and thus unprecedented—foreign policy towards Haiti ("Another factor undermining the administration's position," read the *Globe* report, "is the deep ambivalence about an invasion among Aristide supporters here.") Indeed, some—labelled in the press "Aristide supporters"—opposed the invasion on grounds quite different from those of the Republicans. Noting that the United States had created—through an act of the *U.S.* Congress—the modern Haitian army, then funded it, trained it, then covertly funded it some more, these opponents of the invasion believed that the U.S. had enormous, if unavowed, influence over the Haitian high command.[8] In this view, an invasion masterminded by Washington might do little more than shuffle the cast of characters, leaving the Haitian elite and their military essentially intact.

But at what point would this argument, no matter how reasonable, lose its relevance? Suppose that certain sectors of the Haitian elite convinced Washington that the army was no longer serving the interests of the rich: would Washington then see force as justified? Who would then take the place of those unreliable allies and "intelligence assets" known as the Haitian police and army?

Prior to the invasion, many in Haiti thought the use of force had been justified well before the August 28 assassination of Jean-Marie Vincent, a 49-year-old priest inspired by liberation theology. Best known for his efforts on behalf of the peasants of the area around Jean-Rabel, the priest had narrowly escaped the 1987 massacre there, and was later wounded as he tried to shield Aristide from a would-be assassin shortly after a mass commemorating the victims.

In the establishment press of North America, many wrote of Father Vincent's martyrdom as "the last straw," hardening resolve among those pushing for a military intervention in Haiti and deciding the undecided. The U.S. administration seemed to favor this narrative device, although others noted that the murder of a Haitian priest was an unlikely explanation for a major U.S. foreign policy shift: the killing of progressive priests and nuns, long a staple of Latin American politics, has rarely discomfited Washington's policy makers. A host of similar acts—including the assassination of the Archbishop of San Salvador while in the midst of saying mass—had no discernible effect on U.S. military aid to El Salvador.

Why, then, were U.S. troops being dispatched to Haiti? A couple of hypotheses make more sense than the self-congratulatory tales spun by politicians and opinion-makers. Was the prospect of thousands more poor, black refugees the only threat serious enough to prompt military action by the United States? So claimed the political scientist William Leogrande, offering as a general rule that "Fear of illegal immigration explains, by and large, current U.S. policies in the Caribbean."[9]

Likewise, the editors of *The Progressive* noted that "Aristide's return to Haiti has become essential to America's purposes in the region because it is the only way Washington can stem the flow of Haitian refugees, which transformed Haiti from a problem into a crisis and sent the Clinton Administration into a state of near-hysteria."[10] "Never before," observed Doyle McManus in the *Los Angeles Times*, "has the United States gone to war to stop refugees from coming to our shores."[11] Patrick Bellegarde-Smith added an important detail to this reading:

> On September 15, announcing what he then expected to be an armed invasion of Haiti, Clinton buried in the middle of the speech the most important point: he talked about 'the safety of our borders'—code words. He talked about the 300,000 internal exiles in the mountains of Haiti who could legitimately come to the United States because they are, indeed, political refugees—black people, mostly peasants, who qualify for political asylum. This was the key element, and I think the American public was astute enough to recognize it: we have to protect our borders, so we have to invade Haiti, or Haitians will invade us.[11]

Of course, the focus of Clinton's speech was the human rights abuses committed by the Haitian military, and for once he did not mince words: "Cédras and his armed thugs have conducted a reign of terror, executing children, raping women, killing priests....The message of the United States to the Haitian dictators is clear. Your time is up. Leave now, or we will force you from power."

He did not add, of course, that these thugs were *our* thugs. No mention was made, in his speech, of our seventy-years'-long support of the Haitian army.

By the time of Clinton's speech, it was clear even to doubting Thomases that U.S. troops would soon be going into Haiti. But to what purpose (other than keeping

Haitians in Haiti) and under what conditions? Many in Haiti suspected that the invasion's goals on the ground would be quite contrary to those of the Haitian people. The last-minute mediation by Jimmy Carter, Colin Powell, and Sam Nunn did little to allay these fears. As a result of an invitation extended by *de facto* foreign minister Charles David, the American trio travelled to Port-au-Prince on September 17. They were not there to negotiate, said the Clinton State Department.

The Carter team negotiated for two tense days. Television coverage of the brinkmanship seemed, at times, surreal. Speaking in the hushed, reverent tones usually reserved for commentary on golf tournaments, one journalist reported live from outside military headquarters, noting that Cédras was a man who wanted only to leave Haiti "with dignity and without further bloodshed."

Carter had even more fulsome praise for Cédras (and also his wife, who he termed "impressive, powerful and forceful. And attractive. She was slim and very attractive").[13] Blotting out the very memory of Clinton's recent national speech describing the junta's reign of terror, Carter noted that it was just "plain wrong" to refer to Cédras as a cruel dictator. The former president even invited the "honorable" general to visit his Sunday school class.

Ignoring the arrangements made previously with the Aristide government—that there would be no negotiation with the puppet regime put in place by Cédras—Carter met on September 18 with Emile Jonassaint, the military's latest *pope twèl*, or rag doll. Carter offered an attractive package, including the following selling points: "The Haitian military and police forces will work in close cooperation with the U.S. military mission....A general amnesty will be voted into law by the Haitian parliament....The military activities of the U.S. Military Mission will be coordinated with the Haitian military high command."

As the eleventh hour drew nigh, no deal had yet been signed. The *dilatoire* continued; in the capital and in the countryside, Haitian anxiety peaked. Later that evening, Clinton contacted Carter in Port-au-Prince, and ordered the envoys were to leave Haiti immediately: the first airplanes had been launched, and the invasion was underway. This announcement, it was said, led to the signing of the last-minute deal. And thus one of the most obvious lessons of Jimmy Carter's mission to Haiti was that the military dictators had never taken three years of threats as meaningful. When President Clinton stated at the end of that long, tense day that only "credible and imminent threat" of invasion—the launching of the 82nd Airborne—led Cédras to back down, we are reminded that all our previous threats had been quite incredible, in light of our long support for the military.[14]

But this irony escaped the establishment press, which commented on the Carter mission in tones nothing short of reverent. Many television commentators gushed that Carter was a shoo-in for a Nobel. That most distinguished Nobel recipient Henry Kissinger was one of the evening's commentators. With an uncharacteristic twitch of modesty, Kissinger admitted that he knew little of Haiti, and then proceeded to prove the point. He, too, praised Carter's mission, adding further cause for concern among those favoring democracy in Haiti.

In published commentary about this diplomatic legerdemain, "victory narratives" abounded.[15] Carter, by negotiating with the Haitian military, had saved the day. He was a hero. Speaking to a mass-circulation weekly, the former president demurred:

> Carter says there is no magic to his method, just a willingness to be a sympathetic shoulder for outcast regimes—a kind of celebrity shrink for the dysfunctional global family. 'There is a pent-up yearning among these people to be treated fairly,' says Carter, who turns 70 on Oct. 1. 'I'm kind of a relief valve. They can talk to me.'[16]

Some of the victory narratives were openly dishonest; most were analytically shallow (Carter's transformation of military dictators into an oppressed group "yearning to be treated fairly" was both). And almost all of these narratives failed to question the line that depicted long-suffering U.S. brass working tirelessly on behalf of Haitian democracy. Under the title "The Mouse That Roared Squeaks Back," the *New York Times* ran a front-page story about the trials of working with a fractious little populist priest:

> The strain of trying for three years to restore Father Aristide to power even as he openly griped about American policy, the strain of a weekend when the United States nearly went to war over him, and the strain of a politically and racially charged relationship between the West's richest nation and its poorest—all came to a boil this week in the capital.[17]

The Aristide camp, feeling betrayed by these last-minute deals and amnesties being finalized over their heads, remained silent. Their silence cost them: the next day, September 20, Aristide was barraged by criticism. "The proper response from Aristide," observed Congressman David Obey, Democrat of Wisconsin, "is not to second guess and nitpick. The proper response is two words, 'Thank you.'"[18]

Twenty thousand U.S. troops began landing in Haiti the morning after Carter's mission ended. They entered what in military parlance was called a "permissive environment"—that is, they had been assured that they would not be encountering hostile fire. This seemed to me self-evident: after all, the Haitian military was the step-child of the U.S. military. In its long existence, the Haitian army had no history of engagements with armed opponents. Its only enemies had been unarmed civilians.

These civilians now wanted to see more than a walk-in. More precisely, as Bellegarde-Smith noted, "most Haitians wanted the first wave of invasion to come in and obliterate the Haitian army."[19] Haitians, terrified of their own military, warmly welcomed the U.S. troops whose express intention hours earlier had been to rid the country of its army; U.S. soldiers seemed a bit nonplussed by this jubilatory welcome.

As the first helicopters landed, U.S. special forces, scowling fiercely, leapt out and assumed their stylized offensive crouch, weapons sweeping the horizon for enemies. At one landing site in Port-au-Prince, Haitian onlookers, enchanted and somewhat amused, became more bold. Finally, a man in a faded t-shirt and battered tennis shoes walked over to one of the special forces, ignoring the soldier's command to halt. The Haitian, clearly unarmed and smiling broadly, kept walking towards the crouching soldier, who looked ready to fire. When he reached the soldier, the Haitian man began patting him on the back and even tapping the soldier's helmet. "Relax," said the smiling man. "We're the people. We're the good guys." The soldier didn't understand a word, but got the sentiment. Confused, he smiled back, to the delight of the crowd.

The U.S. soldiers, most of them under 25, had good reason to be confused. Their marching orders—their "Rules of Engagement," or ROEs—had changed a number of times and would continue to change. One minute, the Haitian army and police—the "thugs," "rapists," and "torturers" of Clinton's impassioned speech—were their enemies. The next, the soldiers were asked to work "in close cooperation" with the Haitian armed forces. "Commander's meeting with Haitian general is called cordial," noted the *New York Times* on the morning of the landing. President Clinton elaborated:

> "This is a very different and a much better day than it would have been had we not been able to successfully combine the credible threat of force with diplomacy,"

he said in introducing a White House briefing. "Our troops are working with full cooperation with the Haitian military. We should recognize that we are in a much stronger and safer position to achieve our goals in Haiti today."[20]

Initially, American troops were ordered by Chairman of the Joint Chiefs of Staff General John Shalikashvili not to intervene in "Haitian-on-Haitian" violence. Some of the young Americans soldiers didn't like this, especially after they were asked to stand by as the Haitian military and *attachés* began beating and killing unarmed demonstrators. "It's messing up my head," complained a 20-year-old private. "It's wrong. And every time you have to look into the faces of the people here, the people who thought we were coming to save them from these guys, it breaks your heart."[21]

Soldier after soldier echoed these sentiments, shared by many watching (and I mean *watching*) from the United States.[22] For the first time, the spectacle of Haitian troops firing on unarmed civilians, captured on film many times over the years, captured the American imagination. Millions witnessed the death of Benykel Dédé, a young coconut vendor, as U.S. troops, chafing, stood by. "Four or five nights of it on television would have undone us politically," acknowledged one senior White House official, who then reported with some pride the multiagency "public-relations strategy" crafted in response to American indignation.[23]

Public pressure at home and in Haiti, combined with the complaints of the soldiers, led to another revision of the ROEs. U.S. troops at last began disarming the military and paramilitary groups like FRAPH that had for so long enjoyed the tacit or explicit assistance of certain sectors of the U.S. government.

The extent of this assistance—and its continuation long into the Clinton period of support for the government-in-exile—is only now coming to light. Writing in

The Nation, Allan Nairn quoted FRAPH leader Emmanuel "Toto" Constant who stated that in 1991 he had been encouraged to form FRAPH by U.S. officers:

> [Constant] said that his first U.S. handler was Col. Patrick Collins, the U.S. Defense Intelligence Agency attaché in Haiti, whom he described as 'a very good friend of mine.'... Constant said that Colonel Collins had first approached him while Constant was teaching a training course at the headquarters of the CIA-run National Intelligence Service (SIN) and building a computer database for Haiti's notorious rural Section Chiefs at the Bureau of Information and Coordination in the General Headquarters of the Haitian coup regime.[24]

As noted in Chapter 5, SIN's chief activities in Haiti seemed to have been political terror and drug trafficking. Constant taught its agents two courses: one on liberation theology—with which his American mentors were obsessed—and another entitled "Animation and Mobilization." According to another report, the CIA did not merely sponsor such courses, but also sent U.S. citizens to teach them, including seminars on surveillance, interrogation, and weaponry.[25]

These allegations were denied by the CIA, which did acknowledge paying Constant—for information only. "We draw an important distinction between gathering information from nasty people," objected one intelligence official, "and supporting or encouraging the nasty things they do."[26] Despite Constant's unequivocal statements, both the White House and the CIA categorically denied any relationship with FRAPH:

> 'No agency of the United States government ever funded Fraph; we never directed Fraph; we never had any operational relationship with Fraph,' a senior Administration official said at the White House. Asked whether American intelligence agencies had given support to the operation, R. James Woolsey, the

Director of Central Intelligence, responded with a terse 'no' and then said, 'When I say no, I mean no.'[27]

Unimpressed by the arrival of U.S. troops, FRAPH continued its lethal attacks on pro-democracy demonstrators. Coming after the embarrassing disclosures of CIA support, FRAPH's violence forced the occupying forces to raid FRAPH headquarters on October 3.[28] "This is what we've been waiting for," cheered the thousands of onlookers. Captain J.B. Shattuck was among those who led one of these raids; he and other soldiers were horrified to find not only weapons, but also grisly photos of victims: "They were like pictures you might take on a fishing trip, you know, showing your trophies. But these were human bodies, all mutilated."

Meanwhile, the next day, the U.S. Embassy provided a podium, a sound system, and some advance publicity for a speech by Toto Constant. U.S. troops provided security.[29]

Raids on FRAPH hangouts led to the seizure of significant numbers of weapons. Unfortunately, these raids were limited to certain areas; there remained *macoute* strongholds, as well as U.S. military officers who aligned themselves with the worst of their Haitian counterparts.[30] But where U.S. troops were slow to act, Haitians often sacked the headquarters of either the *attachés* or the military, seizing the arms and turning them over to the U.S. soldiers. The crowds seized *attachés* as well. Most of them were manhandled a bit and then passed on to U.S. soldiers, who quickly "processed" (read, released) them.

This toleration of the *attachés* damaged the goodwill extended to U.S. forces, and undermined official denials of U.S. complicity with FRAPH. At the time of Aristide's return, it was still difficult to state with confidence that the disarming of paramilitary groups in Haiti was underway. The occupation's planners were either wed to the notion of maintaining the paramilitary groups as a counterweight to pro-democracy forces—U.S. claims that "FRAPH is just a political party" lent credence to this hypothesis—or sadly misinformed about popular revulsion towards the Haitian army. The latter hypothesis was supported by the frequent references to Somalia, where it had been difficult for the U.S. forces to locate arms caches. Three weeks after the landing, Jean-Claude Bajeux, director of the Ecumenical Center for Human Rights, observed that

> The campaign waged in the American press and television to present Haiti as a second Somalia bears no relation to reality, because in the case of Haiti, the former military leaders would never find the kind of refuge among the people that would enable them to carry on a guerilla war.[31]

Another example of the confusion of U.S. plans was seen in the efforts to rehabilitate certain soldiers into an interim police force. The cornerstone of the rehabilitation seemed to be a six-day training course and the replacement of the soldiers' hats with baseball caps (this latter detail engendered the most commentary, much of it amusing, on the Haitian radios). The effort was coordinated by the Americans, who in some cities planned elaborate public events to present the first cohort of reeducated, interim police. In one northern town, a crowd gathered as the national anthem was played; people cheered at the proceedings until the new/old Haitian police officers appeared, at which point cheers turned to jeers of *mare yo, nou p'ap janm vle yo* ("tie them up, we never want to see them again").[32]

Of course, it was Aristide the people wanted to see again. On October 15, with Cédras and company departed for golden exile, Aristide became the first deposed Latin American leader ever to be returned to office. From behind a bullet-proof screen, sitting awfully close to Warren Christopher, Aristide spoke not of the power of troops, but of "the power of dreams—your words, your energy." The crowds, which were massive, were clearly overjoyed at the sight of Aristide, expressing displeasure only at the handful of Haitian soldiers foolish enough to show their faces at the investiture. An impromptu street party lasted for days, and the obvious joy of the Haitians called into question all the U.S. press stories of Aristide's waning popularity.

Despite his obvious popular support, there were signs that Aristide was not entirely in step with his people. During his speech, Aristide repeated his mantra of reconciliation—"no to violence, no to violence, yes to reconciliation"—but the banners in Port-au-Prince read, "Reconciliation yes, but justice first."

To tell the truth, Aristide's calls for reconciliation struck one of the few false notes during the course of the celebrations. It is conceivable that, with Aristide back at the helm, the long-suffering poor majority will be willing to let bygones be bygones; forgiveness, after all, is necessarily a thankless job. But the absence of a functioning judiciary has left the family members of coup victims frustrated and angry. During a mass to celebrate the return of Aristide, one elderly priest put it this way: "Shall we have reconciliation? Yes, we must forgo vengeance, but with two things in mind. One, justice needs to be served here. Two, the blood of those who died for the return of democracy has been sown as the seeds of the new Haiti that we must tend carefully, watchfully. Only their martyrdom makes real reconciliation possible."

Given that the chief reasons behind the invasion seem to have been to prevent further outmigration and to restore business as usual, what do we make of Haitians' obviously widespread satisfaction with recent developments? A recent set of commentaries by prominent Haitian intellectuals—all of whom would be regarded as "pro-democracy"—show no attempts to deny this popular satisfaction. "It is an intervention desired and demanded by the mass of Haitian people," noted Jean-Claude Bajeux.[33] Other Haitian intellectuals on the left have warmly endorsed the 1994 occupation in no uncertain terms. Writer René Dépestre, long exiled in Cuba and then France, wrote in *Le Monde:*

> I refuse to rigidly embrace some sort of mystical vision of past U.S. conduct. In the present situation, the landing of U.S. troops, I have good reason to believe that, for once, the interests of the United States join with those of the Haitian people, which are manifest in the person of their president, Father Jean-Bertrand Aristide.[34]

Leftist Caribbean intellectuals *welcoming* a U.S. invasion? Still, these are the comments of intellectuals and expatriates, whose views are no more likely to resemble those of the poor majority than have their lives.

But there is no denying the popular enthusiasm in Haiti for the deployment of U.S. troops. Have the poor been duped? For the victims of the most recent waves of repression, support for the landing might be likened to an endorsement of less painful methods of torture. *Any* change in the balance of power—at times, one thought even a cataclysm of nature would do—represented a potential improvement for the perennial victims of state power. The initial joy and relief in urban slums like Cité Soleil do not admit of multiple interpretations—even if we in the United States would do well to avoid taking that joy and relief as an excuse for self-congratulation.

What of other Haitians, those less directly in the line of fire? I know people who were initially either bitterly opposed to the landing or highly suspicious of U.S. motives and came to soften their criticisms. These Haitians were likely to refer to the history of the Haitian army and its entanglements with the United States. These Haitians were aware of our recent covert assistance to the high command and to the heads of paramilitary organizations such as FRAPH. They saw Jimmy Carter's eleventh-hour shuttle diplomacy as a last-ditch effort to preserve and mollify the Haitian army. But these Haitians, too, came to soften their criticisms of recent developments.

Friends in the United States asked me to explain this change of heart. Even before I had returned to Haiti, four reasons for popular support of a U.S. invasion came immediately to mind. The first two were the departure of the high command (Cédras, François, and Biamby), and the return of Aristide. These long-awaited events, often promised, made Haitians believe that the deployment of U.S. troops was good for something. Third, the spectacle of Haitian soldiers and police being roughed up by anyone, anyone at all, clearly delighted a population weary of the brutality-with-impunity formula that has long been the law of the land. This pleasing reversal did not occur with any consistency until several days into the occupation, when the ROEs were changed and U.S. troops raided FRAPH headquarters. Fourth, many in the poor majority reasoned that if recent events have incensed a portion of the tiny elite, then there must be some benefit for the rest of them.

But just which sectors of the elite are unhappy about the recent turn of events? The Haitian high command was displeased, as were, perhaps, the thousands of officials and politicians who constituted Haiti's *de facto* government for three years. But important sectors of the business elite were not at all displeased. The invasion did have as one of its objectives to restore business as usual in Haiti; and business as usual means doing it with the elite.

As noted in previous chapters, the United States has for the past two decades used Haiti as chattel labor. By 1984, Haiti was the ninth largest assembler of U.S. goods in the world, and this "industry" was quickly exempted from the bogus embargo so often deplored in the establishment press. In fact, U.S. trade with Haiti *increased* substantially after Clinton assumed office.

While Jimmy Carter—who publicly deplored the embargo as "shameful"—was dining with Cédras and company, the news-service wires buzzed briefly with what ought to have been a scandal. As many in Haiti had suspected, both the Bush and Clinton administrations had in essence authorized the shipment of oil to the military and their backers. Even as rhetoric about the "failed sanctions" escalated, U.S. officials from the Office of Foreign Assets Control loudly informed Texaco that the sale of petroleum to Haiti was illegal—but more quietly hinted that the company would not be prosecuted if it made such sales. One high-ranking official later testified that his orders to "go slow on Texaco" came from the Secretary of the Treasury himself.[35] Official U.S. documents, filed in 1993, note at least 26 tanker shipments to Haiti during the preceding year, and report millions of dollars in payments *from* Texaco affiliates to the junta.[36]

These arrangements helped to explain why, throughout the year prior to the occupation, Haitian millionaire Fritz Mevs had been busy building his huge oil tank farm on the outskirts of Port-au-Prince. It helped to explain why many in Haiti's small middle class joined in the anger of Haiti's powerless poor (who had always gone without electricity), but why the military and local gentry—families like the Mevs—had never wanted for much in the way of petroleum products. Except in oil-rich countries, an oil embargo serves as the bite of any serious sanctions. Thus there had, in effect, been *no* embargo against the coup supporters, merely a tightening of the longstanding embargo against the Haitian poor.[37]

Over the course of September, enough facts had been gathered about the leaks in the embargo to embarrass the Clinton administration, which continued to justify its use of troops by noting that all attempts at sanctions had failed. With the exceptions of a few lines in the *Miami*

Herald and the *Wall Street Journal,* however, the scoop of the summer was passed over for the more compelling human-interest stories that surfaced as the special forces, fresh from other areas of conflict, landed in "exotic" Haiti. Stories about Haiti's "MRE"—"morally repugnant elite"—did appear in the international press. But these failed to examine the mechanisms by which, for example, one prominent coup supporter, his U.S. assets supposedly frozen, was in March 1994 able to purchase, with cash and in Miami, a new luxury car.

The tepid exposés of the establishment press tended to focus on local actors and local factors. That is, it dwelt on ties between the *Haitian* elite and the *Haitian* military. To quote the *Financial Times* of London:

> The proximity of businessmen and the military is barely disguised. When Gregory Mevs, president of the infrastructure interests of his family's multi-faceted business, fumbled to find his business card on introduction, he joked: 'I have so many generals and colonels walking through my office every day, I don't need business cards.'[38]

Absent from discussion were investigations of the means by which the tycoons and their military protégés were able to use *U.S.*-based banks and companies in order to grease the cogs of the 1991 coup.

Although the military has been, at times, a loose cannon, it has always been the tool of the Haitian ruling class; the structural violence of Haitian society requires enforcement. The key players here were neither Toto Constant, who is small fry, nor the CIA, which was merely following orders. The reason that those giving the orders are afraid of liberation theology is that its central ideas—such as that so eloquently expressed in the notion of "a preferential option for the poor"—are annoying to the rich. And U.S. policy, whether domestic or foreign, has always been to make an option for the rich.

When the Mevs family terms itself "Aristide's biggest

supporters," distributing in early October 30,000 color posters of the soon-to-be-restored president, and hosts an elegant dinner for members of the Congressional Black Caucus, one senses that the term "democracy" admits to many meanings. Any "democracy" endorsed by Washington is likely to be a version equally acceptable to Haiti's rich.

And so when the *Financial Times* of London asks "Democracy in Haiti—will the rich buy it?," one is tempted to respond, "Of course they'll buy it. They'll even pay cash for it."

It seemed to me that some of the reasons why the U.S. soldiers were so warmly welcomed were fairly obvious, but I knew that a deeper understanding of popular responses would require a chance to interview people who had experienced the invasion first-hand. My subjects were not the various leaders who hold forth in press conferences, but the people whom I'd come to trust in these matters—the rural poor who have for over a decade been my co-workers, confidants, and patients.

Right after the re-installation of Aristide, I returned to Haiti after an unexpectedly protracted—and involuntary—absence. Much had changed. Conditions were perhaps worse than when I had left some months earlier, but morale was immeasurably better—better even than the televised reports had suggested. I found the physical landscape changed, too. The airport was surrounded by massive piles of U.S. military hardware. Heavily-armed American soldiers stood on the tarmac; out-of-uniform police observers kept a watchful eye on the movement of passengers through the airport. The dreaded "black book," containing an ever-growing list of undesirables, had disappeared from the immigration desks.

The occasional Haitian soldier was slinking around, but the ratio of foreign-to-native soldiers seemed to be on the order of 100:1. "So how's it going?" I asked one young

U.S. soldier who looked to be about 20. "It's tough," he replied, grinning sweetly at an elderly Haitian woman who was waving at him. "I haven't had a shower in two weeks. This is worse than Somalia—except that, here, the people love us."[39]

One of my co-workers, who helped me to negotiate the concertina wire surrounding the airport did not disagree. His Titid keychain, long in hiding, was again proudly affixed to his belt. Nodding to the U.S. troops, he observed that "As soon as these guys arrived, the guns stopped singing." My co-workers, who had endured significant intimidation during the coup, seemed to agree that the level of personal security was at an all-time high—especially if you, like they, happened to be poor and a supporter of Aristide.

Port-au-Prince was clean ("The people cleaned it up for Titid," went the refrain). The sky was thick with helicopters; the roads dark with military vehicles, especially the peculiarly-shaped "Humvees." The bone-jarring ride up to the Central Plateau also revealed transformations of a more Haitian nature. It seemed as if every wall and tree and stationary object along the road had been painted. The murals were often mordant and sometimes hilarious: one showed Cédras, his pockets stuffed with cash, weeping as he was led away by a U.S. soldier built like Arnold Schwarzenegger but with facial features like Denzel Washington's. In the mural, a helicopter hovered overhead—and from Cédras' pockets fell a cascade of U.S. dollars.

For the first time in the 12 years I've been working here, there was not a single military checkpoint between Port-au-Prince and Do Kay, the village where I live. No chains barred the way. Not a single Haitian soldier was to be seen—not even at the checkpoint where Chouchou Louis had been beaten and tortured to death less than three years previously. Indeed, I learned on the way home that our regional nemesis was gone. Major Charles

Josel of Hinche—"Commander Z" to those in the region—fled over the Dominican border, narrowly escaping popular justice.

As we drove through Do Kay, people clapped and yelled "*lavalassement!*" at me. In 1990, Do Kay had cast 289 of its 293 votes for Aristide. Over the years, I had learned to trust the analyses of these villagers, and also some of their leaders, more than my own initial reactions. In the heady days after Aristide's return, there was great confusion and dissent—a sort of disarray—in the commentaries of the leaders of the Haitian popular movements. But the presence of the U.S. military evoked little dissatisfaction in the village. *Se sa-n te bezwen,* a number of people remarked: "It's what we needed."

I tried to explore this further with a number of friends and co-villagers whose morale had been boosted in recent days. Everyone queried linked this boost to Aristide's return and to the Haitian army command's departure. As often as not, they mentioned the U.S. soldiers who made this possible. Some people in Do Kay were downright effusive about the U.S. troops and regaled me with stories about the humiliation of certain Haitian officers by U.S. soldiers. Several people have said to me, "This is what we call "*ipokrit yo sezi.*" ("The hypocrites are shocked," or, less literally, "What goes around, comes around").

Nou pran kou, men nou la pi rèd, reported a young man who represented the People's Organization of Do Kay: "We've been hit hard, but we're still here, as tough as ever." His analysis of current events was in many ways typical of the comments I elicited in October and November:

> The Americans would have been happy to have the coup succeed, we know that. The Bush administration was probably involved in it. But they didn't understand Titid's power. He's very small, compared to them, but much smarter. He said to resist, and we

did. The military killed a lot of people, and a lot of
people took to the sea. Americans didn't like that, so
they saw that it would be good for them to give us
back Titid. They made him sign a bunch of bad
papers, but the point is, he's back and the guys who
were killing us are gone. So it's not perfect, but it's a
lot better.

Most other assessments agreed with this one. One
young community organizer who had belonged to political
organizations since the time of Duvalier's flight stated:

The Haitian military has been at the orders of the
U.S. government for a long time. These guys are
always taking money from the Americans. We hate
the [Haitian] army, and always have. What has it ever
done *for* us? It only does things *to* us. So it's the
Americans' responsibility. Look, if someone comes
into your house and dumps garbage in your [living]
room, you can call them and tell them to get it out.
And you don't have to thank them.

The widow of Chouchou Louis was thrilled at
Aristide's return. There was no bitterness in a long interview conducted in the third week of October:

I think [Aristide's return] is a great victory for us little
people (*ti pèp la*). I always knew he'd come back. I
hope to meet him some day, and to tell him what
happened, although he probably already knows I
hope that he takes apart the [Haitian] army so that it
never rises again. What they did to Chouchou, they'd
do to another generation, too.

Indeed, support for Aristide was unwavering, and
there was some impatience with even his loyal critics.
For example, one market woman attended a public meeting on October 16 to hail the return of Chavannes Jean-
Baptiste, head of the region's most important—and
much-persecuted—peasant movement. Delighted to see
Jean-Baptiste, she was troubled by some of his remarks:

Titid is always hurting himself for our sake. He crushes his very body to serve us. Now look at him, obliged to get on an American plane, which is not his way, you know, in order to come back to us. It's what we wanted. Chavannes [Jean-Baptiste] is a good man, but he doesn't pray for the poor as much as Titid does. He's like Titid's little brother, but he needs to listen to Titid more.

A similar disjuncture was noted when comparing comments in *Haïti-Progrès*, the left-of-center weekly most closely aligned with the popular movement, with those of my patients and friends. In its October 26 edition, the newspaper deplored the "golden exile" reserved for the second tier of army officers, who had been posted as military *attachés* in embassies in Europe and Latin America. But people in the Central Plateau seemed to have a different reading of this ploy, as the words of one young woman suggest:

I think it was a great idea. People always talk about reconciliation, but it's [the wealthy and the military] who hate us. They hate us, they want to crush us. Nobody wants to kill another human being, but Haiti's too small for all of these people who want to crush us, crush our movement, crush our hope. They want to kill Titid, obviously—they've said so many times—so how do we get rid of them? I think sending them away to the embassies was a great idea, very smart and very much like Titid to think of such a good idea for us.

Most had charitable comments about the U.S. troops, although some noted with anxiety a disturbing trend: the troops were too quick to believe—and too slow to punish—those who had been most closely aligned with the coup government.

The assassination of one pro-Aristide figure is instructive. In the first week of November, the deputy Mayor of the town of Mirebalais, in the heart of the lower

Central Plateau, was killed when he emerged prematurely from hiding. Everyone in the region knew who killed
him: one of the section chiefs. So why, people asked, was
it so difficult for the U.S. troops then stationed in
Mirebalais to arrest the murderer? When confronted with
complaints about his slowness to act, the U.S. officer
responsible for maintaining order in the region—at this
writing, the lower plateau's highest authority—offered the
following defense of his actions:

> It's difficult to know who the bad guys are around
> here. It's very complicated. Everyone's saying bad
> things about the [Haitian] army and FRAPH, but I
> need details. I can't take action on the basis of
> rumors. In the case you're referring to, I couldn't get
> details—people just said, 'he's a bad person, he's a
> killer.' Then I couldn't get witnesses who'd testify.
> When I finally did, the guy disappeared.

The suspect was eventually apprehended, but only
after many in the region came to believe that U.S. troops
were reluctant to enforce justice equitably.

Still, the U.S. troops seemed, often enough, to
receive the benefit of the doubt. One elderly market
woman who spends a fair amount of time in a nearby
market town responded to my question about alleged collaboration between U.S. troops and *attachés*.:

> What do they know? They're just children (*se ti moun
> yo ye*). They're nice; I've met several of them. They
> just need some help figuring out what's going on
> here, and unfortunately they keep talking to rich peo-
> ple and *macoutes* who speak their language. But
> some of them still understand us, and can tell when
> the rich are lying about us.

Others with close ties to the poor were slow to condemn popular enthusiasm for the presence of foreign
troops. A university student from the area around Do
Kay had this to say:

It's not their fault that they're happy. They've been through so much....Three years of being afraid to sleep, of being afraid to tell even close friends how you really feel. How would you feel if there were a break in this cycle, even if the break was unlikely to lead to something enduringly good? . . . But when they're ready for the *blan* [foreigners] to go, they'll be quick to make their feelings known.

William Smarth, a progressive priest cited elsewhere in these pages, agreed:

Of course people are relieved by the recent changes. The left in the United States doesn't really under- stand the historical moment. Their ideology-driven comments don't incorporate the views of the poor; such analyses rarely do. Haiti is nothing like Somalia. There is absolutely no popular support for the Haitian military, which should be regarded as a proxy army of the United States. It would be great to be rid of it. Above all, it is imperative to disarm the *attachés*—and we can all push for this.

There was, as noted, dissent. But in the last months of 1994 it tended to come from people a level or two removed from the poor themselves. Chavannes Jean-Baptiste startled his peasant supporters (and irritated the U.S. troops) when, on October 16, he announced that "This is not a victory. This is not the way we should have returned. This is not the way that Titid should have returned. We shouldn't have needed a U.S. occupation to bring him back. We should have done it ourselves."[40]

According to one witness, a middle-aged market woman, there was a sort of silence in the crowd. Were they confused? Or crestfallen? It seemed to some in the audience that Jean-Baptiste was blaming them for failing to beat back the U.S.-armed military. "We tried our best to fight back," she protested, later, "but we're so small next to their big weapons." *Haïti-Progrès*, formerly strong-ly pro-Aristide, praised Jean-Baptiste's lucid analyis but railed against his unwillingness to publicly dissociate himself from Aristide, who had, its editors felt, sold out: "how can [Jean-Baptiste] maintain an anti-occupation discourse among the peasants of Papaye and then run back to a government that collaborates fully with the occupying forces?"[41]

Back in the States, *The Progressive* took a similar line: "U.S. Out of Haiti" read the cover of their November issue. "Will Haitians be starved and slaughtered if the U.S. forces leave? They're being starved and slaughtered now, with the active collaboration and connivance of the United States."[42]

There are two problems with this sort of commentary. First, it suggests that *the removal of U.S. troops = "U.S. Out of Haiti."* As I have tried to show—and as the Haitian poor discovered long ago—there are many ways to occupy a country. The United States may have been every bit as much "in Haiti" in the early 1980s, when the covers of progressive magazines did not call for an end to our occupation, which was then conducted through a *proxy* army, the CIA, and even USAID. The second problem is that it may be true that Haitians are being "starved and slaughtered" even now—but the perception here is that this starvation and slaughter are much abated.

I, for one, am sure that the removal of a man like Commander Z will alter the mortality rates of an area like the Central Plateau. It has certainly altered the level of fear. And if you live here, and hear the relief of the poor, you do not make light of these changes.

The Haitian people have fought hard for a measure of justice. That's what they feel they have in the return of Aristide: a sliver of justice, a chance at restoring some degree of democracy. If the poor cheer this as an advance, then perhaps the servants of the poor should join in this cheer—without any illusions. Even on a bad day, you'd have to admit that it's not the worst of all possible outcomes—which is the lot the Haitian poor have consistently drawn.

As the euphoria accompanying Aristide's return died down, it would have been good if Haiti could be considered to have gone back to square one: to February, 1991, when Aristide took office. But there have of course been major changes, all of them bad, during the past three years. The first has been the decapitation of the Haitian popular movement: many of its key leaders have been killed since the coup. Others have sold out, in small ways or in large. A second change has been a deepening of the emnity between Haiti's tiny elite and the rest of the population. The elite always seemed to have little but disdain for Haiti's poor majority; after the past three years, the feeling, it would seem, is more sharply mutual. As anthropologist Michel-Rolph Trouillot has recently noted, "The Haiti that Jean-Bertrand Aristide inherited with the presidency is one in which the cleavage between classes is wide enough to be called social apartheid."[43]

Third, there is the continued decline of Haiti's infrastructure and the hobbling of the economy. If in 1991 the "human suffering index" could describe Haiti, alone among the hemisphere's nations, as characterized by "extreme human suffering," imagine how much worse conditions have become since then. The devastation recently wrought by Tropical Storm Gordon, which in mid-November may have killed up to 2,000 people, is more an index of Haiti's fragility than of the storm's fury. This fragility is not the result of the embargo, but of the unfettered ability of investors, whether foreign or homegrown, to use Haiti as they see fit.

A fourth change is to be found in the neo-liberal economic development plan that is not at all in keeping with the wishes of the Haitian electorate. In a very real sense, the World Bank, the IMF, USAID, and the U.S. State Department have their hands on the reins of state in Haiti today. Careful review of their past policies here is only now beginning, and gives little cause for hope. Even internal reviews, such as those by the U.S. Government Accounting Office, have been scathing; independent assessments marvel at the cynicism of many USAID projects in Haiti.[44]

There can be little doubt about the dominant ideology underpinning the new administration in Haiti. "Aristide Chooses a Premier Who Has Free-Market Ideas," ran the headline of a *New York Times* article reporting that "Businessmen have been clamoring for a Prime Minister able to oversee a new economic plan acceptable to the World Bank, the International Monetary Fund and top business leaders here."[45] They got their man in Smarck Michel, described by the *Times* as "pragmatic, pro-market." *Haïti-Progrès* put a different spin on the appointment, giving it the banner headline, "Smarck Michel chargé d'appliquer le plan américain."[46]

These developments, although certainly an improvement over the bloodletting of the past three years, alarm many of those most committed to democracy in Haiti. In Chapter 5 of this book I sketched a history of the coup of 1991, reporting the actions of a courageous nurse who took over the university hospital when frightened doctors, responding to threats from the military, jumped ship. In mid-October, 1994, she closed a note to me with the following observation:

> I'm deeply distressed about the ways in which democracy is being subverted. What pacts did Aristide have to sign to return here? These IMF plans are only going to further impoverish the poor masses. And now USAID is the king of the hill here. It's *enkontounab*, unstoppable.

Many people feel that the huge international organizations are *enkontounab*. Some argue that this is the reason that Aristide *should* comply with their wishes; he has no choice. The uses of Haiti are now augmented to include

Haiti as object lesson in geopolitics: thou shalt not defy the New World Order.

How new all this is may be debated. Perhaps Aristide has already reviewed what happened to others leaders, such as Michael Manley of Jamaica, who tried to wrangle with the IMF. Manley, in his memoirs, writes of a meeting of 2,500 delegates affiliated with his government. The purpose was to discuss the structural adjustment programs proposed by the IMF: "They saw an absolute and disabling contradiction between the philosophy of the IMF and the model of development on which its programmes were predicated, on the one hand, and the goal of a socially controlled, egalitarian society seeking to maximize its independence of economic action, on the other."[47] By the late 1970s, there was open conflict between Manley and the IMF, with advisors from the fund going so far as to suggest the resignation of the government.[48]

We know what happened. The IMF, indeed *enkontounab*, won the day. Manley's version of democratic socialism went under in a spasm of violence unprecedented in modern Jamaica. When, years later, Manley returned to the political scene, it was as a chastened reformer.

Which brings us to the fifth change, that in Aristide himself. Poor Titid: imagine the journey he's been on. The author of a text entitled "Capitalism is a Mortal Sin" now meets regularly with representatives of the World Bank, the IMF, and USAID. "Aristide puts aside liberation theology to make peace with the elite," ran the headline of a recent story in *U.S. News and World Report.*[49] Whether in the United States or Haiti, most published commentary nods approvingly on this alleged transformation. Many speak of Aristide as having "matured"; others discern a new "realism." Even his staunchest advocates in diplomatic and business circles applaud the prophet's metanoia: "I think the best thing that has happened to

Aristide and his administration-in-exile is that they have had a crash course in democracy and capitalism," observed former ambassador Robert White, "and come to understand that too much revolution scares away investors. Small countries can't afford too much social experimentation."[50]

Once, Father Aristide was once the priest of the poor. Now, for a few more months, he's the president of a beleaguered nation run into the ground by a voracious business elite and their military *attachés*—all receiving generous outside assistance. President Aristide owes a considerable debt to and is engaged to parley with the very people and institutions he once deplored from the pulpit.

But how much, really, has Aristide changed? Quite remarkable is the faith of the Haitian poor in this man, who seems so transformed to the jaded eye—and so unchanged to those who believe in him. A slogan decorating a wall along the road to the Central Plateau reads: *Titid, se senbol demokrasi epi se fini.* The best translation of this is, "Titid is the symbol of our democracy, and that's all there is to it." It's quite clear. But in a moment of doubt, the slogan could be read in ways unintended by the graffitist: Aristide is the symbol of democracy, but democracy's over.

In theory, there is always the possibility of a sixth change: better reporting on Haiti. Throughout this book, I have criticized mainstream media coverage of Haiti. During the course of the past few months, new and helpful investigative reporting seemed, at times, to change the margins of acceptable discourse about what has happened here. As noted, Allan Nairn, writing in *The Nation*, reported that U.S. officials were present in Haitian military headquarters at the time of the coup, and also that the CIA may have helped to sponsor the creation of FRAPH.

The issue here is not whether or not the long arm of the CIA was at work in Haiti. The facts are clear on this. In *The Uses of Haiti*, I complained less about U.S. government denials of CIA involvement in Haiti—after all, it's their job to lie about such endeavors—and more about the U.S. press, which for years took these blandishments at face value. The key issue is, rather: how much truth are establishment journalists willing to tell? What are the margins of acceptable discourse and debate now?

To answer this question, one does not turn to *The Nation*, but to the many dailies and weeklies cited throughout this book. In the October 17 edition of *Newsweek*, we can read about all our alleged enemies— Toto Constant, the head of FRAPH, Michel François, the head of the death squads—and learn that they were in fact our friends:

> Constant, according to U.S. intelligence sources, was a paid CIA informer from 1987 until last spring [1994], despite allegations that he is a major drug smuggler. Even François, who left Haiti denouncing Cédras for betraying the country to the Americans, has reportedly been a paid CIA asset; his brother Evans François, according to *Newsweek* sources, has been on the payroll for years.[51]

Similar stories ran in *Time* magazine and in the major dailies.

Less than a year ago, Haitians were branded "paranoid" for making these allegations. So *has* there been a shift towards more accurate reporting about Haiti? A more sound hypothesis is that this "improvement" in reporting, which was quite striking during the weeks prior to Aristide's return, represents shifts in State Department pronouncements about Haiti and Aristide. Now that the junta is no longer in business, its misdeeds make excellent copy—and to allow that copy to be printed gives the current alliance the appearance of a new day of truth.

Throughout the crisis, the *New York Times* showed

its usual deference in transmitting officialdom's outlandish claims. On September 28, an article by Elaine
Sciolino informed readers that the "CIA [was] Reportedly
Taking a Role in Haiti." The piece did mention controversy about the agency's role here in years past. But in her
version of the debate, "the chief objections raised were
that the CIA was already doing so much for Aristide—
radio programming, leafletting—that more assistance
might give the impression of an overly partisan stance."
Without irony, the *Times* ran the following subheading
over the article: "After all the overt help for Aristide, he
may get a little covert help, too."

As noted, the story of high-level footdragging in all
efforts to keep Texaco from getting fuel to the Haitian
junta was suppressed in the press, receiving passing
mention in a handful of local or industry papers, but not
an inch in the major dailies and newsmagazines devoting
pages to human-interest stories about the experiences of
our troops in an exotic land.[52]

In addition to subservience to state power, one readily finds, in the establishment press, the usual hostility
to popular movements. An interesting understanding of
"chaos" emerges from journalistic commentaries on the
social responses to the events of September and October.
Crowds of poor people were regularly depicted as "plun-
dering and pillaging," when in fact something quite different—a political statement, say—was going on:
"Hundreds of Haitian civilians ransacked the four police
stations and central military headquarters here today
and marched through the streets with captured rifles,
plunging Haiti's second-largest city into chaos."[53] What
chaos ensued after the seizure of military arms was
never made clear, but the accompanying photograph
suggests that the captured weapons were handed over to
the occupying forces, as requested by the Aristide government.

The curious equation of popular democracy and

chaos comes through more clearly in an October 12 article, also in the *New York Times*, by Catherine Manegold. She reported that "Business Owners Fear Chaos at the Hands of Mobs When Aristide Returns," devoting almost an entire page to the fears of the rich. Manegold writes of the Haitian elite, who "speak French, not Creole," but half of those cited were U.S. businessmen residing in Haiti. One of them referred to Cédras as "probably the one person in that group who should have stayed. He kept us out of civil war."

The international press was scarcely more critical. In *World Press Review*, which openly praised its selection of articles as representing "a wide geographical and ideological spectrum of views," U.S. motives were taken at facevalue: the cover of the December 1994 issue, which shows a concerned U.S. soldier giving water to a supine Haitian man, asks "Can Haiti Be Saved"?

The past decade has been, as the Haitians say, marked by "event after event." The most significant of these has been the irruption of the poor as they have fought to change the primary uses of Haiti. This is the central meaning of the popular movement that brought down the Duvalier dynasty, fought the successor juntas, and, in one of the few democratic elections the area has known, elected a disciple of liberation theology as president.

With these changes and processes in mind, how might we assess recent developments in Haiti? What is likely to happen next? Three likely scenarios—one of them much more probable than the others—can be sketched:

The best-of-all-worlds scenario

Aristide returns as the advocate of the poor majority. In this utopian scenario, there would certainly be reconciliation and peace, but peace with justice. A Truth Commission documents the nature of the recent killings and massacres, families of victims are remunerated, the perpetrators are punished. Complete disarmament of the military and paramilitary forces follows. Many would hope for an abolition of the army, and radical restructuration of the police force. The School of the Americas is closed, and the CIA shuts up shop in Haiti.

In this scenario, the Aristide government becomes strong enough to offset the ability of the IMF/World Bank/USAID axis to determine Haiti's future, leaving that delicate task to the Haitian people themselves. As for the rest of the world, we would forge new links of "pragmatic solidarity" with the Haitian poor. Reflection on Haiti's $800 million debt would lead to the (obvious) conclusion that Haiti doesn't owe the rest of the world a penny; quite the contrary.

Haiti would take a uniquely Haitian path towards democracy, with the increased participation of the poor masses promised by Aristide during his 1990 campaign. Aristide, after serving a full five-year term *in Haiti,* is replaced by another strong voice for social justice.

The most-likely scenario

Aristide returns, significantly constrained by his debts to Washington and to international diplomatic and business circles. The most brutal killing stops, but a failure to disarm fully the military and paramilitary forces will mean repeated, if isolated, acts of violence, usually against the popular organizations. The Haitian security forces are "restructured," with little real change in numbers, and will remain strongly influenced by the United States even after a transfer of authority to U.N. peacekeeping forces.[54] The CIA continues to operate in Haiti.[55]

Haiti works at whittling down its $800 million debt, but has great difficulty doing this. The IMF/World Bank/USAID axis pours money into the country—and sucks it out, too, through a structural adjustment program that favors exports and offshore assembly. People who are genuine advocates of popular democracy will deplore this subversion of the Haitian people's aspirations; they will be marginalized. In the event that Aristide continues to call for social justice in a meaningful way, then he too will be marginalized in international circles as he was previously.

The worst-case scenario

Aristide is assassinated, either literally or morally. The popular movement sustains further decline through assassinations, discouragement, and cooptation—the latter usually accomplished with cash from what is ostensibly "aid" money. Haiti's profoundly anti-democratic elite continues to call the shots, and either the military and paramilitary structures of the past remain in place, or new and similar ones are erected; the *attachés* remain armed, and the CIA continues its hijinks in Haiti as elsewhere in Latin America. The Haitian agricultural economy continues to decline, and those who control the state apparatus rely increasingly on narcotrafficking, contraband, and intimidation in order to keep their coffers full (In other words, the worst-case scenario is precisely the one that has prevailed here over the past three years.)

How can we tell which of these is now taking shape? If the Clinton State Department were to express regret over the invasions of Panama and Grenada and Guatemala and Chile, and also our murderous past policies towards El Salvador and Nicaragua, then this would certainly lend more credibility to those who argue that policies have changed. But recall that the first two of these adventures were used by Clinton as *justifications* for his Haiti policy. Can we expect the powerful to recant? The chances for such penitence have never seemed more remote.

A mere two months after Aristide's return, the first, utopian scenario is passing from improbable to impossible. The question thus becomes: which of the two sad scenarios is more likely?

As I write from rural Haiti at the close of 1994, conditions are terrible and morale is good. But the military-diplomatic deal that was recently brokered, and the return of Aristide, cannot *create* democracy. Popular democracy is created peacefully by ordinary citizens seeking to shape, to some meaningful extent, their own destinies. It is not created by foreign troops any more than it is created by military aid or by offshore assembly plants.

Three years of brutal dictatorship, and the attendant disruption of social services and legal commerce, have compounded the already endemic suffering of Haiti in ways that are quite obvious and most disturbing. At the same time, there is a renascent sense of possibility in Haiti, one not sensed under military rule. Haitians, at least the ones I work with, believe that they can and must rebuild Haiti. This humbling *faith* in the possibility of collective action—however quixotic in the face of facts—should move us and fuel our own commitment to making common cause with the Haitian poor.

In fact, this combination of poor conditions and good morale marks an excellent opportunity for forging a new and unprecedented way of relating to the Haitian people. The first task, in my opinion, is to be honest about the history of our past relations. A second might be to forge new and stronger links with "ordinary citizens" in the Haitian popular movement. Who are these ordinary citizens? They are the rural and urban poor who constitute the vast majority of the Haitian people. Their hopes and needs should determine, in large part, Haiti's future course. What's more, they are even today clamoring for their rightful role in their country's reconstruction.

A third step would be to oppose anti-democratic programs now in place in Haiti. The rural and urban poor do not endorse the structural adjustment program that will now determine their fates. Those concerned with such radical notions as democracy—that is, the right of the majority to control their own affairs—would do well to counter the bankers' program with a pragmatic solidarity that both respects the will of the Haitian poor and is cognizant of the enormous difficulties that face them.

Certainly, such efforts would be dwarfed by the standard approaches to "development," those advocated, for example, by USAID, the World Bank, and IMF. As the new world order takes shape, there emerges a sort of international *de facto* world government, in which these agencies do indeed seem *enkontounab*, unstoppable.[56] Hearing their jargon—with much talk of "austerity measures"—it is clear that pragmatic solidarity is not their primary concern.

Austerity measures in Haiti? What could be more austere than the lives of the Haitian poor?

Many in these large institutions share the opinion of foreign policy expert Michael Mandelbaum, who recently asserted in the *New York Times* that, in Haiti, "Prosperity will require not only indulging the rich but also frustrating the poor." He further informs us that "social justice may just have to wait."[57] This formula for prosperity—indulging the rich, frustrating the poor—sounds curiously familiar in Haiti, for surely it was also the formula for this country's long misery. But the struggle for justice—sometimes spectacular and heartrending, sometimes prosaic, often inspired—will continue here, as it has for more than 500 years.

Central Plateau
December 1994

Diagnosis*

U.S. Government Has Chronic Allergy to Haitian Democracy

I guess you think you know this story.
You don't. The real one's much more gory.
The phoney one, the one you know,
Was cooked up years and years ago.

—Roald Dahl, *Revolting Rhymes* [1]

On August 28th, as a long day in clinic was winding down, my friend and colleague Fernet sent me a note. "You should come and meet a new patient." Since I was sitting only a few feet away from Fernet, I knew I should walk over to his consulting room now. I found him talking to a teenager named Nicole. At first glance, she appeared less ill than most of the patients we'd seen that day. When I walked in, she was engaged in energetic conversation with Fernet. And unlike most of the other patients, she wore nail polish (such details stand out in our clinic, which serves the poor of Haiti's Central Plateau). Looking closer, however, I thought I could make out certain stigmata of chronic disease—hair too silky, the whites of her eyes too white—but wouldn't have been sure she was sick without glancing at her medical chart. And I realized that in the noisy, dim bars of the dirt-poor provincial capital of Hinche, her hometown, Nicole would have appeared as a pretty, lithe young woman, with large expressive eyes and a ready smile.

---

*For assistance in updating this book, I am grateful to Haun Saussy, Michelle Karshan, Brian Concannon, Nancy Dorsinville, Leslie Fleming, Tracy Kidder, and Nicole Gastineau.

This last image is no idle fancy: Nicole, only 17 years old and living with AIDS, was telling us that she was turning tricks for food. Nicole described her modus operandi: she would ask someone judged a potential customer for money to buy a beer but would instead save the money and buy *fritay*, the cheap and dusty fried food sold alongside every major road in Haiti. She'd been doing this since she was 15, she said. Interruptions from a nurse (who'd already met Nicole and given her a shot of penicillin for syphilis and was drifting in and out of the exam room, picking up medical records) didn't change Nicole's cadence at all. In fact, she launched into her sad story, which began when her mother died, took a turn for the worse when she was raped by a policeman at 11 or 12, and continued downhill from there. "How long did you go to school?" I asked, at one point. "Never, really. I attended now and then, but could never pay the school fees. I can sign my name, but that's it."

Even after almost 20 years here and hearing a lot of sad stories from young people with HIV, I was shaken. Calm and dispassionate Fernet, with whom I've worked for years, was also dismayed, I could tell. "Do something," I said to him softly, in English, as we walked out of the clinic with Nicole. "Make sure she has enough to live on until we can make some sort of plan." We invited Nicole to come back on Friday, when we and the rest of the clinic staff were to hold our annual conference on health and human rights. We were expecting a big crowd.

On August 30th, with more than 3,000 people packed inside the church and another 1,000 outside, it would have been difficult for Nicole to get in. But Fernet, who was watching for patients near the entrance, escorted her to where I was sitting, up close to the podium. Several times I wondered what Nicole was making of all this. She laughed heartily at the skits and jokes, clapped after all the songs, and seemed absorbed by the speeches and presentations—some of them pretty grim—on health and human rights. After it was over, I asked her what she thought. "It's the best party I've ever seen," she said. "And now we're all going to eat." She melted into the crowd with a wave that said, "see you soon."

The past few days say a lot about everyday life in Haiti, a place where most people's daily routine has been driven into the ground by the processes described in this book. Indeed, not much imagination is required to write another afterword to *The Uses of Haiti* (1994), since Haiti is still being used in most of the ways described in that first edition. Alas, most of the more dire predictions made in the postscript written in December of 1994 (but first published in this edition) have come to pass. We have seen ongoing and readily documented obstructionism on the part of the most powerful governments in the world; we have seen ongoing sabotage of the democratic process by the traditional Haitian elite. But we have also witnessed the poor majority's insistence that they have a say in the future of their nation. Since the obstructionism and sabotage have been effective at making Haiti even poorer (amazingly), the structural violence documented in *Uses* continues to generate episodic violence. I would be failing my friends and neighbors—and guilty of intellectual dishonesty—if I did not try to make the links between the two explicit.

Since episodic violence is the traditional fare of the print media, it's easy to offer a sampling of what is going on as this updated edition goes to press. On the very same day that Nicole attended our "party" (and received a meal) for which she had to offer nothing in return, the Organization of American States made their own link between health and human rights:

> PORT-AU-PRINCE, Haiti, Aug 30 (Reuters)— The Organization of American States has released a grim assessment of deteriorating human rights in Haiti, saying armed gangs act with impunity while health conditions were worsening.
>
> The organization's Inter-American Commission on

Human Rights said in a report released on Thursday that it was "deeply preoccupied by the weakness of human rights in Haiti, the lack of an independent judiciary... the climate of insecurity, the existence of armed groups that act with total impunity and threats to which some journalists have been subjected."

The rights delegation, which met with government, police and judicial officials, also cited higher rates of illiteracy, maternal-infant mortality and undernourishment in the Caribbean nation of 8 million which, it said, "represent by themselves human rights violations."[2]

It's certainly progress when the OAS comes to understand that illiteracy, poverty, and disease constitute human rights violations. More specifically, these are violations of *social and economic rights*, which the OAS and its powerful patron in Washington seem to oppose at every turn. The Haitian poor, on the other hand, have made social and economic rights their primary struggle, as the next few days' events suggest. On Sunday, September 1st, there was a report of riots—some said a police station in a coastal town was set on fire—when taxi drivers raised their fares by one gourde. At current exchange rates, a gourde now amounts to four cents. Violence continues to smoulder in the slums around Port-au-Prince, where "gang wars" are taking a toll on lives and nerves. By some reports, there were 10 deaths during the past weekend alone. Tension is also high in the city of Gonaïves, where a dramatic jailbreak in August undermined a five-year-long process that brought to justice the authors of the Raboteau massacre perpetrated during the military coup of 1991-1994.[3] Over 160 prisoners, some of them ex-militiamen, escaped when a bulldozer crashed through a wall of the dilapidated prison.[4] An article from the September 3rd edition of *The Village Voice* described the outcome of the prison break in the following terms:

> The tension between the two worlds exploded last month when Amiot Metayer, a political militant and gang leader, was freed by machine-gun-wielding members of his "Cannibal Army," who attacked the Gonaïves jail he was being held in with a bulldozer. Metayer had been arrested on suspicion of ordering buildings torched during an outbreak of violence with a rival gang leader. Upon his release, he denounced Aristide, vowing to "fight to the death" any attempt to put him back in prison.[5]

Attempts to put Metayer back in prison won't be easy, even though most of the Raboteau convicts were recaptured. One of the first things that Aristide did upon returning to Haiti was to dismantle the Haitian army—which in over a century had known no enemy other than the Haitian populace—there were no troops to call in to quell the riot. And could the police, underpaid and poorly trained, go into an area where the escaped prisoners themselves belonged to local gangs, some of them armed with the very same automatic weapons described in the previous edition of *The Uses of Haiti*, weapons the U.S. Special Forces were supposed to recover and remove?

But the press articles did not mention the U.S. troops' failed disarmament program. In fact, most coverage blamed the violence, the lack of police protection, and the poverty on the Aristide government. When Haitian officials averred that they were reluctant to use force to respond to the jailbreak, they were promptly denounced by their detractors as failing to uphold the rule of law. Force or no force, Aristide was sure to be accused—certainly by the Bush administration and by its ever-ready tool, the OAS. But sectors of the international "human rights community"—unaware, it would seem, of U.S. complicity in both the successful armament and unsuccessful disarmament—have also denounced the Haitian government for its failure to act decisively to bring the escaped prisoners to justice. "Impunity is worse than ever," complained representatives of several such organizations. Here in central Haiti, such commentary from remote, misinformed or interested parties caused bitter laughter. As one villager here put it, "Sounds like [the human rights organizations] want a Duvalier-style response to the jail break." A lawyer based in Port-au-Prince, who approved of the government's temperate response to the jailbreak, wondered if the critics "were hoping to see another Waco?"

It's the same story with the investigation of the murder of journalist Jean Dominique, also in the news this week. Dominique and one of his employees were murdered on April 3, 2000, and their killers have yet to be brought to justice.[6] Although it took five years to prosecute the authors of the very public Raboteau massacre, the slow pace of the Dominique investigation has already cost Aristide many supporters abroad. The judge assigned to the case left the country in "voluntary exile," citing death threats and a lack of cooperation from above—this in spite of the fact that the government acceded to his long list of requested perks: a chauffeur, new lodging, bodyguards. The Aristide government, branded by such organizations for its failure to create—out of whole cloth, since there was certainly no such thing in Haiti prior to 1991[7]—an independent judiciary, tried to coax the judge back from Miami. But the judge, quite popular among the aforementioned human rights organizations, preferred voluntary exile in Miami to the risk of exercising justice in Haiti. Another report last month announced that the self-exiled judge is planning to cash in on his celebrity by starting a radio show there. The hapless Haitian government finally assigned the case to a new judge.

In fact, with the notable exception of the sad story of Nicole and others like her, all of these events have been on the radio; they have also made the rounds of the papers and the Internet. There is now no place in the hemisphere—not Medellín, not South-Central Los Angeles, not São Paulo—where the poor endure worse conditions, even though police violence is far worse elsewhere.[8] And Haiti's gang wars and murders and drug trafficking and general misery are now making the papers, even in the United States. But most commentaries made in English and French are conspicuously uninterested in the *origins* of this violence, when they don't collude to obscure them. Reporters who work in Haitian Creole find it harder to ignore the root causes, since they are obvious to everyone here: worsening poverty and deepening inequality that grow out of centuries of exploitation. No honest account of such exploitation could ever restrict its frame of view to the immediate scene: the last hold-up, the latest jailbreak, the latest mortality statistics. Yet honest and comprehensive accounts of the context of this violence are hard to find. We can't let the present and local context mesmerize us; the root causes, as I argued about related events in the 1994 edition of this book, are often far away and decades, if not centuries, removed from their brutal upshots. The proximal causes, as I'll try to show here, are the result of ill-conceived or malevolent policies that we must challenge if Haiti is to be allowed to survive.

The Uses of Haiti was written almost a decade ago. It's now 10 years later, 200 years later, 500 years later. Afterwords are supposed to be commentaries tacked onto the end of a book in order to shed light, drive home a point, or bring to a close a narrative that was incomplete. Books on the recent past tend to trail off into hazy generalities (or decontextualized particulars): "only the future will tell," they often say in their last lines. When I wrote this book, I made an effort not to trail off. And here I am, after two prefaces by eminent scholars I respect and after a long, long afterword of my own: how much more *Uses* can one take?

I'd be happy to think that *Uses* serves a purpose, and since I (like any author) think I had something important say when I wrote it, every copy it sells is good news to me—even though I know it will probably never achieve bestseller status. But writing the history of contemporary Haiti is not my main concern. Taking care of patients like Nicole means more to me and is more likely to bring me satisfaction (I will, as we say in the United States, keep my day job). Noam Chomsky, good enough to write the preface to the first edition, predicted, accurately (as usual), that "this is a book slated for oblivion." Bad marketing ploy, perhaps, but good judgement: the book has indeed been difficult to obtain for several years.

Would that it were out of date as well. This new afterword is, regrettably, mostly more of the same, with some notable exceptions. On February 7, 1996, exactly ten years after Jean-Claude Duvalier handed over power to another U.S.-supported dictatorship, Jean-Bertrand Aristide became the first president in Haitian history to step down from office after passing power to another democratically elected president. Although most Haitians felt that Aristide had not been permitted to serve out his mandate (having spent most of it in exile), they were eager to re-elect him. From 1996 on, the running joke here in the Central Plateau was that surely Haiti was the only country in which the year 2001 was more significant than the end of the millennium. After Titid was re-elected, again by a landslide, the next transition was in many ways as significant: on February 7, 2001, President René Préval became the first Haitian president ever to serve his entire original mandate, no more and no less, and relinquish power voluntarily.

The return of Aristide was contemporaneous with the return of another George Bush. Rather than reviewing positive developments, especially in terms of U.S. policies towards Haiti, this afterword reports terrible continuities. If you've read the first edition, you can have a spirited exchange with those journalists who have been discovering Haiti in recent years. If a journalist were to tell you that the INS has recently singled out Haitians for racist and exclusionary treatment, you, a close reader of *Uses*, could laugh and respond, "Looks like you did not read Chapter 8 very closely. The INS has routinely singled out Haitians for racist and exclusionary treatment for a half a century and more." If the same journalist were to note that the U.S. government and its Latin American allies were initiating an embargo against the Republic of Haiti, you, the astute reader, would point out that this was also the case from 1804 to 1862, during which time the United States, itself a major slave economy, refused to extend diplomatic recognition to the first country to ban slavery.[9] But the slave-owning republic to the north of Haiti was not content merely to refuse to receive a Haitian ambassador. In a series of actions with loud echoes today, we also pressured other American republics to refuse to recognize Haiti:

> The United States blocked Haiti's invitation to the famous Western Hemisphere Panama Conference of 1825 and refused to recognize Haitian independence until 1862. This isolation was imposed on Haiti by a frightened white world, and Haiti became a test case, first, for those arguing about emancipation and then, after the end of slavery, for those arguing about the capacity of blacks for self-government.[10]

And if that enterprising journalist were to label recent coup attempts "the new violence" in Haiti while deploring the twin scourges of racism and bad policies, you the reader would probably retort, "See *Uses of Haiti*, passim."

But despite the continuities, there have been some fascinating new twists and turns. The nature of the war against the Haitian poor has changed in important ways. Much of *The Uses of Haiti* described how, during the 20th century, the U.S. government occupied Haiti militarily (1915-1934), created the modern Haitian army through an act of the *U.S.* Congress, and then continued to support it and the Duvalier dictatorships in the style to which they had become accustomed from the time of the pull-out of troops in 1934 until Haiti's first free and fair elections, held on December 16th, 1990. *Uses* also tells the tragic story of the military coup of 1991, the bloody years that followed, and the restoration of constitutional rule in 1994. The long afterword, written shortly after U.N.-led forces entered Haiti in 1994, described how we, the United States, tried to condition the assistance necessary to rebuild ravaged Haiti on U.S. political objectives. The objectives were unattractive to the Haitian poor, who continued to vote for the social-justice platform that emerged in the late eighties.

As for aid to the governments of Haiti, it flowed most freely during the Duvalier dictatorships and the violent military juntas. Now that Haitians possess at long last a democratically elected government, the U.S. government has decided to bypass normal channels and instead distribute its aid (and influence) via non-governmental organizations (NGOs) alone. Worse still, it has again engaged its allies—and who dares oppose us?—to follow suit. For example, the administration of George W. Bush has exercised its authority to veto already-approved aid loans from the Inter-American Development Bank— loans earmarked to improve health, education, and water in Haiti. A few outside of Haiti seem to be paying attention, but human rights organizations have had little to say about the hypocrisy and disregard for other humans and their rights apparent in such decisions— there is widespread awareness within Haiti of what it means to be so generous to dictators and military juntas and to subsequently block a series of loans for clean water, education, and health care. The OAS has been the major cheerleader of the blockade against Haiti under Aristide's presidency, which brings us back, with something between stupefaction and anger, to its statement of August 30th: of course Haiti's health and sanitary disasters "represent by themselves human rights violations." That's why it's wrong for the hemisphere's most powerful nation to block humanitarian aid to the most impoverished and wronged one. The violations are caused not by Haiti, but by its powerful neighbor to the north.

What is the justification for this latest act of arrogant hostility toward the Haitian poor? Trumped-up charges regarding improper methods of tallying ballots during the May 2000 legislative elections are the avowed reason for this particular embargo. Certainly, Americans are right to be concerned about electoral justice, but let us be clear about the need for an international standard. Ironically, charges of election irregularities were being leveled against the Haitian government at about the same time that more serious allegations concerning the U.S. electoral process, most notably in Florida, were being investigated. In fact, two years later, Florida's inefficient and corrupt electoral machinery continues to make headlines.

Are there solid reasons to believe, for example, that Aristide didn't win the 2000 elections fair and square? No, the complaints this time were about the *legislative and local* elections that took place in May 2000, months before Titid was reelected by yet another landslide. The May elections fielded some 20,000 candidates. Critics seeking to impugn the elections, which delivered, as predicted by Gallup polls, a massive victory for the party associated with Aristide, argued that the votes for eight Senate seats had not been counted correctly. A run-off was in order, argued the OAS and its liegelord in Washington. So, presto, official foreign aid to Haiti—necessary to rebuild the country's ravaged infrastructure—was frozen.

Subsequently, the Haitian government followed all of the stipulations set down in a series of accords advanced by the OAS in June, 2001:[11] the seven senators involved (one of the seats had already expired, and was re-run) not only agreed to a run-off with their second place challengers, but resigned so that new elections could be held. One would be gratified and amazed to see such behavior among American legislators. But despite concessions here in Haiti, the aid embargo remains, suggesting that perhaps the actual reason for it was not really U.S. concern over local elections. Those who study patterns of U.S. giving to Haiti and to other countries would certainly be a bit suspicious. The U.S. government had, as noted, little trouble running hundreds of millions of dollars through the Duvalier dictatorship; rarely questioned the purposes for which the "aid" was spent, never asked for much in the way of accountability (except, of course, in terms of promises to repay loans). We were unstintingly generous to the post-Duvalier military, whose spectacular exploits, including the torching of Aristide's church during mass, are chronicled in this book. And even during the leaky, half-hearted embargo against the men in uniform who ousted Aristide (a junta eventually found guilty of crimes against humanity), the United States was providing training, on U.S. soil, to the officers of that very regime.[12]

Suspicions about the real reasons behind the U.S. aid embargo against Haiti are only fanned when one looks elsewhere for links between the extent to which adherence to certain electoral procedures determines whether or not U.S. aid flows. To say that "double standards" exist is a considerable understatement. Take Pakistan, which until recently was under a similar embargo but with some justification, since General Pervez Musharraf had come to power in a military coup.[13] But all of this changed as of mid-September, 2001. "My personal objective when I got here in August," [Ambassador] Ms. Chamberlin said in a November, 2001 interview, "was to work very hard to improve Pakistani-American relations, with the aim that at the end of my three years here we could lift American sanctions on Pakistan. I could never have dreamed that we'd have accomplished so much in my first three months."[14] What's a coup between good friends? All those unpleasantries were quickly forgotten when new uses for Pakistan were found.[15]

The hypocrisy of U.S. justifications for imposing trade and aid sanctions has been noted by almost all neutral observers.[16] But what are the immediate, lived effects of this hypocrisy among the poor? The current U.S.-sponsored embargo against Haiti targets the most vulnerable population in all of the hemisphere, the poorest people with the most fragile economy, ecology, and society. Its impact has been profound, as a report from the Inter-American Development Bank notes. Bank officials themselves concluded that "overall, the major factor behind economic stagnation is the withholding of both foreign grants and loans, associated with the international community's response to the critical political impasse. These funds are estimated at over U.S.$500 million."[17]

If the Bank itself can come to such a conclusion, why is it among the institutions punishing Haiti? U.S. Congresswoman Barbara Lee answered this question earlier this year:

> The U.S. has used its veto powers on the IDB's Board of Directors to stop all loans designated to Haiti and has chilled funding opportunities at the other financial institutions, like the World Bank and IMF, pending a resolution of the political situation in Haiti. This situation is unique because the loans in question have been approved by the bank's board of executive directors, and the Haitian Government has ratified the debt and signed contractual documents.
>
> This veto is particularly disturbing since the charter of the IDB specifically states that the Bank shall not intervene in the politics of its member states. The Bush Administration has decided to leverage political change in a member country by embargoing loans that the Bank has a contractual obligation to disburse.[18]

Since I am particularly interested in the welfare of the sick, allow me to chart the history of Inter-American Development Bank Loan No. 1009/SF-HA, "Reorganization of the National Health System." The "national health system" was designed to be the primary provider of basic health care of the poor majority. On July 21, 1998, the Haitian government and the IDB signed a $22.5 million loan for Phase I of a project to "decentralize and reorganize" the Haitian health care system. The need to improve the health care system then, as now, was urgent: there are 1.2 doctors, 1.3 nurses and .04 dentists per 10,000 Haitians (for comparison, there are 27.9 doctors for every 10,000 U.S. inhabitants and 58.2 doctors for every 10,000 Cuban inhabitants).[19] Forty percent of the Haitian population is without access to any form of primary health care; HIV and tuberculosis rates are by far the highest in the hemisphere, as are infant, juvenile, and maternal mortality. To use its jargon, the IDB project would target eighty percent of the population for access to primary health care through the construction of low-cost clinics and local health dispensaries. The funds would be used to train community health agents and to purchase medical equipment and essential medicines. To be gauged successful by its own criteria, the project must lead to a drop in the infant mortality rate from 74 to 50 deaths per 1,000 live births; a drop in the juvenile mortality rate from 131 to 110 deaths per 1,000 births: a drop in the birth rate from 4.6 to 4; and a drop in the general mortality rate attributable to the lack of proper health care from 10.7 per 1,000 to 9.7 per 1,000. These were not overly ambitious goals. Most who evaluated the project thought it feasible and well designed. And the need speaks for itself.

So what's the hold-up? In order for funds to be disbursed by the IDB, the loan agreement had to be ratified by the Haitian parliament. In October 1998, the Haitian Minister of Health presented the project to Haiti's famously obstructionist 46th Legislature, which included many people who now constitute the Convergence "Démocratique" (the coalition opposed to Aristide) and soon to be voted out of office. For weeks, the Parliament simply failed to meet. When it did meet, it failed to obtain a quorum. The legislators also rejected three prime ministers proposed by then-president René Préval. The goal was clear enough within Haiti: paralyze all social services, including health care, in order to undermine every effort of the Executive branch, which was still associated with the party founded by Aristide, to improve the living conditions of the poor majority that had elected him by a landslide in 1990 and would do so again in November 2000. The Haitian people had had enough of this kind of parliamentary gridlock, which is why they voted a straight ticket that supported the party associated with Aristide in the May 2000 parliamentary elections.

In October 2000, after the installation of the more representative 47th Legislature, the new parliament voted immediately to ratify the health project along with the three other vital IDB loan agreements. No money yet, but it was on the way, the Haitians were told by an official decree published in the Government's newspaper on January 8, 2001. By early March, the IDB had not yet disbursed the loan but announced that it intended to work with the new Aristide government, reelected a few months previously, and to finance projects already in the pipeline. It demanded, however, that a number of conditions be met. The Government must pay $5 million dollars in arrears to the IDB. On May 15, 2001, notwithstanding the fact that not one penny of this or any other IDB loan had been disbursed, the Bank advised the Haitians that the government would be required to pay what it called a "credit commission" of 0.5% on the entire balance of undisbursed funds effective twelve months after the date of approval of the loans. As of March 31, 2001, Haiti already owed the IDB a $185,239.75 "commission fee" on a loan never received. The total amount of fees owed on five development loans from the IDB, all of them taken out in previous decades, was $2,311,422. The Bank advised the Government that payment must begin on September 15, 2001 with the balance due October 5, 2001. In mid-May, amidst rumors that the IDB was shutting down its offices in Haiti, the Bank announced that the country representatives and top staff were being recalled to Washington "for consultations."

The "consultations" could not have been too heartening. According to the title of an AP wire story, "Haiti clamors for release of blocked loans that might take years to disburse." The chief IDB officer in Haiti called for the payment of "$20 million in loan arrears and reform [of government] economic practices" before Haiti could gain access to the already-approved credit. Many of these loans on which arrears are "owed" were of course made to the dictatorships and military juntas described in the previous chapters. Even supposing the educational loan were to go through, the IDB officer allowed that "If other loans are not added, Haiti will probably be paying out more than it is getting."[20]

Alas for the Haitian poor, the lives of hundreds of thousands hang in the balance: the loans are for three things—water, health care, and education—that they need desperately. What would Nicole's fate have been, one wonders, if she had been able to attend school? What will her future be if she does not drink clean water and receive proper medical care?

And proper medical care is awfully hard to deliver under these conditions. The courtyard around our hospital remains overflowing with patients. Over the past year, our general ambulatory clinic has seen an enormous increase in demand. We are staffed to receive about 35,000 visits annually, but if trends hold will this year see an estimated 180,000 patients. Meanwhile, our visits to most neighboring facilities show them to have very few patients, since the services they offer are too expensive for the destitute sick. We have registered a rise in trauma cases due in large part to road accidents (which relate to lack of road upkeep and other infrastructural deficits). The sequelae of accidents are more serious, since patients are required to travel farther to receive care and because many require, but do not get, the care of orthopedic and trauma surgeons. Malaria remains, in our facility, the leading single diagnosis during the rainy season. Malaria deaths continue to occur, even though Haiti has not yet registered chloroquine-resistant cases. There's no great mystery as to why: lack of access to care remains the primary problem, as noted in the initial IDB proposal, drafted years ago.

As for the impact of the other embargoed loans on the Haitian poor, what might one expect if the public infrastructure of the country were run into the ground and there were now no money to provide clean water and at least primary education? As the Haitians say, you can't get blood out of a rock. The situation here is as bad as any I've seen, with an international aid embargo leveled against a democratically elected government. Journalists and other diverse analysts expending all of their energies, it would seem, criticizing David, not Goliath. When I pointed these things out at a recent conference sponsored by the Pan American Health Organization, I was rebuked by an irate IDB official for my "rude and inappropriate" comments. But a couple of months later, as the dimensions of the humanitarian crisis became apparent even within the corridors of power, U.S. Senator Christopher Dodd was not very delicate, either. Speaking from the Senate floor on July 31, 2002, Dodd noted the obvious:

Ironically it is the United States that has taken the lead in preventing Haiti from receiving assistance from the [Inter-American] Development Bank—the institution that is supposed to be the premier regional development agency.

Proponents of withholding crucial IDB funding point to Haiti's weak institutions, to the need for drastic and timely economic and administrative reforms, as a prerequisite to restarting assistance. True, Haiti is an impoverished nation with weak institutions. True, there is corruption at high levels. Yes, there is a serious need for reform in these areas. But it is also true that poor countries breed weak institutions, and seek to strengthen themselves and help their people with the assistance of international humanitarian aid.

But that is not the real reason that assistance is being withheld. The real reason funds are being withheld is political—namely as leverage in ongoing OAS negotiations to resolve issues related to the May 2000 Haitian elections.

The Secretary General of the Organization of American States (OAS) has endeavored over the last two years to resolve the political stalemate in Haiti over the disputed 2000 parliamentary elections. He has put on the negotiating table a balanced and credible proposal for resolving the election dispute and is working to ensure that security and other matters of concern to Haitian society are being taken seriously by the Government of Haiti.

That said, has Haiti had flawed elections? Absolutely!

Mr. President, we are talking about a country without a long historical tradition of democracy, and while the squalor worsens, and public faith in government is reduced to zero, what remains of their fragile democracy is eroded further.

Even the United States, with our proud history of peaceful transitions of power, orderly elections, and representative governance, has had significant troubles with our own elections in very recent years. Surely we do not expect Haiti to live up to a standard of electoral perfection that we ourselves have not achieved, much less to use this standard as a benchmark of worthiness to receive desperately needed international aid.

I have always strongly opposed linkage between the ongoing political dialogue and Haitian access to the resources of the Inter-American

Development Bank (IDB). These monies have been held hostage for too long and the damage to the Haitian economy has been devastating. The good faith efforts of the Haitian government in responding to the OAS initiative should be more than enough justification for beginning the process of loan disbursements from the IDB, although the state of despair in Haiti is all the justification that should be needed for an institution whose primary obligation is to promote economic and social development in the hemisphere.

Shame on the Inter-American Development Bank for allowing itself to be used in this manner. It does not speak well of an institution that for the most part has a very good reputation. Shame on the United States for pressuring the IDB to do so.[21]

Until very recently, the OAS has hewn whatever line the Bush administration saw fit to trace. A few days ago, however, there were signs that such repugnant policies were making even the diplomats uneasy. Yesterday, September 4th, the OAS passed Resolution Number 822, which called for an end to the negotiations between the Haitian government and the opposition.[22]

Who, exactly, constitutes this all-powerful opposition, capable of blocking the lifelines of development assistance to the very country (their own country) most in need of it? Inside Haiti, the main political opposition is the same motley group described in the first edition of Uses. These tiny grouplets have banded together in a still small coalition called, without irony, the Convergence "Démocratique." Although mostly rightwingers, its leadership comes from several quarters of the political map. The Convergence is, however, united in its unswerving opposition to Aristide—and thus, one must conclude, to the poor majority's right to have a say in Haiti's affairs. The level of support of the groups composing the Convergence, as gauged by polls, has run between 4 and 12 percent.[23] It is the "intelligentsia" of the Convergence who come up with cockamamie stories about how each attack or attempted coup against Aristide is really a sham authored by himself, accusations which echo their comments regarding the attempts on his life in the eighties.[24]

Although the Convergence has scant popular support within Haiti, it has strong and unambiguous support in Washington. And it is to Washington that its leaders turn. For example, the "Movement for National Salvation" has just set in motion rumors, subsequently denied by an official State Department spokesman, that the United States has endorsed a "plan for political transition" involving Aristide's forced departure.[25] The Convergence is funded, at least in part, by the U.S. International Republican Institute, which is associated, unsurprisingly, with the U.S. Republican Party and obtains funding from Congress through the National Endowment for Democracy.[26] In this sense, then, Haitians do feel that they suffer from a system which offers privileged people impunity. But it comes from our government, not theirs.

What about the "Haiti solidarity community" that should have been able to convey a coherent critique of the policies of the powerful to the citizens of the rich countries that now decide the fates of the bottom billion? Alas, this community—to which I belong—has been almost as fractured as the Haitian political class itself. Perhaps this is unsurprising, from a sociological point of view. In an incisive book, Michael Ignatieff makes an important point for those seeking to sift through the incoherent commentaries flying around the Internet:

> The phrase "global civil society" implies a cohesive moral movement when the reality is fierce and disputatious rivalry among the nongovernmental organizations. These groups frequently claim that they represent human interests and

human rights more effectively than governments, and while this is sometimes true, NGOs
are not necessarily more representative or
more accountable than *elected* governments.[27]

Within Haiti and without, the "Haiti solidarity community" is divided on just about everything. The "human
rights community" is certainly full of strange bedfellows.
Two of the human rights groups most vocal in their
denunciations of the "Aristide regime" have just won an
award presented within the U.S. Embassy.[28] In truth,
this "community" is riven by deep division, particularly
over social and economic rights—the rights of the poor—
and their relation to legal rights. The so-called progressive commentary from outside Haiti can also erase history to make a point. One of the biggest anti-Aristide gripes
of the sectarian left is that he allegedly "sold out" in order
to bring in aid money to rebuild Haiti. Calls to ignore the
results of democratic elections are not usually involved in
democratic niceties. One self-proclaimed radical, who
launches endless e-mails from Canada, recently titled
one "Jean-Bertrand Aristide, *bay talon-w!*" (Jean-
Bertrand Aristide, get lost!"). Now there's a true democrat
speaking: she wants the people's choice to disappear
from the scene. Most of these complaints come, as noted
in the epilogue written at the close of 1994, from the self-
appointed leaders of various small movements, each with
their sponsors in Europe or North America. But how can
you rebuild Haiti without massive resources, perhaps
something on the scale of half of what has been drained
from Haiti in recent years? It will require, as noted, hundreds of millions of dollars to rebuild ruined health, educational, and sanitary infrastructure here. And until that
happens, there will be misery and hunger and inequality,
and their consequences, here. Such "structural violence,"
which has been perpetrated from above and without, will
be reflected in local violence, just as it is everywhere in
the world.

You'd think that progressive observers, at least,

would make this connection. But many don't. The "human rights community" rarely dares to criticize the United States government and its obedient appendages (e.g., the OAS). But critical analysis should be following the chain of command and asking why it is, for example, that the "International Republican Institute" and the "National Endowment for Democracy" are so keen on financing the Haitian opposition with their slender democratic qualifications. Much recent commentary sidesteps the David-versus-Goliath story, focusing almost exclusively on the inevitable results (viz., episodic violence) of the awful poverty that Haitian are now forced to endure. It's important to add that missing the David-versus-Goliath story means missing the story, period. The U.S. press is, as usual, self-righteous and short-memoried. The Haitian for-profit media, we read today, are claiming that the government's call for them to pay taxes is "yet another attempt to muzzle the press."[29]

So we hear endless complaints about the corruption of the Haitian government, with no mention of the industrial-strength corruption of the United States and its vassals. (I'm not asking, here, where is that missing $4.8 billion taken from an IMF loan to Russia.[30] Nor am I asking how Enron, WorldCom or Martha Stewart came up with their creative accounting methods. I'm focusing, rather, on U.S. corruption concerning Haiti. Why did the Haitian government have to lobby the U.S. government to recover 160,000 pages of documents taken from the headquarters of FRAPH and from other military installations in Haiti?).[31] The U.S. press descries in great detail the "thugs" and "armed gangs" and "Lavalas goons" and the violence they perpetrate but with little recollection of how it was that Haiti came to be armed. Reports of narcotrafficking appear in the print media with little discussion of the destination to which such cocaine transshipments are bound.[32] Haiti's "flawed electoral processes" are dissected while more serious allegations of disenfranchisement in Florida are given short shrift—again, a scandal quickly forgotten because, we're told, we're now at war against terrorism.

Then there are the miscarriages of justice for which we are even more directly responsible, because they're occurring on U.S. soil. One update since *Uses*: Emmanuel "Toto" Constant, the founder of FRAPH and found guilty of murder in the Raboteau trial, is still living as a free man in Queens, New York despite a 1995 deportation order. U.S. officials have admitted that Constant was paid by the CIA and discussed his paramilitary activities with them. He now remains under an order of deportation, but this has been delayed under State Department advisement.[33]

The Haitian government is concerned about such individuals, and with good reason. In the past year, former Haitian military officers have staged coup attempts from the Dominican Republic and perhaps from other countries. In July, 2001, five police officers were killed in the line of duty in the town closest to our clinic. On 17 December 2001, a more ambitious effort succeeded in penetrating the presidential palace and were headed towards Aristide's residence with heavy artillery mounted in the back of a pick-up. And even when they fell short of their mission, such attempts have not been wholly unsuccessful. Their goal is to create chaos and thus complement "political" efforts to discredit and destabilize the elected government. After the assault, the homes of Convergence members were attacked by angry mobs. The OAS made clear where its concerns lay. Rather than condemn the coup, it issued a call to indemnify members of the Convergence—and the cash-strapped government did so.

The Uses of Haiti described the process by which Haiti was driven into the ground. Ten years after its publication, I would like to close by underlining the following point. When something is driven into the ground, resources are required to rebuild it. A person who has been kicked to the ground must expend energy to get back up again. This was clear in 1986, more so in 1990 and 1994, and clearest of all right now. "A Marshall Plan for Haiti" some said. "Reparations," observed the more historically minded (A few truly ahistorical ideologues have argued that "Haiti needs no aid. It can recover on its own.")

The real reason we have an embargo against Haiti, in my view, is that every time the Haitians are allowed to elect who they want they make the mistake of not electing the kind of people the U.S. government wants. They keep electing, in fact, the same guy, the one who is pushing social and economic rights for the poor. The same one who is vilified by the establishment press (when Aristide was recently given an award by the U.N.Food and Agricultural Organization, the *Wall Street Journal* said, "what next—a U.N.Medal of Freedom for Fidel Castro?").[34] In almost all of his public utterances, Aristide brings forth the significance of social and economic rights. To cite again the article from *The Village Voice*, which is not flattering to the Aristide government:

> In May, three local activists were shot dead by police, who later claimed to have been attacked by gangs. Local residents, for their part, charged the activists were shot while arriving at an arranged meeting with police. The killings triggered two days of shooting between police and gangs, leaving a pervasive suspicion among locals that, having outlived their usefulness, the militants have become targets.

> When asked about the situation at a recent press conference, Aristide replied: "The people of Cité Soleil are the sons and daughters of the country. Their rights are violated when they cannot eat; their rights are violated when they cannot go to school. We must work with all sectors, the opposition and the elite, to improve

their lives. We are committed to working with
them and we will not rest until we do that."[35]

The *Wall Street Journal* might deny the relevance of
Aristide's comments to the situation, but any inhabitant
of Haiti would see the connection: without social and
economic rights, political rights have no soil to grow in.
The brutality in Haiti's streets will not be tamed by legal
reforms or by extralegal police action, but by confronting
poverty and disease.

As of today, all significant aid to the public sector
remains blocked, although smaller amounts are being
routed through non-governmental organizations (some of
them doing excellent work, but on a local scale), through
right-wing political parties, and through churches, some
of them also quite conservative. Haitians abroad continue
to send home remittances, but remittances, though vital
to the survival of many families here, cannot substitute
for the aid necessary to rebuilt the country. Conditions
here on the ground are akin to the battlefield of an unde-
clared war on the poor. Now that the OAS seems to be
calling for an end to the embargo, it's tempting to predict
that the current U.S. administration will find other ways
to make sure the money doesn't get through, masking
political goals under "technical considerations."

War, $500 million in aid, connections between rich
nations and poor ones, irresponsible analyses—why does
this all sound so familiar? Well, it could be that it's the
same story told in the first edition of *Uses*. Or perhaps
it's the figure itself, linked to the inaccuracy—if blind-
ness to the big picture amounts to inaccuracy—of the
press? That constellation should be reminding us of El
Salvador two decades ago, which was the absolute opposite, in my view, of the current Haitian situation. There,
the murderous Salvadoran government was under no
embargo, although it should have been isolated in the
manner that Haiti is now. In that instance, $500 mil-
lion—that nice round, recurring number—went to the

Salvadoran army, which had as its sole enemy the Salvadoran people (and a few dozen nuns and priests who were accompanying them). The first edition of *Uses* recounted in some detail the massacre of hundreds of men, women and children cowering in the hamlet of El Mozote. As in Haiti, official press coverage averted its gaze from the complicity of the powerful:

> From January 1983 through December 1989, "El Mozote" was cited in a mere fifteen articles published in major U.S. and Canadian newspapers. (During this same period the U.S. government provided the Salvadoran military with more than $500 million in direct military assistance.)... The coverage of El Mozote shows us that for the journalists, no less than for most people of the West, the daily lives of billions of people in the rest of the world do not exist outside the parameters of crisis or scandal: hurricanes, earthquakes, volcanic eruptions, droughts, crop failures, and civil wars.[36]

Our understanding of the dramas of Haiti and El Salvador are dim, at best. And yet understanding the causes and consequences of such tragedies is perhaps the most important challenge now facing all of us. Allow me to close with a final reconsideration of the human rights situation here in Haiti. I heard on the radio, just today, that although the IDB was considering releasing the blocked funds, the World Bank had no plans for extending credit to Haiti. In fact, the World Bank complained that Haiti owed it $18 million in arrears. Because I'd gone to the World Bank to ask, as a concerned citizen, why there was an international embargo against the government of Haiti, I was able to meet with a high-ranking official there. It was my first visit to the Bank; I was received with courtesy. The senior official with whom I met congratulated me for my interest in Haiti and told me that he too had experience there. He had negotiated a loan with "the Haitian government in the past."

Anxiously, I asked him "when was that?" "In 1987," he replied. In 1987, Haiti was ruled by the murderous military junta, the authors of the attack on Saint-Jean Bosco at the very time Father Aristide himself was saying mass. What happened that day is described in detail in these pages. The World Bank is in essence asking the Aristide government to repay the loan it made to those who tried to kill him.

On the day Nicole attended our conference on health and human rights, Aristide was off to Johannesburg, where the world's leaders were addressing, they said, the problems of the planet. It's worth citing Aristide's remarks, which were brief:

> ...Whereas every day 24,000 people die of hunger (that makes 4 deaths every second), 1.1 billion poor people live without access to clean drinking water. And yet 70% of the surface of the earth is covered with water. Diseases associated with this precious liquid are the cause of one third of the deaths recorded in developing countries....As for tropical forests, they are disappearing at a rate of 11.3 million hectares per year [27.9 million acres]. Between 1940 and 2002, Haiti's forest cover shrank from 40% to 1%. Our compatriots, fleeing the disastrous consequences of economic sanctions unjustly applied to Haiti, rush, like the soil, towards the sea....

> Soon, in 2004, we will celebrate the bicentenary of our independence, not on our knees but standing on our feet. Standing in the shadow of Toussaint Louverture, Dessalines, Martin Luther King and alongside you, dear and true friends of Haiti. From this day forward, let us all stand up with dignity and courage, together with the 800 million hungry people and the 854 million illiterate people on our planet to revive its social, economic, and ecological fabric.[37]

"Dignity" is no abstract moral label in this vision; it grows out of tolerable economic and ecological conditions. Those who make common cause with the poor, in Haiti and elsewhere, have every reason to hope that Aristide's vision comes to pass. In the interim, however, the bottom billion will continue to go without clean water, adequate nutrition, and even a modicum of basic medical care. Many will die—erased by the mean-spirited policies of those who abuse their power. I will close this Afterword, and return to our clinic, where Nicole and many others await us.

Cange, Haiti
September 5, 2002

"I declare in overthrowing me they have uprooted the trunk of the tree of peace, but it will grow back because the roots are Louverturian,"

—Jean Bertrand Aristide

What Happened in Haiti?

Where Past is Present

Paul Farmer

March 12, 2004

On the night of February 28, 2004, Haitian president Jean-Bertrand Aristide was forced from power, in part by an armed uprising of former members of the military, disbanded in 1995. Aristide claimed he was kidnapped and did not know where he was being taken until the very end of a 20-hour flight, when he was informed that he and his wife would be landing "in a French military base in the middle of Africa." He found himself in the Central African Republic.

Whenever Haiti does intrude into America's consciousness, people like me—old Haiti hands who have lived and worked here and written about the place over the years—are consulted on "the current crisis." The current crisis isn't something that started in January 2004: it has been going on for the past couple of decades and longer. I've found, however, that if you try to discuss the roots of the problem, journalists and policymakers are likely to cut you off, saying: "Let's not dwell on the past. What should be done about Haiti's future?"

Nonetheless, a quick review of Haiti's history is indispensable to understanding the current muddle. We begin in the eighteenth century, when a slave colony on Haiti, then called Saint-Domingue, became France's most valuable colonial possession. According to historians, Saint-Domingue stands out as perhaps the most brutal slave colony in human history. It was the leading port of call for slave ships during the latter half of the eighteenth century, and a third of new arrivals died within a few years of reaching the colony. On the eve of the French Revolution, the bit of real estate now dismissed as a failed state was producing two-thirds of Europe's tropical produce. Many of France's beautiful coastal cities, including Bordeaux, are monuments to the slave trade. These facts are already forgotten outside Haiti.

Haitians remember: they consider themselves living legacies of the slave trade and the bloody revolt, starting in 1791, that finally removed the French. Over a decade of war followed, during which France's largest expeditionary force was sent to quell the rebellion. As the French containment operation flagged, the Haitian slave general Toussaint Louverture, victorious in battle, was invited to a parley. No parley ensued: Toussaint was kidnapped and taken away to a prison in the mountains of France; he died there of exposure and tuberculosis. Every Haitian schoolchild knows by heart his last words: "In overthrowing me, you have cut down in San Domingo only the trunk of the tree of black liberty. It will spring up again by the roots for they are numerous and deep." Among those whose imaginations were fired by these events was William Wordsworth, who addressed Toussaint:

> Though fallen thyself, never to rise again,
> Live, and take comfort. Thou hast left behind
> Powers that will work for thee; air, earth, and skies;
> There's not a breathing of the common wind
> That will forget thee; thou hast great allies;
> Thy friends are exultations, agonies,
> And love, and man's unconquerable mind.

Wordsworth was wrong about allies. The slaves in revolt had few friends, and the war continued in Haiti, with Europe's chief colonial powers—France, England and Spain—caught up in the fray. In November 1803, the former slaves won what proved to be the war's final battle and on January 1, 1804 declared the independent republic of Haiti. It was Latin America's first independent country and the only nation ever born of a slave revolt. Virtually all of the world's powers sided with France against the self-proclaimed Black Republic, which declared itself a haven not only for all runaway slaves but also for indigenous people (the true natives of Haiti had succumbed to infectious disease and Spanish slavery well before the arrival of the French). Hemmed in by slave colonies, Haiti had only one non-colonized neighbor, the slaveholding United States, which refused to recognize Haiti's independence.

Haiti's leaders were desperate for recognition, since the only goods the island had to sell were sugar, coffee, cotton, and other tropical produce. In 1825, under threat of another French invasion and the restoration of slavery, Haitian officials signed what was to prove the beginning of the end of any hope of autonomy: King Charles X agreed to recognize Haiti's independence only if the new republic paid an indemnity of 150 million francs and consented to the reduction of import and export taxes for French goods.

It may be impossible to put a price on the toll taken by slavery—the destruction not only of lives and families, but of cultures and languages—but the same cannot be said about "the French debt." One hundred fifty million gold francs amounts to about half a billion U.S. dollars in the most conservative estimate, without attempting to calculate 175 years of interest and inflation. Unusually, reintroducing slavery was not legal at the time, even under French law. The "debt" that Haiti recognized was incurred by the slaves' having deprived the French owners not only of land and equipment but of their human "property." The threat of force made it more akin to extortion than compensation.

By any account, the impact of the debt repayments—which continued until after World War II—was devastating. Assessments by Haitians are severe: anthropologist Jean Price Mars, referring to the Haitian leaders who yielded to French threats, complained in 1953 that their "incompetence and frivolity... made a country whose revenues and outflows had been balanced up to then into a nation burdened with debt and trapped in financial obligations that could never be satisfied." French abolitionist Victor Schoelcher argued that "imposing an indemnity on the victorious slaves was equivalent to making them pay with money that which they had already paid with their blood." Even those who profited from the deal knew that Haiti's economy was being dealt a lethal blow.

When capital moves up a steep grade of inequality—from a war-devastated colony of former slaves to one of the world's most powerful nations—the greater happiness of the greatest number is not being served; rather, those who have little to spare are forced to give up essentials so that others can add to their luxuries. Such transfers from the poor to the rich continue to this day, with some of the international financial institutions serving as cheerleaders for analogous—albeit more subtly practiced—processes.

In the late nineteenth century, the United States eclipsed France as a prevailing force in Haitian affairs. A U.S. military occupation (1915-1934) brought back *corvée* labor and introduced aerial bombing, two symptoms of the vast disparity in power between occupier and occupied. Officials sitting at desks in Washington, D.C. created institutions that Haitians would have to live with. For example, the Haitian army that today claims to have the country "in its hands" and seeks to be reestablished was created not by Haitians but by an act of the U.S. Congress. From its founding during the U.S. occupation until it was demobilized by Aristide in 1995, the Haitian army has never known a non-Haitian enemy. Internal enemies, however, it had aplenty.

This state of affairs—military-backed governments, dictatorships, chronic instability, repression, the heavy hand of Washington over all—continued throughout the 20th century. When I first traveled to Haiti in 1983, the Duvalier family dictatorship had been in place for a quarter of a century. There was no free press—and no dissent, to be sure, from radios or newspapers; no politicians declaring themselves the heads of parallel governments. The Duvaliers and their military dealt with all such threats ruthlessly, while the judiciary and the rest of the world looked the other way. Haiti was already the poorest country in the Western world, and those who ran it argued, with a certain sociological confidence, that force is required to police deep poverty.

By the mid-1980s, however, the hunger, despair, and disease that are the lot of most Haitians was beyond management, even by force. Baby Doc Duvalier, named "President for Life" at age 19, fled the country in 1986. A first attempt at democratic elections, in 1987, led to a massacre at the polling station. An army general declared himself in charge. In September 1988, the mayor of Port-au-Prince—himself a former military officer—paid a gang to burn down a downtown Roman Catholic church while it was packed with people attending mass. At the altar was none other than Father Jean-Bertrand Aristide, nemesis of the dictatorship and the army and a proponent of liberation theology. This stream of Catholic thought had been sweeping Latin America with its injunctions that the Church proclaim "a preferential option for the poor." It had its adversaries: Pope John Paul II, for one, and President Ronald Reagan. Members of Reagan's brain trust, participating in a 1980 meeting in Santa Fe, New Mexico, declared liberation theology less Christian than Communist and recommended that "U.S. policy must begin to counter (not react against)... the 'liberation theology' clergy."

Aristide's rise from slum priest to presidential candidate took place against a backdrop of right-wing death squad activity and threatened military coups. He rose quickly in the eyes of the Haitians, but his stock plummeted with the United States and its press. The *New York Times*, which relies heavily on informants who speak English or French instead of only Haitian Creole, had few kind words for the priest: "Among the business community, pessimistic reactions run stronger," ran a news story published three days prior to Haiti's first elections. "'He is a cross between Ayatollah and Fidel,' one downtown businessman said in a typical assessment of Father Aristide from those in the entrepreneurial class. 'If it comes to a choice between the ultra-left and the ultra-right, I am ready to form an alliance with the ultra-right.'" Such coverage gave the impression that it might be a tight race. But Haitians knew that Aristide would easily win any democratic election, and on December 16, 1990, the priest won 67% of the popular vote in a field of 12 candidates.

The United States might not have been able to prevent Aristide's landslide victory, but there was much they could do to undermine him. The most effective method, adopted by the first Bush administration, was to fund the opposition—its poor showing at the polls was no reason, it appears, to cut off aid to them—and the military. Declassified records now make it clear that the CIA and other U.S. organizations helped to create and fund a paramilitary group called FRAPH, which rose to prominence after the September 1991 military coup that ousted Aristide. Thousands of civilians were killed outright and hundred of thousands fled onto the high seas and across the border to the Dominican Republic.

Whether it was the refugee question or a change of heart in foreign policy—Bill Clinton mentioned the Haitian refugees in many of his campaign speeches—Aristide became, in October 1994, the first exiled Latin

American president to return to office, with a little over a year left in his term. Although the 1994 U.S. military intervention was authorized by the United Nations and indisputably stopped bloodshed and restored constitutional rule, other forces were at play: the restoration of Aristide was basically a United States show. Then, seven weeks after Aristide's return, Republicans took control of the U.S. Congress. From that day forth, influential Republicans worked to block or burden with conditions aid to impoverished, strife-torn Haiti.

The aid through official channels was never very substantial. Counted per capita, the U.S. was giving Haiti one-tenth what it was distributing in Kosovo. Claims heard recently from the mouths of former ambassadors and the second Bush administration—that hundreds of millions of dollars flowed to Haiti—are correct, though misleading. Aid did flow, just not to the elected government. A great deal of it went to non-governmental organizations and to the anti-Aristide opposition. A lot went to pay for the U.N.occupation and Halliburton support services. U.S. organizations like the International Republican Institute and even the U.S. Agency for International Development funneled hundreds of thousands, perhaps millions, of dollars to the opposition. The cuts in bilateral aid and the diversion of monies to the opposition meant there could be, in a country as poor as Haiti, little effort to build schools, health care infrastructure, roads, ports, telecommunications, or airports.

When the anti-Aristide opposition cried foul over a handful of contested parliamentary seats in the 2000 election, the U.S. quickly acted to freeze international aid as well. Take, for example the case of the Inter-American Development Bank loans. These loans—one for health care, another for education, one for potable water, and one for road improvement: areas of greatest need in Haiti, the timeliness of which would seem obvious to anyone— had been approved by the Haitian government and by the Bank's board of directors. The loans were then delayed for "political reasons." Haiti held local and parliamentary elections in May 2000, and eight parliamentary seats— out of approximately 7,500 posts filled that day—were disputed, even though all went to those with the greatest number of votes (those unhappy with the results demanded a run-off). Sources both Haitian and American confirmed to me that it was the United States that asked the Inter-American Development Bank to block the loans until these electoral disputes had been resolved. Since seven of the Senators in question resigned in 2001, and the other's term expired shortly thereafter, that should've been the end of the aid freeze. Instead, it continued throughout Aristide's tenure.

The IDB later claimed that this funding freeze occurred as the result of a consensus reached by the Organization of American States in something called "the Declaration of Quebec City." Interestingly enough, the Declaration is dated April 22, 2001, and the letter from the United States representative to the IDB asking that the loans not be disbursed was dated April 8, 2001. To quote the conclusion of one of the rare journalists to find this scandal worthy of inquiry, "it would seem that the effort became concerted after it was made."

International financial institutions have time and again engaged in discriminatory and probably illegal practices towards Haiti. According to the Haiti Support Group, "Haiti's debt to international financial institutions and foreign governments has grown from U.S.$302 million in 1980 to U.S.$1.134 billion today. About 40% of this debt stems from loans to the brutal Duvalier dictators who invested precious little of it in the country. This is known as 'odious debt' because it was used to oppress the people, and, according to international law, this debt need not be repaid." There has been relative silence in the press and among human rights groups on this score.

The story gets worse. In order to meet the renewed demands of the IDB, the cash-strapped Haitian government was required to pay ever-expanding arrears, many of them linked to loans paid out to the Duvalier dictator-ship and to the brutal military regimes of 1986-1990. In July 2003, Haiti sent over 90% of all its foreign reserves to Washington to pay these arrears. Yet as of today, less than U.S.$4 million of the four blocked loans mentioned above has flowed to Haiti in spite of many assurances to the contrary from the IDB.

This startling echo of illegal practices in the nine-teenth century—for the IDB payments will strike both lawyers and the Haitian poor as reminiscent of France's indemnity shakedown—is of a piece with many other dis-criminatory practices towards Haiti and its people. You'd think this might be newsworthy: the world's most power-ful nations joining forces to block aid and humanitarian assistance to one of the poorest. But for three years this story was almost impossible to place in a mainstream journal of opinion. It was not until March 2004 that one could read in a U.S. daily the news that the aid freeze might have contributed to the overthrow of the penniless Haitian government. In its one and only investigative piece about the three-year-long aid embargo, the *Boston Globe* finally stumbled upon the facts:

> WASHINGTON—For three years, the US gov-ernment, the European Union, and international banks have blocked $500 million in aid to Haiti's government, ravaging the economy of a nation already twice as poor as any in the Western Hemisphere.
> The cutoff, intended to pressure the govern-ment to adopt political reforms, left Haiti struggling to meet even basic needs and weakened the authori-ty of President Jean-Bertrand Aristide, who went into exile one week ago. Today, Haiti's government, which serves 8 million people, has an annual budget of about $300 million—less than that of Cambridge, [Massachusetts] a city of just over 100,000. And as Haitians attempt to form a new government, many say its success will largely depend on how much and how soon aid will flow to the country... Many of

Aristide's supporters, in Haiti and abroad, angrily contend that the international community, particularly the United States, abandoned the fledgling democracy when it needed aid the most. Many believe that Aristide himself was the target of the *de facto* economic sanctions, just as Haiti was beginning to put its finances back in order.

The Aristide Question

The view that the United States and France undermined Aristide is not a fringe opinion. Nobel Laureate and former president of Costa Rica Oscar Arias wrote in the *Washington Post* that, "in the case of Haiti, not only was the struggling democracy cut off from outside aid but an armed insurrection of former military and death-squad leaders was in the end endorsed by the U.S. and French governments." The Caribbean nations grouped under CARICOM and the African Union have called for a formal investigation of Aristide's removal, and Gayle Smith, an Africa specialist on the National Security Council staff under President Bill Clinton, observed that "most people around the world believe that Aristide's departure was at best facilitated; at worst, coerced by the U.S. and France."

Why such animus towards Haiti's leader from American and French officialdom? Answering this question helps reframe the one that is always asked by the press. Journalists never ask, for example, how much 150 million gold francs are worth today or what their loss might have meant for a struggling tropical economy. They ask, rather, "Is Aristide a good guy or a bad guy?" Certainly, Aristide is the sort of person who would and did say, "France extorted this money from Haiti by force and you should give it back to us so that we can build primary schools, primary health care, water systems, and roads." Aristide is also the sort of person who will do the math on the French debt, adding in interest and

adjusting for inflation. He came up with a startling figure: France owes Haiti U.S.$21,685,135,571.48 and
counting, at five percent annual interest.

This figure was scoffed at by some French, the
whole affair seen as some sort of comical farce mounted
by their disgruntled former subjects; others in France,
it's increasingly clear, were insulted or angered when the
point was pressed in diplomatic and legal circles.

Aristide pressed the point. The figure of $21 billion
was repeated again and again. The number 21 appeared
all over the place in Haiti, along with the word "restitution." On January 1, 2004, during Haiti's bicentennial
celebrations, Aristide announced he would replace a 21-
gun salute with a litany of 21 points about what had
been achieved in spite of the embargo and what would be
done when restitution was made. The crowd went wild.
The U.S. and French press by and large dismissed his
comments as silly, even though lawyers saw the case as
not without legal merit.

It's hard to have even a brief conversation about
Haiti without Aristide's personality coming up. What's
more, it's usually easy to tell within minutes how one's
interlocutor feels about him. Haiti is almost always
referred to as polarized, but this is not true in every
sense. Most Haitians have a lot in common: poverty, disease, mistrust of the great powers. Haiti's elections and
polls, even recent ones, show that the poor majority still
support Aristide. What's polarized are the middle classes
and the traditional political elites—which together seem
to constitute what human rights groups and political
analysts term "civil society," a grouping that for some
ineffable reason does not include the poor majority.
Equally polarized are people like me: non-Haitians who
concern themselves with that country's affairs for a
whole host of reasons. Among those who can read and
write, among the chattering classes, there is no more
divisive figure than Aristide.

Given all the *coups* and assassination attempts and

spectacular crimes mentioned above—given all the complexity—what is the standard storyline in the mainstream press? That Aristide had the chance to be "Haiti's Mandela," but instead "cruelly disappointed" his supporters who then defected in droves. Nothing could be further from the truth, as even a superficial review of the facts will show. First, Haiti is not South Africa. There can be no lofty figure who survives terrible mistreatment in order to lead his nation into the sunlit uplands of democracy, because in order to preside over such transitions, or even to survive them, leaders have to be able to deliver on campaign promises. Haiti's legendary poverty makes this impossible without repatriated resources or access to credits and assistance. Aristide knew this, hence his attempts to free up development assistance for health, roads, water, and primary education. When outside assistance was blocked by Washington and Aristide's first strategy failed, the restitution of the French debt was moved to the fore.

This broader background helps explain why the two superpowers in the Caribbean region—the United States and France—are united on Haiti, if not on Iraq.

None of this is new, as even a cursory review of the past decade or so shows. On the eve of his 1990 election, under the banner headline "Front-Running Priest a Shock to Haiti," we read in the *New York Times* that "the former Salesian priest, long known for his strident brand of liberation theology, has sent profound shock waves through many of the sectors of this society that have traditionally made or broken presidents since Haiti's independence in 1804. From the business community, the army, and the Catholic and Protestant churches to Voodoo priests and rural landowners, sentiment is strongly, if not uniformly, set against him." In other words, everyone was always against Aristide—except the poor majority.

Between the coup that followed Aristide's inauguration and his return to Haiti, the coverage and debates

were the same. Our nation's "paper of record" is especially revealing. On September 22, 1994, the *New York Times*
ran a front-page piece about Aristide entitled "The Mouse
That Roared." From it, we get a keen sense of Aristide as
irritant: "The Clinton crowd has had to work hard to justify him to lawmakers who were unnerved by the October
1993 closed-door CIA briefing to Congress, in which the
intelligence agency offered information—later proven
false—that Father Aristide had received psychiatric treatment at a Montreal hospital in 1980. Senator Jesse
Helms, Republican of North Carolina, left the briefing
and branded him a 'psychopath'—a slur it has been hard
for Father Aristide to get over."

It would be convenient for the traditional elite and
other allies and overseas funders if Aristide, who has
indeed been forced to preside over unimaginable penury,
were to be abandoned by his own people. But what of
suppressed Gallup polls, conducted with the hope of
showing that Aristide is no longer popular? In fact, these
2002 polls indicate that Aristide is far and away Haiti's
most popular and trusted politician. What is to be done
about the Haitian voters who, to the horror of their elites
and to the Republican right, keep voting for Aristide?

In truth, the protégés of Senator Jesse Helms have
had more say in Aristide's fate than have the Haitian
electorate. Aristide claims he had no idea where he was
being taken on the night of February 28, 2004 until minutes before landing at, he was told, "a French military
base." He found himself in the Central African Republic,
a place he'd never visited before. Although U.S. officials
stated initially that he had been "taken to the country of
his choice," Aristide's version of events surely seems
more plausible. The Central African Republic is a country
in not much more than name. About the size of Texas
and with a population of only three million, it is subject
to French military and economic interests. It is also, in
spite of natural resources (diamonds, gold, oil, timber,
and uranium) that any Haitian might envy, one of the

world's poorest countries and highly unstable. A March 2003 BBC story reported that the capital, Bangui, was the world's most dangerous city. The United States has issued a travel advisory banning its citizens from traveling to the Central African Republic; our embassy there was closed two years ago. The Central African Republic "government" seized power in a military coup a little over a year ago.

When the poorly-briefed Aristide walked off the plane and across the tarmac, he found a single journalist waiting. What did he have to say after a 20-hour flight during which he did not know where he was bound? First, he thanked the Africans for their hospitality, and then he said only the following: "I declare in overthrowing me they have uprooted the trunk of the tree of peace, but it will grow back because the roots are Louverturian."

It's no surprise that Aristide would echo Toussaint Louverture, who is one of his heroes. In one of the few measured and informed pieces written about the current Haitian crisis, Madison Smartt Bell, writing in *Harper's Magazine*, linked the past to the present, as Haitians readily do:

> Toussaint did not live to see the result of his struggle: the emergence of Haiti as an independent black state, founded by slaves who had broken their own chains and driven off their masters. After his deportation to France, the torch he'd carried was passed to Jean-Jacques Dessalines, a man of more ferocious spirit, whose watchword was *Koupe tet, boule kay*— "Cut off heads and burn down houses." Papa Doc Duvalier had systematically associated himself and his regime with the spirit of Dessalines, as he deployed Dessalinien tactics on his own people: ruthless application of overwhelming force. Aristide seemed more attracted to the spirit of Toussaint, who had a real distaste for useless bloodshed, political and diplomatic skills to match or surpass his remarkable military talent, a delicately evolved sense of Haiti's relationship with the sur-

rounding colonial powers, a devout Catholicism able to coexist with the Vodou he also practiced, and a social vision, based on harmonious cooperation among the races, a good two hundred years ahead of his time.

Bell observes that, in the end, "Toussaint was undone by foreign powers, and Aristide also had suffered plenty of vexation from outside interference." Since Bell's essay was published, Aristide is, like Toussaint, in something of a French prison.

The Who's Who

Who are the other players in these high-stakes games, games in which history weighs so heavily? For many years it's been the same cast of characters on both sides of the sea. Starting with the U.S. *dramatis personae* helps to make things clearer on the Haitian side. The current Bush administration has put in charge of Latin American diplomacy two men who have been at it for a long time; their views are well-documented. As the "Special Presidential Envoy to the Western Hemisphere," Otto Reich is the United States' top diplomat in the region even though he has never survived a House or Senate hearing; he was appointed by Bush during a Congressional recess. In the 1990s, Reich was a lobbyist for industry (among his current deals: selling Lockheed-Martin fighter planes to Chile), but prior to that he had a long record of government service. In a recent *New Yorker* profile of Reich, William Finnegan gives us more background on his *curriculum vitae*:

> Reich first went to work for the Reagan Administration at the Agency for International Development, in 1981. As the civil war in Nicaragua heated up, he moved to the State Department, where, from 1983 to 1986, he headed a Contra-support program that operated out of an outfit called the Office of Public Diplomacy. The office arranged

speeches and recommended books to public libraries, but it also leaked false stories to the press—that, for instance, the Sandinista government was receiving Soviet MiG fighters, or was involved in drug trafficking. A declassified memo from one of Reich's aides to Patrick Buchanan, the White House communications director, boasted about the office's "White Propaganda" operations, including op-ed pieces prepared by its staff, signed by Contra leaders or academics, and placed in major newspapers. (Reich's spokesman denied this.) The office employed Army psychological-warfare specialists, and worked closely with Lieutenant Colonel Oliver North, at the National Security Council.

During the course of the Iran-Contra investigation, the U.S. Comptroller General concluded that Reich's office had "engaged in prohibited, covert propaganda activities." But by then Otto Reich had been named U.S. Ambassador to Venezuela, where he laid the groundwork for future efforts to destabilize President Hugo Chavez. Mind you, these are not all covert efforts: less than a year ago, Reich was on record hailing a *coup* against the left-leaning Chavez, urging the State department and opinion-makers—including the *New York Times*—to support "the new government." The *Times* complied. There was only one problem with this plan: the Venezuelan majority failed to fall into step. There was not adequate public support, in Venezuela or elsewhere in Latin America, for the *coup*, and so Chavez remained in his seat. Following Aristide's ouster, Chavez has promised that, should the U.S. government try anything similar in Venezuela again, they will meet with two responses: an interruption in Venezuelan oil and another "hundred years' war" from all Latin Americans who respect self-determination and sovereignty.

When the Bush administration sent a certain Roger Noriega as its envoy to "work out" the Haitian crisis in February 2004, not everyone knew who he was, for Noriega's career has flourished in the back of Senate committees. For the better part of a decade, Noriega worked for Jesse Helms and his allies. Although it is no secret that Noriega has had Aristide in his sights for years, none of this history made it into the mainstream media until recently. Then things became clearer. On CNN on March 1, after Aristide's departure from Haiti, Congresswoman Maxine Waters "accused Undersecretary of State for Latin America Roger Noriega—whom she called 'a Haiti hater'—of being behind the troubles there." The CNN report continued: "Noriega was a senior aide to former Senator Jesse Helms, who as chairman of the Senate Foreign Affairs Committee was a backer of long-time dictator Jean-Claude Duvalier and an opponent of Aristide."

When I share these biographical details and the names of other people who are driving these policies—I refer to Otto Reich, Jesse Helms, Jeane Kirkpatrick, Elliot Abrams, John Poindexter, Bush *père* and *fils*— and then mention Iran-Contra, Honduras, Venezuela, the Declaration of Quebec City, liberation theology, and the International Republican Institute, the Haiti story starts to hang together. Haiti policy is determined by a small number of people who were prominent in either Reagan's or George H.W. Bush's cabinets. Most are back in government today after an eight-year vacation in conservative think tanks, lobbying firms, and the like. Elliot Abrams, convicted of felony during the Iran-Contra hearings, serves on the National Security Council; Reagan's national-security advisor John Poindexter is now heading the Pentagon's counterterrorism office; John Negroponte, former Ambassador to Honduras, is now Ambassador to the United Nations. Jeane Kirkpatrick is on the board of the International Republican Institute, a prime source of funds for the political opposition to Aristide and, credible sources suggest, for the demobilized army personnel who provided the muscle for the Haitian opposition in early 2004. The far right of the U.S. Republican party has been the key determinant of Haiti policy.

What about U.S. Secretary of State Colin Powell? The Washington-based Council on Hemispheric Affairs, writing of events in Haiti, offers the following summary: "Powell's vision for Latin America is now indistinguishable from that of his junior hemispheric policymaking ideologues, Noriega and Reich. The battle for the Secretary of State's soul has ended in a rout for those who had highly regarded the man they thought he was, in contrast to the man he turned out to be."

On the Haitian side, naming the players is again a relatively easy exercise because they fall into a small set of categories. To sum up the opposition, you have Haiti's business elite, including those who own the Haitian media, and the former military and paramilitary—the very persons who were involved in the 1991-94 *coup*. Many were in jail for murder, drug trafficking, and crimes against humanity, and now every single one of them is free.

Among those released by the rebels is former General Prosper Avril, a leader of the notorious Presidential Guard under both François and Jean-Claude Duvalier. Avril seized power by a *coup d'état* in September 1988; he was deposed by another *coup* in March 1990. A U.S. District Court found that Avril's regime had engaged in "a systematic pattern of egregious human rights abuses." It found him personally responsible for enough "torture and cruel, inhuman, or degrading treatment" to award six of his victims U.S.$41 million in compensation. His victims included opposition politicians, union leaders, scholars, and even a doctor trying to practice community rural medicine. Avril's repression was not subtle: three torture victims were paraded on national television with faces grotesquely swollen, limbs bruised, and clothing covered with blood. He also suspended thirty-seven articles of the Constitution and declared a state of siege.

The U.S. started protecting Avril shortly after the 1994 restitution of Haiti's elected leaders. In November,

Secretary of State Warren Christopher relayed to the U.S. Ambassador intelligence reports that the "Red Star Organization," under Mr. Avril's leadership, was "planning [a] harassment and assassination campaign directed at the Lavalas Party and Aristide supporters. The campaign is scheduled to commence in early December 1995"—right before the election that would allow Aristide to become the first president in Haitian history to peacefully hand over power to another elected civilian. This information was not passed on to the Haitian authorities, and that same month an assassination attempt was made against prominent Lavalas legislators. In December the Haitian police team investigating the case sought to arrest Mr. Avril at his home. A U.S. Embassy official admitted that he had visited Avril the day before the arrest; immediately after the Haitian police arrived at Avril's house, U.S. soldiers arrived. They tried to dissuade the Haitian police from making the arrest, and it was only after Haiti's president intervened personally on the police radio that the police were able to enter Avril's house. By the time they entered the premises he had fled to the neighboring residence of the Colombian ambassador. Police searching Avril's house found military uniforms, illegal police radios, and a cache of weapons.

Avril escaped to Israel but later returned to Haiti, where his international support and feared military capacity deterred further arrest attempts. He founded a political party, which has never fielded candidates for elections but was nevertheless invited by the International Republican Institute to participate in developing an opposition to Aristide. In May 2001, after U.S. troops had withdrawn from Haiti and while Avril was at a book signing away from his home and his guns, the Haitian police finally seized the opportunity to execute Avril's arrest warrant. The successful arrest was greeted with applause by the vast majority of Haitians and by human rights and justice groups in Haiti, the United States, and Europe. Amnesty International asserted that the arrest "could mark a step forward by the Haitian justice system in its struggle against impunity," and that "the gravity of the human rights violations committed during General Avril's period in power, from his 1988 *coup d'état* to his departure in March 1990, cannot be ignored." France's Committee to Prosecute Duvalier concluded that "the General must be tried."

On December 9, 2003, the investigating magistrate in the case of the Piatre Massacre, a March 1990 attack in which several peasants lost their lives, formally charged Avril in the case. He was in prison awaiting the termination of pre-trial proceedings when freed on March 2, 2004—three days after Aristide was deposed.

The list goes on. Rebel leader Guy Philippe is also a former soldier who received, during the last *coup*, training at a U.S. military facility in Ecuador. When the army was demobilized, Philippe was incorporated into the new police force, serving as police chief in the Port-au-Prince suburb of Delmas and in the second-largest city, Cap-Haïtien. During his tenure, the United Nations International Civilian Mission learned that dozens of suspected gang members were summarily executed, mainly by police under the command of Philippe's deputy. The U.S. Embassy has implicated Philippe in drug smuggling during his police career. These crimes, committed in large part by former military incorporated into the police force, are often pinned on Aristide even though he sought to prevent *coup*-happy human rights abusers from ending up in these posts in the first place.

Philippe fled Haiti in October 2000 when Haitian authorities discovered him plotting a *coup*, together with a clique of fellow police chiefs. Since that time, the Haitian government has accused Philippe of masterminding terrorist attacks on the Haitian Police Academy and the National Palace in July and December 2001, as well as lethal hit-and-run raids against police stations in Haiti's Central Plateau over the past two years.

In February 2004, Philippe's men bragged to the U.S.

press that they had executed Aristide supporters in Cap-Haïtien and Port-au-Prince, and many have indeed been reported missing. Philippe's declaration—"I am the chief, the military chief. The country is in my hands"—triggered the following response from Oscar Arias: "Nothing could more clearly prove why Haiti does not need an army than the boasting of rebel leader Guy Philippe last week in Port-au-Prince. The Haitian army was abolished nine years ago during a period of democratic transition, precisely to prevent the country from falling back into the hands of military men." On March 2, 2004, Philippe told the Associated Press that he would use his new powers to arrest constitutional Haiti's prime minister, Yvon Neptune, and he proceeded to lead a mob in an attack on Neptune's residence. Philippe has been quoted as saying that the man he most admires is Augusto Pinochet.

Louis-Jodel Chamblain was a sergeant in the Haitian army until 1989 or 1990. He reappeared on the scene in 1993 as one of the founders of the paramilitary group FRAPH. Formed during the 1991-94 military regime, FRAPH was responsible for numerous human rights violations before the 1994 restoration of democratic governance. Chamblain organized attacks against democracy supporters, issued FRAPH identity cards, and obtained official recognition for FRAPH from the dictatorship. Among the victims of FRAPH under Chamblain's leadership was Haitian Minister of Justice Guy Malary, ambushed and machine-gunned to death with his bodyguard and a driver on October 14, 1993. According to an October 28, 1993 CIA intelligence memorandum, "FRAPH members Jodel Chamblain, Emmanuel Constant, and Gabriel Douzable met with an unidentified military officer on the morning of 14 October to discuss plans to kill Malary." (Constant, the leader of FRAPH, is now living as a free man in Queens, New York.)

In September 1995, Chamblain was among seven senior military and FRAPH leaders convicted in absentia

and sentenced to forced labor for life for their involvement in the September 1993 extrajudicial execution of
Antoine Izméry, a well-known pro-democracy activist. In
November 2000, Chamblain was convicted *in absentia* in
the Raboteau massacre trial. In late 1994 or early 1995,
Chamblain went into exile to the Dominican Republic in
order to avoid prosecution. He was regularly spotted in
public by Haitian expatriates and international journalists.

All of these biographies have been a matter of public
record for years, but one could mark the day—I marked
it as February 28, as the coup was unfolding—that the
New York Times and other newspapers began offering a
bit more background on the men who now control Latin
America's oldest and most volatile nation. These sketches
give an idea, too, of why the Haitian people were enthusiastic about demobilizing the army. Writing in the
Washington Post, Oscar Arias underlined the degree of
popular support for demilitarization: "Since Aristide said
that he could not abolish the army without the support
of the Haitian people, the Arias Foundation for Peace and
Human Progress commissioned an independent polling
firm to gauge popular support for the idea. The results
were stunning: 62 percent of Haitians were strongly in
favor of abolition and only 12 percent were against."

As for the traditional political elite, surely they're a
mixed bag? Some have wanted to live in the National
Palace, Haiti's executive mansion, since the time it was
occupied by Papa Doc. Some are more marginal but just
as destructive. When recently you saw one man destroying
artwork on display in Port-au-Prince, you could read that
he was a "pastor from the Party of God." In fact this man,
a perennial presidential candidate, is delighted to burn, in
full view of international cameras, precious objects linked
with voodoo and other aspects of Haitian culture.

Who are these people? What unites them beyond
their hatred of Aristide? They've all been around a long
time but were not permitted to speak out or form political

parties during the Duvalier or military dictatorships. One penetrating analysis, by an academic named Robert Maguire, noted that "we should remember that from the first day of Aristide's term, the opposition set up a provisional government. My own observation then was that things in Haiti had changed. This never would have been permitted before. It was a sign that Haiti seemed to be becoming a more tolerant place." Again, this is another social fact missed by the mainstream human rights groups.

The leaders of the Haitian "civil society" groups include U.S.-born André Apaid, Jr., the founder of a television station and owner of Alpha Corp., a garment manufacturer that was prominently featured in news reports about Disney's sweatshop suppliers. Aristide's relentless push to raise the minimum wage above 72 gourdes a day—about $1.60—cut into the massive profits of the offshore assembly industry, since its principal resource is the desperate joblessness of the Haitian population. The U.S. Congress has passed a measure to build new garment factories in Haiti and encourage American companies to contract out more sweatshop labor—an answered prayer for Apaid.

As for the owners of the media in Haiti, they behave as owners often do when surrounded by the poor, the famished, and by *chimères*, described in the foreign press as armed thugs working for the Aristide government. But who are the *chimères*? Again, Madison Smartt Bell provides a better answer to this question than what we read in journalistic accounts or human rights reports:

> Before that term was coined, Haitian delinquent youths were called *maleleve* ("ill brought up") or, still more tellingly, *sansmaman* ("the motherless ones"). They were people who'd somehow reached adulthood without the nurture of the traditional *lakou*—communities that the combined forces of poverty and global-

ization had been shattering here for the last few decades. That was what made them so dangerous. The *Chimè* were indeed chimeras; ill fortune left them as unrealized shadows. With better luck they might have been human beings, but they weren't. These were the people Aristide had originally been out to salvage; "*Tout moun se moun*" was his earliest motto ("Every man is a man").

Coup d'Etat as a Source of Amusement

This human salvage operation exploded in February 2004 as "rebels" continued to "take cities." I work in these towns and know the rebels' *modus operandi*. They came in, shot the police—who usually numbered no more than two or three—and left. Only a similarly equipped counterforce could have stopped them, and there you have it: Haiti has no army. But Haiti is no more Costa Rica, "the Switzerland of Central America," than it is South Africa. Haiti has so few friends. The beleaguered government appealed for help in the U.N.Security Council, but this was delayed by the Bush administration—delayed long enough for the government to fall or be pushed out.

Whatever we do learn about the events of February 2004, we know that the *coup* makes bemused commentary. The idea of the Central African Republic as Aristide's "country of choice" triggered good copy, certainly. One "news analysis" of these events in the *New York Times*, with a South African byline, reads as follows:

> Jean-Bertrand Aristide, Haiti's latest strongman-in-exile, wants to lick his wounds in South Africa, a land of world-beating beauty, Mediterranean weather, American-quality freeways and Paris-luxe shops fit for any deep-pocketed ex-ruler of an impoverished land. Instead, he whiles his days away in the Central African Republic, a Texas-size nation of flat plains, Amazonian humidity, just

400 miles of Afghan-quality paved roads and cheap butterfly-wing art at the capital's K-Cinq market. Contrast him with his most illustrious predecessor, Jean-Claude Duvalier, known as Baby Doc. Forced out of power in 1986 after 29 years, he now lives on the Côte d'Azur. If there is an art to landing a cushy post-dictatorial sinecure, Mr. Aristide seems to have mastered only part of it in his dozen years as Haiti's president—which began with his election but ended with his using increasingly forceful methods of rule. Perhaps he simply lacked the right stuff.

Some of the journalists writing about Haiti seem to lack the right stuff. Aristide has never been able to serve out as much as half of his elected term before being overthrown by military figures with close ties to the United States, notwithstanding the "dozen years as Haiti's president" cited by this reporter. And the attempt to line up Aristide with "deep-pocketed ex-rulers" relies on malicious inference belied by the facts.

Did the U.S. and France have a hand in Aristide's forced removal? Were President and Mrs. Aristide being held in the Central African Republic against their will? How could they answer one way or another, being the guests of a government that threatened them after they criticized the United States and France in statements to friends and to the press? As the American lawyer for the government of Haiti put it, "Who can or will corroborate their story? The gardener? The janitor?" It is not that eyewitnesses are unavailable, but rather that few among them are willing to go on record against the U.S. and France, and that when they do, their words are dismissed. One eyewitness report, from a "concierge" at the Aristide's home, was buried in *Libération*, a French daily: "In Creole, he tells a story that contradicts the official version, which says that the head of state freely accepted his departure. In a voice still haunted by fear, Joseph Pierre insists that the ex-president was kidnapped in the night between [Saturday and Sunday] by the American army: 'American white men came to get him in a helicopter. They took away his security guards too. It was around 2 in the morning. He didn't want to go. The American soldiers forced him to. Because they had their guns trained on him, he had to follow them. Only God is stronger than the Americans.'"

Perhaps. But most of Aristide's claims, initially disputed by U.S. officials from Assistant Secretary of State Noriega to Donald Rumsfeld, are now acknowledged to be true. U.S. claims that Aristide met with officials in Antigua—Aristide denied this—were undermined by reports from Antigua. After having claimed that the Aristides were taken to the "country of their choice," Noriega acknowledged during a House hearing that Aristide did not know of his destination until less than an hour before landing in the Central African Republic. Even officials there acknowledge that no Haitian authorities were involved in the choice of Aristide's destination.

Many more questions remain unanswered. We know that U.S. funds overtly financed the opposition. But did they also fund, even indirectly, the rebellion that so prominently featured high-powered U.S. weapons only a year after 20,000 such weapons were promised to the Dominican Republic army? Senator Christopher Dodd is urging an investigation of U.S. training sessions of 600 "rebels" in the Dominican Republic and also wants to investigate "how the International Republican Institute spent $1.2 million of tax payer money" in Haiti. Answering these and related questions will require an intrepid investigative reporter willing to take on hard questions about U.S. policies in Latin America.

Oscar Arias concludes that, "were the international community now to stand by as the rebels reinstated the army, it would surely destroy the seeds of peace and self-rule that have been planted with great sacrifice by the Haitian people." But about the return of the military, there can be little doubt. The man sworn as Haiti's new prime minister announced in his first public statement that Aristide's order to replace the military with a civilian police force violated Haiti's constitution; he promised to name a commission to examine the issues surrounding its restoration. The *de facto* prime minister also named a former general to his new government.

More guns and more military may well be the time-honored prescription for policing poverty, but violence and chaos will not go away if the Haitian people's hunger, illness, poverty, and disenfranchisement are not addressed.

Afterword
Life Since the Coup
Larry Birns and Jessica Leight

As the first anniversary of the ousting of President Jean-Bertrand Aristide came and passed, not a word emerged from the Bush administration explaining, defending, or apologizing for the role it had played in the violent unseating of the first of only two democratically elected presidents in Haiti's troubled history. Nor has the U.S. seen fit to publicly criticize the egregious excesses of the rump government led by interim Prime Minister Gerard Latortue, which Washington had invested shortly after it had brought on Aristide's February 29, 2004 flight into exile.

There is a growing international awareness of Latortue's indulgent treatment of the anti-Aristide armed gangs and ex-militia which had spearheaded the final weeks of the anti-Aristide rebellion, which eventually led to his ouster. As Haitian authorities continue to persecute pro-Aristide Haitians, the Bush administration could not appear less concerned, a fact that a U.N.Security Council delegation saw for itself in its April 2005 visit to the country. The violence perpetrated by such groups—who were described as a gang of "thugs" by U.S. Secretary of State Colin Powell during the waning days of the Aristide administration—as well as the repeated basic human rights violations sanctioned by Latortue—who subsequently praised Powell's "thugs" as "freedom fighters"— was not sufficient to prompt a word of rebuke from the State Department. Instead, it maintained the time-honored tradition underlying U.S. policy toward Haiti: periodic interventions to crush any overt democratic manifestations on the part of the populace, followed by long periods of either benign or malign neglect. Similarly, Washington set patently lower standards and expectations when it came to issues of social justice and quality of life in regard to the black republic than for any other Latin American country. As a result, Washington's continued laid-back approach to this tormented land has mainly meant for Haiti's suffering population, at best, faux democracy rather than the real thing.

Haiti's Disloyal Opposition

In the six months prior to the coup, the Haitian "democratic" opposition was led primarily by two unrepresentative and elite-dominated political coalitions with overlapping memberships, the Convergence "Démocratique" and the Group of 184. Both bodies were single-mindedly driven by the desire to oust Aristide by any means. The president's liberation gospel and energetic attacks on Haiti's traditionally oligarchic political system had generated widespread odium against him among the elite. Ultimately, with generous backing from the U.S. embassy and the U.S. government-funded International Republican Institute, via the National Endowment for Democracy, these opposition groups, long on cash and short on votes, began to organize for a power grab through supposedly non-violent anti-Aristide demonstrations that became increasingly venomous as the months swept by without a political resolution.

An already explosive political stalemate between the government and the opposition noticeably worsened starting in September 2003, when anti-Aristide forces turned to a violent street strategy while holding firm to their intransigent policy of non-negotiation with the president.

Haiti's desperate struggle to preserve its hard-won democracy was given low priority by the State Department. Secretary Powell evinced an almost Delphic languor in the face of fierce daily melées in the gutters of Port-au-Prince, despite the potential disastrous impact on the U.S. if tens of thousands of impoverished Haitian rafters were to wash up on Florida's shores seeking refuge. Moreover, to further disable his ability to govern, the Bush administration embargoed the sale of riot control equipment to the besieged and cash-strapped Aristide regime, seriously crippling its ability to control civil unrest through non-lethal means.

In the violent final three-week period leading up to Aristide's ouster, Washington also tightened its policy of economic asphyxiation which continued a freeze on tens of millions of dollars in previously pledged international aid to Port-au-Prince. This vindictive stance against Aristide was only the culmination of a misguided, if not a misanthropic, strategy that had dominated Washington's relations with Haiti since Aristide's first inauguration in 1991. Egged on by now retired Senator Jesse Helms' unqualified hatred for Aristide, first the Clinton and then the Bush administrations not only aborted disbursement of desperately needed economic assistance pledged by the U.S., but also imposed a series of untenable political conditions on the Haitian leader, and then persuaded Canada, the European Union and the Organization of American States, as well as the international lending agencies, to join in the aid cut-off.

Aristide repeatedly agreed to all of the onerous conditions demanded of him, including power-sharing with what proved to be an unyielding opposition that refused to participate in any of the various mechanisms designed to pave the way for new elections, most notably the formation of a new electoral council. Though only one word from Washington—the opposition's ultimate ideological patron—would have been more than sufficient to soften the Group of 184's obdurate non-negotiation position, no such suasion was forthcoming. On the contrary, the State Department took no action to address the rapidly deteriorating economic, political, and security conditions on the island, utterly unaffected by the fact that the hemisphere's most vulnerable democracy was at total risk.

Aristide's Foreign and Domestic Enemies

As political instability in Port-au-Prince worsened, armed fugitives from the era of military rule (1991-1994), individuals such as ex-police chief Guy Philippe and FRAPH death squad leader Louis-Jodel Chamblain (who were among those whom had just been sprung from jail by their confederates or had crossed over the border with the Dominican Republic), launched a final phase of their insurrection in early February 2004. Against only resistance from Aristide's ragtag forces, they took control of the entire country save the capital. The thin firewall between these violent gangs and sweatshop millionaire businessman André Apaid, Jr., the leader of the so-called "non-violent" opposition Group of 184, rapidly evaporated when the latter, a dual U.S. and Haitian citizen, urged the armed rebels in the northern city of Gonaïves to keep their weapons. He pointedly observed that "armed resistance" was a legitimate action.

It was at this moment that the purportedly non-violent opposition's sinister political strategy emerged. It hoped to take by force what it had failed to achieve at the ballot box since it lacked anything near the numerical strength to win an election.

Thus the opposition's elitist leaders—who had long despised Aristide for his radical message and his hero status among Haiti's long-neglected poor—refused to alter their strategy of non-negotiation with Aristide by any means, thereby vouchsafing the eventual destruction of his presidency. Meanwhile, there was not a whisper of dissention coming from Washington regarding this nefarious strategy. Without the resources to professionalize its intimidated, outnumbered and chronically disloyal police force, the now unprotected Aristide government rapidly unraveled as the rebels advanced on Port-au-Prince for their final three-week offensive.

At the same time, Washington was maintaining its carefully calculated posture of inaction, allowing the situation in Haiti to deteriorate into a freefall. Assistant Secretary of State Roger Noriega, then-White House advisor Otto Reich, and Noriega's assistant Daniel Fisk, all former protégés of ex-Senator Helms—Aristide's most deadly foe—were said to have made a series of off-the-record remarks to the press that, despite Powell's statements to the contrary, the Bush administration would in fact countenance "regime change" in Haiti.

Powell, meanwhile, publicly clung to the bankrupt formula that an agreement between Aristide and the opposition was a mandatory precondition for any deployment of an outside peacekeeping force. This was a green light for the political opposition to continue stalling as the armed rebels approached the gates of the presidential palace. At this point, the pressure on Aristide became unbearable. Ultimately, it was U.S. embassy officials as well as a detachment of Marines stationed there, who ordered the discharge of Aristide's private U.S. security force, leaving him alone at the Port-au-Prince airport. There, a U.S. embassy-chartered jet was waiting to whisk him to the then-unknown destination of the Central African Republic. At that point, State Department spin doctors, inspired by Powell's account, promulgated a sanitized version which presented Aristide as almost eagerly opting for resignation and exile. His departure coincided with the belated arrival the same day of U.S. peacekeeping forces.

Targeting Lavalas

Within days of the president's ouster, the U.S. embassy in Port-au-Prince took a lead role in hand-picking the government that would replace him on an interim basis with Latortue as acting prime minister. Almost from the start, Latortue's gross ineptitude became apparent to Haitians and the international community alike. For example, his bumbling response to Tropical Storm (later Hurricane) Jeanne in September 2004, a natural tragedy that accounted for the deaths of several thousand on the island and cost tens of millions of dollars in property loss, was perhaps the most dismal of his numerous failures. While Jeanne was raging, Latortue and his confederates lacked the competence to take even the rudimentary step of establishing an emergency national radio grid over which they could broadcast calls to the populace to seek higher ground in order to escape the flooding. This abdication of responsibility alone justified the many calls made for his and his colleagues' resignations.

Even more damaging, Latortue, joined by Bernard Gousse, his tarnished justice minister and one of the most condemnable figures now holding power in Haiti, have directed an increasingly violent campaign aimed at squashing dissent and exorcising Aristide's Lavalas party from the Haitian political process. Beginning with Latortue's earliest days in office, members of Aristide's Lavalas Party—rather than renegade ex-police and known military assassins—became his principal target. Latortue's relentless anti-Aristide rhetoric from the start was aimed at constructing an airtight case against Lavalas' participation in the scheduled October and November 2005 general elections. Gousse did this primarily by incarcerating a wide swath of distinguished Aristide leaders and supporters, usually on trumped-up charges, or none at all.

The victims of these purges included the country's most highly revered priest, Father Gerard Jean-Juste (who was later freed after weeks of public outcry), former Prime Minister Yvon Neptune (whose March 2005 hospitalization by U.N. forces prompted further calls for his release), Interior Minister Jocelerme Privert, Senator Yvon Feuille, and Deputy Rudy Herivaux. The Latortue government was also guilty of gunning-down pro-Aristide street protestors without even the pretense of professional restraint on the part of the authorities, all the while making the captious charge that Aristide himself was orchestrating the ongoing demonstrations from South Africa, where he remains in exile. For such sedulous abuses, the

Caribbean Community (CARICOM), with Barbados breaking rank, has refused to restore normal relations with the Latortue regime until a free and fair election is staged. Additionally, the Inter-American Commission on Human Rights is but one of a number of international and regional bodies that have moved to condemn the government-sanctioned transgressions now occurring throughout Haiti with near-daily regularity. As one international human rights monitor observed, "the contrast between the Haitian government's eagerness to prosecute former Aristide officials and its indifference to the abusive record of certain rebel leaders could not be more stark."

Based on Latortue's affability toward the ex-military and police, known for their long history of terrorizing ordinary Haitians, one must conclude that the interim prime minister would have few problems with trying to reconstitute the brutal Haitian army at a later date. These same forces were responsible for most of the more than 6,000 civilian fatalities dating back to the era of military rule from 1991-1994.

In recent months, Latortue has dealt with the problem of alienated former military personnel by pledging to compensate almost 6,000 of them with individual bonuses of $5,000, regardless of how murderous their records were, for having been demobilized by Aristide in 1995. This process would involve a disbursement of about $29 million, a huge sum for Haiti. While most Haitians still have no access to clean water or jobs and barely survive on an average of less than a dollar per day, Latortue is hard-pressed to justify paying such a huge amount to one of Haiti's most reprehensible groups of human rights violators.

Simultaneously, it can be expected that both Latortue and U.S. authorities will help advance the electoral prospects of Haiti's business-led conservative groups, headed by the island's unscrupulous André Apaid, Jr., as well as Leslie Manigat, a conservative former international lending agency official whose democratic credentials have been severely compromised by his ebullient opportunism.

The U.N.'s Mixed Record in Haiti

At first, the U.N.'s Secretary General Kofi Annan, along with Canadian, French and U.S. officials, either turned a blind eye to the human rights abuses perpetrated by the Latortue regime, or went so far as to shower favoritism on his hapless extra-constitutional government. In general, the OAS and the U.N., along with Canada and France have fully supported the Bush administration's highly skewed vision of island realities, based on the commonly-held misconception that Aristide had presided over a "failed state," and had to be replaced. While they prated on about the "democratization" of the hemisphere, none of their officials were prepared to dispatch peacekeepers in a timely fashion to protect Aristide's constitutional rule, nor made any attempt to free up frozen foreign aid pledged to the country. These mean-spirited decisions helped to rule out any prospects for Aristide's political survival and the country's meager democratic structure to be preserved.

The killing of two U.N. peacekeepers in March 2005 by ex-members of Haiti's military transformed the attitude of the Brazilian-led U.N. peacekeeping force, MINUSTAH, and its civilian overseers. These deaths offered further confirmation of the high cost the international community would have to pay for its lack of a clear design for going the necessary distance to guarantee a secure Haiti along with the installation of a genuine democratic system. Less than a week after the *de facto* February 29, 2004 *coup* against Aristide, the Brazilian government declared that it would volunteer to lead MINUSTAH and allocate 1,100 of its own troops to form its core. MINUSTAH's commander assumed control of the operation in June.

On November 29, 2004, the U.N. Security Council

announced that the peacekeepers would extend their stay until June 2006, although this date was disputed by China, but it took several months more before the force reached its authorized strength of 7,400 troops and national police. Brazil's stated mission for its presence in Haiti was to provide support for the decisions of the Security Council and to aid the Haitian people. "It is natural for Brazil to be in Haiti," said a Brazilian embassy source at the time. "There was no alternative to involvement [there]." However, a number of independent observers have argued that President Luiz Inácio Lula da Silva's reasons for his country's leadership role in fact could not be more self-centered, stemming from his desire to advance Brazil's standing internationally. In a *quid pro quo* with Washington, he had hoped on obtaining U.S. backing for Brazil's bid for a permanent U.N. Security Council seat.

In spite of its seemingly straightforward role as "peacekeeper," the presence as well as the performance of the MINUSTAH force (particularly initially) was criticized on a number of grounds. Given that Haiti's current regime was not elected, but imposed, some critics have contended that, by authorizing a peacekeeping force to Haiti which acted almost exclusively in liaison with the Latortue regime, the United Nations was implicitly condoning an illegitimate cabal. Fundamentally, MINUSTAH up to now has been serving less to implement a peaceful resolution to a serious political crisis than to help inaugurate a post-Aristide era in which a way would be found whereby the Lavalas Party would be disqualified from participating in the 2005 presidential balloting, either by being banned outright or by its refusing to participate for security reasons. Needless to say, if Lavalas is allowed to field candidates with safety, it will almost certainly win by a landslide—something the Bush administration would find intolerable. At the present time, Lavalas has decided not to participate in the elections because of the non-stop harassment and intimidation directed at its members, ending up with many of it's partisans being assassinated.

Until the tragic incident in Gonaïves and at another location in which two U.N. peacekeepers lost their lives, MINUSTAH had been reluctant to face down the ex-militia who remain armed with automatic weapons. Instead, the U.N. force at first preferred to take on sketchily armed slum dwellers in gritty pro-Aristide neighborhoods. Moreover, for several months MINUSTAH commanders and their political supervisors in New York assumed a noticeably complacent approach towards Latortue's mounting human rights toll, failing to voice sufficient outrage over the government's glaring abuses—particularly those of Gousse's—or to urgently speak out for the full application of the U.N. mandate. On several occasions, U.N. forces even joined with the local regime's uniformed brigands in military operations that cost the lives of innocent Aristide supporters.

Last August, Annan selected Juan Gabriel Valdès as his special representative to Haiti. Valdès had been a distinguished Chilean former foreign minister and his country's U.N. ambassador who earlier had been recalled by Santiago because of his opposition to the U.S. war in Iraq. After a disturbingly slow start, Valdés finally began to speak out against the Latortue regime's excesses.

In the crucial areas of demobilization and containment, U.N. military commanders initially declared that their mission's instructions did not include the neutralization of armed gangs, despite the fact that MINUSTAH's original mandate called for the disarmament and the establishment of a stable environment required for new elections. Such a declaration of extreme caution at a time when armed rebel factions threatened the very fabric of the already tattered Haitian state, demonstrated MINUSTAH's initial relative disengagement from the country's harsh political realities. The situation somewhat improved after the peacekeepers became acculturated to Haiti's exoic habitat and commenced to be more operational and professional.

In the initial absence of a sufficient degree of political will and commitment behind the international peacekeeping force, as well as confusion over the scope of its task, there was no guarantee that an increase in MINUS-TAH's force level would successfully invigorate its capacity. Without an expanded commitment, the risk is that the Port-au-Prince regime will continue to crumble and that Latortue and his confederates, particularly Justice Minister Gousse, should properly be seen as caricatures of good governance—smug, arrogant, insensitive to instances of corruption and ultimately a source for lawless behavior.

The façade of legitimacy furnished by the U.N.'s role in Haiti could very well continue to be used as a smoke-screen for ongoing repression by the likes of Gousse, who has operated a reign of terror against those he perceives as his political enemies. This can only further discredit the U.N.'s already circumscirbed efforts and further confirm the deprivation and poverty that Haiti's poor continue to suffer—while at the same time possibly triggering a new surge of "boat people" desperate to reach Florida's shores.

—June 2005

Larry Birns and Jessica Leight

Larry Birns is the director of the Council on Hemispheric Affairs. Educated at Bates, Columbia and Oxford, he taught and lectured for fifteen years at a number of U.S. and British universities before serving as a public affairs official, senior grade, with the U.N.'s Economic Commission on Latin America. He is the author of over 350 articles and papers on U.S.-Latin American relations. Jessica Leight serves as a COHA Research Fellow and is chief of its Haiti and Venezuelan sections. A Yale University researcher, she is the author of multiple articles on Venezuela and Haiti; her works have appeared in the *Los Angeles Times*, *Foreign Affairs*, the *Foreign Service Journal*, the *Baltimore Sun*, the *St. Louis Dispatch*, and the *Sunday Guardian*, among many other publications.

Endnotes

Introduction by Noam Chomsky

1. Thomas Friedman, *NYT* Week in Review, June 2, 1992; David Fromkin, *NYT Magazine*, Feb. 27, 1994.

2. Huntington, *International Security*, 17:4, 1993.

3. *Boston Review*, "U.S. Reported to Intercept Aristide Calls," February/March 1994; I am honored to be the chosen target, p. 1.

4. Kaplan, *New Republic*, Dec. 28, 1992. Sciolino, *NYT*, July 22; Danner, *New York Review of Books*, Nov. 4, 1993. Harrison, "Voodoo Politics," *Atlantic Monthly*, June 1993; a detailed response by Paul Farmer was not published. Landes, Ryan, see my *On Power and Ideology* (South End, 1987). For sources throughout, see my *Year 501* (South End, 1993), chap. 8.

5. *Haiti Info*, May 23, 1993; personal interviews, Port-au-Prince, June 1993. Trouillot, *Haiti: State against Nation* (Monthly Review, 1990), 102f.

6. Trouillot, *op. cit.*; McNamara to Bundy, *On Power and Ideology*, chap. 1.

7. *Labor Rights in Haiti*, International Labor Rights Education and Research Fund, April 1989; *Haiti After the Coup: Sweatshop or Real Development*, National Labor Committee Education Fund (New York), April 1993, a report based on visits and research by U.S. labor union fact-finders, entirely ignored in the mainstream.

8. See *On Power and Ideology*, 69f; *Year 501*, chap. 8. *WSJ*, Feb. 10, 1986.

9. Editorial, *NYT*, Jan 17, 1993.

10. French, *NYT*, Oct. 22, 1991; Jan. 12, 1992.

11. Americas Watch and National Coalition for Haitian Refugees, *Silencing a People* (Human Rights Watch, Feb. 1993). *Haiti After the Coup*.

12. COHA, "Sun Setting on Hopes for Haitian Democracy," Jan. 6, 1992.

13. Hyland, "The Case for Pragmatism," *Foreign Affairs*, *America and the World*, 1991-92; Wolfowitz, *ibid.*, Jan.-Feb. 1994; Harrison, *Christian Science Monitor*, Feb. 23, 1994.

14. Wolfowitz, see *Counterpunch* (Institute for Policy Studies),

March 1, 1994; Pezzullo-Carter, see my *Deterring Democracy* (Verso, 1991; Hill & Wang, 1992), chap. 10. Harrison, *CSM, op. cit.*

15. COHA's *Washington Report on the Hemisphere*, Dec. 14, 1993; Jan. 26, 1994.

16. Carothers, in Abraham Lowenthal, ed., *Exporting Democracy* (Johns Hopkins, 1991); *In the Name of Democracy* (U. of California, 1991).

17. *Haiti After the Coup.*

18. Wilentz, *Reconstruction*, vol. 1.4 (1992).

19. Diebel, *Toronto Star*, Oct. 10, 1991; Nov. 14, 1993. See chapter 5, "The Coup of 1991," below.

20. French, *NYT*, Sept. 27; Oct. 8, 1992.

21. Canute James, *FT*, Dec. 10, 1992.

22. Douglas Farah, *WP weekly*, Nov. 1–7, 1993; *Birmingham Catholic Press*, Oct. 15, 1993, citing Father Antoine Adrien, who is close to Aristide.

23. *WP weekly*, Feb. 17, 10, 1992 (Lee Hockstader, editorial); Barbara Crossette, *NYT*, May 28, 1992. See my "Class Struggle as Usual," *Letters from Lexington* (Common Courage, 1993); reprinted from *Lies of Our Times*, March 1993.

24. Crossette, *NYT*, Feb. 5, 1992.

25. *USA Today*, March 2, 1994.

26. *WP*, Dec. 20, 1992; *NYT*, Jan. 9, 1993.

27. Americas Watch, *Op. cit.*

28. *NYT*, Jan. 15, 1993.

29. AP, *BG*, July 18, 27; *NYT*, July 26; Reuters, *BG*, July 27, 1993.

30. Eyal Press and Jennifer Washburn, letters, *NYT*, March 3, 1994.

31. George Graham, *FT*, Feb. 20, 1994; Report of National Labor Committee Education Fund, Feb. 15, 1994. Note that the increases are not attributable to the rescinding of the embargo from July to October 1993.

32. AP, *NYT*, March 6, 1994.

33. Howard French, *NYT*, Feb. 9; Robert Greenberger, *WSJ*, Feb. 15, 1994. Norman Kempster, *LA Times*, Dec. 18, 1993.

34. French, *NYT*, Feb. 24, 1994; Diebel, *Toronto Star*, Nov. 14, 1993.

What's At Stake in Haiti

1. The *Washington Post*, June 17, 1992, p. A33.

2. Gutiérrez, 1983, p. 97.

3. I use these terms following anthropologist Sally Falk Moore, who has suggested that the research task of the anthropologist, these days, is to search for "the large scale in the local." Moore writes of a "processual ethnography," which would "show how local events and local commentary on them can be linked to a variety of processes unfolding simultaneously on very different scales of time and place, and to note what might be called the 'foreground preoccupation' of the actors or commentators on these events, and the 'background conditions' informing their situation that figure much more prominently in the preoccupations of the historically minded ethnographer" (Moore, 1987, p. 731). My analysis is also indebted to the frameworks advanced by Immanuel Wallerstein, Sidney Mintz, and Orlando Patterson (see bibliography).

4. See, for example, "Images for an Anti-Autobiography," where the Haitian poet René Dépestre points an accusing finger at "the coffee exporter/Who exports on the very same boat/Fresh peasant blood." (*Poète à Cuba*, 1976).

5. Cited in Hagen, 1982, pp. 166-167.

6. For more details, see Abbott, 1988, Farmer, 1992, Hagen, 1982, and Leibowitch, 1987. The facts gruesomely evoked another element of Haitian popular culture, the zombies reanimated by evil sorcerers: "Cambronne also dealt in cadavers, in almost as much demand. To save the living, medical students must dissect the dead, and obtaining corpses in sufficient quantity is the perennial problem of medical schools. Haitian cadavers, readily available once Cambronne entered the business, had the distinct advantage of being thin, so the student had no layers of fat to slice through before reaching the object of the lesson. Cambronne, using the refrigerated container service recently introduced into Haiti, supplied these corpses on demand. When the General Hospital failed to provide him with enough despite the $3.00 he paid for each body, he simply stole them from various funeral parlors" (Abbott, 1988, p. 171).

7. Cited in Saint-Gérard, 1984, p. 111 n7. The scam was finally denounced, if timidly so, by the local press, but it was not the exposé that led to an end to Hemo-Caribbean and Co. New and improved technologies simply rendered it uncompetitive.

8. Immerman, 1982, p. 7.

9. Chomsky, 1985, p. 2.
10. Cited in Nelson-Pallmeyer, 1992, p. 14.
11. Lally Weymouth, "Haiti vs. Aristide," the *Washington Post*, December 18, 1992.

Part I: The Uses of Haiti

1. Wolf, 1982, p. 4.
2. Langley, 1989, p. 175.
3. Harrison, 1993, p. 102.
4. Trouillot, 1986, p. 57.
5. Harrison, 1993, p. 105.

The Template of Colony

1. See Moreau de Saint-Méry, 1984 (1797), p. 28. Estimates regarding the indigenous population of Hispaniola vary widely. This variation reflects the controversy currently raging among physical anthropologists, archaeologists, and ethnohistorians: although all agree that the European discovery touched off devastating epidemics (of smallpox, measles, typhus, scarlet fever, and other highly contagious diseases) in previously unexposed native populations, there is no agreement as to the size of pre-Columbian populations. Cook and Borah, 1971, have reviewed all contemporary sources at length, and have settled on the tragic figure of 8,000,000 as the aboriginal population of Hispaniola in 1492. There is, in contrast, more widespread agreement on the 1510 figure.
2. Cited in Williams, 1970, p. 45.
3. See, for example, the account of Benítez-Rojo, 1992, pp. 43-49.
4. Benítez-Rojo, 1992, p. 5.
5. Benítez-Rojo, 1992, p. 9.
6. See Debien, 1962, p. 50.
7. Moreau de Saint-Méry, 1984 (1797), p. 25.
8. James, 1980, p. 50.
9. Moreau de Saint-Méry, 1985, p. 42.
10. Benítez-Rojo, 1992, p. 70.
11. Cited in Heinl and Heinl, 1978, p. 26-27.
12. Brown, 1989, p. 67.
13. Métraux, 1972, p. 365.
14. Williams, 1970, p. 246.

15. Pluchon, 1987, p. 176.
16. Cited in Heinl and Heinl, 1978, p. 37.
17. Williams, 1970, p. 247.
18. Auguste and Auguste, 1985, p. 9.
19. Schoelcher, 1982, p. 357
20. Cited in Auguste and Auguste, 1985, p. 236.
21. Lowenthal, 1976, pp. 656-657.
22. Mintz, 1974, p. 60.
23. Cited in Lawless, 1992, p. 95.
24. Paquette, 1988, p. 211.
25. Cited in Paquette, 1988, p. 180.
26. Jordan, 1974, p. 147.
27. Jordan, 1974, p. 147.
28. Mintz, 1974, p. 61.
29. Benítez-Rojo, 1992, p. 67.
30. Cited in Lawless, 1992, p. 48.
31. Lawless, 1992, p. 56.
32. Auguste, 1987, p. 3.
33. Cited in Nicholls, 1985, p. 92.
34. Cited in Jordan, 1974, pp. 148-149.
35. Nicholls, 1985, p. 89.
36. Cited in Schmidt, 1971, p. 28.
37. Logan, 1968, p. 32.
38. Logan, 1968, pp. 34, 36, 39-40.
39. Price-Mars, 1953, tome II, p. 180.
40. St. John, 1884, p. 134.
41. Trouillot, 1986, p. 89.
42. Cited in Heinl and Heinl, 1978, p. 312.
43. In 1889, according to historian Rayford Logan, "the United States government made its first efforts to gain Môle St. Nicolas by force of arms" (Logan, 1968, p. 111). But most Haitian leaders used the Môle as an enticement; this practice continued until quite recently. François Duvalier, who liked to call himself a fierce nationalist, "on at least four occasions while president invited the United States to establish a base at Môle St. Nicolas" (Heinl and Heinl, 1978, p. 618).
44. Georges Adam, 1982, p. 34.
45. Georges Adam, 1982, p. 209.
46. Rotberg, 1971, p. 110.
47. Heinl and Heinl, 1978, p. 256.

48. In Menos, 1986 (1898), p. 375.
49. See Prince, 1985, p. 18.
50. Castor, 1988, p. 21.
51. Cited in Lawless, 1992, p. 108.
52. Heinl and Heinl, 1978, pp. 404-405.
53. Cited in Logan, 1968, p. 119.
54. Dulles, 1954, p. 76.
55. Plummer, 1988, pp. 220-221.
56. His dismemberment has been described in great detail by several foreign historians. As Castor (1988:54-55) notes, "This event was much discussed as an example of Haitian savagery. Yet the people's anger had legitimate foundations. By killing those directly responsible for the odious prison massacre, people wished to revenge themselves and at the same time to show their determination to break with a past dominated by those ubiquitous satraps who, having committed their crimes, left [Haiti] to peacefully enjoy their money stolen from the country." Her comments have great resonance today.
57. Cited in Orenstein, 1993, p. 5.
58. Cited in Orenstein, 1993, p. 5.
59. See "Haiti and its Regeneration by the United States," *National Geographic* 38 (1920), p. 505.
60. See the account of "A Plebiscite Under the Boot" offered by Roger Gaillard, 1982, pp. 125-138.
61. Cited in Chomsky, 1993c, p. 19.
62. Chomsky, 1993c, p. 19.
63. Castor, 1988, p. 93.
64. Cited in Castor, 1988, p. 94. Castor also argues that the occupation aggravated the misery of the peasantry, leading to massive outmigration—some 250,000 Haitians emigrated to Cuba alone during the occupation.
65. See "Haiti and its Regeneration by the United States," *National Geographic* 38 (1920), p. 509.
66. Heinl and Heinl, 1978, pp. 463, 470.
67. Cited in Prince, 1985, p. 21.
68. Heinl and Heinl, 1978, p. 462; emphasis added.
69. See Schmidt, 1971, p. 103n.
70. Gaillard, 1983, pp. 261-262. The studies of Gaillard and Suzy Castor, referenced in the bibliography, offer important correctives to many U.S. accounts of the occupation. Unfortunately, these studies are not available in English translation.

71. Cited in Heinl and Heinl, 1978, p. 489.

72. Cited in Lawless, 1992, p. 65.

73. Castor, 1988, p. 117.

74. See also Gaillard, 1983, p. 282. Gaillard states that 12 were killed and 23 were wounded at Marchaterre. Heinl and Heinl (1978, pp. 495-497) also recount the story, underlining that the Marines—one of whom was bitten by a peasant—fired in self-defense.

75. See "Haiti and its Regeneration by the United States, *National Geographic* 38 (1920), p. 510.

76. Heinl and Heinl, 1978, p. 516.

77. Lowenthal (1976:663) puts it mordantly: "Nine-tenths of the population still manages to produce nine-tenths of the total value of national exports *in addition to* their own needs, by working an inadequate amount of worn-out land, with an archaic technology, in the absence of functioning credit services, so that the other one-tenth of the population may continue to consume nine-tenths of all imported goods and the finest agricultural products, from fresh eggs to scotch whiskey."

78. Trouillot, 1986, p. 23.

79. Cited in Lawless, 1992, p. 140.

80. Galeano, 1988, p. 107. I have changed the passage to the past tense.

81. Galeano, 1988, p. 108.

From Duvalierism to Duvalierism
Without Duvalier

1 Greene, 1980, p. 269.

2. Lawrence Harrison's recent (1993) commentary, for example, twice reminds us that the United States cut off all aid to François Duvalier in 1963. He neglects to mention, however, that aid was suspended only after a series of massacres was denounced in the international press.

3. Heinl and Heinl, 1978, p. 618. Colonel Heinl refers, of course, to orders that he himself received.

4. Cited in Kamber, 1991, p. 26.

5. Cited in Immerman, 1982, p. 101.

6. Cited in Galeano, 1988, pp. 207-208.

7. Lawless, 1992, p. 5.

8. Blasphemy was not a big concern of Papa Doc's, who in 1964

issued the Catechism of the Revolution. In it, as noted, was his own version of the Lord's Prayer: "Our Doc, who art in the National Palace for life, hallowed be Thy name by present and future generations. Thy will be done in Port-au-Prince and in the countryside. Give us this day our new Haiti, and never forgive the trespasses of those traitors who spit on our country each day. Lead them into temptation, and poisoned by their own venom, deliver them from no evil."

9. Similar conditions had been laid out in the original Haiti-Vatican Concordat, signed in 1860, but Haitian rulers had rarely interfered with a task that often fell to the powerful papal nuncio.

10. Abbott, 1988, p. 140.

11. Smarth, 1989, p. 142.

12. Smarth, 1989, pp. 152-153.

13. O'Neill, 1993, p. 93.

14. Lawless, 1992, p. 160.

15. Trouillot, 1990, p. 200.

16. Chinchilla and Hamilton, 1984, p. 230; paragraphing altered.

17. In reference to the country's violent atmosphere (and on the increasing boldness of Haitian death squads), Massing (1988) has recently written of the "salvadorization" of Haiti.

18. Burbach and Herold, 1984, p. 196.

19. Cited in Kamber, 1991, p. 26.

20. Grunwald, Delatour and Voltaire, 1984, p. 232.

21. Grunwald, Delatour and Voltaire, 1984, p. 232.

22. Cited in Lawless, 1992, p. 116.

23. O'Neill, 1993, p. 93.

24. Stepick, 1984, pp. 178-179.

25. Lawless, 1986, p. 42.

26. Abbott, 1988, p. 275.

27. Abbott, 1988, p. 276.

28. *The New York Times*, February 4, 1986.

29. Trouillot, 1990, pp. 224-225.

30. Wilentz, 1989, p. 63.

31. Hurbon, 1987c, p. 8.

32. *Time Magazine*, February 24, 1986, p. 45.

33. "Getting to know the bouncing general," *The Times* (London), February 12, 1986.

34. "Haiti's New Era Is Unfolding Slowly," *The New York Times*, February 24, 1986.

35. See "8 Dead in Clash in Haiti Capital," *The New York Times*, April 27, 1986, p. 18.

36. Trouillot, 1990, p. 222.

37. Wilentz, 1989, p. 237.

38. Massing, 1987, p. 49.

39. Hurbon, 1987c, p. 22.

40. Aristide, 1990, p. 78.

41. Wilentz, 1989, p. 140.

42. Aristide, 1990, p. 46.

43. Massing, 1987, p. 45.

44. Wilentz, 1989, p. 298.

45. Wilentz, 1989, p. 298.

46. Cited in Allman, 1989, p. 109.

47. Cited in Wilentz, 1989, p. 308.

48. Aristide, 1990, p. 47.

49. Wilentz, 1989, p. 323.

50. See "CIA Formed Haitian Unit Later Tied to Narcotics Trade," *The New York Times*, November 14, 1993,   p. 1.

51. The *New York Times*, December 1, 1987, p. 27.

The Power of the Poor in Haiti

1. Wilentz, 1989, p. 327.

2. Wilentz, 1989, p. 335,

3. Cited in Lawless, 1992, p. 167.

4. Aristide, 1990, p. 55.

5. Aristide, 1990, p. 17.

6. Cited in Danner, 1993a, p. 29.

7. See "CIA Formed Haitian Unit Later Tied to Narcotics Trade," *The New York Times*, November 14, 1993,   p. 1.

8. Aristide, 1990, p. 98.

9. Subsequent quotations from this article are to be found in Howard French, "Front-Running Priest a Shock to Haiti," *The New York Times*, December 13, 1990.

10. The Lawyers Committee for Human Rights further noted that "voter turnout was an astounding 75%, despite formidable logistical challenges. The dirt roads and mountain paths of rural Haiti where 75% of the population lives made the distribution of election materials—registration cards, voting lists, ballot boxes and ballots—treacherous and uncertain. The high illiteracy rate among Haitians compounded the challenges of

registering and voting. Yet despite these obstacles, approximately 3.2 million Haitians registered to vote and more than 2.4 million voted on election day" (See p. 2 of "Haiti: A Human Rights Nightmare," a report published in 1992 by the Lawyers Committee for Human Rights).

11. Kamber, 1991, p. 31.

12. Radio address, January 4, 1991.

13. "It is said, usually with more sadness than amusement, that the western media covers the Third World only in cases of coups, calamities, and communism. Historical accuracy will suffer only slightly by saying that the press covers Haiti only in cases of coups, calamities, communism, and cannibalism" (Lawless, 1992, p. 1).

14. Aristide, 1990, p. 87.

15. Howard French, "Haiti's New Leader Takes on Army," *The New York Times*, February 9, 1991, p. 3.

16. Stumbo, 1991, p. 12.

17. O'Neill, 1993, p. 106.

18. Aristide, 1992, pp. 151-152.

19. Moïse and Ollivier, 1992, p. 161.

20. Joseph, 1993, p. 458.

21. See pp. 22, 25 of "Haiti After the Coup: Sweatshop or Real Development," published in April 1993, by the National Labor Committee.

22. Harrison, 1993, pp. 101-102.

23. Cited in Chomsky, 1993a, p. 211.

24. Cited in Chomsky, 1993a, p. 210.

25. See p. 4 of "Haiti: A Human Rights Nightmare," a report published in 1992 by the Lawyers Committee for Human Rights.

26. See pp. 4-5 of "Haiti: A Human Rights Nightmare," a report published in 1992 by the Lawyers Committee for Human Rights.

27. The diary of a young woman who had grown up in a Brazilan slum bears eloquent testimony to widespread sentiments regarding traditional politicians: "When I am hungry I want to eat one politician, hang another, and burn a third" (De Jesus, 1962, p. 40).

28. See Isabel Hilton, "Aristide's Dream," *The Independent* (London), October 30, 1993, p. 29.

29. Shahin, 1991, p. 95.

30. See Isabel Hilton, "Aristide's Dream," *The Independent* (London), October 30, 1993, p. 29.

31. See "What Does Haiti Want? An Interview with Jean-Claude Martineau." *The Central America Reporter*, Nov.–Dec., 1993, p. 1.

32. Shahin, 1991, p. 102.

The Coup of 1991:
The Power of the Rich in Haiti

1. Aristide, 1992, p. 183.

2. Aristide, 1992, p. 184.

3. Unattributed quotations are drawn from my own interviews. In most cases, those interviewed have asked not to be identified.

4. From a speech delivered by Bishop Romélus to the National Convention of the Haitian Apostolate (USA), in Boston, on May 28, 1992, and reprinted in *America*, July 25, 1992, p. 28.

5. After the broadcast, the reporters were themselves subject to death threats. On October 5, the UPI wire service reported that "journalists who reported on a grisly massacre by mutinous Haitian soldiers have gone into hiding for fear that they may be the military's next victims."

6. *The New York Times*, October 8, 1991, p. A10.

7. The *Philadelphia Inquirer*, October 8, 1991, p. 3A.

8. *The New York Times*, October 9, 1991, p. A1.

9. See, for example, the essay by former USAID chief Lawrence Harrison (1993).

10. See David Corn, "Beltway Bandits," *The Nation*, November 29, 1993, p. 648.

11. Chomsky, 1993d, p. 153.

12. In "What Price Democracy?" by David Peterson, *Lies of Our Times*, November 1991, p. 7-8.

13. From documents compiled by The Haiti Commission, 36 East 12th Street, New York, NY 10003.

14. The French story was widely distributed; this version is taken from the *Palm Beach Post*, October 22, 1991, p. 18A.

15. Amy Wilentz, "The Oppositionist," *The New Republic*, October 28, 1991, pp. 16-20.

16. Jean-Bertrand Aristide, "Restore the Road to Democracy," *The New York Times*, October 27, 1991.

17. See p. A16 of the *San Francisco Chronicle*, October 22, 1991.

18. See "Foes vow to replace Aristide," *Palm Beach Post*, October 31, 1993, p. 1A, and "The CIA can be a poor judge of charac-

ter," *Boston Globe*, October 26, 1993, p 15.

19. Cited in *The Progressive* 57 (December, 1993), p. 8.

20. Americas Watch, 1993, p. 22.

21. Pamela Constable, "In Haiti, gas is short but not patience," the *Boston Globe*, December 9, 1991, p. A2.

22. I have interviewed or treated dozens of peasants who suffered at the hands of soldiers and other representatives of state power; this matter is discussed further in Chapter 8.

23. Scott, 1985, p. xvi.

24. Cited in the *Washington Post*, November 10, 1991, p. C1.

25. See p. 14 of "Haiti After the Coup: Sweatshop or Real Development," published in April, 1993, by the National Labor Committee.

26. See the *Boston Globe*, April 8, 1992.

27. "Washington To Haiti: Democracy Or Die," the *Washington Post*, April 24, 1992.

28. What greased this machinery? To some extent, U.S. tax dollars: the group organizing the ratification had in 1990 received $500,000 from the National Endowment for Democracy, through the program of which Lawrence Harrison was so proud (See David Corn, "Beltway Bandits," *The Nation*, November 29, 1993, p. 648).

29. In Joseph, 1993, p. 460.

30. In Joseph, 1993, p. 459.

31. Yanique Joseph (1993, p. 456) sums it up succinctly: The Bazin "package represented a compromise between sectors wielding power: high-ranking army officers, rich businesspeople wishing to preserve their monopolies, ambitious politicians, and assorted profiteers. They united behind Marc Bazin, a former official of the World Bank and the American favorite during the election of December 1990. Bazin was installed as prime minister and the office of president was left vacant."

32. See "CIA Formed Haitian Unit Later Tied to Narcotics Trade," *The New York Times*, November 14, 1993, p. 1.

33. See pp. 10-11 of "Haiti: A Human Rights Nightmare," a report published in 1992 by the Lawyers Committee for Human Rights.

34. From "Aristide calls on U.N.to step up embargo," the *Boston Globe*, September 28, 1992, p. 2A.

35. *The New York Times*, September 27, 1992. My italics.

36. Chomsky, 1993d, p. 155.

37. Chomsky, 1993d, p. 149.

38. From a speech delivered by Bishop Romélus to the National Convention of the Haitian Apostolate (USA) on May 28, 1992, and reprinted in *America*, July 25, 1992, p. 28.

39. In April, an Associated Press story reported that "Haiti's largest trafficker of U.S.-bound cocaine operates freely while American drug agents stand by helplessly, federal law enforcement files showed. They know his name—Fernando Burgos Martinez—and his address and have witnessed shipments, but Haiti's military government won't intervene" (from the *Charlotte Observer*, Sunday, April 4, 1993, p. 24A). The chief DEA officer in Haiti subsequently received, on his private embassy line, telephoned death threats. He left the country shortly thereafter.

40. Danner, 1993a, p. 25.

41. Orenstein, 1993, p. 4.

42. Danner, 1993a, p. 26.

43. See Colum Lynch, "In Aristide's hesitation, assurances won," the *Boston Globe*, July 5, 1993.

44. See "Frontline: Showdown in Haiti," produced and written by June Cross and first screened on November 9, 1993.

45. Given the presence of uniformed soldiers, this was not a difficult conclusion to draw. The U.N./OAS mission came to an even more obvious one: that the execution was "painstakingly planned" by the army. See "Izméry: u.n. assassinat 'minutïeusement planifié' par l'armée," *Haïti Progrès*, December 1–7, 1993, p. 1. Other Haitians, including a bystander, were killed by this same group of *attachés*, and a pro-Aristide army officer was similarly dispatched that afternoon.

46. See "Gunmen and Police Brutally Enforce Strike in Haiti," *The New York Times*, October 8, 1993.

47. Cited in *The New York Times*, October 15, 1993, p. A8.

48. Cited in *The New York Times*, October 15, 1993, p. A1.

49. "Baby Doc's right-hand man back in business," *The Independent* (London), November 1, 1993, p. 10.

50. "Failure of Haiti Operation Backs Initial Pentagon Skepticism," in *The New York Times*, October 15, 1993, p. A8.

51. See "CIA Formed Haitian Unit Later Tied to Narcotics Trade," *The New York Times*, November 14, 1993,   p. 1.

52. See "CIA Formed Haitian Unit Later Tied to Narcotics Trade," *The New York Times*, November 14, 1993,   p. 1.

53. Lee Hockstader, writing in the *Washington Post*, June 17,

1992, p. A33.

54. "Document suggesting Aristide unstable likely a forgery," the *Palm Beach Post*, October 31, 1993, p. 18A.

55. See Harrison, 1993, p. 103.

56. For more on the effects of the coup to date, the reader is referred to reports by Pax Christi, the Washington Office on Haiti, Americas Watch, the Haiti Commission on the Coup d'État of September 30, 1991, and the Lawyers Committee for Human Rights.

57. See "Ron Brown's Haiti Policy: The Early Years," in *Harper's Magazine* 288 (1725), February, 1994, pp. 15-16.

58. After the 1993 publication of "Haiti After the Coup," the National Labor Committee was threatened with a lawsuit by the lawyers of one of Haiti's wealthiest families.

59. See "A 'Shadow' darkens Aristide's image," the *Boston Globe*, November 5, 1993, p. 29.

60. Mr. Garrison's memos to General Cédras are written in crisp English, if we are to believe a facsimile published in *Haïti en Marche* in the edition of November 17-23, 1993, p. 1. The memorandum, dated November 11, concerns "release of fuel supply." Mr. Garrison explains that "SHELL's lawyers in London have indicated that they must demonstrate some resitance to the Haitian effort to get the fuel released." Garrison has just spoken to "a high-level American source," and offers the following advice: "One policeman, with whatever court official is necessary, must take a copy of the Court Order to the Director of SHELL and ask him whether or not he is going to recognize it...and release the fuel. If he refuses, you simply arrest him." The note concludes by predicting that "this action will be accepted by the international community." Mr. Garrison's advice was followed, and his prediction shortly thereafter was proven correct.

61. Chomsky, 1989, p. 10.

The Uses of Haiti (Reprise)

1. Léger, 1907, p. 300.

2. Weinstein and Segal, 1984, p. 109.

3. Trouillot, 1990, p. 229.

4. St. John, 1889, p. xi.

5. St. John, 1889, p. xiv.

6. St. John, 1889, p. xiii (emphasis added).

7. See "Haiti and its Regeneration by the United States," *National*

Geographic 38 (1920), p. 497.

8. See "Haiti and its Regeneration by the United States," *National Geographic* 38 (1920), p. 500.

9. See "Haiti and its Regeneration by the United States," *National Geographic* 38 (1920), p. 505.

10. Lawless, 1992, p. 51.

11. Lawless, 1992, p. 38.

12. Even the geographic designation is of interest, as Benítez-Rojo suggests: "This designation might serve a foreign purpose— the great powers' need to recodify the world better to know, to dominate it..." (Benítez-Rojo, 1992, p. 1).

13. Wilentz, 1989, p. 299.

14. Cited in Allman, 1989, p. 112.

15. See *The New York Times*, August 3, 1993, p. A2.

16. Orenstein, 1993, p. 4. Beaulieu is a famous Duvalierist.

17. Lynn Garrison, "For Haitians, a countdown to death," the *Miami Herald*, December 3, 1993, p. 35A. The editorial was smartly illustrated by Fian Arroyo.

18. Cited in Chomsky, 1993a, p. 209.

19. Chomsky, 1993c, p. 14.

20. From an interview on February 8, 1991. Yanique Joseph put it more starkly: "As a symbol, Aristide was a threat to the existing order in the Caribbean and Latin America, predominantly a region of states with democratic facades bolstered by menacing armies" (Joseph, 1993, p. 455).

21. David Corn, "Beltway Bandits," *The Nation*, November 29, 1993, p. 648.

22. Liss, 1991, p. 29.

23. Immerman, 1982, p. 183.

24. Liss, 1991, p. 30.

25. Immerman, 1982, p. 58.

26. Cited in Pearce, 1982, p. 29. Eisenhower must have been referring to some philosophy other than the one advanced by Moscow, spoofed Juan Arévalo, bitterly: "Kommunism with a 'k' is every political and social democratic movement that tries to defend the interests of the working masses, the humble, and the exploited all over the world, or speaks of sovereignty and nationalism or dares to criticize the United States" (Cited in Liss, 1991, p. 25).

27. Immerman, 1982, p. 71.

28. Pearce, 1982, p. 28.

29. Woodward, 1985, p. 237. Note that Woodward emphasizes the importance of "communist infiltration" much more than does the study by Immerman. Immerman's monograph is more in-depth and is based largely on declassified documents not consulted by Woodward. For an excellent overview of Arévalo's thought and of the role of radicals in his and the Arbenz governments, see the study by Sheldon Liss (1991).
30. Pearce, 1982, p. 28.
31. Cited in Pearce, 1982, p. 29.
32. Cited in Liss, 1991, p. 42.
33. Cited in Immerman, 1982, p. 183.
34. Immerman, 1982, p. 111.
35. Immerman, 1982, p. 112.
36. Immerman, 1982, p. 101.
37. Immerman, 1982, pp. 158-159.
38. Immerman, 1982, p. 179.
39. Immerman, 1982, p. 181.
40. Immerman, 1982, p. 178.
41. Galeano, 1988, p. 154.
42. Pearce, 1982, p. 29.
43. Woodward, 1985, p. 244.
44. Immerman, 1982, p. 200.
45. Immerman, 1982, p. 201.
46. Liss, 1991, p. 35.
47. Galeano, 1988, p. 255. One of the victims was the father of Rigoberta Menchú.
48. Cited in Pearce, 1982, p. 176.
49. Immerman, 1982, p. 201.
50. Cited in Trudeau, 1984, p. 60.
51. For reviews of U.S. foreign policy in El Salvador, see Chomsky, 1985, LeFeber, 1984, Pearce, 1982, and Sklar, 1988.
52. Reported by Wilentz, 1989, pp. 308-309.
53. Again, the Guatemalan experience confirms the pattern: "Thousands of innocent peasants died at the hands of death squads such as the Mano Blanco [White Hand], which was directed by Mario Sandoval Alarcon, who had led the overthrow of Arbenz. Yet the government maintained the fiction that the deaths resulted from confrontation between left- and right-wing extremists" (Liss, 1991, p. 34).
54. Danner, 1993b, p. 59.
55. Cited in Chomsky, 1985, p. 15.

56. Danner, 1993b, p. 61.
57. Danner, 1993b, p. 67.
58. Cited in Danner, 1993b, p. 101.
59. Danner, 1993b, p. 98.
60. Elliott Abrams, known to be contemptuous of Congressional input into U.S. foreign policy, was nonetheless sure that the El Mozote case would not amount to more than a tempest in a tea pot. "After all, the question would come down to—as Abrams put it to me—do you believe the Embassy, an agency of the United States government, or Americas Watch?" (Danner, 1993b, p. 118).
61. Danner, 1993b, p. 104.
62. Cited in Danner, 1993b, p. 106.
63. Cited in Danner, 1993b, p. 117.
64. Danner, 1993b, p. 132.
65. Chomsky, 1985, p. 122.
66. See Clements, 1984, for an eyewitness account.
67. Chomsky, 1985, p. 112.
68. Chomsky, 1985, p. 105.
69. Gutiérrez, 1983, p. 88.

Part II: A User's Guide to Haiti

1. With the exception of Yolande Jean, the Haitians introduced in these following chapters are given pseudonyms; I have likewise changed certain geographical designations.

On Guantánamo

1. The words of Yolande Jean and of other Haitians quoted in this chapter derive from interviews conducted by the author in the summer of 1993.
2. In 1912, the annual rent was raised to $5,000. For the text of the Platt Amendment, which formalized these arrangements, see Eric Williams, 1970, pp. 420-421.
3. Annas, 1993, p. 592.
4. Scheper-Hughes, 1993, p. 29. The page numbers to which I refer are those of the manuscript, which is in press.
5. Cited in O'Neill, 1993, p. 115.
6. Johnson, 1993, p. 37.
7. *The New York Times,* November 28, 1991, p. A6
8. Cited in *The Nation,* January 4/11, 1993, p. 5.

9. Powell, 1993, p. 59.

10. Schoenholtz, 1993, p. 71.

11. McCormick, 1993, p. 157.

12. McCormick, 1993, p. 159.

13. Annas, 1993, p. 590.

14. Cited in Annas, 1993, p. 590.

15. Annas, 1993, p. 590.

16. Depo-Provera is an analogue of the hormone progesterone, and is prescribed as a long-acting contraceptive. The *forced* use of such an agent has been discussed—theoretically—by many medical ethicists, and adamantly rejected on moral grounds. In legal terms, the forced injection of any substance represents the felony crime of assault.

17. Powell, 1993, p. 64. As noted above, forced treatment fulfills the legal criteria for the crime of assault.

18. Clinton and Gore, 1992, pp. 119-120.

19. Clinton and Gore, 1992, p. 119.

20. *USA Today*, Vol. 121, No. 2568.

21. Cited in *The Nation*, January 4/11, 1993, p. 5.

22. See "South Florida braces for Haitian time bomb," the *Orlando Sentinel*, Monday, January 11, 1993,   p. A1.

23. See the article filed by Philip Hilts on February 15, 1993.

24. Powell, 1993, p. 60.

25. The Centers for Disease Control had previously changed the criteria by which AIDS is defined to include all persons with less than 200 T-lymphocytes per cubic millimeter, whether or not these patients had a history of opportunistic infections. Judge Johnson later found "that military physicians had told the Immigration and Naturalization Service that detainees with CD4 counts of 200 per cubic millimeter or below 'should be medically evacuated to the United States because of the lack of facilities and specialists at Guantánamo' and that the government had 'repeatedly failed' to act on this recommendation" (See Annas, 1993, p. 591).

26. Cited in Powell, 1993, p. 68.

27. If we are to believe a recently published scholarly book on the Cuban health care system, "Quarantine is voluntary, according to a ministry official, but considerable pressure is brought to bear on those who resist. It is contended that most people decide to enter the sanitoriums because they desire treatment, fear infecting family and friends, and fear rejection. The complex of homes provided to those quarantined is luxurious

by Cuban standards, the food abundant, and the treatment humane, but the conditions most likely do not compensate for the loss of freedom. Those living at these sanitoriums have unlimited but controlled contact with their families and friends, are allowed to go out for various social purposes, and get weekend passes to go home, but only under the watchful eye of a relative or a designated medical student" (See Feinsilver, 1993, p.83).

28. Scheper-Hughes, 1993, pp. 15-16.

29. Feinsilver, 1993, p. 84.

30. "SIDA" is the Spanish-equivalent acronym for AIDS.

31. Fogel and Rosenthal, 1993, p. 359.

32. Cited in Feinsilver, 1993, p. xii.

33. Scheper-Hughes, 1993, p. 28.

34. For example, Chapter 20 of *AIDS and Accusation* (Farmer, 1992) is devoted to this subject.

35. Scheper-Hughes, 1993, p. 7.

36. O'Neill, 1993, p. 117.

37. Powell, 1993, p. 58.

38. McCormick, 1993, p. 160.

39. McCormick, 1993, p. 151.

40. Powell, 1993, p. 64.

41. Glick-Schiller and Fouron, 1990, p. 337.

42. Cited in Smart, 1993, p. 52.

43. Annas, 1993, p. 590.

44. Powell, 1993, p. 65.

Chouchou Louis and the Political Economy of Brutality

1. Americas Watch, 1993, p. 20.

2. O'Neill, 1993, p. 106.

3. See George Black and Robert O. Weiner, "A 'Process' Blind to the Cost in Blood," the *Los Angeles Times*. (Washington Edition), October 19, 1993, p. A11.

4. Haitians have often noted that U.S. foreign policy has dictated the U.S. popular press' reading of what is at stake in Haiti. Poet Jean-Claude Martineau put it succinctly: "Duvalier, under the nose of the United States, has killed more than 30,000 people without the American press even mentioning a thing about it. In Cuba, even one injustice is recorded by the American press." See "What Does Haiti Want? An Interview with Jean-Claude Martineau." The *Central America Reporter*,

Nov.-Dec., 1993, p. 9.

5. Wilentz, 1989, p. 353.

6. "What Does Haiti Want? An Interview with Jean-Claude Martineau." The *Central America Reporter*, Nov.-Dec., 1993, p. 9.

7. Chomsky, 1993a, p. 32.

8. Graham Greene gets to the heart of the matter in *The Power and the Glory*, a novel set in Mexico during a period of state repression of the Catholic Church. The protagonist of the story, a hard-drinking priest, is fleeing the authorities. There is a price on his head, and the Judas figure who will betray him is a poor mestizo with malaria and bad teeth. The priest accuses the man of plotting his betrayal, and laughs at the honesty of the feverish man's response: "A poor man has no choice, father. Now if I was a rich man—only a little rich—I should be good."

9. Gaillard, 1982, p. 220.

10. Gaillard, 1983, pp. 261-262.

11. Chomsky, 1993a, p. 204.

12. Chomsky, 1993a, p. 202.

13. Trouillot, 1986, pp. 23-24.

14. See "What Does Haiti Want? An Interview with Jean-Claude Martineau." The *Central America Reporter*, Nov.-Dec., 1993, p. 1.

15. See, for example, "CIA-funded Haiti unit reported tied to drugs, terror," the *Boston Globe*, November 14, 1993, p. 15. For further evidence of collaboration between drug rings and the Haitian army, see also Chapter 5.

16. Amy Wilentz puts it trenchantly: "During the four regimes that preceded Aristide, international human rights advocates and democratic observers had begged the State Department to consider helping the democratic opposition in Haiti. But no steps were taken by the United States to strengthen anything but the executive and the military until Aristide won the presidency. Then, all of a sudden, the United States began to think about how it could help those Haitians eager to limit the powers of the executive or to replace the government constitutionally." (Cited in Chomsky, 1993a, p. 211).

17. See James Carroll, "U.S. School That Teaches Militaries How To Torture," the *Boston Globe*, October 5, 1993.

18. Howard French, "Power Means Brutality; Practice Makes Perfect," *The New York Times*, October 17, 1993, Section 4, p. 1.

19. French is not alone in failing to make the connections. Writing in *Vanity Fair*, T.D. Allman observes, "To visit any other country the United States has occupied is to visit a country profoundly shaped, whether for good or ill, by America's corruptions and by its ideals. But on the heart, mind, and soul of Haiti, the U.S. occupation left not a trace, not a single trace" (Allman, 1989, p. 111). Compare this assessment with that of historian Suzy Castor, author of *L'Occupation Américaine d'Haïti*: "Haiti's 19 years of military occupation by the United States profoundly marked national life. After this period, all of the country's economic, political, and social development bears the stamp of this occupation, which shook, in enduring ways, the very foundations of the nation" (Castor, 1988, p. 215).

20. *The Nation*, May 3, 1993.

21. Harrison, 1993, p. 102.

22. See "What Does Haiti Want? An Interview with Jean-Claude Martineau." The *Central America Reporter*, Nov.-Dec., 1993, p. 9.

23. "Advocates warn of human rights emergency in Haiti," the *Palm Beach Post*, October 30, 1993, p. 12A.

24. Cited in "Advocates warn of human rights emergency in Haiti," the *Palm Beach Post*, October 30, 1993, p. 12A.

Acéphie

1. Métraux, 1972, p. 274.

2. See Farmer, 1992, for an in-depth exploration of these questions.

3. Guérin *et al*, 1984, p. 256.

4. Murray and Payne (1988: 25-26) question the relevance of gay tourism in the Haitian AIDS epidemic: "Insofar as gay travel can be estimated from gay guidebooks, Haiti was one of the least-favored destinations in the Caribbean for gay travelers during the 1970s and the less-favored half of the island of Hispaniola." His assessment is based only on "frequency of listing in gay guidebooks," surely a less significant indicator of the relevance of such tourism than the cluster studies which revealed direct sexual contact between Haitian men and North American gay tourists. It is important to note that the introduction of an epidemic of sexually transmitted disease need not involve some critical mass of sexual contact, but requires only that the infectious agent be introduced into a sexually active population (in this case, Haitian men). The Guérin *et al*

(1984) study does this.

5. Osborn, 1989, p. 126; emphasis added.

6. Bartholemew *et al*, 1987, p. 2606.

7. See Koenig *et al*, 1987, Pape and Johnson, 1988, and Merino *et al* 1990. For a fairly thorough review of this and related literature, see Farmer, 1992.

8. See the International Monetary Fund's summaries of "Directions of Trade Statistics" in that organization's *Yearbook 1984.*

9. Liautaud, Pape, and Pamphile, 1988, p. 690.

10. Oppenheimer, 1988, p. 282.

11. Choi, 1987, p. 19.

12. Choi, 1987, p. 19.

13. Treichler, 1989, p. 34.

14. Albert, 1986, pp. 174-175.

15. Viera, 1985, p. 97.

16. Viera, 1987, pp. 121-122.

17. Moore and LeBaron, 1986, pp. 81, 84.

18. Fee, 1988, p. 127.

19. Derrick Jackson, "Opening the Door to Racial Hatred," the *Boston Globe*, April 15, 1992, p. 23.

New Myths for Old

1. Howard French, "Power Means Brutality; Practice Makes Perfect," *The New York Times*, October 17, 1993, Section 4, p. 1.

2. Harrison, 1993, p. 105.

3. Harrison, 1993, p. 106.

4. Rotberg, 1971, p. 370.

5. Harrison, 1993, p. 104.

6. See "Washington To Haiti: 'Democracy Or Die,'" the *Washington Post*, April 24, 1992, p. A27.

7. Wilentz, 1989, p. 115.

8. Orenstein, 1993, p. 4.

9. Colum Lynch, "In Aristide's hesitation, assurances won," the *Boston Globe*, July 5, 1993.

10. Hancock, 1989, p. 180.

11. Lappé, Collins and Kinley, 1980, p. 97.

12. See DeWind and Kinley, 1988.

13. Hancock, 1989, p. 180.

14. Cited in Chomsky, 1991, p. 386.

15. Chomsky, 1991, pp. 386-387.

16. Isabel Hilton, "Aristide's Dream of Haiti," *The Independent* (London), October 30, 1993, p. 29.

17. Immerman, 1982, p. 136.

18. Chomsky, 1987 (1968), p. 83.

19. See "Washington To Haiti: 'Democracy Or Die,'" the *Washington Post*, April 24, 1992, p. A27.

20. Howard French, "Study Says Haiti Sanctions Kill Up to 1,000 Children a Month," *The New York Times*, November 9, 1993, p. 1.

21. The longstanding economic sanctions by the United States against Cuba also give the lie to this basic thesis. The sanctions have fettered Cuba's trade significantly. But they have not had a significant impact on the health of infants and children. In fact, Cuban mortality rates in these age groups have declined throughout this embargo, dropping from over 100 deaths per 1,000 live births in 1958 to just under 10 deaths per 1,000 births in the first half of 1993. Cuba's health indices are by far the most favorable in Latin America, and are very similar to those from the United States.

22. "Physicians' group says a Harvard study erred on dying Haiti children," the *Boston Globe*, November 24, 1993, p. 2.

23. Pamela Constable, "Haitian politics: cruelty and myths," the *Boston Globe*, October 21, 1993.

24. Lee Hockstader, "Haitians See U.S. Hand In All That Befalls Them," the *Washington Post*, June 17, 1992, p. A33.

25. Déjean, 1993, p. 270.

26. Chomsky, 1989, pp. 11, 8-9.

27. Chomsky, 1985, reviews this coverage in detail.

28. Danner, 1993b, p. 120-121.

29. Danner, 1993b, p. 121.

30. Immerman, 1982, p. 112.

31. Cited in Immerman, 1982, p. 125.

32. Immerman, 1982, pp. 5-6.

33. Kownacki, 1993, p. 14.

34. Cited in Chomsky, 1991, p. 387.

35. Arthur Jones, "Haiti, Salvador links viewed," the *National Catholic Reporter*, November 19, 1993, p. 5.

36. Aristide, 1990, p. 67.

37. Chomsky, 1993d, p. 158.

Epilogue to the New Edition

1. A number of friends and interlocutors have influenced my readings of what's happening now in Haiti, and I'd like to thank them: Greg Bates, Ophelia Dahl, Mary Healy and the folks at the Washington Office on Haiti, Elaine Cleeton and her students at SUNY Geneseo, Mark Pavlick, Burt Wechsler, Jorge Cortiñas, Rudi Stern, William Smarth, Antoine Adrien, Jane Regan, Roseanne Auguste, Papa Frico, Marie-Flore Chipps, Didi Bertrand, Maxi Raymonville. Thanks, too, to the U.S. soldiers who were willing to be interviewed. As ever, this work has been read and critiqued by Haun Saussy, Bill Rodriguez, Jim Kim, and, especially, Noam Chomsky.

2. See Laënnec Hurbon, "The Hope for Democracy," the *New York Review of Books*, November 3, 1994, p. 38.

3. See Paul Quinn-Judge," the Boston Globe, September 8, 1994, p.

4. A few weeks earlier, over an editorial extolling the "recolonization of Africa," the *Sunday Telegraph*—one of Britain's most widely circulated papers—ran an editorial about Aristide under the title "Prophet of Hate." In it, we learn that Aristide was "little better than the notorious Duvalier dynasty, which ruled with an iron fist from 1957 to 1986....During [Aristide's] brief rule some estimates suggest that hundreds died in the course of such disorders." See also "America should not send men to die for this priest," the *Sunday Times* [London], September 18, 1994./

5. See Douglas Jehl, "Clinton Plans Speech to Head Off Clash With Congress," the *New York Times*, September 15, 1994, p. A8.

6. See "Patrick Bellegarde-Smith" (interview), *The Progressive*, November, 1994 (Vol. 58, No. 11), p. 32.

7. See Allan Nairn, "Aristide Banks on Austerity," *Multinational Monitor*, July/August, 1994, pp. 8–9. It is of note that Nairn's excellent reporting from Haiti appeared well outside of the mainstream.

8. I was one of those who argued this point. See "Should the U.S. invade Haiti?" the *Miami Herald*, July 24, 1994, pp. C1, 5. As an aside, after receiving my initial draft, the editor with whom I spoke asked only that I delete my allegation that the U.S. was still funneling covert aid to the military or paramilitary groups in Haiti. I changed my accusation to the conditional, but suspect that we will soon uncover the paper trail of this assistance, which violates a number of U.S. laws.

9. See William Leogrande, "Washington et l'écueil haïtien," *Le Monde Diplomatique*, October 1994, p. 1.

10. See "Imposing 'Democracy' in Haiti," *The Progressive*, November, 1994 (Vol. 58, No. 11), p. 8.

11. Cited in *The Progressive*, November, 1994 (Vol. 58, No. 11), p. 8. See also William Safire, "Haiti: Much Ado About Something," the *New York Times*, September 19, 1994.

12. See "Patrick Bellegarde-Smith" (interview), *The Progressive*, November, 1994 (Vol. 58, No. 11), p. 32.

13. For a sample of Carter's commentary on the Cédras family, see "Ex Hits the Spot," *People*, October 3, 1994, pp. 44–47. Carter's appreciation for Mme. Cédras was widely reported. See, for example, the wry "La diplomatie cacahuete," *Le Monde*, September 23, 1994, p. 30. The former president found Ethiopian dictator Mengistu's wife equally alluring: "I found him to be charming, his wife is one of the most beautiful women I've ever seen in the world, she was like King Solomon's daughter" (cited in "Jimmy Carter, Despite Acclaim for Haiti Role, Says He Feels Unappreciated," the *New York Times*, September 21, 1994, p. A17).

14. In a devastating essay written in early October, Noam Chomsky put it this way: "Cédras, police chief Francois, and the rest were informed with great clarity that they could continue their work of decimating the popular organizations, secure in the knowledge that when the time came for them to hand the work over to others, they would either be flown out on an American jet with what remained of the country's wealth in their pockets, like Somoza and Duvalier, or allowed to stay on in the rich suburbs enjoying the fruits of their labors and awaiting the next opportunity, which may not be too long delayed" (See "Democracy Restored," *Z Magazine*, November, 1994 (Vol. 7, No. 11), p. 51).

15. The structure and content of these victory narratives is discussed in my editorial, "Let's be honest about our history with Haiti," the *Tri-Valley Herald*, September 30, 1994, p. A-21.

16. See "Ex Hits the Spot," *People*, October 3, 1994, p. 47. Such statements from "the human rights president" should not surprise, given many similar pronouncements (such as that in which he noted that we have no debt to the Vietnamese since "the destruction was mutual.")

17. See Maureen Dowd, "The Mouse That Roared Squeaks Back," the *New York Times*, September 22, 1994, p. 1.

18. For some, these were not the two words that came most readi-

ly to mind. *The National Catholic Reporter,* in a more charitable vein, suggested that we should have only two words for Haiti: "I'm sorry." See "In Haiti's strange hour, U.S. could learn needed lesson," *National Catholic Reporter,* September 30, 1994, p. 20.

19. See "Patrick Bellegarde-Smith" (interview), *The Progressive,* November, 1994 (Vol. 58, No. 11), p. 33.

20. See John Cushman, Jr., "Haitian Police Crush Rally as American Troops Watch," the *New York Times,* September 21, 1994, p. 1.

21. See Rick Bragg, "G.I.'s Voice Disgust at Orders Not to Interfere With Beatings," the *New York Times,* September 22, 1994, p. A14.

22. One soldier, Captain Lawrence Rockwood of military intelligence, making the mistake of taking Clinton's speech at face value, believed that U.S. forces had been deployed in Haiti in response to the deteriorating human rights. As the days went by, Captain Rockwood became increasingly disturbed by the U.S. forces' failure to prevent the killing of civilians and prisoners by Haitian military and paramilitary groups. He sought action through the proper channels. After being stonewalled at every level of command, the soldier finally, on September 30, filed a complaint with the command Inspector General, citing "subversion of the President's primary mission intent concerning human rights by the command." Having filed the complaint, Captain Rockwood decided to take matters into his own hands, forcing his way into the main prison in Port-au-Prince, where conditions were as he feared. The Haitian command called their friends at the U.S. embassy, who reported to the prison and escorted to Rockwood to his unit, where he was placed under arrest. Captain Rockwood was then subjected to a thorough psychiatric evaluation, and, when this proved unremarkable, escorted out of Haiti. At this writing, he has been asked to resign or face court martial.

23. See Douglas Jehl, "Clinton Orders U.S. Troops to Take Steps", the *New York Times,* September 22, 1994, p. A12.

24. See Allan Nairn, "Behind Haiti's Paramilitaries," *The Nation,* October 24, 1994, p. 458. Also in Nairn's important report: "When I asked Constant . . . about the anti-Aristide coup, he said that as it was happening Colonel Collins and Donald Terry (the CIA station chief who also ran the SIN) `were inside the [Army General] Headquarters.' But he insisted that this was `normal': The CIA and D[efense] I[ntelligence] A[gency] were always there."

25. See, for example, Allan Nairn's "The Eagle is Landing," *The Nation*, October 3, 1994, p. 346.

26. Cited in "Lying Down With Dogs," *Time*, October 17, 1994, p. 28.

27. See Doug Jehl, "Clinton Exults in Swift Success of U.S. Military Force in Haiti," the *New York Times*, October 7, 1994, p. A14.

28. A previous raid, suggested by an *attaché* working with the U.S. troops, led to the discovery of a dance troupe, but no arms (see John Kifner, "A U.S. Raid in Haiti Discovers Dancers, Not a Weapons Cache," the *New York Times*, October 3, 1994, p. A1.

29. See Larry Rohter, "Haiti's Military Power Structure Is Showing Signs of Falling Apart," the *New York Times*, October 5, 1994, Pp. A1, A16.

30. In a late-October interview, Father William Smarth made the following observation: "Two cities with big and persistent macoute problems are Cayes, in the south, and Port-de-Paix, in the northwest. Here U.S. troops have worked with the bad guys, including FRAPH and the worst military torturers....In Port-de-Paix, a [Haitian] journalist was recently arrested with the connivance of the U.S. military. Attachés continue to extort and rob, but are clever enough to blame these events on lavalas. Why do the U.S. soldiers buy this sort of rubbish? Still, the people will denounce this, so there's hope."

31. See Jean-Claude Bayeux, "An Embarrassing Presence," the *New York Review of Books*, November 3, 1994, p. 37.

32. Again, the popular response was entirely predictable, but had been dismissed by Washington: "At first, Father Aristide resisted having so many former soldiers in the police force, but [Clinton] Administration officials said they persuaded him to accept them" (the *New York Times*, September 19, 1994).

33. See Jean-Claude Bajeux, "An Embarrassing Presence," the *New York Review of Books*, November 3, 1994, p. 37.

34. See René Dépestre, "Une parole de vérité," *Le Monde*, September 23, 1994, p. 2.

35. See the detailed and well-documented account in Chomsky's "Democracy Restored," *Z Magazine*, November 1994 (Vol. 7, No. 11), p. 53.

36. Why the flow of funds in this direction? Local Texaco officials are said to have paid the junta in order to buy and sell petroleum, because the military, not Texaco, controlled the arrival of all ships to Haitian ports. In official company reports, these

hefty payments, dwarfed by the distributors' even larger mark-ups, will no doubt be called "taxes."

37. This helps to explain General Cédras' take on the embargo at the outset of 1994: "Nor does he seem much concerned by the embargo. The first one, imposed by President Bush after the coup `had no adverse effects—the population was very indifferent.' And the latest one? `It's just another day of the week,' he says with a shrug" (Bella Stumbo, "A Place Called Fear," *Vanity Fair*, February 1994, p. 76.

38. See "Democracy in Haiti—will the rich buy it?", the *Financial Times* (London), October 16, 1994, p. 1.

39. I further asked him if he knew where the Haitian high command had been trained. "Yup, the School of the Americas, Fort Benning. Bad guys. I don't know why we had to protect them like that when they were leaving."

40. See "Les époustouflants paradoxes de Chavannes Jean-Baptiste," *Haïti-Progrès*, Oct. 26–Nov. 1, 1994 (Vol. 12, No. 31), p. 4.

41. Ibid.

42. See "Imposing `Democracy' in Haiti," *The Progressive*, November, 1994 (Vol. 58, No. 11), p. 8.

43. See Michel-Rolph Trouillot, "Aristide's Challenge," the *New York Review of Books*, November 3, 1994, p. 39.

44. The Washington Office on Haiti (110 Maryland Avenue NE, Washington, D.C., 20002) offers important and critical documentation regarding USAID projects in Haiti. See also Jane Regan's "A.I.D.ing U.S. Interests in Haiti," *CovertAction Quarterly* 51 (Fall–Winter 1994), pp. 7–13, 56–58. Since *The Uses of Haiti* was first published, an excellent collection of essays about U.S. policies towards Haiti has appeared: *The Haiti Files*, edited by James Ridgeway. The pieces by John Canham-Clyne and the Haiti Information Bureau are particularly useful.

45. From the *New York Times*, October 25, 1994, p. 1.

46. *Haïti-Progrès*, October 26–November 1, 1994, p. 1.

47. Manley, 1982, p. 184.

48. See Kaufman, 1985, p. 184: "Advisors from the IMF also suggested that the government resign."

49. See "A Haitian about-face," *U.S. News and World Report*, December 19, 1994, pp. 48, 50.

50. See Randolph Ryan, "Aristide's Plans for Reform May Face Opposing Tensions," the *Boston Globe*, September 25, 1994, p. 20.

51. See "We'll hunt you down like a dog," *Newsweek*, October 17, 1994, p. 28.

52. For classic examples of the genre, see Rick Bragg's well-written "I Never Seen Nothing Like That," the *New York Times Magazine*, November 6, 1994, pp. 52–57. Bella Stumbo "gained rare access" to General Raoul Cédras in order to paint a sympathetic portrait of him in "A Place Called Fear," *Vanity Fair*, February 1994, pp. 74–77, 117–121. The photograph of the author gazing adoringly upon the general—"so mildly pleasant and tediously thoughtful," she found—is punishment enough.

53. See Eric Schmitt, "Haitian Crowds Loot Police Buildings," the *New York Times*, September 26, 1994, p. 1; my italics.

54. Aristide has pledged to reduce the Haitian army from a force of 7,500 to one of 1,500. "The U.S. agency assigned to rebuild the Haitian police force is called ICITAP, which is an offshoot of the FBI. According to its chief Haitian planner, ICITAP is due to stay for three years, bringing in several hundred U.S. trainers to mold a 5,000-man Haitian force" (Allan Nairn, "The Eagle is Landing," *The Nation*, October 3, 1994, p. 344). ICITAP was created in 1986 to help train police forces in El Salvador and Guatemala. In summary, then, the Haitian security forces will be reduced from 7,500 to 6,500, and be trained by the very U.S. agency that helped to train two of Latin America's most notorious police forces.

55. Colonel Patrick Collins, who may have helped to create FRAPH, has been recalled to Haiti by the Clinton administration, and Allan Nairn recently reported that "Today, the CIA is beefing up its Haiti station, bringing in more operatives and recruiting new Haitian assets" (Allan Nairn, "The Eagle is Landing," The Nation, October 3, 1994, p. 346). The CIA is said to have recently received a $5 million "emergency grant" to counter Aristide's opponents—a novel project for the agency.

56. Over a decade ago, Tanzanian President J.K. Nyerere put it trenchantly: "When did the IMF become the International Ministry of Finance?" (Cited in Kaufman, 1985, p. 243).

57. See Michael Mandelbaum, "Can Aristide Be Haiti's Mandela?", the New York Times, October 14, 1994, p. A35.

Diagnosis

1. Dahl, R. 1982. *Revolting Rhymes*. London: Cape.

2. Deibert, M. 2002. "Human Rights Deteriorating in Haiti, OAS

Says." Reuters 30 August.

3.   For more on the Raboteau trial, see Concannon, B. 2000. "Beyond Complementarity: The International Criminal Court and National Prosecutions, A View from Haiti." *Columbia Human Rights Law Review* 32(1): 201-50.

Concannon, B. 2001a. "Justice for Haiti: The Raboteau Trial." *International Lawyer* 35(2): 641-47.

Concannon, B. 2001b. "No Reconciliation Without Justice." *Criminal Justice Matters* 44: 21-24.

Farmer, P. 2003. *Pathologies of Power: Health, Human Rights, and the New War on the Poor.* Berkeley: University of California Press, forthcoming.

4.   As jail breaks and general lawlessness go, Haiti has nothing on the Dominican Republic. A recent riot in La Vega, about 75 miles northwest of the Dominican capital, left at least 29 dead. More striking, to those interested in justice, "as many as eighty percent of the men, women, and even children who fill Dominican jails have never been tried for the crimes they've been accused of committing." See Ottey, M.A.W. 2002. "Dominican Republic Jail Riot Revives Human Rights Issue." *Miami Herald* 26 September, p. 10A.

5.   Deibert, M. 2002. "Aristide's Tinderbox." *The Village Voice* 28 August – 3 September.

6.   "The government provides an update on the progress of the investigations into the killings of Jean Dominique and Brignol Lindor." 2002. Agence Haïtienne de Presse, 13 September (English translation).

7.   Mildred Aristide, traces the history of Haiti's justice system in her remarks at the graduation ceremony of L'École de la Magistrature on September 13, 2002. Available at: http://www.haiti.org/mta-discours-sept13.html.

8.   Violent death is the third most common cause of death in São Paulo—in 1999, ten percent of deaths were the result of homicide. The police were responsible for roughly ten percent of these murders. Between 1981 and 2001, 11,692 people have died at the hands of the military and civil police forces.

See Caldeira, T. 2002. "Police Violence in Democratic Brazil." *Ethnography* 3(3): 235-263.

Caldeira, T. 2000. *City of Walls: Crime, Segregation, and Citizenship in São Paulo.* Berkeley, CA: University of California Press.

Ouvidoria da Polícia do Estado de São Paulo. 2001. *Relatório Annual de Prestação de Contas de 2000.* São Paulo: Ouvidoria da Polícia.

Ouvidoria da Polícia do Estado de São Paulo. 2002. *Relatório*

Annual de Prestação de Contas de 2001. São Paulo: Ouvidoria da Polícia.

9. Cited in Schmidt, H. 1971. *The United States Occupation of Haiti, 1915-1934.* New Brunswick, NJ: Rutgers University Press; p. 28.

10. Lawless, R. 1992. *Haiti's Bad Press.* Rochester, VT: Schenkman Books; p. 56.

11. See "Government of Haiti Makes Decisive Move to End Political Impasse." 2002. PR Newswire 19 July.

12. See Carl Hiaasen's editorial decrying the U.S. "hypocrisy" described here. Hiassen notes that "Haiti wouldn't be as abysmal as it is today if the United States hadn't looked the other way for 28 years while the Duvaliers looted the national treasury, pocketed foreign aid and assassinated their critics. When it comes to demanding democracy and human rights abroad, though, the United States has extremely flexible standards." Hiassen, C. 2002. "U.S. Denies Crucial Funds to Help Haiti." *Miami Herald* 16 June. Available at: http://www.miami.com/mld/miamiherald/news/columnists/carl_hiaasen/3471462.htm

13. Just a few weeks ago, on August 21, 2002, Musharraf "unilaterally" amended Pakistan's Constitution to expand his control of the country even further. In these amendments, he claims the right to dissolve the elected Parliament and to make additional amendments at his own discretion. See Rohde, D. 2002. "Musharraf Redraws Constitution, Blocking Promise of Democracy." *New York Times* 21 August, p. A1.

14. Burns, J.F. 2001. "U.S. Envoy Sees Her Role Reverse." *International Herald Tribune,* 26 November.

15. An example closer to home is Nicaragua, where in 1996, Arnoldo Alemán of the Liberal Constitutionalist Party (PLC) was elected president. Despite the fact that Alemán headed what was possibly the most corrupt executive branch in Latin America, the PLC retained power in the elections of November 2001. Many attribute PLC candidate Enrique Bolanos' win to U.S. support and intimidation. The pro-Sandinista daily *El Nuevo Diario* reported that U.S. Ambassador Oliver Garza spoke in "a threatening tone" when discussing the repercussions of a win by Sandinista party candidate Daniel Ortega. In the month prior to the election, Governor Jeb Bush of Florida write, in an editorial in the *Miami Herald,* an attack on Ortega: "it would seem inconceivable that a people would choose to return to a totalitarian past...[Daniel Ortega] is a foe of the values for which the United States stands." This article was translated and run in the conservative Nicaraguan daily *La*

Prensa, and may have reversed the lead Ortega—not without his own checkered past—had in the polls. See Campbell, D. 2001. "Getting the Right Result: Nicaragua's Election Showed the U.S. Still Won't Allow a Free Vote." *Guardian,* November, p. 17.

See also Council on Hemispheric Affairs. 2001. "Upcoming Nicaraguan Elections." Press release, 30 October. Available at http://www.coha.org/Press Releases/01-21-Nicaragua(extended).htm.

16. Gibbons, E.D. 1999. Sanctions in Haiti: Human Rights and Democracy Under Assault. Westport, Conn.: Praeger.

17. Robert, D., and R. Machado. 2001. "Haiti: Economic Situation and Prospects." Inter-American Development Bank, Country Economic Assessment. Available at http://www.iadb.org/regions/re2/sep/ha-sepg.htm.

18. "Statement of Congresswoman Barbara Lee: New Partnership for Haiti Resolution," 23 May 2002. Lee also introduced House Congressional Resolution 382, "Urging the President to end any embargo against Haiti and to no longer require, as a condition of providing humanitarian and development assistance to Haiti, the resolution of the political impasse in Haiti, and for other purposes." (107th Congress 2nd session H. Con. Res. 382, 2002).

19. These numbers reflect 1999 data. See the Country Health Profiles of the Pan American Health Organization, available at: http://www.paho.org/Project.asp?SEL=HD&LNG=ENG&CD=COUNT.

20. Norton, M. 2002. "Haiti Clamors for Release of Blocked Loans That Might Take Years to Disburse." Associated Press, 11 March.

21. Dodd, C. 2002. "Concerning the Crisis in Haiti." Statement before the U.S. Senate, 31 July. Available at: http://www.senate.gov/~dodd/press/Speeches/107_02/0731.htm

22. "The OAS adopted today Resolution CP/Res. 822, which puts an end to the blockage of international aid to the poorest country in the American hemisphere. Ever since the OAS's election observers and the political parties associated with Convergence démocratique raised objections to the legislative and local elections of May 2000, the European Union, the World Bank, the Inter-American Development Bank and the wealthy countries have blocked several hundred million dollars' worth of aid to Haiti. In all the resolutions adopted by the OAS concerning Haiti, the release of funds has been conditioned on Fanmi Lavalas [the party founded by Aristide] and Convergence démocratique reaching an agreement. By making

this resolution [822], the OAS has tacitly put an end to the process of agreement between Fanmi Lavalas and Convergence démocratique." (Bonneau, L. 2002. *Le Nouvelliste* 4 September, p. 18.)

23. CID/Gallup. 2000. Haiti Public Opinion Poll, October. See also Brian Concannon's essay on the subject at:
http://www.uchastings.edu/boswell_01/Brian%20on%20Dec%201 7.htm.

24 Amy Wilentz wrote a wonderful account of these years: "As Namphy's regime became weaker and more violent, such groundless rumors against Aristide—which you could hear from the mouths of bishops and ambassadors...grew wilder and more fantastic. Eventually, whisperers would accuse him of involvement in the attack on the [1987] presidential elections, would say that he had invented out of whole cloth various Church orders against himself, would even go so far as to claim that Aristide himself had paid a band of men to feign an assassination attempt against him. In other words, every action of the right-wing forces was accompanied by a rumor blaming Aristide for the thing. The campaign seemed organized—each rumor popped up whole and was reiterated each time by the same bunch of people." See Wilentz, A. 1989. *The Rainy Season: Haiti After Duvalier*. New York: Simon and Schuster; p.115.

25. "The Bush Administration denies rumors circulated by the MPSN asserting that the United States Would Contribute to the Removal from Power of the Legitimately-Elected President of Haiti." 2002. Agence Haïtienne de Presse, 29 August (English translation).

26. See the National Endowment for Democracy's website at: http://www.ned.org/about/faq.html.

27. Ignatieff, M. 2001. *Human Rights as Politics and Idolatry*. Princeton: Princeton University Press; p. 8-9.

28. "Un diplomate américain crée des remous dans le domaine des droits humains" ("An American Diplomat Creates a Stir in the Realm of Human Rights"). 2002. *Le Nouvelliste*, 31 July, p. 26. The prize recipient was Pierre Espérance, on behalf of the National Coalition for Human Rights.

29. "La D.G.I. prend les médias par la peau du portefeuille." ("The National Tax Bureau Grabs the Media by the Scruff of Their Wallets.") *Le Nouvelliste*, 6-8 September, p. 1.

30. See Whittell, G. 2000. "Russian Leader Faces Pounds 3bn Questions." *The Times* (London), 25 July, p. 15.
    "Russia Still Investigating Fate of 1998 IMF Loan." 2002. Associated Press, 21 April.

31. See Patricia Hayner's discussion of this subject:
    "When U.S. forces invaded Haiti in the fall of 1994, they drove trucks straight to the offices of the armed forces and the brutal paramilitary group, the Front for Haitian Advancement and Progress (FRAPH), hauling away documents, photos, videos, and other material that contained extensive evidence of the egregious abuses of these forces, including gruesome 'trophy photos' of FRAPH victims. Some foreign rights advocates in Haiti who came into possession of some of this material also handed it over to U.S. troops, relieved that it would be in safer hands. 'There wasn't a photocopier working in the entire country, so you couldn't make copies of things, and in the chaos of the moment nowhere else was secure,' one person told me. But everyone assumed the material would be returned to Haiti when things settled down. On the contrary, none of these approximately 160,000 pages of documents, photographs, videotapes, or audiotapes have been released by the United States back to the country to which they belong. They remain in U.S. government hands, under the control of the Department of Defense. The assumed reason for this intransigence is not flattering: the United States provided direct support to some of those directly implicated in abuses, paying key FRAPH leaders as intelligence sources, and these documents would almost certainly reveal these connections and the complicity of the U.S. government in supporting known thugs. The United States eventually offered to return the documents only if the Haitian government would agree to restrictions on the use of the material, and after certain portions were blacked out, but the Haitians refused these conditions. Despite formal requests to the U.S. government for access to the documents, the Haitian truth commission completed its work, and a number of important trials have gone forward, without the benefit of any of this damning documentary evidence."

    Hayner, P. 2001. *Unspeakable Truths: Confronting State Terror and Atrocity.* New York and London: Routledge; p. 203-204.

32. In President Bush's annual report to Congress regarding illicit drug producing countries, he cited Haiti, Afghanistan, and Burma as the three countries that have " 'failed demonstrably . . . to make substantial efforts' during the previous twelve months to adhere to international counternarcotics agreements." Taking a similar tone, the U.S. State Department's

International Narcotics Control Strategy Report (2002) bashed Haiti for failing to cooperate with international law enforcement, despite stating in the same report that the Drug Enforcement Agency had "reported very good cooperation" during the counternarcotics "Operation Hurricane" of September 2001; that Justice Minister Lissade "acted quickly in a few cases to extradite non-Haitian traffickers"; and that during 2001, the Haitian National Police seized 446 kilograms of cocaine, up from 238 kilograms in 2000 (p. VI-34, VI-36). Available online at http://www.state.gov/g/inl/rls/nrcrpt/2001/. See also http://usinfo.state.gov/topical/global/drugs/02022505.htm for the Press Release of President Bush's report to Congress, 25 February 2002.

33. Grann, D. 2001. "Giving 'the Devil' His Due." *Atlantic Monthly* 287(6): 54-75.
34. "No Hero to Haitians." 2002. *Wall Street Journal*, 29 April, p. A18.
35. Deibert, M. 2002. "Aristide's Tinderbox." *The Village Voice* 28 August.
36. Binford, L. 1996. *The El Mozote Massacre.* Tucson: University of Arizona Press; p. 4.
37. *Le Nouvelliste.* 6-8 September 2002, p. 22. Paragraphing altered.

Bibliography

Abbott, Elizabeth
  1988 *Haiti: The Duvaliers and Their Legacy.* New York: McGraw-Hill.

d'Adesky, Anne-Christine
  1991 "Silence + Death = AIDS in Haiti." *The Advocate* 577:30-36.

Albert, Edward
  1986 "Illness and Deviance: The Response of the Press to AIDS." In *The Social Dimensions of AIDS: Method and Theory.* Feldman, Douglas, and Thomas Johnson, eds. New York: Praeger. Pp. 163-178.

Allen, John
  1930 "An Inside View of Revolutions in Haiti." *Current History* 32:325-329.

Allman, T.D.
  1989 "After Baby Doc." *Vanity Fair* 52(1):74-116.

Americas Watch
  1991 *El Salvador's Decade of Terror.* New Haven: Yale University Press

Americas Watch and the National Coalition for Haitian Refugees
  1993 *Silencing a People: The Destruction of Civil Society in Haiti.* New York: Human Rights Watch.

Annas, George
  1993 "Detention of HIV-Positive Haitians at Guantánamo." *New England Journal of Medicine* 329(8):589-592.

Anonymous
  1993 Kalfou Danjere! Akò Pou Remanbre Leta Reyaksyonè a (Kayè Popilè 11). Port-au-Prince: Edisyon Près Pwoletè.

Anvers, Paul
  1992 *Rizières de sang.* Paris: L'Harmattan.

Aristide, Jean Bertrand
  1990 *In the Parish of the Poor: Writings from Haiti.* MaryKnoll, New York: Orbis.
  1992 *Tout Homme est un Homme.* Paris: Editions du Seuil.

Auguste, C., and M. Auguste
1985 *L'Expédition Leclerc 1801-1803*. Port-au-Prince: Imprimerie Henri Deschamps.

Auguste, Yves
1987 *Haïti & Les États Unis*. Port-au-Prince: Imprimerie Henri Deschamps.

Bartholomew, Courtenay, Saxinger, W. Carl, Clark, Jeffrey W., Gail, Mitchell, Dudgeon, Anne, Mahabir, Bisram, Hull-Drysdale, Barbara, and Cleghorn, Farley.
1987 "Transmission of HTLV-1 and HIV Among Homosexual Men in Trinidad." *Journal of the American Medical Association*. 257: 2604-2608.

Bastien, Rémy
1961 "Haitian Rural Family Organization." *Social and Economic Studies* 10(4):478-510.
1985 (1951) *Le Paysan Haitien et sa Famille: Vallée de Marbial*. Paris: Karthala.

Benítez-Rojo, Antonio
1992 *The Repeating Island: The Caribbean and Postmodern Perspective*. James Maraniss, trans. Durham, NC: Duke University Press.

Boff, Leonardo
1991 *Faith on the Edge: Religion and Marginalized Existence*. Robert Barr, trans. Maryknoll, NY: Orbis Books.

Boff, Leonardo, and Clodovis Boff
1987 *Introducing Liberation Theology*. Paul Burns, trans. Maryknoll, NY: Orbis Press.

Bonhoeffer, Dietrich
1972 *Letters and Papers from Prison*. New York: Macmillan.

Bonnardot, M.-L., and G. Danroc
1989 *La Chute de la Maison Duvalier*. Paris: Editions Karthala.

Brown, Karen McCarthy
1989a "Afro-Caribbean Spirituality: A Haitian Case Study" *Second Opinion* 11:36-57.
1989b Systematic Remembering, Systematic Forgetting: Ogou in Haiti. In Africa's Ogun: Old World and New.

Sandra Barnes, ed. Bloomington: Indiana University Press. Pp. 65-89.

Burbach, Roger, and Marc Herold

1984 "The U.S. Economic Stake in Central America and the Caribbean." In *The Politics of Intervention: The United States in Central America.* Roger Burbach and Patricia Flynn, eds. New York: Monthly Review Press. Pp. 189-211.

Campbell, Mavis

1976 *The Dynamics of Change in a Slave Society: A Socio-Political History of the Free Coloured of Jamaica 1800-1865.* London: Associated Universities Press.

Carpenter, Frank

1930 *Lands of the Caribbean.* Garden City, NY: Doubleday, Doran and Co.

Castor, Suzy

1988 *L'Occupation Américaine d'Haiti.* Port-au-Prince: Imprimerie Henri Deschamps.

Cauna, Jacques

1984 "L'État Sanitaire des Esclaves sur une Grande Sucrerie (Habitation Fleuriau de Bellevue 1777-1788). *Revue de la Société Haitienne d'Histoire et de Géographie* 42 (145):18-78.

Chierici, Rosemarie

n.d. Lifting the Veil of Anonymity: A Haitian Refugee's Tale of Rejections, a Lesson for the Anthropologist. Unpublished ms., collection of the author

Chinchilla, Norma, and Nora Hamilton

1984 "Prelude to Revolution: U.S. Investment in Central America." In *The Politics of Intervention: The United States in Central America.* Roger Burbach and Patricia Flynn, eds. New York: Monthly Review Press. Pp. 213-249.

Choi, Keewhan

1987 "Assembling the AIDS Puzzle: Epidemiology." In *AIDS: Facts and Issues.* Victor Gong, ed. New Brunswick, NJ: Rutgers. Pp. 15-24.

Chomsky, Noam

1985 *Turning the Tide: U.S. Intervention in Central America and the Struggle for Peace*. Boston: South End Press.

1987 "Objectivity and Liberal Scholarship." In *The Chomsky Reader*. James Peck, ed. New York: Pantheon. Pp. 83-120.

1989 *Necessary Illusions: Thought Control in Democratic Societies*. Boston: South End Press.

1991 *Deterring Democracy*. London: Verso.

1993a *Year 501: The Conquest Continues*. Boston: South End Press.

1993b *The Prosperous Few and the Restless Many*. Berkeley: Odonian Press.

1993c *Rethinking Camelot: JFK, the Vietnam War, and U.S. Political Culture*. Boston: South End Press.

1993d *Letters from Lexington: Reflections on Propaganda*. Monroe, Maine: Common Courage Press.

Clements, Charles

1984 *Witness to War*. New York: Bantam Books.

Clinton, Bill, and Albert Gore

1992 *Putting People First*. New York: Time Books.

Cook, Sherburne, and Woodrow Borah

1971 *Essays in Population History: Mexico and the Caribbean*. Berkeley: University of Californa Press.

Danner, Mark

1989 "A Reporter at Large: Beyond the Mountains I." *The New Yorker*, November 27, 1989. Pp. 55-100.

1993a "Haiti on the Verge." *The New York Review of Books* XL(18):25-30. [November 4, 1993]

1993b "The Truth of El Mozote." *The New Yorker* LXIX (41): 50-133. [December 6, 1993].

De Jesus, Carolina Maria

1962 *Child of the Dark*. New York: Dutton.

Debien, Gabriel

1962 "Plantations et esclaves à Saint Domingue: Sucrerie Cottineau." *Notes d'Histoire Coloniale* 66:9-82.

Déjean, Paul

1993 *Haiti: Alerte, On Tue*. Montreal: CIDIHCA.

Delince, Kern

1979 *Armée et Politique en Haiti*. Paris: Editions l'Harmattan.

Dépestre, René
    1988 "La Revolution de 1946 est pour demain." In *Pouvoir Noir en Haiti*. Frantz Voltaire, ed. Montreal: CIDIHCA. Pp. 57-94.

Désinor, Carlo
    1988 *De Coup d'État en Coup d'État*. Port-au-Prince: l'Imprimeur II.

Desvarieux, M., and J. W. Pape
    1991 "HIV and AIDS in Haiti: Recent Developments." *AIDS Care* 3(3):271-279.

DeWind, Josh, and David Kinley
    1988 *Aide à la Migration: l'Impact de l'Assistance Internationale à Haïti*. Montreal: CIDIHCA.

Diederich, Bernard, and Al Burt
    1986 *Papa Doc et les Tontons Macoutes*. Henri Drevet, trans. Port-au-Prince: Imprimerie Henri Deschamps.

Dulles, Foster
    1954 *America's Rise to World Power 1898-1954*. New York: Harper Torchbooks.

Farmer, Paul
    1992 *AIDS and Accusation: Haiti and the Geography of Blame*. Berkeley: University of California Press.

Feinsilver, Julie
    1993 *Healing the Masses: Cuban Health Politics at Home and Abroad*. Berkeley, CA: University of California.

Ferguson, James
    1987 *Papa Doc, Baby Doc: Haiti and the Duvaliers*. Oxford: Basil Blackwell.

FIC (Frères de l'Instruction Chrétienne)
    1942 *Histoire d'Haïti*. Port-au-Prince: Editions Henri Deschamps.

Flynn, Patricia
    1984 "Central America: The Roots of Revolt." In *The Politics of Intervention: The United States in Central America*. New York: Monthly Review Press. Pp. 29-64.

Fogel, Jean-François and Bertrande Rosenthal,
    1993, *Fin de Siècle a la Havane*, Paris: Seuil.

Frank, André Gunder
   1969 *Latin America: Underdevelopment or Revolution.* New
      York: Monthly Review Press.
   1979 *Dependent Accumulation and Underdevelopment.* New
      York: Monthly Review Press.

Gaillard, Roger
   1974 *Les Cent-jours de Rosalvo Bobo, ou une Mise à Mort
      Politique.* Port-au-Prince: Imprimerie Le Natal.
   1981a *Premier Ecrasement du Cacoïsme.* Port-au-Prince:
      Imprimerie Le Natal.
   1981b *La République Autoritaire.* Port-au-Prince:
      Imprimerie Le Natal.
   1982 *Hinche Mise en Croix.* Port-au-Prince: Imprimerie Le
      Natal.
   1983 *Le Guerilla de Batraville.* Port-au-Prince: Imprimerie
      Le Natal.

Galeano, Eduardo
   1973 *Open Veins of Latin America.* Cedric Belfrage, trans.
      New York: Monthly Review Press.
   1987 *Memory of Fire II: Faces and Masks.* Cedric Belfrage,
      trans. New York: Pantheon.
   1988 *Memory of Fire III: Century of the Wind.* Cedric
      Belfrage, trans. New York: Pantheon.

Geggus, David
   1989 "The Haitian Revolution." In *The Modern Caribbean.*
      Franklin Knight and Colin Palmer, eds. Chapel Hill, NC:
      University of North Carolina Press. Pp. 21-50.

Georges Adams, A.
   1982 *Une Crise Haïtienne 1867-1869: Sylvain Salnave.*
      Port-au-Prince: Editions Henri Deschamps.

Girault, Christian
   1982 *Le Commerce du Café en Haiti: Habitants,
      Spéculateurs et Exportateurs.* Paris: Editions CNRS.

Gisler, Antoine
   1981 *L'Esclavage aux Antilles Françaises (XVIIe-XIXe siè-
      cle).* Paris: Editions Karthala.

Glick-Schiller, Nina, and Georges Fouron
   1990 "Everywhere we go, We are in danger": Ti Manno and
      the emergence of a Haitian transnational identity.

American Ethnologist 17(2): 329-347.

Gramsci, Antonio
  1971 *Selections from the Prison Notebooks.* Q. Hoare and G. Nowell Smith, trans. and ed. New York: International Publishers.

Greene, Graham
  1940 *The Power and the Glory.* London: Heinemann.
  1966 *The Comedians.* New York: Viking.
  1969 *Collected Essays.* New York: Viking.

Grunwald, J., Delatour, L., and K. Voltaire
  1984 "Offshore Assembly in Haiti." In *Haiti—Today and Tomorrow: An Interdisciplinary Study.* Foster, C. and A. Valdman, eds. Lanham, MD: University Press of America. Pp. 231-252.

Guérin, J., Malebranche, R., Elie, R., Laroche, A., Pierre, G., Arnoux, E., Spira, T., Dupuy, J., Seemayer, T., and C. Péan-Guichard
  1984 "Acquired Immune Deficiency Syndrome: Specific Aspects of the Disease in Haiti." *Annals of the New York Academy of Sciences:*254-263.

Gutiérrez, Gustavo
  1983 *The Power of the Poor in History.* Robert Barr, trans. Maryknoll, NY: Orbis.
  1988 *A Theology of Liberation: History, Politics, and Salvation* (15th Anniversary Edition). Sr. Caridad Inda and John Eagleston, trans. Maryknoll, NY: Orbis.

Hagen, Piet
  1982 *Blood: Gift or Merchandise.* New York: Alan R. Liss

Haitian Refugee Center
  1990 *Affidavits Concerning Conditions in INS Detention.* Miami: Haitian Refugee Center

Hancock, Graham
  1989 *The Lords of Poverty: The Power, Prestige, and Corruption of the International Aid Business.* New York: Atlantic Monthly Press.

Harrison, Lawrence
  1985 *Underdevelopment is a State of Mind.* Lanham, MD: University Press of America.
  1993 "Voodoo politics." *The Atlantic Monthly.* 271(6): 101-

108.

Hazard, Samuel
    1873 *Santo Domingo, Past and Present; With a Glance at Haiti.* New York: Harper and Brothers.

Heinl, Robert, and Nancy Heinl
    1978 *Written in Blood.* Boston: Houghton Mifflin Co.

Hurbon, Laënnec
    1979 *Culture et Dictature en Haiti: L'Imaginaire sous Contrôle.* Paris: Editions Harmattan.
    1987a *Le Barbare Imaginaire.* Port-au-Prince: Editions Henri Deschamps.
    1987b *Dieu dans le Vaudou Haitien.* Port-au-Prince: Editions Henri Deschamps.
    1987c *Comprendre Haïti: Essai sur l'État, la Nation, la Culture.* Paris: Editions Karthala.
    1989 "Enjeu politique de la crise actuelle de l'Eglise." *Chemins Critiques* 1(1): 13-22.

Immerman, Richard
    1982 *The CIA in Guatemala: The Foreign Policy of Intervention.* Austin: University of Texas Press.

International Monetary Foundation
    1984 "Directions of Trade Statistics." In *Yearbook 1984.* Washington, D.C.: IMF.

James, C.L.R.
    1980 *The Black Jacobins.* London: Allison and Busby.

Janvier, L.-J.
    1883 *La République d'Haiti et ses Visiteurs (1840-1882).* Tome 1. Paris: Marpon et Flammarion. 393 pp.

Joachim, Benoit
    1979 *Les Racines du Sous-Developpement en Haïti.* Port-au-Prince: Henri Deschamps.

Johnson, Kevin
    1993 "Judicial Acquiescence to the Executive Branch's Pursuit of Foreign Policy and Domestic Agendas in Immigration Matters: The Case of the Haitian Asylum Seekers." *Georgetown Immigration Law Journal* 7(1):1-37.

Jordan, Winthrop
    1974 *The White Man's Burden: Historical Origins of Racism*

in the United States. London: Oxford University Press.

Joseph, Yanique
  1993 "Haiti: At the Crossroads of Two World Orders. In *Altered States: A Reader in the New World Order.* Phyllis Bennis and Michel Moushabeck, eds. New York: Olive Branch Press. Pp. 455-461.

Kamber, Mike
  1991 "Haiti: The Taiwan of the Caribbean Breaks Away." *Z* (February): 24-31.

Kaufman, Michael
  1985 Jamaica Under Manley: Dilemmas of Socialism and Democracy. London: Zed.

Klein, Herbert
  1986 *African Slavery in Latin America and the Caribbean.* New York: Oxford University Press.

Koenig, Ellen, Pittaluga, Juan, Bogart, Marie, Castro, Monolo, Nunez, Francisco, Vilorio, Israel, Delvillar, Luis, Calzada, Manuel, and Jay Levy.
  1987 "Prevalence of antibodies to Human Immuno-deficiency Virus in Dominicans and Haitians in the Dominican Republic" *Journal of the American Medical Association* 257(5); 631-634.

Kownacki, Mary Lou OSB
  1993 *Love Beyond Measure: A Spirituality of Nonviolence.* Erie, PA: Benet Press.

Labelle, Micheline
  1987 *Idéologie de Couleur et Classes Sociales en Haïti.* Montreal: CIDIHCA.

Lacerte, Robert
  1981 "Xenophobia and Economic Decline: The Haitian Case, 1820-1843." *The Americas* 37(4):499-515.

Langley, Lester
  1989 *The United States and the Caribbean in the Twentieth Century* (Fourth Edition). Athens, GA: University of Georgia Press.

Lappé, Frances, Collins, Joseph, and David Kinley
  1980 *Aid as Obstacle.* San Francisco: IFDP.

Lawless, Robert
  1992 *Haiti's Bad Press*. Rochester, Vermont: Schenkman Books.

LeFeber, Walter
  1984 *Inevitable Revolutions*. New York: Norton.

Leger, J.
  1907 *Haiti et ses Détracteurs*. New York: Neale.

Leibowitch, Jacques
  1985 *A Strange Virus of Unknown Origin*. New York: Ballantine Books.

Leyburn, James
  1966 *The Haitian People*. New Haven: Yale University Press.

Lionet, Christian
  1992 *Haïti: l'Année Aristide*. Paris: L'Harmattan.

Liss, Sheldon
  1991 *Radical Thought in Central America*. Boulder, CO: Westview Press.

Logan, R.
  1968 *Haiti and the Dominican Republic*. London: Oxford University Press.

Lwijis, Janil
  1993 *Entè/OPD: Kalfou Pwojè*. Port-au-Prince: Le Natal.

Manley, Michael
  1982 Jamaica: Struggle in the Periphery. London: Third World
  Media/Writers and Readers Publishing Cooperative.

McCormick, Elizabeth
  1993 "HIV-Infected Haitian Refugees: An Argument Against Exclusion." *Georgetown Immigration Law Journal* 7(1):149-171.

de Matteis, Arthur
  1987 *Le Massacre de 1937: Une Succession Immobilière Internationale*. Port-au-Prince: l'Imprimeur II.

Menos, Solon
  1986 *L'Affaire Luders*. Port-au-Prince: Les Editions Fardin.

Merino, Nhora, Sanchez, Ricardo, Munoz, Alvaro, Prada,

Guillermo, Garcia, Carlos, and B. Frank Polk.
  1990 "HIV-1, Sexual Practices, and Contact with Foreigners in Homosexual Men in Colombia, South America. *Journal of the Acquired Immune Deficiency Syndroms* 3:330-334.

Métraux, Alfred
  1972 *Haitian Voodoo.* Hugo Charteris, trans. New York: Schocken.

Midy, Franklin
  1989a "Haiti, la religion sur les chemins de la démocratie." *Chemins Critiques* 1(1):23-44.
  1989b "L'Affaire Aristide en perspective: Histoire de la formation et du rejet d'une vocation prophètique." *Chemins Critiques* 1(1):45-60.

Millet, Kethly
  1978 *Les Paysans Haïtiens et l'Occupation Américaine 1915-1930.* La Salle, Québec: Collectif Paroles.

Mills, C. Wright
  1956 *The Power Elite.* Oxford: Oxford University Press.

Mintz, Sidney
  1966 Forward to Leyburn, James, *The Haitian People.* New Haven: Yale University Press.
  1974a *Caribbean Transformations.* Baltimore: Johns Hopkins University Press. 355 pp.
  1974b *The Caribbean Region.* In *Slavery, Colonialism, and Racism,* S. Mintz, ed. New York: Norton. Pp. 45-72.
  1977 "The So-Called World System: Local Initiative and Local Response." *Dialectical Anthropology* 2(4):253-270.
  1985 *Sweetness and Power: The Place of Sugar in Modern History.* New York: Viking Penguin. 274 pp.

Moïse, Claude, and Emile Ollivier
  1992 *Repenser Haiti: Grandeur et Misères d'un Mouvement Démocratique.* Montreal: CIDIHCA.

Moore, Alexander, and Ronald LeBaron
  1986 "The Case for a Haitian Origin of the AIDS Epidemic." In *The Social Dimensions of AIDS: Method and Theory.* Douglas Feldman and Thomas Johnson, eds. New York: Praeger. Pp. 77-93.

Moore, Sally Falk
1987 "Explaining the present: theoretical dilemmas in processual ethnography." *American Ethnologist* 14(4):727-736.

Moreau de Saint-Méry, Médéric-Louis-Elie
1984 *Description Topographique, Physique, Civile, Politique et Historique de la Partie Française de l'Isle Saint-Domingue (1797-1798)*. 3 vols. (New edition, B. Maurel and E. Taillemite, eds). Paris: Société de l'Histoire des Colonies Francaises and Librairie Larose.

Murray, Stephen, and Kenneth Payne
1988 "Medical Policy Without Scientific Evidence: The Promiscuity Paradigm and AIDS." *California Sociologist* 11(1-2): Pp. 13-54.

Nachman, Steven
1993 "Wasted Lives: Tuberculosis and Other Health Risks of Being Haitian in a U.S. Detention Camp." *Medical Anthropology Quarterly* 7(3):227-259.

Nelson-Pallmeyer, Jack
1992 *Brave New World Order: Must We Pledge Allegiance?* Maryknoll, NY: Orbis Books.

Neptune-Anglade, Mireille
1986 *L'Autre Moitié du Développement: À Propos du Travail des Femmes en Haïti*. Petion-Ville, Haïti: Editions des Alizes.

Nicholls, David
1985 *Haiti in Caribbean Context: Ethnicity, Economy, and Revolt*. New York: St. Martin's Press.

Nicolas, H.
1957 *L'Occupation Américaine d'Haïti*. Madrid: Industrias Graficas Espana.

O'Neill, William
1993 "The Roots of Human Rights Violations in Haiti." *Georgetown Immigration Law Journal* 7(1):87-117

Onoge, Omafume
1975 "Capitalism and Public Health: A Neglected Theme in the Medical Anthropology of Africa." In *Topias and Utopias in Health*. S. Ingman and A. Thomas, eds. The Hague: Mouton. Pp. 219-232.

Oppenheimer, Gerald
1988 "In the Eye of the Storm: The Epidemiological Construction of AIDS: In *AIDS: The Burdens of History*, E. Fee and D. Fox, eds., pp. 267-300. Berkeley, CA: University of California Press.

Orenstein, Catherine
1993 "Haiti's Curse." *Lies of Our Times* 4(12):3-5.

Osborn, June
1989 "Public Health and the Politics of AIDS Prevention." *Daedalus* 118(3):123-144.

Pape, Jean, and Warren Johnson
1988 "Epidemiology of AIDS in the Caribbean." *Baillière's Clinical Tropcial Diseases* 3(1):31-42.

Paquette, Robert
1988 *Sugar is Made with Blood: The Conspiracy of La Escalera Conflict between Empires over Slavery in Cuba.* Middletown, CT: Wesleyan University Press.

Patterson, Orlando
1987 "The Emerging West Atlantic System: Migration, Culture and Underdevelopment in the U.S. and Circum-Caribbean Region." In *Population in an Interacting World,* William Alonzo, Ed. Cambridgem MA: Harvard University Press, pp. 227-260.

Pearce, Jenny
1982 *Under the Eagle: U.S. Intervention in Central America and the Caribbean.* Boston: South End Press.

Pluchon, Pierre
1980 *La Route des Esclaves: Négriers et Bois d'Ebène au XVIIIe Siècle.* Paris: Hachette.
1987 *Vaudou, sorciers, empoisionneurs: de Saint-Domingue à Haïti.* Paris: Karthala.

Plummer, Brenda Gayle
1988 *Haiti and the Great Powers, 1902-1915.* Baton Rouge: Louisiana State University Press.

Plummer, Brenda
1992 Haiti and the United States: The Psychological Moment.
Athens, GA: University of Georgia Press.

Powell, Cathy
    1993 "'Life' at Guantánamo: The Wrongful Detention of Haitian Refugees. *Reconstruction* 2 (2): 58-68.

Price-Mars, Jean
    1953 *La République d'Haïti et la République Dominicaine: Les Aspects Divers d'un Problème d'Histoire, de Géographie et d'Ethnologie.* (2 volumes). Lausanne: Imprimerie Held.

Prince, Rod
    1985 *Haiti: Family Business.* London: Latin American Bureau.

Ridgeway, James, ed.
    1994 The Haiti Files: Decoding the Crisis. Washington, D.C.:
    Essential Books/Azul Editions.

Rotberg, Robert
    1971 *Haiti: The Politics of Squalor.* Boston: Houghton Mifflin.

Saint-Gérard, Yves
    1984 *L'Etat de Mal: Haïti.* Toulouse: Eche.

Scheper-Hughes, Nancy
    1992 *Death Without Weeping: The Violence of Everyday Life in Brazil.* Berkeley: University of California.
    1993 AIDS and Human Rights in Cuba— A Second Look. In *Festschrift in honor of Charles Leslie*, Zimmermann, ed. Manuscript in collection of author.

Schmidt, Hans
    1971 *The United States Occupation of Haiti, 1915-1934.* New Bruswick, NJ: Rutgers University Press.

Schoelcher, Victor
    1982 [1889] *Vie de Toussaint Louverture.* Paris: Editions Karthala.

Schoenholtz, Andrew
    1993 "Aiding and Abetting Persecutors: The Seizure and Return of Haitian Refugees in Violation of the U.N. Refugee Convention and Protocol." *Georgetown Immigration Law Journal* 7(1):67-85.

Scott, James
    1985 *Weapons of the Weak: Everyday Forms of Peasant*

Resistance. New Haven: Yale University Press.

Shahin, Jim
   1991 "Island of Hope." *American Way* 24(19):54-61, 92-102.

Sklar, Holly
   1988 *Washington's War on Nicaragua.* Boston: South End Press.

Smart, Barry
   1993 *Postmodernity.* London: Routledge.

Smarth, William
   1989 "L'Église sous la dictature de Duvalier en Haïti, de 1957 à nos jours." In *Le Phénomène Religieux dans la Caraïbe.* Laënnec Hurbon, ed. Montreal: CIDIHCA. Pp. 137-170.

Smith, Carol
   1978 "Beyond Dependency Theory: National and Regional Patterns of Underdevelopment in Guatemala." *American Ethnologist* 5(3): 574-617.

St. John, Spenser
   1884 *Hayti: Or the Black Republic.* London: Smith and Elder.

Starn, Orin
   1992 "Missing the Revolution: Anthropologists and the War in Peru." In *Rereading Cultural Anthropology.* George Marcus, ed. Durham, NC: Duke University Press. Pp. 152-180.

Stepick, Alex
   1984 "The Roots of Haitian Migration." In *Haiti—Today and Tomorrow: An Interdisciplinary Study.* Foster, C. and A. Valdman, eds. Lanham, MD: University Press of America. Pp. 337-349.

Stepick, Alex, and Alejandro Portes
   1986 "Flight into Despair: A Profile of Recent Haitian Refugees in South Florida." *International Migration Review* 20(2):329-350.

Treichler, Paula
   1988 "AIDS, Gender, and Biomedical Discourse: Current Contests for Meaning." In *AIDS: The Burdens of History,* Elizabeth Fee and Daniel Fox, eds., pp. 190-266

Berkeley, CA: University of California Press.

Trouillot, Michel-Rolph

1986 *Les Racines Historiques de l'État Duvaliérien.* Port-au-Prince: Editions Deschamps.

1990 *Haiti, State Against Nation: The Origins and Legacy of Duvalierism.* New York: Monthly Review Press.

Trudeau, Robert

1984 "Guatemala: The Long-Term Costs of Short-Term Stability." In *From Gunboats of Diplomacy.* Richard Newfarmer, ed. Baltimore: Johns Hopkins University Press. Pp. 54-71.

Viera, Jeffrey

1985 "The Haitian Link." In *Understanding AIDS: A Comprehensive Guide.* Victor Gong, ed. New Brunswich, NJ: Rutgers.

1987 "The Haitian Link." In *AIDS: Facts and Issues.* Victor Gong, ed. New Brunswick, NJ: Rutgers. Pp. 117-123 (second edition).

Wallerstein, Immanuel

1974 *The Modern World-System: Capitalist Agriculture and the Origins of the European World-Economy in the Sixteenth Century.* San Diego, CA: Academic Press.

Weinstein, Brian, and Aaron Segal

1984 *Haiti: Political Failures, Cultural Successes.* New York: Praeger.

Wilentz, Amy

1989 *The Rainy Season: Haiti After Duvalier.* New York: Simon and Schuster.

1990 Forward to Aristide, *In the Parish of the Poor.* Maryknoll, NY: Orbis Books.

Williams, Eric

1970 *From Columbus to Castro: The History of the Caribbean, 1492-1969.* London: Andre Deutsch.

Wolf, Eric

1982 *Europe and the People Without History.* Berkeley: University of California Press.

Woodward, Ralph

1985 *Central America: A Nation Divided* (Second Edition). New York: Oxford University Press.

Index